Welcome to Seattle

Seattle is a city of many personalities: eclectic, urban, outdoorsy, artsy, gritty, down-to-earth, or posh—it's all here, from the quirky character of the eccentric "Republic of Fremont," to hipsters walking baby carriages past aging mansions on Capitol Hill. There's something for just about everyone within this vibrant Emerald City. Taking a stroll, browsing a bookstore, or enjoying a cup of coffee can feel different in every one of Seattle's neighborhoods. This book was produced in the middle of the COVID-19 pandemic. As you plan your upcoming travels to Seattle, please confirm that places are still open and let us know when we need to make updates by writing to us at this address: editors@fodors.com.

TOP REASONS TO GO

★ **Fresh Seafood:** Shop for local produce and seafood at the Pike Place Market, and then eat at Seattle's renowned restaurants.

★ **Craft Beer:** Seattle is so obsessed with the stuff that its annual Beer Week lasts for two.

★ **Art and Architecture:** Chihuly Garden and Glass is located at the base of the Space Needle.

★ **Coffee Culture:** Seattle may be the birthplace of Starbucks, but you'll find cool local coffee shops on every corner.

★ **Gardens and Parks:** Visit Alki Beach or stroll through the Olympic Sculpture Park.

Contents

MAPS

Fodor's Features

Chapter 1

EXPERIENCE SEATTLE

20 ULTIMATE EXPERIENCES

Seattle offers terrific experiences that should be on every traveler's list. Here are Fodor's top picks for a memorable trip.

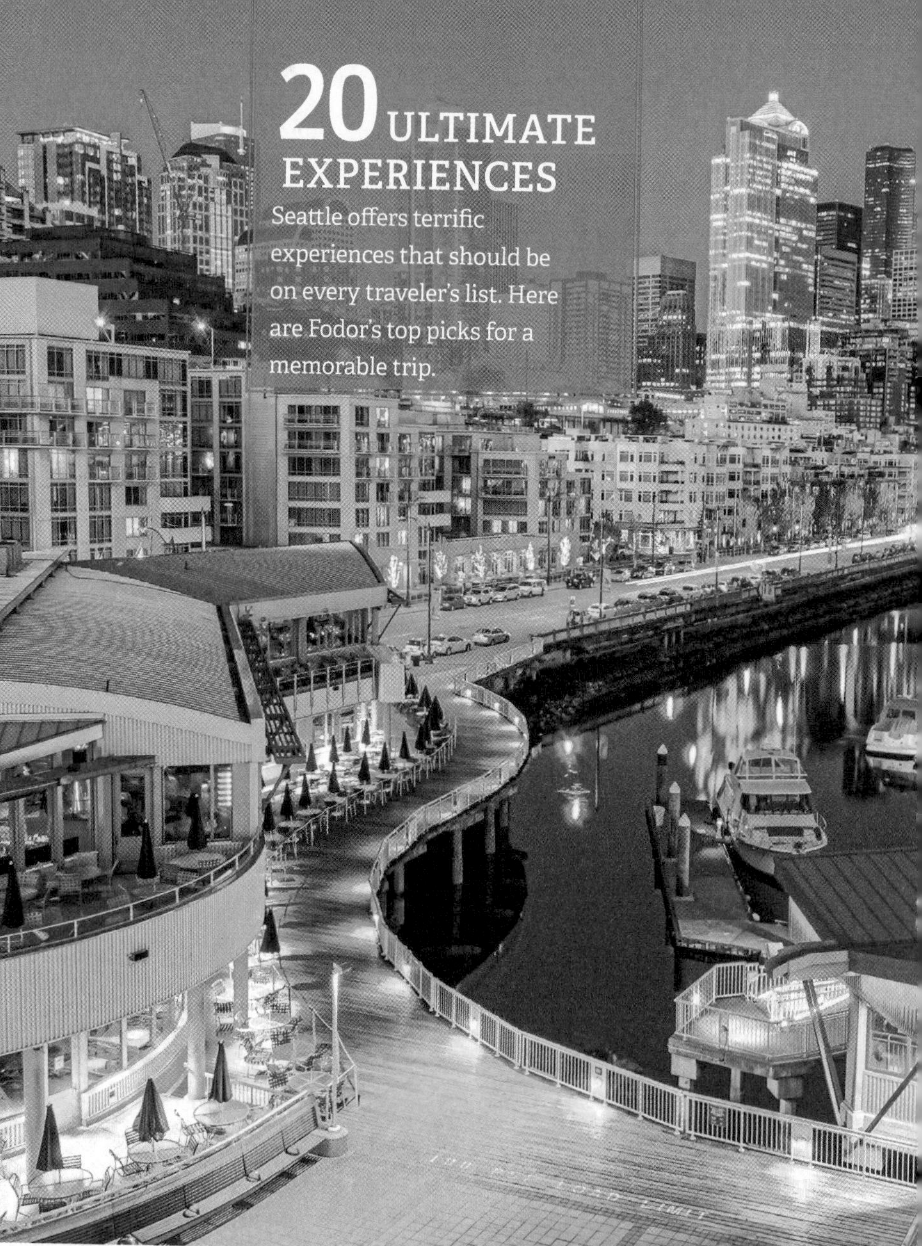

1 Seattle Waterfront

At the Waterfront area, stretching across Elliott Bay from Pioneer Square to the Olympic Sculpture Park, you can walk the piers to catch the Washington State Ferry, grab a cup of chowder, check out the Seattle Aquarium or hop on the Seattle Great Wheel. *(Ch. 3)*

15 Fremont Troll

Inspired by Scandinavian folklore, this towering mixed media statue is the work of four local artists and large enough to clutch a full-sized Volkswagen Beetle. *(Ch. 9)*

16 Volunteer Park

Seattle's largest park is 534 acres of winding woodland trails, picturesque sea cliff views, sprawling open meadows, and other natural landscapes. *(Ch. 8)*

17 Smith Tower Observatory

Travel back in time at this scenic 35th floor historic skyscraper lounge with a Prohibition-era speakeasy and scenic views for miles from an open-air deck. *(Ch. 5)*

18 Seattle Aquarium

The ninth largest aquarium in the U.S, the big showstopper here is a 360-degree-view, 400,000-gallon glass tank showcasing the life swimming around Puget Sound. *(Ch. 3)*

14 Pioneer Square

Anchored between Chinatown and SODO District just steps away from the Waterfront, Pioneer Square is considered the heart of Seattle's historic downtown. *(Ch. 5)*

10 Woodland Park Zoo

Come get up close and personal with more than 1,200 animals representing more than 300 species at this historic zoo dating back to 1899. *(Ch. 9)*

11 Space Needle

Erected for the 1962 World's Fair, this 602-foot-tall internationally renowned Space Age era relic remains a quintessential Seattle experience. *(Ch. 4)*

12 The Seattle Public Library

This 11-story building has a distinctive design with tremendous space that can hold up to 1.45 million books, along with an innovative "Books Spiral," that winds up four stories. *(Ch. 3)*

13 Underground Tours

Underneath the streets lies a whole subterranean layer of tunnels, bypasses, and secrets. See the gritty underground via a fascinating tour. *(Ch. 5)*

8 Chihuly Gardens + Glass

Considered to be among the modern masters in glasswork, artist Dale Chihuly' is behind Seattle's unique and vibrant technicolor sculptural garden. *(Ch. 4)*

9 Visit the Original Starbucks

Opened in 1975 across from Pike Place Market, the "Original Starbucks" is technically its second location, but it's a badge of honor to pay respects to the storefront. *(Ch. 3)*

2 Pike Place

A tradition since 1907, Pike Place is among the oldest continuously operated public farmers' markets in the U.S. and draws locals and tourists alike. *(Ch. 3)*

3 Burke Museum of Natural History

Founded by a team of Naturalists, the Burke Museum has living exhibits touching on paleontology, archaeology, biology, and contemporary culture. *(Ch. 12)*

4 The Children's Museum

Let your children wander through an immersive world of imagination in this 18,000-square-foot exhibition. If they can dream it, they can be it. *(Ch. 4)*

5 The Seattle Center

Here you can enjoy the city's cultural spoils. If nine museums and attractions aren't enough to whet your palate, there is plenty of food to try. *(Ch. 4)*

6 Sky View Observatory

Head 902 feet up to the 73rd floor of the Columbia Center downtown for incredible 360-degree views of Seattle's magnificent skyline attractions. *(Ch. 3)*

7 Olympic Sculpture Park

This nine-acre outdoor sculpture art park is filled with enormous works within a sprawling natural path weaving past Elliott Bay. *(Ch. 3)*

19 Museum of Pop Culture

Learn the stories behind the ascension of rock stars like Prince and Nirvana; see props and costumes from *A Nightmare on Elm Street* and *Buffy the Vampire Slayer*. *(Ch. 4)*

20 Museum of Flight

If it flies, then it's probably here at this 185,000 square-foot aviation museum that's home to 175 aircraft and spacecraft vehicles. *(Ch. 13)*

WHAT'S WHERE

1 Downtown. Seattle's popular tourist spots, including the evolving waterfront, recently expanded Pike Place Market, and Seattle Art Museum are here. Belltown is home to the Olympic Sculpture Park.

2 South Lake Union and Queen Anne. Queen Anne rises up from Denny Way to the Lake Washington Ship Canal. At the bottom are the Space Needle and the Seattle Center. South Lake Union has the REI superstore, and lakefront.

3 Pioneer Square. Seattle's oldest neighborhood has historic redbrick and sandstone buildings.

4 International District. Once called Chinatown, the I.D. is a fun place to shop and eat. The stunning Wing Luke Museum anchors the neighborhood.

5 First Hill and the Central District. Nicknamed "Pill Hill", the First Hill neighborhood has the Frye Art Museum. Farther east is the Central District, with beautiful churches and street art.

6 Capitol Hill and Madison Park. On one side, it's young and edgy, full of artists, musicians, and

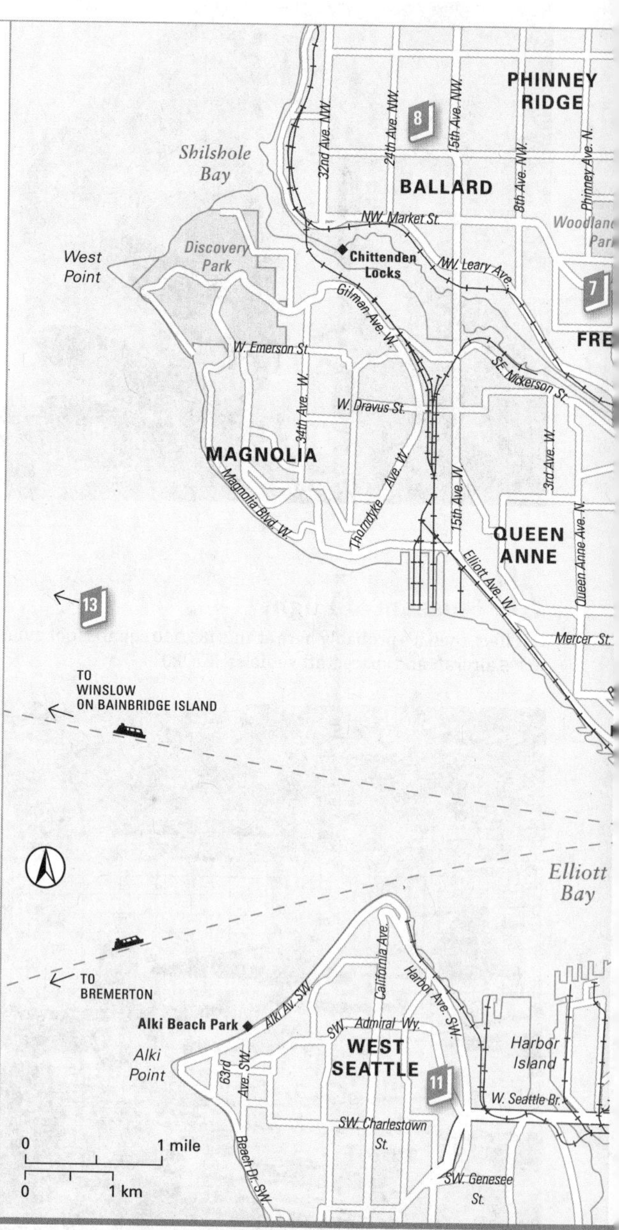

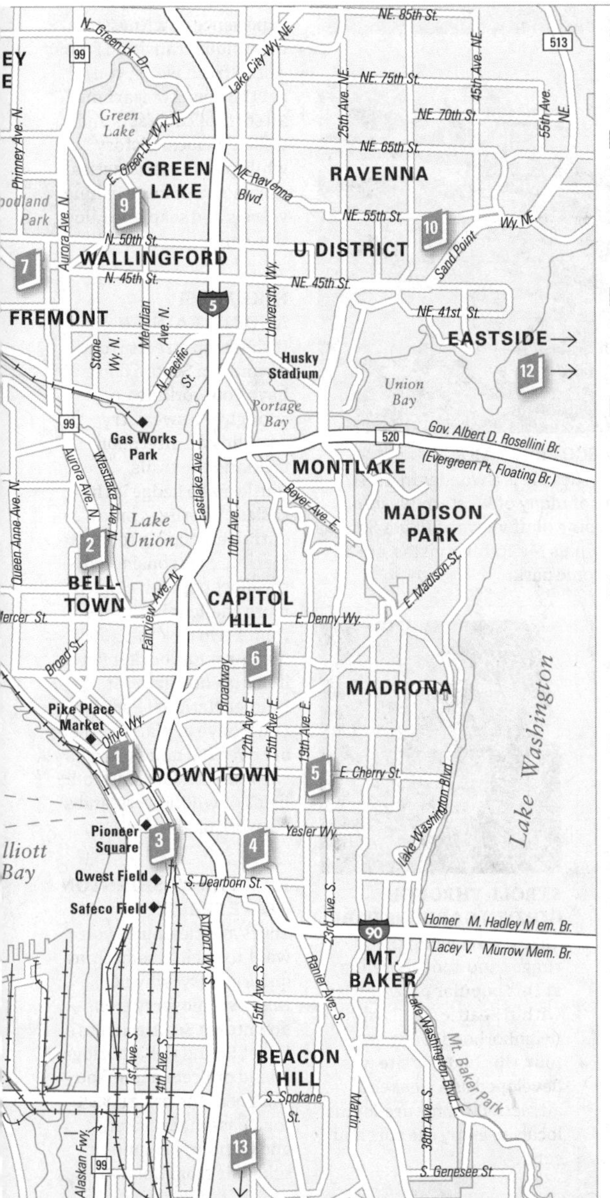

students. On the other side, it's elegant and upscale, with 19th-century mansions.

7 Fremont and Phinney Ridge. Fremont is a mix of pricey boutiques and restaurants. Phinney Ridge includes the Woodland Park Zoo.

8 Ballard. This historically Scandinavian neighborhood is now booming with new builds.

9 Wallingford and Green Lake. Wallingford starts at the ship canal with Gas Works Park. Green Lake's park has a 3-mile paved path that circles the lake.

10 The "U District." The University of Washington's vast campus is lovely, and the surrounding neighborhood can be both gritty and inviting.

11 West Seattle. On a peninsula west of the city proper, West Seattle's California Avenue has some appealing shops and restaurants.

12 Eastside. The Eastside suburbs are home to Microsoft. Bellevue is the most citylike, with its own skyline, an art museum, and high-end shops.

13 Side Trips From Seattle. Visit the Islands, plus Mount Rainier and Olympic National Parks.

Experience Seattle's Natural Wonders

TAKE IN VIEWS FROM DISCOVERY PARK
Of course, the largest park in Seattle is a wonder in itself, but it also offers views of all of many of Western Washington's natural wonders: sweeping bluff views of Puget Sound and the Olympic Mountains, plus Mt. Rainier vistas, are all visible from points at this iconic park.

HIT THE SLOPES
Those majestic mountains surrounding Seattle have some function to their form. Hit the slopes for alpine skiing and snowboarding, Nordic skiing, and winter tubing. Situated on the crest of the Cascade Range, Stevens Pass features 125 acres of skiable terrain, including 52 major runs.

STROLL THROUGH GOLDEN GARDENS PARK
Take a walk along the rugged 300-foot shoreline at this popular park nestled within Seattle's Ballard neighborhood. Built in 1907, this historic site was developed as a weekend attraction for nature-loving locals to enjoy the surf and sand.

CRUISE THE LOCKS
On a nice day, the open deck views off the Argosy Cruises Locks tour between Elliott Bay and Lake Union are downright magical. Aside from the very cool experience of witnessing the unique transition from salt to fresh water, you get the bonus of learning all sorts of cool facts and tidbits on local history while passing the nautical rush hours of large fishing vessels and seaplanes along the water.

HIKE MT. SI AND MT. RAINIER
If the steep streets from downtown Seattle don't have you working up enough of a sweat, try spending an afternoon trekking the trails. Rattlesnake Ledge is the easiest, offering 4 miles of trail ascending to 2,078 feet. Mt. Si is considered the most popular, albeit a more challenging 8-mile round-trip trek to 3,900 feet. As far as bucket list items go, however, Mt. Rainier National Park is one you'll have to plan for: there are over 260 miles of trails with forests, lakes, streams, fields of wildflowers, and a network of glaciers.

RIDE THE WASHINGTON STATE FERRIES
Tours are nice, but if you want to pack in something quick 'n' easy: why not take a scenic ferry from downtown Seattle across Puget Sound to Bainbridge Island or Bremerton? You can't beat the price ($8.65 for a passenger ticket), and its hourly commuter schedule from Colman

Mt. Si and Mt. Rainier

Dock on the prime strip of the Seattle waterfront makes it easy to arrange an impromptu boat ride without the hassle.

KAYAK OR PADDLEBOARD AT THE NORTHWEST OUTDOOR CENTER

If you'd rather navigate the water than be a passenger, head to the Northwest Outdoor Center to rent a kayak or paddleboard for an afternoon around Lake Union and Puget Sound. Kayak rentals are reasonable for budget-conscious travelers, ranging from $18 to $30 per hour, with kayak instructors and organized trips available if you'd like to join a crew. Northwest Outdoor Center offers classes in sea and river kayaking, as well as standup paddleboarding. The company has been around since 1980, so you can be sure you're in good hands with them.

GO WHALE-WATCHING

The whale-watching in Puget Sound and the San Juan Islands is legendary—a dream that many will still travel the world for. There are many ways to have an encounter, including boat rides, seaplanes, and guided kayak tours.

BIKE ALONG THE WATERFRONT

For Seattle denizens, biking is more than just a mode of transportation or a leisurely pastime—it's a way of life. When visiting, expect to share the road when you hit the 8.5-mile Seattle Waterfront Pathway. Smooth pavement and endless views of the Elliott Bay shoreline make this bike path a must for experiencing the best of coastal nature and city sights on wheels. The trail careens past the Pike Street Hillclimb and the Lenora Street Bridge through the Olympic Sculpture Park and Myrtle Edwards Park. Plus, access to downtown makes it easy to hop on and hop off.

Seattle's Best Cafés

LA MARZOCCO CAFÉ
Washington state is home to the only U.S. location of this well-known coffee brand, which is situated in the Seattle Campus Center. More than a café, La Marzocco operates as a permanent pop-up with a monthly rotating selection of coffee roasters and brands.

ANCHORHEAD
Anchorhead's wholesale coffee garnered such a local cult following that it demanded its own retail store. Hence, this 1,000-square-foot café opened in the middle of downtown Seattle in 2016, going strong ever since. Along with expertly pulled espresso, cold brew, and other craft coffee drinks, the café has its own gourmet pastries and snacks including a "quaffle": a croissant dough cinnamon roll pressed in a waffle iron.

LIGHTHOUSE ROASTERS
The dream of the '90s is alive at this cozy coffee shop and roastery that has been keeping the Fremont neighborhood caffeinated with small-batch artisan brews since 1993. Using a vintage cast-iron roaster, Lighthouse is all about the slow drip. In addition to its expertly curated and meticulously roasted brews, the café features a rotating roster of local artists, playing into its community-driven spirit.

CHERRY STREET COFFEE HOUSE
You can't throw a coffee cup without hitting one of Cherry Street Coffee House's 11 locations. Community is key at this coffee micro-chain, which has anchored Seattle's coffee scene since 1997. For two decades the family-owned business has attracted a loyal following for its serious dedication to coffee and mention a killer food menu — think: Turkish börek or falafel sandwich.

SLATE COFFEE ROASTERS
Come for the coffee, stay for the snacks at this small coffee roaster chain with locations scattered throughout the trendy Ballard, Pioneer Square, U District, and Callus neighborhoods. Sip on expertly pulled shots and stock up on small-batch single origin beans, paired with creative artisan pastries like twice-baked pistachio croissants, house-made waffles, and avocado toast. Their coffee is hand-brewed, and their signature item is the deconstructed espresso and milk.

CAFÉ PRESSE
This longstanding French-style café in Capitol Hill comes from the owners of award-winning restaurant, Le Pichet. Grab a magazine from the rack and sit by the window with a creamy espresso and house made pastries like croissants, brioche, and pain au chocolat. You might even find it charming enough to stay for lunch, happy hour or dinner, when they serve delicate French classics.

MR. WEST
No, it's not the famous Mr. West you're probably thinking of — though this café-bar concept is certainly cool enough to name-drop. With two locations in downtown and University Village, this trendy all-day café serves breakfast and lunch items

Mr. West

like toasts topped with aged cheddar, honey and sea salt; local market Greek yogurt topped with apple compote; and an herbed pork meatball sandwich with fontina and mornay on demi-baguette. Their sleek, plant-filled interior is inviting; you might even want to stay and wind down after coffee with some beer or wine.

BAUHAUS STRONG COFFEE

Bauhaus (opened in 1993) is both a coffee shop and a cultural homage to its music-loving community — hence sharing its name with Peter Murphy's legendary goth rock band. While its original scrappy Capitol Hill shop on Pine has closed, its newer Ballard reigns on with the same DIY aesthetic, making this a great spot to chill out with a cup of coffee and a 'zine.

VICTROLA COFFEE ROASTERS

Celebrating its 20th anniversary this year, Victrola is among Seattle's must-see destinations for coffee geeks. Named for the Victrola phonograph that was popular in the '20s, this roaster and café pays homage to the 1920s through their aesthetic and vibe of their spaces. Top-notch latte art and sumptuous small batch roasted brews make this among the best places for a coffee tasting. Coffee might be taken seriously here, but the vibe is laid back with plenty of room to bring a group without worrying about a table. And if you're planning a caffeinated crawl, locations scattered among Capitol Hill, Pike Place, and Beacon Hill make it easy to tackle at least one spot on your bucket list.

ELM COFFEE ROASTERS

Modern with a touch of twee, this sunny contemporary roastery and café nestled in Pioneer Square isn't just a great place to café a solid brew — it's a place to get educated on coffee beans from around the world. Learn to cup and brew like a certified barista or come see how beans are roasted on site through windows that offer views into the back room. Grab a freshly baked doughnut courtesy of local favorite, General Porpoise, and take a seat at the long marble bar where you can sip on lightly roasted brews and chat with friendly baristas. Elm Coffee Roasters are committed to showcasing vibrant blends from places like Ethopia, Rwanda, and Colombia. If you have a discerning palate, you're sure to taste the subtle notes of their unique blends. The space itself is minimal and filled with natural light.

What to Eat and Drink in Seattle

SEATTLE DOG

The city's signature late-night food can be found at hot dog carts outside bars in Capitol Hill, Belltown, and Pioneer Square. Though it may seem like an innocuous snack, Seattle dogs are a little different: the classic topping is not ketchup or mustard, but cream cheese.

LOCALLY ROASTED COFFEE

Seattle's coffee reputation has long been tied to Starbucks as its original location exists in Pike Place, but it's smaller independent roasters like Slate, Vivace, and Caffe Vita that locals love, and that keep the city caffeinated.

FRESHLY SHUCKED OYSTERS

The cold, clean waters of the Pacific Northwest are also nutrient-rich, and produce crisp, briny oysters that are the pride of the region. The Olympia oyster, specifically, garners the most praise. Not only is the state home to America's largest shellfish farm, you can also find these flavorful delights throughout Seattle. Look for weekday-afternoon happy hours for a discounted dozen paired with a delicious beverage.

RAINIER CHERRIES

Washington's apples might make headlines, but Seattleites wait all year for Rainier cherries, the two-tone (golden and pink), ultrasweet gems named, of course, for the nearby landmark. The eponymous delights arrive midsummer.

WILD SALMON

Seattle is undeniably a seafood town, and its most famous product might just be wild salmon, whose color is a rainbow of pink, orange, and red. The dish graces many menus and sushi bars.

GEODUCK

Less famous than the salmon and oysters, but the most symbolic for locals as it is specific to the Northwest, eating this giant saltwater clam (pronounced gooey-duck) is the purest taste of local merroir (flavor of the sea). Its flavor is surprisingly sweet and crunchy. You can eat it cooked or raw, though you might be put off by its unique appearance.

Washington State wine

PHO

If you've ever wondered how Seattle survives the damp and dark of winter here, this subtle, fragrant Vietnamese noodle soup, found every few blocks, is the answer. Vietnamese food in general is very popular in the city, but hot soup complements rainy days, especially as many of the pho eateries are warm and cozy inside. Enjoy the slow-cooked, thick or thin noodles with beef or vegetables.

CRAFT-BREWED IPA

Craft breweries serve as a second home for most Seattleites, and nobody dare open one without serving their version of the hoppy Northwest imperial pale ale. Ballard is a certified brewery destination, though of course there are excellent small-batch beers made across various Seattle neighborhoods.

TERIYAKI

Lesser known than some of the others on this list, Seattle-style teriyaki is a classic workday lunch here, an affordable package of grilled meat with sweet sauce, a pile of fluffy white rice, and a crisp salad generally served in a corner store.

WASHINGTON WINE

Woodinville is the destination for oenophiles in the Pacific Northwest, with many wineries to tour and vintners to learn from. If you can't make it out for a tasting in Woodinville, check menus for sips of Washington's acclaimed wines, including Walla, which is often compared to Napa Valley in quality.

Free and Almost Free

WASHINGTON PARK ARBORETUM
Get lost in over 230 acres and 10,000 native plants at Seattle's premier oasis for flora and fauna fanatics. Explore gardens brimming with indigenous plants, shoreline marshes and wetlands, paved woodlands, flowering cherries and dogwoods, plus one of the largest Japanese maple collections in North America.

KERRY PARK

Don't judge Kerry Park by its small size on the map—it's unanimously agreed upon that this is where you'll find the best panoramic views of Seattle. In fact, you might get a little deja vu while up there; it's actually the backdrop featured in '90s pop culture classics like *Frasier* and *10 Things I Hate About You*. Located on Queen Anne Hill's south side, from here you can see the Space Needle and Elliott Bay. It's a moderately steep hike, and more of a lookout than a park, but everyone will tell you that it is well worth the visit. The park also features an abstract sculpture made of steel by artist Doris Totten Chase, entitled "Changing Form." The sculpture was installed here in the early 1970s.

PINBALL MUSEUM
This Chinatown gem falls into the "almost free" category; for $18 admission, you have your pick of 54 classic pinball machines, spanning from the '60s to the 2000s. Their website lists the current machines; retro sodas and beer are served on site.

HIRAM M. CHITTENDEN LOCKS
Watch boats lowered and raised on these historic locks that separate Lake Washington, Lake Union, and Salmon Bay from the tidal waters of Puget Sound. Underground is a viewing area where large spawning varieties of salmon migrate throughout the year.

FRYE ART MUSEUM
Soak up daring contemporary art from late 19th- and early-20th-century local and international masters at this innovative art museum located in Seattle's First Hill neighborhood. Frequently rotating exhibitions bring life to contemporary issues, where you can discover famous and emerging voices.

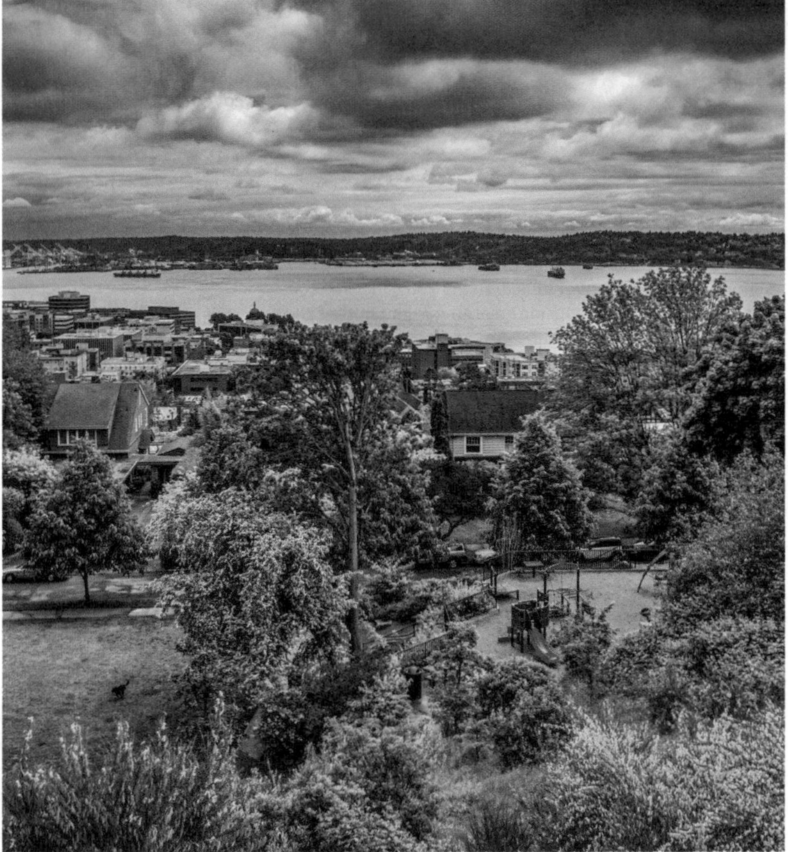

Kerry Park

VOLUNTEER PARK
This iconic urban park was designed by the influential landscape architectural firm, the Olmsted Brothers. This is where you'll find one of Seattle's first reservoirs built in 1900, along with the Volunteer Park Conservatory, the Seattle Asian Art Museum, a water tower with an observation deck hotly contested by locals voted to offer one of the best free views in Seattle, and a seasonal wading pool during the summer.

DISCOVERY PARK
Boasting 534 acres of winding woodland trails, picturesque sea cliff views, sprawling open meadows and other natural landscapes all nestled right in the heart of the Magnolia neighborhood, Discovery Park lays claim to being the largest park in Seattle and is considered its natural crown jewel. Here there are two miles of protected tidal beaches, and it acts as a sanctuary away from the busy city life.

COAST GUARD MUSEUM
Seattle is the last frontier onto the Pacific ocean, so make time to stretch those sealegs exploring its incredible shipping history — all free of charge. Nestled within the Seattle waterfront at Pier 36, the Coast Guard Museum is where you can find discover over 15,000 photographs dating from the mid-1800s, the largest public collection of Coast Guard patches, historic memorabilia, vintage uniforms, and restored artillery.

Seattle's Best Music Venues

Burlesque, vaudeville, jazz, R&B, punk, grunge, indie rock, and everything in between — Seattle has no shortage of legendary musicians that have put the city on the map as a seminal place to discover music. Today you can catch top national touring acts alongside emerging talent at these renowned venues.

THE SHOWBOX AND THE SHOWBOX SODO
The Showbox has hosted many famous names on its stage over the past 80 years. This stunning art deco theater situated right near Pike Place has stood the test of time, providing a stage for stadium headliners like Pearl Jam and Prince. Its sister theater, The Showbox Sodo, opened in 2007. Formerly a warehouse, this converted concert venue has a more industrial vibe.

NEUMOS AND BARBOZA
Neumos (née Neumos Crystal Ball Reading Room), is a scrappy little mid-size club pulling in Capitol Hill's indie crowd for its dance parties, trivia nights, and live shows. In the basement is bar and club Barboza.

THE CROCODILE
This long-running indie rock club has beencling-ing to grunge since 1991. Over the years the club has cleaned up a bit, but the headlining talent remains among the best. Catch national acts, local bands, and karaoke and trivia nights. In the Back Bar, fuel up on wood-fired pizzas before or after the show.

TRACTOR TAVERN
If your vibe leans more rock and country, Tractor Tavern is your down home destination for live music. Anchoring Ballard's historic district for the past 20 years, they host acts from reggae and bluegrass to rockabilly and folk.

SUNSET TAVERN
A former Chinese restaurant turned dive bar and club, this trendy watering hole in the Ballard neighborhood is a destination for cool up-and-coming indie shows and craft cocktails and beers. In the front is Betty's Room, a wood-paneled cocktail lounge inspired by a tiki/dive basement lounge that belonged to the owner's family friends.

NECTAR LOUNGE
Seattle's largest indoor/outdoor music venue in Freemont, this is where you can catch national touring acts and local heavyweights from all genres. Unlike smaller clubs, it's nearly impossible to fight over bar space (there are three full-service ones) and plenty of room to spread out onto an upper mezzanine and covered outdoor patio.

THE NEPTUNE
Neptune dates back to 1921 when it first operated as The U-Neptune Theatre playhouse screening silent films and live performances. As it approaches its 100-year anniversary, the theater is now used as a performing arts space for music, comedy, cinema, lectures, and more.

THE MOORE
Seattle's oldest operating theater, this local relic dates back to 1907 when it opened as Moore Theatre — an opulent social venue of its time dripping with onyx, marble, stained glass, and its own pipe organ. The 1,800-seat theatre remains Seattle's premier venue for top national talent.

THE PARAMOUNT
Over its nearly century-long tenure, this French baroque-style performing arts ballroom and theater on the National Historic Register has featured a never-ending line up of epic shows including Pink Floyd and The Grateful Dead.

TRIPLE DOOR
Triple Door first opened as a vaudeville house in 1926, transformed into a cinema, and eventually became the dinner-music theater of today in 2002. Chow down on food from its from sister restaurant Wild Ginger while watching jazz, cabaret, and reggae.

What to Listen to by Decade

From funk to punk to grunge and everything in between, Seattle's music scene has grown and evolved over the past few decades. The list of artists who discovered their sound here is long and varied—here is just a sampling of some of the best artists from the 1960s to today. If you're searching for musical inspo, tune into local radio station KEXP for the latest and greatest sounds of Seattle.

'60S AND '70S

The Seattle funk scene, though not as prevalent today, was very much alive in the mid-'60s to early '70s, with about 20 clubs hosting live soul and funk acts on any given night. Famed local performers of the time included Quincy Jones and Ray Charles. In the rock realm, Seattle-born Jimi Hendrix has gone down in history as one of the greatest guitarists and songwriters of all time. His legacy is still honored in Seattle today.

'80S

Punk was alive in the '80s in Seattle, with influence from other Pacific Northwest cities like San Francisco. Famous bands like Heart, who are from Bellevue, and Soundgarden, gained international recognition in the '80s.

'90S

Seattle will always be proud of its association with Kurt Cobain, the late great golden boy of grunge. Nirvana was signed to iconic Seattle label Sub Pop, which gave rise to the grunge movement, and was also the home of bands like Mudhoney. Alice in Chains and Pearl Jam also formed in the mid-'90s. Hole, fronted by the infamous Courtney Love, came out with *Live Through This* in 1994, their best-known and most accessible album. Tracks like "Miss World" were written in Seattle. Kathleen Hanna of Bikini Kill, the Julie Ruin, and Le Tigre is credited as being one of the most influential female punk artists; not just in the Pacific Northwest but everywhere. The birthers of the Riot Grrrl movement, Bikini Kill put out the perfectly '90s punk album *Revolution Girl Style Now!* in 1991, inspiring acts like Sleater-Kinney (also originally out of Olympia, Washington), and influencing contemporaries like Nirvana. Hip-hop was also prevalent at this time, with one of most notable PNW-based acts being Sir Mix-A-Lot.

2000S

Grunge dissipated and evolved into indie pop, and the Seattle sound favored ethereal production over rawness. Joining the Sub Pop label were bands like Fleet Foxes, Sunny Day Real Estate, Postal Service, Death Cab for Cutie, and more.

TODAY

Rapper Mackelmore is probably one of the most famous contemporary artists out of Seattle, but the city's somewhat insular indie scene is one of its most prominent; Hardly Art is the label home to many associated indie/punk acts like Chastity Belt, Childbirth, Tacocat, Lisa Prank, and Dude York. For a different and harder to classify sound, listen to the refreshingly singular rapper DoNormaal (you'll definitely read about her if you pick up a copy of the city's alt-weekly The Stranger). Rising pop/R&B artist Parisalexa is another Seattleite to watch out for.

Space Needle 101

Ready for a 42-second elevator ride to the future? When it was built for the future-focused "Century 21" World's Fair in 1962, the Space Needle symbolized Seattle's innovative spirit and technological might. Today, the 605-foot spire is one of the world's most recognizable skyline landmarks and the city's most popular tourist attraction, with a revolving restaurant and an observation deck in the flying saucerlike Tophouse.

WHAT WENT INTO THE NEW-AND-IMPROVED SPACE NEEDLE?

Many years in the planning, the Century Project involved a large global team of experts and the creation of a new kind of glass. More than 100 crew members worked around the clock during the installation phase of the renovation, which was done in sections to keep the Space Needle open to visitors. To install the floor-to-ceiling glass enclosure for the observation deck, a special crane hoisted glass panels weighing more than a ton around 520 feet in the air, where the panels were set in place using a custom robotic arm with giant suction cups. It's a true feat of engineering, as is the glass rotating floor that's the first of its kind in the world.

IS IT WORTH THE CROWDS AND THE PRICE?

The Space Needle has always been a popular tourist attraction, with crowds zipping up the elevator hundreds of times a day to take in epic 360-degree views of the city, mountains, and Puget Sound. The original observation deck design included a solid guardrail and horizontal metal safety cables that got in the way of a seamless panorama. Now there's nothing between you and the bird's-eye views but glass. Wrapping all the way around the observation deck at 520 feet, a series of 11-foot-tall, 7-foot-wide glass panels start at the floor and tilt outward. Glass benches around the perimeter follow the angle of the transparent walls, making a jaw-dropping backdrop for selfies. Even on cloudy days, you can see for what seems like forever. A striking grand staircase leads down to the 500-foot level, where floor-to-ceiling glass walls and a high-tech glass revolving floor overlook the ground below.

SHOULD I GO IF I'M AFRAID OF HEIGHTS?

That depends. Do you just get a little nervous or are we talking full-on acrophobia? Space Needle tours start in an elevator that holds 25 people and has windows so you can watch your rapid ascent. Your stomach might drop a little on the 42-second ride up. Once you've reached the Tophouse, you'll be surrounded by glass, so there's no getting around how high off the ground you are, especially inside the 500-foot level with glass floors. Looking down isn't for the faint of heart.

WHY WOULD I VISIT TWICE IN ONE DAY?

The Space Needle offers a two-visit package that's well worth it if you have the time. On a clear day, you'll enjoy sweeping views of the city, the mountains, and the glittering Puget Sound. Even when it's gray and drizzly, the city and water views are unparalleled. For your second visit, there are a couple of options. During the summer, Seattle sunsets are sublime, and there's no better perch than the needle for watching the sun go down over the sound. If you can't swing sunset, return after dark, when the city sparkles all around you. You can even glimpse ferries gliding through the inky waters of Elliott Bay on their way to the islands in the distance.

WHERE CAN I GET THE BEST SHOTS OF THE SPACE NEEDLE FROM THE GROUND?

You can spot the Space Needle from many parts of the city, but the most famous vantage point is Kerry Park on the south slope of Queen Anne. In a posh part of town, the park features a large terrace that overlooks the city and bay and offers an unobstructed view of the Space Needle. On especially clear days, snow-capped Mt. Rainier rises behind the city just to the right of the Space Needle. Alki Beach in West Seattle also boasts a panoramic view starring the famous landmark.

DO LOCALS EVER VISIT?

Most Seattleites have been to the Space Needle at least a few times, often with out-of-town visitors in tow or to celebrate special occasions at the revolving restaurant. On the Fourth of July and New Year's Eve, locals pour into Seattle Center to ooh and aah at fireworks above the Space Needle. World-famous local radio station KEXP, which has its HQ in Seattle Center, provides music for the elaborate explosions of light and color.

SHOULD I BUY TICKETS IN ADVANCE?

There are definitely advantages to buying tickets in advance, especially during the peak summer season. Tickets are timed so you don't have to wait in line for long. The downside? You might pick a day with lousy weather (though it's still worth going!). You can pre-purchase tickets the day of your visit, as well, to save a bit of cash and guarantee your spot.

ARE THERE ANY DISCOUNTS OR PACKAGE DEALS?

If you plan to do a lot of exploring, you'll save up to 45 percent using the popular Seattle CityPASS ticket booklet. For $108 (or $84 for kids 12 and under), the pass, which lasts for nine days from first use, includes a day/night admission (good for two visits in 24 hours) to the Space Needle, as well as tickets to the Seattle Aquarium, the Argosy Harbor Cruise, and two option tickets for either MoPOP or the Woodland Park Zoo, and either the Pacific Science Center or the Chihuly Garden and Glass.

HOW DO I GET THERE?

The Seattle Center Monorail must've seemed so futuristic when it was built for the World's Fair in 1962. Today it's a charming throwback that whisks tourists from Westlake Center–close to many of Seattle's hotels–to Seattle Center. One-way fares are $3 for adults and $1.50 for kids 5 to 12 (kids under 5 are free). You can also get to the Space Needle by foot, bus, or car, but riding the monorail is a classic part of the experience.

Seattle Today

Seattle is a city that doesn't stand on convention. From its well-earned reputation for quirky music and art to its laid-back population of obsessive foodies, this is a place that defies easy categorization. You're as likely to see millionaires riding the bus as PhDs behind the counter at a coffee shop. Grizzled fishermen mingle at Ballard bars alongside mustachioed hipsters, techies in performance clothing, and tattooed moms. It's an international city, with a strong Asian influence and a history of innovation. This is a place that successfully rallied for the statewide legalization of marijuana, yet people still refuse to jaywalk, even during protests.

TODAY'S SEATTLE

... is influenced by its environment. The Seattleite way of life is shaped by the mountains, water, and massive evergreen trees that hang like verdant shrouds over Craftsman homes. You can see it in Seattleite fashion—for many, waterproof gear and sensible shoes take precedence over trends. You can see it in the hobbies—with the most sailors per capita, nearly everyone has a boat or knows someone who does. REI started here for a reason: this outdoorsy, active population is constantly on a hike, bike, or paddle adventure. With such a connection to nature, Seattleites are rabid recyclers and composters and the city has enacted a ban on both plastic bags and plastic straws. The rain makes the population introspective, and dark—which they channel into wildly imaginative writing, art, and music.

... is highly educated. This is a city of nerds. Go ahead, make that obscure reference to Hessian fighters or binary code—you'll find an appreciative audience. Seattle is the most educated city in the country, and constantly vies for most literate with Minneapolis. It has always attracted educated, creative people, from the first influx of Boeing engineers and University of Washington students to today's high-tech innovators.

... is liberal, progressive, and alternative. One of the most liberal cities in the country, Seattle can be counted on to vote overwhelmingly Democrat in any given election. This progressive hotbed is also host to one of the largest LGBT populations, one of the highest mixed-race populations nationwide, and a hugely influential alternative press—including *The Stranger* and various neighborhood blogs. Which is not to say they're always tolerant, especially when it comes to politicizing treatment of marginalized and houseless people.

... is growing. Fast. With a near-constant influx of newcomers arriving, the population is growing ahead of the national average. Newbies now outweigh natives—a fact many old-timers lament. Hemmed by the geographical limits of mountains and water, the city has had no choice but to expand skyward. Density is growing, as are light-rail and other forms of mass transit. And not a moment too soon—Seattle now boasts the fifth-worst traffic in the country. Luckily, the city is walkable and bikeable, and most neighborhoods are well equipped with all the necessities within walking distance. With all this expansion, housing costs are sky-high, and Seattle is fast becoming one of the most expensive cities. Understandably, you won't see a lot of kids—only San Francisco boasts fewer families with children. Dogs, however, are another story. The canine-to-kid ratio is decidedly in Fido's favor.

Seattle Then and Now

THE EARLY DAYS

"There is plenty of room for one thousand settlers. Come at once." Upon receiving his brother's note, Arthur Denny set out from Portland on the schooner *Exact* with two dozen settlers. It landed at Alki Point on November 13, 1851.

The Denny party wasn't the first to arrive at the wild land that would become the Emerald City, though: the Duwamish tribe had been living there for millennia, and British explorers surveyed the same spot in 1792. But Arthur Denny was the first of Seattle's many mad visionaries. He dreamed of creating a future endpoint for the transcontinental railroad, one to rival the already steadily developing Portland. The party moved to Elliot Bay's eastern shore in 1852; in 1853, the first boundaries of the city were marked on present-day Pioneer Square and Belltown, and Seattle—named after Chief Seattle (Si'ahl) of the Duwamish and Suquamish tribes—was born.

THE GOLD RUSH

Amid all the growth came a series of disasters. In 1889, the Great Fire burned 64 acres. Then the "Panic of 1893" stock-market crash crippled the local economy. Seattle seemed down on its luck until, in 1897, a boat docked carrying gold from the Klondike, heralding the last Gold Rush.

The city quickly repositioned itself as the "Gateway to Alaska" (Alaska being the preferred point of entry into the Klondike). The assay office that journalist Erastus Brainerd convinced the federal government to open was just part of the city's Gold Rush revenue—Canada's Northwest Mounted Police required that each prospector show up with a year's worth of supplies, and Seattle merchants profited heavily from the edict.

FLOATPLANES AND POSTWAR PROSPERITY

William E. Boeing launched his first floatplane from Lake Union in 1916. This marked the start of an industry that would define the city and long outlast timber. World War I bolstered aircraft manufacturing enough that Boeing moved south to a former shipyard.

Seattle was devastated by the Great Depression, with its only growth the result of New Deal programs that built parks, housing, and roads, including the floating bridge that links Seattle and Mercer Island. But entry into World War II again buoyed shipbuilding and aircraft industries. Boeing produced the B-29 bomber, the aircraft used to drop atomic bombs on Hiroshima and Nagasaki.

Seattle's renewed prosperity, which prompted it to host the 1962 World's Fair, remained tethered to Boeing, and the early '70s "Boeing Bust," when loss of federal funding caused Boeing to lay off tens of thousands of employees, sunk the city back into recession. After that, although Boeing would remain an influential employer, new industries would start to take its place. In 1963, Seattle had spent $100 million to upgrade its port in a successful bid to lure cargo traffic from Asia away from Portland and San Francisco. In 1970, six Japanese shipping lines started calling at Seattle.

THE TECH BOOM AND TODAY'S SEATTLE

The tech boom may have defined the '90s, but it planted its roots in Seattle in the '70s. In 1978, Microsoft moved from Albuquerque to the Eastside suburb of Bellevue, bringing the first influx of tech money—even today "Microsoft money" is shorthand for wealthy techies (Microsoft moved to its current Redmond campus in 1986). In 1994, Amazon.com became incorporated in the State of Washington; it is now one of Seattle's largest employers and has such a significant presence in South Lake Union that many locals refer to it as Amazonia. Although the dot-com bust temporarily took the wind out of Seattle's entrepreneurial sails, the city has continued to define itself as a major tech player, with companies such as Facebook, Google, and Zynga having local offices. And an increasing number of other companies are basing themselves here, including Expedia, Zillow, AllRecipes, and Redfin. Today, the metro area of almost 4 million holds a diverse portfolio: one part of the port is dominated by container ships while the other side welcomes Alaska-bound ships to Smith Cove Cruise Terminal. The food and beverages industries are a major part of the economy, with coffee giant Starbucks and Redhook Ale Brewery standing alongside such major seafood companies as Trident Seafoods. Like tech, the gaming industry is huge here, with Big Fish Games, PopCap, Nintendo of America, and Wizards of the Coast based in the metro area. T-Mobile's national headquarters is here, too, as is a long list of hardware companies. The University of Washington is a national leader in medical research, and a biotech hub is rising in the city center. Retail giants Nordstrom, Tommy Bahama, REI, Costco, and, of course, Amazon, keep money flowing into the area.

IMPORTANT DATES

1851 Denny party arrives in Seattle.

1861 University of Washington is established.

1889 Seattle's Great Fire destroys the commercial core.

1889 Washington becomes the 42nd state.

1903 John C. Olmsted arrives; his master plan creates most of the city's parks.

1910 Washington women get the vote, 10 years before the rest of the nation; of course it would be another 50 years until women of color gained suffrage nationwide.

1941 After Pearl Harbor is attacked, 8,000 Japanese immigrants are sent to internment camps.

1962 The World's Fair (and Space Needle) opens and runs for six months.

1982 Visitors Bureau starts using nickname "Emerald City." Seattle has also been called Queen City, Jet City, Rat City, and, of course, Rain City.

2001 Sesquicentennial coincides with a 6.8 earthquake that causes more than $1 billion in damage.

2004 The Central Library opens, the crown jewel in the city's massive "Libraries for All" project.

2015 *The New Yorker* publishes Pulitzer-winning "The Really Big One," which predicts a devastating PNW earthquake.

2016 The city celebrates a newly expanded light-rail system and passes a $54 billion transit bill to keep the improvements coming.

2017 Pike Place Market debuts a new expansion, and Seattle continues to develop a new, tourist-friendly waterfront.

With Kids

Seattle is great for kids. After all, a place where floatplanes take off a few feet from houseboats and where harbor seals might be spotted on a routine ferry ride, doesn't have to try too hard to feel like a wonderland. And if the rain falls, there are plenty of great museums to keep the kids occupied. A lot of child-centric sights are easily reached via public transportation, and the piers and the aquarium can be explored on foot from most Downtown hotels. A few spots (Woodland Park Zoo, the Ballard Locks, and the Discovery and Gas Works parks) are easier to visit by car.

MUSEUMS

Several museums cater specifically to kids, and many are conveniently clustered at the Seattle Center. The Center's winning trio is the **Pacific Science Center,** which has interactive exhibits and IMAX theaters; the **Children's Museum,** which has exhibits on Washington State and foreign cultures plus plenty of interactive art spaces catering to kids ages 10 months to 10 years; and, of course, the **Space Needle.** For older, hipper siblings there's a skate park; the Vera Project, a teen music and art space; and **MoPOP**.

Downtown there are miles of waterfront to explore along the piers. The **Seattle Aquarium** is here and has touch pools and adorable otters—what more could a kid want?

PARKS AND OUTDOOR ATTRACTIONS

Discovery Park has an interpretive center, a Native American cultural center, easy forest trails, and accessible beaches. **Alki Beach** in West Seattle is lively and fun; a wide paved path is the perfect surface for wheels of all kinds—you can rent bikes and scooters, or take to the water on rented paddleboats and kayaks. **Gas Works Park** has great views of the skyline, floatplanes over Lake Union, and the evocative rusty remnants of the old machinery. **Volunteer Park** and Green Lake have wide lawns and shallow pools made for splashing toddlers.

The **Woodland Park Zoo** has 300 different species of animals from jaguars to mountain goats, cheap paid parking, and an adjacent playground; stroller rentals are available. Watching an astonishing variety of boats navigate the ship canal at the **Ballard Locks** will entertain visitors of any age.

HOTELS

Downtown, the **Hotel Monaco** offers a happy medium between sophisticated and family-friendly. The colorful, eccentric decor will appeal to kids but remind adults that they're in a boutique property. Fun amenities abound, like optional goldfish in the rooms and toys in the lobby. Surprisingly, one of the city's most high-end historic properties, the **Fairmont Olympic,** is also quite kid-friendly. The grand staircases in the lobby will awe most little ones, and there's a great indoor pool area. In addition, the hotel offers babysitting, a kids' room-service menu, as well as toys and board games.

Several properties offer kitchenette suites that help families save some money on food costs. The **Silver Cloud Inn** in Lake Union has suites with kitchens. It's north of Downtown on Lake Union, but the South Lake Union streetcar is across the street and gets you into Downtown and to bus connections quickly.

Seattle's Best Parks

Mountain ranges, ocean waters, and islands may surround the city, but Seattleites are often content to stay put on sunny weekends. Why? Because the incredible park system makes for fantastic outdoor adventures, offering everything from throwing beach rocks into the ocean against the backdrop of the Olympics to hiking under canopies of old growth, and from eating ice cream next to gurgling fountains in the center of town to wandering pathways of traditional Japanese gardens.

Luckily for today's residents, more than a century ago, the city's Board of Commissioners had the wisdom to hire the Olmsted Brothers (who had inherited the firm from Frederick Law Olmsted, designer of New York's Central Park) of Brookline, Massachusetts, to conduct a survey of the potential for a park system. J.C. Olmsted's visionary plan not only placed a park, playground, or playing field within walking distance of most homes in Seattle, it also created a 20-mile greenway connecting many of the urban parks, starting at Seward Park on Lake Washington and traveling across the city to Woodland Park and Discovery Park. Later the architect created plans for the campus of the University of Washington and the Washington Park Arboretum.

What follows are our top picks for best parks in the city. *(See also the Neighborhoods listings for more in-depth reviews of top parks.)*

BEST FOR FAMILIES AND PICNICS

Cal Anderson Park. An urban park in every sense, this Capitol Hill expanse has a lovely water sculpture, a playing field, and green space. Grab an ice cream at nearby **Molly Moon's** (*917 E. Pine St.*) and enjoy. *1635 11th Ave., Capitol Hill.*

Gas Works Park. Reachable by the Burke-Gilman Trail, this Wallingford park gets its name from the remains of an old gasification plant. Twenty acres of rolling green space look out over Lake Union and the city skyline. *North end of Lake Union at N Northlake Way and Meridian Ave. N, Wallingford.*

Volunteer Park. Capitol Hill's best green spot houses a plant conservatory, the Asian branch of the Seattle Art Museum, a water tower, paths, and an Isamu Noguchi sculpture (along with a great view). *14th Ave. E at Prospect St., Capitol Hill.*

(See also Carkeek Park, Marymoor Park, Olympic Sculpture Park, and Warren G. Magnuson Park.)

BEST FOR SEASONAL BLOOMS

Kubota Garden. It may be far south, but Kubota Garden is striking, with 20 acres of landscaped gardens blending Japanese and native plants and techniques. *817 55th Ave. S, South Seattle.*

Washington Park Arboretum. The park system's crown jewel may well be this 230-acre expanse, with flowering fruit trees in early spring, vibrant rhododendrons and azaleas in late spring and early summer, and brightly hued trees and shrubs in fall. *2300 Arboretum Dr. E, Washington Park.*

(See also Bellevue Botanical Gardens.)

BEST VIEWS

Alki Point. West Seattle comes to life in summer, and there's no better way to enjoy it than walking along this beachfront path to enjoy the sparkling views of Puget Sound, the Seattle skyline, and the Olympics. *1702 Alki Ave. SW, West Seattle.*

Carkeek Park. North of Ballard, Carkeek has awe-inspiring views of Puget Sound and the Olympics. Its Pipers Creek, playgrounds, picnic areas, and forest trails make this a fun family spot. *950 NW Carkeek Park Rd., Broadview.*

Discovery Park. Seattle's largest park, in Magnolia, is all about variety, with shaded forest, open meadows, pebbled beach stretches, and even sand dunes. A lighthouse, plus sweeping views of Puget Sound and the mountains make this an extremely picturesque spot. *3801 W Government Way, Magnolia.*

Golden Gardens. This Ballard park, perched on Puget Sound, is the best place for beachcombers. Loads of facilities and a pretty pathway make this spot even more special. *8498 Seaview Pl. NW, Ballard.*

Myrtle Edwards. Adjacent to the Olympic Sculpture Park, Myrtle Edwards has a short bike and pedestrian path along Elliott Bay, with vistas of the sound and the mountains. *3130 Alaskan Way W, Downtown.*

Olympic Sculpture Park. The Seattle Art Museum's 9-acre outdoor playground, located in Belltown, has fabulous views of Elliot Bay and the Olympics, complemented by huge works of art by the likes of Alexander Calder. *Western Ave. at Broad St., Belltown.*

(See also Gas Works Park.)

BEST WALKING TRAILS

Green Lake. The almost 3-mile loop around the lake is a favorite spot for joggers, bikers, kids, and dog walkers alike. You can rent a paddleboat and explore the waters. *E Green Lake Dr. N and W Green Lake Dr. N, Green Lake.*

Seward Park. Old-growth forest, views of the mountains and Lake Washington, and a very fun walking loop make this a beloved spot at the southwest side of Lake Washington. *5902 Lake Washington Blvd.*

Warren G. Magnuson Park. Northeast of University District, this large green space has great playgrounds, walkable trails, and one of the largest off-leash dog parks in the city. *Sand Point Way NE at 65th St., Sand Point.*

(See also Discovery Park.)

BEST SOUND-SIDE PARKS

Lincoln Park. With old-growth forest and rocky beaches, as well as facilities like a pool and tennis courts, this is a West Seattle favorite. *5551 SW Admiral Way, West Seattle.*

(See also Alki Point, Discovery Park, Golden Gardens Park, Lincoln Park, and Myrtle Edwards Park.)

BEST PARKS ON THE EASTSIDE

Bellevue Botanical Gardens. Perennial borders, colorful rhododendron, rock gardens, and the lovely Lost Meadow Trail fill the 36 acres of this spot in Bellevue. *510 Bellevue Way NE, Bellevue, Eastside.*

Marymoor Park. Six hundred and forty acres of fun can be found at this huge Redmond green space, including a climbing rock, tennis courts, game fields, an off-leash dog area, and a path along the Sammamish River. *6046 W Lake Sammamish Pkwy. NE, Redmond, Eastside.*

Chapter 2

TRAVEL SMART

Updated by
Naomi Tomky

POPULATION:
724,745

LANGUAGE:
English

$ CURRENCY:
U.S. Dollar

AREA CODES:
206

EMERGENCIES:
911

DRIVING:
On the right

ELECTRICITY:
120–220 v/60 cycles; plugs have two or three rectangular prongs

TIME:
Three hours behind New York

WEB RESOURCES:
www.visitseattle.com
www.thestranger.com

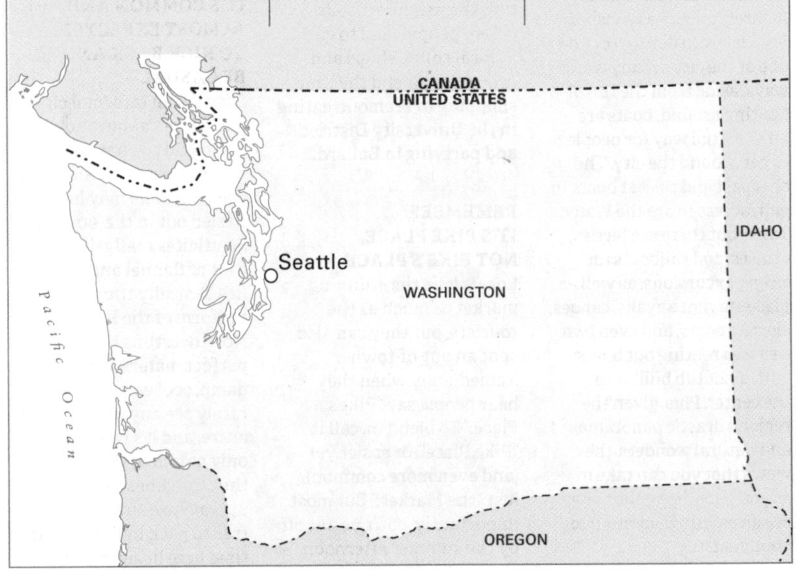

Know Before You Go

Here are some trip-planning tips from locals to get you fully prepared for your Seattle vacation. Wondering about the city's rainy reputation, which sights are free, and whether or not weed is legal? Answers to all that and more below.

IT ONLY RAINS MOST OF THE TIME

That might sound like a bad thing, but let us explain: Seattle has a bad rap when it comes to weather, but on the ground it tends to be rather pleasant year-round. Summer is dry from mid-June to mid-September, and while winter is wet, it's rarely cold. What rain does fall tends to be light and easily ignored. The takeaway? Bring a raincoat, not an umbrella, and you'll be comfortable in Seattle.

BOATS ARE THE BEST

It barely counts as a visit to Seattle if you don't go out on one of the city's many waterways: aside from the fun of floating around, boats are an essential way for people to get around the city. The cheapest and easiest boats to gain access to are the Water Taxis, but there are ferries, cruises, and sailboats for longer excursions, as well as places to rent kayaks, canoes, electric boats, and even two services renting out boats with a hot tub built into the center. Plus, given the region's drastic panoramas and natural wonders, the views that you can take in as you glide along the water are an essential addition to your visit.

GET OUT OF (DOWN)TOWN

Seattle likes its neighborhoods, and getting in and out of Downtown is hard enough that most people don't go there for anything but work or a special occasion. As a visitor, the inclination might be to congregate downtown, which is chock-full of attractions and presumably closest to the action. But there is more to explore than just the area surrounding the Great Wheel. The best way to meet locals is to head out into the neighborhoods, where people tend to gather at local coffee shops and breweries. Spend the time shopping in Fremont, eating in the University District, and partying in Ballard.

REMEMBER: IT'S PIKE PLACE, NOT *PIKE'S* PLACE

Locals love the stunning market as much as the tourists, but they can also spot an out-of-towner immediately when they hear people say "Pike's Place." To blend in, call it "Pike Place," or easier yet (and even more common), just "the Market." But most importantly, don't be put off by the summer afternoon crowds that gather here. Join the folks who live here by grabbing breakfast and watching the vendors set up for the day.

MARIJUANA IS LEGAL, SO CHILL OUT

Sales of marijuana for recreational use are completely legal in Seattle (as long as you're 21 years or older), so you'll see pot shops all over town. How can you tell which is the right place for you to shop? They're a little like liquor stores in that you'll find higher-end ones with nicer products, and divey ones with the cheap stuff. Almost all are staffed by friendly "budtenders" that have the answers to all your pressing questions. However, keep in mind that it's not technically legal to smoke in any hotel rooms or public spaces, though, so if you're visiting you should still exercise some caution.

IT'S COMMON AND ALMOST EXPECTED TO KICK BACK AND BE CASUAL

Seattle's an informal city and there's almost nowhere you could go that you'd be out of place in a T-shirt and jeans. Grunge may have fizzled out in the '90s, but Seattleites really do wear a lot of flannel and fleece (it's basically the unofficial uniform of the Pacific Northwest), as they are the perfect materials for the damp, cool weather. You'll rarely see anyone in formal attire, and it's required only at two or three of the city's finest and most upscale restaurants. Feel free to pack light for your time here bringing only comfortable attire, or stop by REI in South Lake Union to buy something that'll help you blend in.

BRING ALONG BARKSLEY

Seattle has more dogs than it has children, and businesses know that Fido is everybody's best friend. Hotels, bars, and even some restaurants have made their dog-friendliness not just policy, but a point of pride. Even if you don't bring your own pup on vacation with you, expect to see a lot of them at Seattle's breweries where they are welcome. (If dogs aren't your thing, stick to brewpubs, which are less likely to have roaming Rovers.)

WHAT THEY SAY IS TRUE: TRAFFIC IS TERRIBLE

Seattle's narrow geography, resistance to embracing public transportation, and recent astronomic growth has made for horrific traffic. Rush hour lasts through much of the day, and there's always a chance for a snafu to snarl roads for hours anytime. Pack your patience and check in with the traffic cameras on 🌐 *www.wsdot.com/traffic/seattle*. With the limited amount of the city covered by light rail (which does run on roads in south Seattle, thus subject to traffic as well), there is no way to avoid traffic, but looking for the Rapid Ride buses will help—they mostly run in their own lane during heavy traffic times.

THE BEST THINGS IN LIFE (AND SEATTLE) ARE FREE

Seattle's Space Needle might get the big press and the most attention from tourists, but the city hardly looks like herself from the top (since you can't see the needle itself). Make a point to also head up to Kerry Park for the free and quintessential skyline view. But wait, there's more. Like dips in Lake Washington, visits to the Central Library, and majestic Discovery Park, Seattle's beauty can mostly be found in its nature, so there is no need to pay big bucks to do great things in Seattle. For folks on a strict budget, there are also free museum days on the first Thursday of the month; the Center for Wooden Boats offers free sailing on Sundays; and the Pike Place Market never costs a dime (and you can probably even snag a few samples while you're there).

IT'S MORE SLEEPY THAN SLEEPLESS

For all the growth Seattle's had in recent years, the town can still be a bit sleepy when it comes to the hours it keeps: most restaurants close by 10 pm, and bars are mandated to be completely shut by 2 am. If you're looking for spots open past then, you'll find a few restaurants in the International District that serve food past closing time, and scattered diners that stay open around the clock. The flip side of this is that in the morning you'll find coffee shops bustling by 7 am.

DON'T MISS THE MOUNTAINS

In the Seattle area, you might hear the phrase "the mountain is out," which simply means that majestic Mt. Rainier is visible—a bright and beautiful focal point that is a welcome distraction from the crowded freeway traffic. More stunning mountain views are also within your reach. The entire northwest coast corridor all the way to southern Oregon is paralleled by the Cascade mountain range to the east, and western Washington also has the Olympics to the west.

Getting Here and Around

Hemmed in by mountains, hills, and multiple bodies of water, Seattle is anything but a linear, grid-lined city. Twisty, turny, and very long, the city can be baffling to navigate, especially if you delve into its residential neighborhoods—and you should. A good map or phone app can help you confidently explore, and you can use the transportation advice in this section to plan your wanderings around the city's sometimes confusing layout. One thing to keep in mind: Seattle's boomtown status shows in the construction sites that seem to dot every block, which can mean closed-off streets and extra traffic snarls. The Washington State Department of Transportation (WSDOT) features helpful real-time updates and camera footage of local traffic (🌐 *www.wsdot.com/traffic*).

 Air

Nonstop flying time from New York to Seattle is approximately 5 hours; flights from Chicago are about 4–4½ hours; flights between Los Angeles and Seattle take 2½ hours; flights between London and Seattle are about 9½ hours; flights from Hong Kong are 13 hours.

Seattle is a hub for regional air service, as well as air service to Alaska, Hawaii, Canada, and Iceland. It's also a convenient North American gateway for flights originating in Australia, New Zealand, and the South Pacific. Nonstop flights between Seattle and Europe are available, though most transatlantic service involves a connection in Atlanta; Boston; Chicago; New York; or Washington, D.C. Several nonstop flights to Asia are offered.

AIRPORTS

A wide-ranging $650 million expansion plan for Sea-Tac airport has made some improvements but will not finish until 2024. In the meantime, travelers should leave plenty of time for long security lines and to reach faraway gates.

While the present Sea-Tac doesn't offer a particularly impressive array of shops and restaurants, there are enough sit-down cafés, fast-food joints, and quirky shops to keep you entertained between flights. Comfort-food lovers should proceed directly to Beecher's for their world-famous mac and cheese, while Floret offers upscale vegan food. Sub Pop, the iconic Seattle music label that helped launch Nirvana, has a shop stocked with albums from bands on its roster. And for longer layovers, stop into Butter London for a manicure or the Massage Bar for a quick, no-appointment-necessary back or foot massage. Charter flights and small carriers, such as Kenmore Air, that operate shuttle flights between the cities of the Pacific Northwest land at Boeing Field, which is between Sea-Tac and Seattle.

Paine Field, which until recently was mostly used by the nearby Boeing Company, reopened for commercial air service in 2019. With just three gates and nine destinations around the western United States, it's calm, clean, modern and a breeze to navigate. The only downside are the minimal amenities and almost nonexistent ground transportation.

FLIGHTS

American, Delta, Southwest, and United are among the many major domestic airlines that fly to Seattle from multiple locations. Alaska Airlines and its affiliate Horizon Air provide service from many states, including Alaska and Hawaii.

Frontier Airlines has direct flights from Denver and Austin to Seattle. JetBlue has nonstop service to Seattle from New York, Los Angeles, and Boston. Hawaiian

Airlines flies daily from points in Hawaii. Air Canada flies between Seattle and Vancouver, Calgary, Toronto, and Montreal. Kenmore Air has scheduled and chartered floatplane flights from Seattle's Lake Union and Lake Washington to the San Juan Islands, Victoria, and the Gulf Islands of British Columbia.

Major global carriers such as Emirates, Cathay Pacific, and Air France, along with domestic and budget airlines serve 28 international destinations including Singapore, Dubai, and Paris.

Bus

ARRIVING AND DEPARTING

Greyhound Lines and Northwestern Trailways have regular service to points throughout the Pacific Northwest, the United States, and Canada. Only a few years old, the regional Greyhound/Trailways bus terminal, located in SoDo ("South of Downtown") just east of the Downtown stadiums at 503 South Royal Brougham Way, is convenient to all Downtown destinations. Bolt Bus, which serves Vancouver, and Portland, stops outside the nearby International District light-rail station. Quick Shuttle runs buses from Sea-Tac Airport and Downtown to Bellingham and Vancouver, BC.

Car

Access to a car is *almost* a necessity if you want to explore the residential neighborhoods beyond their commercial centers. If side trips to the Eastside (besides downtown Bellevue, which is easily reached by bus), neighborhoods north of the Lake Washington Ship Canal, Mt. Rainier, the San Juan Islands, or pretty much any sight or city outside the Seattle limits (with the exception of Portland, Oregon, which is easily reached by train) are on your agenda, you will definitely need a car. Before you book a car for city-only driving, keep in mind that many high-end hotels offer complimentary town-car service around Downtown and the immediate areas.

In 2016, Seattle was ranked the fourth-worst American city for traffic, which is as frustrating as it sounds. The worst tangles are on I–5 and I–90, and any street Downtown that has a major on- or off-ramp to I–5. The Fremont Bridge and the 15th Avenue Bridge also get tied up. Aurora Avenue/SR 99 gets very busy. The Mercer East section that accesses South Lake Union, near where much of Seattle's construction boom is happening, can be so backed up that the bottleneck is nicknamed the Mercer Mess. Though you'll come across the occasional road-rager or oblivious driver who assumes driving an SUV makes one invincible, drivers in Seattle are generally courteous and safety-conscious. Also be on the lookout for the city's many bicyclists; though most obey the rules of the road and are easy to spot, sometimes they seem to come out of nowhere. Designated bike lanes are clearly marked throughout the city.

Ferry

Ferries are a major part of Seattle's transportation network, and they're the only way to reach such points as Vashon Island and the San Juans. Thousands of commuters hop a boat from Bainbridge Island, Bremerton, and other outer towns to their jobs in the city each day—which makes for a gorgeous and unusual commute. For visitors, ferries are one of the best ways to get a feel for the region and its ties to the sea (plus, they're just plain fun). You'll also get outstanding views of

Getting Here and Around

the skyline and the elusive Mt. Rainier from the ferry to Bainbridge.

Passenger-only King County Water Taxis depart from Seattle's Pier 50 weekdays during rush hours on runs to Vashon Island and West Seattle. The Vashon Water Taxi is $6.75 each way in cash (discounts for ORCA card users, seniors, and youth). The West Seattle Water Taxi makes a quick journey from Pier 50 Seacrest Park in West Seattle for $5.75 each way. Pier 50 is served directly by several Metro bus routes—even if you've rented a car, it's a major hassle to park on the waterfront so busing is the way to go. **■ TIP→ Two free Metro shuttles take passengers directly from the West Seattle dock to the West Seattle Junction and Admiral neighborhoods.** For a great, inexpensive outing, hop on the water taxi to West Seattle, take the free shuttle, and spend the afternoon enjoying the great shopping and restaurants in West Seattle.

Clipper Navigation operates the passenger-only *Victoria Clipper* jet catamaran service between Seattle and Victoria year-round (except Christmas through mid-January) and between Seattle and the San Juan Islands, May through September. These longer journeys are a little pricier: $115–$160 round-trip to Victoria, $100–$139 round-trip to the San Juans. Note that *Victoria Clipper* fares are less expensive if booked at least one day in advance. Be sure to ask about any promotions or deals, and there are also some great package deals available online. In general, package deals are your best bet for Clipper trips. You'll get greatly reduced transportation rates for staying even one night in Victoria.

The Washington State Ferry system serves the Puget Sound and San Juan Islands area and is the largest ferry network in the country and the third largest in the world. Peak-season fares are charged May 1 through September 30. However, ferry schedules change quarterly, with the summer schedule running mid-June through mid-September. Ferries around Seattle are especially crowded during the city's weekday rush hours and holiday events, while San Juan Islands ferries can be jammed on weekends, holidays, and all of May through September. A tiered reservation system releases a portion of San Juan Island ferries at various increments leading up to travel dates. Check the Washington Department of Transportation's 🌐 *www.wsdot.com/ferries* website as soon as you know your travel dates and be prepared to book the minute they open to grab a coveted reservation. Without one, plan to be at the ferry, or have your car in line, at least 20 minutes before departure—but prepare to wait several hours during heavily traveled times (on nice days, the ferry lines can take on something of a party feel, and impromptu, multicar Frisbee games are not unheard of). Walk-on space is always available; if possible, leave your car behind.

You can pick up sailing schedules and tickets on board the ferries or at the terminals, and schedules are usually posted in local businesses around the docks. The Washington State Ferry (WSF) automated hotline also provides travel details, including weekly departure and arrival times, wait times, cancellations, and seasonal fare changes. To ask questions or make international reservations for journeys to Sidney, British Columbia, call the regular WSF hotline. Note that schedules often differ from weekdays to weekends and holidays, and departure times may be altered due to ferry or dock maintenance, severe weather or tides, and high traffic volume.

Regular walk-on fares from Seattle are $8.65 to Bainbridge and Bremerton, and from Edmonds to Kingston; $5.65 from Fauntleroy in West Seattle, Point Defiance in Tacoma, or Southworth to Vashon Island; $5.10 from Mukilteo to Clinton, on Whidbey Island; $3.50 each way between Port Townsend and Coupeville; and $6.75 round-trip between Fauntleroy and Southworth. Round-trip rates from Anacortes to any point in the San Juan Islands run $14. If you'd rather head to Sidney, British Columbia, from Anacortes, it will cost you $20.65. You'll need reservations to visit Sidney. Senior citizens (age 65 and over) and those with disabilities pay half fare; children 6–18 get a smaller discount, and those under age six ride free.

Peak-season vehicle fares (including one adult driver) are $19.15 from Seattle to Bainbridge and Bremerton, and from Edmonds to Kingston; $24.25 from Fauntleroy, Point Defiance, or Southworth to Vashon; $14.80 from Port Townsend to Coupeville, and from Fauntleroy to Southworth; and $11.40 from Mukilteo to Clinton. From Anacortes, peak-season vehicle and driver round-trip fares through the San Juans are $47.15 to Lopez Island, $56.55 to Orcas and Shaw islands, $67.15 to Friday Harbor, and $70.65 (one way) to Sidney, British Columbia. Shoulder-season rates are lower. The following routes accept reservations in advance (highly recommended) during summer and fall through the Save a Spot program (visit the ferries section of *www.wsdot.wa.gov* for more information): Port Townsend/Coupeville, Anacortes/San Juans, and Anacortes/Victoria, British Columbia. For all fares, you can pay with cash, ORCA card, major credit cards, and debit cards with MasterCard or Visa logos.

Light-Rail

The popular Central line runs from Angel Lake, just south of the airport, through Downtown, and continues on to Capitol Hill and the University of Washington. Stations in the University District, Roosevelt Neighborhood, and at Northgate are on track to open in 2021. If the funding comes through, plans also are afoot to extend the system north to Lynnwood, south to Federal Way, and east to Mercer Island, Bellevue, and Microsoft's main campus in Redmond over the next couple of decades. So eventually travelers should have a reliable rail route to get them around instead of the hodgepodge of transit options currently offered. For now, definitely take advantage of the easy and inexpensive route from Sea-Tac airport to Downtown, Capitol Hill, and the University District. Simply head to the Link light-rail station on the fourth floor of the airport parking garage and arrive in Downtown in 36 minutes for just $3 (youth fare is $1.50 and senior/disabled fare is $1). Trains depart every 6 or 15 minutes, depending on the time of day and run from 5 am to 1 am Monday through Saturday and 6 am to midnight on Sunday.

Monorail

Built for the 1962 World's Fair, the country's first full-scale commercial monorail is a quick, convenient link for tourists, though it travels an extremely short route between the Seattle Center and Downtown's Westlake Mall, located at 4th Avenue and Pike Street. Most travelers could walk the 1-mile route without much of a struggle, but the Monorail is nostalgic, retro fun. Making the journey in just two minutes, the Monorail departs both

Getting Here and Around

points every 10 minutes. Hours vary by season, but in summer it runs Monday through Friday 7:30 am to 11 pm; Saturday and Sunday it runs 8:30 am to 11 pm; it's closed Thanksgiving and Christmas Day. The round-trip fare is $3; youth and senior citizens receive a discount and children age four and under ride free, and can be paid for with Orca Card or Transit Go Ticket app.

 Streetcar

The city's cute-as-a-button Seattle Streetcars are a fun way to explore the Downtown core. The South Lake Union Streetcar (SLUS) links South Lake Union and Downtown, with seven stops along the 1½-mile line and connections to light-rail and the Monorail. The 10-stop First Hill line connects Capitol Hill, First Hill, Yesler Terrace, Central Area, Chinatown-International District, and Pioneer Square. Streetcar frequencies vary; the South Lake Union line runs at 10-minute intervals from 7 am to 7 pm on weekdays, while the First Hill line runs every 12 minutes from 9 am to 4 pm. Both run more frequently during rush hour and less often in the late evening (the South Lake Union line stops service at 11 pm; First Hill runs until 1 am). A single fare costs $2.25 (senior/disabled $1, youth $1.05, children under six are free). Tickets can be purchased from a ticket vending machine (coins and credit cards are accepted), on the Transit GO Ticket app, or deducted from an ORCA card. Streetcar-only unlimited day passes cost $4.50 ($2 senior/disabled, $3 youth).

 Taxi

Seattle has a smaller taxi fleet than most major cities do, and it's not the most reliable. Taking a cab is not a major form of transportation in the city, and the number of taxis is highly controlled by the city; accordingly, you'll find that rates run higher here. Most people take cabs only to and from the airport and when they go out partying on weekends. You'll often be able to hail cabs on the street in Downtown, but anywhere else, you'll have to call. Expect long waits on Friday and Saturday night.

Metered taxis all run the same rate, $2.70 per mile, plus a $2.60 meter drop, and 50¢ per minute stuck in traffic. Unless you're going a very short distance, the average cost of a cab ride in the city is $10–$25 before tip. The nice thing about Seattle metered cabs is that they almost always accept credit cards, and an automated system calls you on your cell phone to let you know that your cab has arrived. Visit 🌐 *www.taxifarefinder.com* before your trip to see roughly how much the fare will be and the best route to tell your driver to take. Some of the taxi companies have apps, but none are very functional: they still all work best to call.

Metered cabs are not the best way to visit the Eastside or any destination far outside the city—if you get stuck in traffic, you'll pay for it. Take the bus when possible, and ask your hotel for car-service quotes concerning short side trips outside city limits.

Many locals avoid cabs entirely and take advantage of app-based ride services like Uber or Lyft, both of which boast large fleets of drivers in Seattle. The rides tend to be cheaper than cabs and have less of a wait time. You'll need to download the apps in advance and register with a credit card; fares will be automatically deducted at the end of your ride. Before you book, be sure to check the current rates, which fluctuate with demand; during major events, even a short ride can cost a small fortune thanks to surge pricing.

 Train

Amtrak, the U.S. passenger-rail system, has daily service to Seattle from the Midwest and California. The *Empire Builder* takes a northern route from Chicago to Seattle, with a stop in St. Paul. The *Coast Starlight* begins in Southern California, makes stops throughout western Oregon and Washington, including Portland, and terminates its route in Seattle. The *Cascades* travels from Eugene, Oregon, up to Vancouver, British Columbia, with several stops in between. If you want to spend a day or two in Portland, taking the train down instead of driving is a great way to do so. It's fast and comfortable, and the Amtrak station in Portland is centrally located. Sit on the left side of the train on the way down for stunning views of Mt. Rainier. All Amtrak trains to and from Seattle pull into King Street Station off South Jackson Street in the International District.

Trains to and from Seattle have regular and business-class compartments. Cars with private bedrooms are available for multiday trips (such as to Chicago), while business-class cars provide more legroom, quieter cars, and complimentary newspapers. Reservations are necessary (you can book up to 11 months in advance), and major credit cards are accepted.

Sounder Trains, run by Sound Transit, run between Seattle and Everett and Seattle and Lakewood and travel only during peak hours on weekdays. Trains leave Lakewood about every 20 minutes between 4:36 am and 6:46 am, and then again at 10:16 am, with stops in Tacoma, Puyallup, Sumner, Auburn, Kent, and Tukwila, prior to Seattle. A shortened route from Tacoma runs a few more times in the morning and three times during evening rush hour. Southbound trains leave Seattle thrice during early-morning rush hour and then regularly from 2:35 pm to 6:30 pm. Sounder Trains from Everett have four morning departure times between 5:45 and 7:15 am, stopping in Mukilteo and Edmonds, and offer four return trips from Seattle between 4:05 and 5:35 pm. (Note that there is daily Amtrak service from most of these cities, offering more departure times.)

Fares are based on distance traveled, starting at $3.25 and running up to $5.75 for the Seattle-to-Tacoma trip; youth, senior citizens, and the disabled receive a discounted fare, and kids under six ride free. Tickets can be purchased at machines inside the stations before you board, or you can use your ORCA card or the Transit GO Ticket app.

 Cruises

Seattle's expanding cruise industry now welcomes some of the world's largest ships to docks on Elliott Bay. The city's strategic location along the West Coast means that it's just a day's journey by water to Canada or California, and you can reach Alaska or Mexico in less than a week. In addition to the six major cruise lines that operate weekly service out of

Getting Here and Around

Seattle, you can also sail around Elliott Bay, Lake Union, Lake Washington, or along a combination of local waterways in smaller sightseeing boats like Argosy Cruises *(see Day Tours)*.

Norwegian Cruise Line, Carnival Cruise Line, Celebrity Cruises, Holland America Line, Princess Cruises, and Royal Caribbean all offer seven-day summer cruises from Seattle to Alaska. Some offer additional destinations, such as Princess's 16-day Hawaiian Island trip or Carnival's 17-day one through the Panama Canal. Holland America Line, Princess Cruises, Celebrity Cruises, Carnival Cruise Line, and Royal Caribbean leave from the Smith Cove Cruise Terminal on Pier 91; Norwegian Cruise Line and Oceania Cruises depart from the Bell Street Pier Cruise Terminal at Pier 66. For a smaller, less traditional cruise experience, UnCruise leaves from Fisherman's Terminal for trips to Alaska and the San Juan Islands.

Bicycling

Seattle's hills and its streets designed for cars aren't inherently bike-friendly, but recent expansions of separated bike lines like the one along 2nd Avenue through Downtown, bike paths, and the use of electronic-assisted bikes have made it much easier to get around by pedal power.

Essentials

 Accommodations

There's something for everyone, accommodation-wise, in this city, from high-end luxury hotels to clever boutique hotels and environmentally friendly options to historic properties and brand-new digs. Seattle also has a number of bed-and-breakfasts, though rooms at them tend to go quickly since they represent the best deals in the city during high season. Many of the favorite B&Bs are in Capitol Hill (although you'll find teeny-tiny ones we don't even list just about anywhere in the city), whereas almost all hotels are in the greater Downtown area. The best rule of thumb to get the room that you want is to book as far in advance as possible.

For more information about lodging options and for prices, see hotel listings within each chapter.

Most hotels and other lodgings require you to give your credit-card details before they will confirm your reservation. If you don't feel comfortable booking your hotel online, call the property to give them this information over the phone or ask if you can fax it. However you book, get confirmation in writing and have a copy of it handy when you check in.

Be sure you understand the hotel's cancellation policy. Some places allow you to cancel without any kind of penalty—even if you prepaid to secure a discounted rate—if you cancel at least 24 hours in advance. Others require you to cancel a week in advance or penalize you the cost of one night. Small inns and B&Bs are most likely to require you to cancel far in advance. Most hotels allow children under a certain age to stay in their parents' room at no extra charge, but others charge for them as extra adults; find out the cutoff age for discounts.

■ TIP→ **Assume that hotels don't include breakfast in the cost of your room unless we specify that breakfast is included.**

Another option for visitors that continues to grow in popularity is Airbnb (🌐 *www.airbnb.com*). Using Airbnb's website, you can browse and book apartments and houses all over the city, from budget-friendly spare bedrooms to truly beautiful and spacious digs. Airbnb is a unique way to experience Seattle like a local, and its vast offerings feature a broad range of amenities and prices. VRBO (Vacation Rental By Owner; 🌐 *www.vrbo.com*) offers a similar service.

Earthquakes

Seattle is earthquake country, and the idea of an impending "big one" has received a lot of press recently. It could happen next week and it could happen in 50 years, though, so there is no reason to spend too much time thinking about it. It is far more likely that you might be here when the land gives a gentle rustle. The last major earthquake in the area was in 2001 (6.8 on the Richter scale), with only one related death (a heart attack). Following that, the city tore down the Alaskan Way Viaduct, a major earthquake hazard. So the good news is that because of it being earthquake country, most buildings are built to withstand a pretty severe shaking. If you are here during an earthquake, follow the locals, in whom earthquake protocol has been trained since a very young age: duck and cover. Get as low as you can to the ground and try to stay under a table or at least between pieces of furniture.

Essentials

Health and Safety

A new novel coronavirus brought all travel to a virtual standstill in the first half of 2020. Although the illness is mild in most people, some experience severe and even life-threatening complications. Once travel started up again, albeit slowly and cautiously, travelers were asked to be particularly careful about hygiene and to avoid any unnecessary travel, especially if they are sick.

Older adults, especially those over 65, have a greater chance of having severe complications from COVID-19. The same is true for people with weaker immune systems or those living with some types of medical conditions, including diabetes, asthma, heart disease, cancer, HIV/AIDS, kidney disease, and liver disease.

Starting two weeks before a trip, anyone planning to travel should be on the lookout for some of the following symptoms: cough, fever, chills, trouble breathing, muscle pain, sore throat, new loss of smell or taste. If you experience any of these symptoms, you should not travel at all.

And to protect yourself during travel, do your best to avoid contact with people showing symptoms. Wash your hands often with soap and water. Limit your time in public places, and, when you are out and about, wear a cloth face mask that covers your nose and mouth. Indeed, a mask may be required in some places.

Given how abruptly travel was curtailed in March 2020, it is wise to consider protecting yourself by purchasing a travel insurance policy that will reimburse you for any costs related to COVID-19 related cancellations. Not all travel insurance policies protect against pandemic-related cancellations, so always read the fine print.

Taxes

There is a 15.6% hotel tax in Seattle for hotels with more than 60 rooms, plus an additional $2 per room charge per night. In Bellevue the rate is 14.4%. Renting a car in Seattle will set you back 9.7% in tax, and there are additional taxes for renting cars at the airport.

The sales tax in Seattle is 10.1% and is applied to all purchases except groceries and prescription drugs.

Tipping

Tips and service charges are usually not automatically added to a bill in the United States (except when your party is over six people). If service is satisfactory, customers generally give waitstaff, taxi drivers, barbers, hairdressers, and so forth, a tip of from 15% to 20% of the total bill. (Be aware that tipping waitstaff less than 18% is considered a sign that service was bad.) Bellhops, doormen, and porters at airports and railway stations are generally tipped $1 for each item of luggage. In Seattle there is no recognized system for tipping concierges. A gratuity of $2–$5 is suggested if you have the concierge arrange for a service such as restaurant reservations, theater tickets, or car service, and $10–$20 if the service is more extensive or unusual, such as having a large bouquet of roses delivered on a Sunday.

Events

The Seattle Convention and Visitors Bureau has a full calendar of events at *www.visitseattle.org/things-to-do/events*

Tours

Bike rentals are becoming increasingly common in the city, and many hotels and hostels offer daily and hourly rates to tour the city on wheels. If you'd rather go with a guide, there are a few bicycle touring companies in Seattle. **■TIP→ Seattle is a city built on hills, so bike tours are recommended for riders with moderate to advanced skills only.**

Seattle Cycling Tours
BICYCLE TOURS | Tours explore Pioneer Square, the Waterfront, and Seattle Center, West Seattle, Ballard, or Bainbridge Island. ✉ *714 Pike St., Downtown* ☎ *206/356–5803* 🌐 *www.seattle-cycling-tours.com.*

Seattle Bicycle Tours
BICYCLE TOURS | Explore the city by standard or electric bicycle, the latter of which makes even the local hills rideable for all levels. Reservations are required and can be made via phone or email. ✉ *Vine St Storage Unit, 11 Vine St., Belltown* ☎ *206/697-9611* 🌐 *seattlebicycletours.com.*

Show Me Seattle
DRIVING TOURS | Show Me Seattle offers a huge variety of tours, but their basic orientation tour takes up to 14 people in vans on three-hour tours of the major sights. This is an extremely touristy program that makes stops at places like the flagship Nordstrom store, the first Starbucks, and the *Sleepless in Seattle* floating home, but it also stops by a few sites many tourists miss, like the Fremont Troll and the north-end neighborhoods. ✉ *8110 7th Ave. S* ☎ *206/633–2489* 🌐 *www.showmeseattle.com* 🎫 *$63.75.*

Seattle CityPASS
EXCURSIONS | CityPASS provides admission to many of the top attractions at a steeply discounted rate. The booklet of tickets comes with a map, coupons, and a guide to the Space Needle, Seattle Aquarium, Argosy Cruises Harbor Tour, either the Chihuly Garden of Glass or the Pacific Science Center, and either the Museum of Pop Culture (MoPOP, formerly EMP) or the Woodland Park Zoo. Your pass is good for nine days and allows you to skip most ticket lines. Note that tickets must be removed from the booklet by attraction staff to be valid. ☎ *888/330–5008* 🌐 *www.citypass.com/seattle* 🎫 *$99.*

Chinatown Discovery Tours
WALKING TOURS | Tours of Seattle's Chinatown and International District by the Wing Luke Museum of the Asian Pacific Experience give visitors a sense of the history and importance of the neighborhood, including (in certain tours) a sample of the food that has contributed to making the neighborhood a destination. The daily hotel tour is included in museum admission, but all other tours book up quickly, so reserve ahead. ✉ *Wing Luke Museum, 719 S King Street, International District* ☎ *206/623–5124* 🌐 *www.wingluke.org/visit.*

Savor Seattle Food Tours
WALKING TOURS | Options include a Chocolate Indulgence tour, a Gourmet Seattle tour, and a Pike Place Market tour. ✉ *1st Ave. and Pike St., Downtown* ☎ *888/987–2867* 🌐 *www.savorseattletours.com.*

Seattle Free Walking Tours
WALKING TOURS | Follow the tour guide with a flag around Pike Place Market or through Pioneer Square down to the Waterfront district. Reservations are required and, while there's no charge, tips are definitely appreciated. ✉ *Seattle* ☎ *425/770–6928* 🌐 *www.seattlefreewalkingtours.org.*

Great Itineraries

Seattle Highlights

Though Seattle's not always the easiest city to navigate, it's small enough that you can see a great deal of it in a week. If you've only got a long weekend here, you can easily mix and match any of the days in this itinerary. Before you explore, you'll need three things: comfortable walking shoes, layered clothing, and a flexible mind-set: it's easy and advisable to meander off track.

DAY 1: PIKE PLACE MARKET AND DOWNTOWN'S MAJOR SIGHTS

Spend the first day seeing some of the major sights around Downtown. Get up early and stroll to Pike Place Market. Grab a latte or have a hearty breakfast at a café, then spend the morning wandering through the fish, fruit, flower, and crafts stalls. When you've had your fill, head a bit south to the Seattle Art Museum or take the steps down to the docks and visit the Seattle Aquarium. Other options include taking a stroll to Belltown to take in the views at the Olympic Sculpture Park or getting a roving view of the landscape from atop the new Seattle Great Wheel. Stop for a simple lunch at Il Corvo or Le Pichet. If you're not too tired, head to 1st Avenue in Belltown or to Downtown's Nordstrom and thereabouts for some late-afternoon shopping. Have dinner and drinks in either Belltown or Downtown—both have terrific restaurants that will give you a first taste of that famous Pacific Northwest cuisine.

DAY 2: SEATTLE CENTER OR PIONEER SQUARE

Take the two-minute monorail ride from Downtown's Westlake Center to the Seattle Center. Travel up the Space Needle for 360-degree city views. Then take in one of Seattle Center's many ground-level attractions: the Pacific Science Center, the Children's Museum, the Chihuly Garden and Glass exhibit, or the Museum of Pop Culture (MoPop). If you didn't visit it the day before, walk southwest down Broad Street to the Olympic Sculpture Park. From there, take a cab or the bus to the International District. Visit the Uwajimaya superstore, stroll the streets, and have dinner in one of the neighborhood's many restaurants.

Option: If you don't need to start out with the Space Needle, skip Seattle Center and start your day in Pioneer Square. Tour a few galleries (most of which open late morning), peek into some shops, and then head to nearby International District for more exploring—don't miss the Wing Luke Museum of the Asian Pacific American Experience. If you still want to see the Space Needle, you can go after dinner; the observation deck is open late in summer.

DAY 3: SIDE TRIPS FROM THE CITY

Now that you've seen some of the city, it's time to get out of town and get closer to nature. Hikers have almost too many options, but Mt. Rainier National Park never disappoints. Alternatively, Crystal Mountain, a popular ski resort (from Highway 410, the left-hand turnoff to Crystal Mountain Boulevard is just before the entrance to the national park), offers gondola rides to the summit, where you can take in unparalleled views of Mt. Rainier and the Cascade Range (to get back to the base, hop back on the gondola or hike down). Plan a whole day for any hiking excursion—between hiking time and driving time, you'll probably need it. When you return to the city, tired and probably ravenous, grab a hearty, casual meal and maybe an art flick—Capitol Hill is a great neighborhood for both, as is Wallingford and the University District.

If you'd rather take to the water, get on a ferry and visit either Bainbridge or Vashon islands. Bainbridge is more developed, but it's pretty and has large swaths of protected land with trails. The Bloedel Reserve is a major attraction, with trails passing through a bird refuge, forest, and themed gardens (a Japanese garden and a moss garden are just two). It's always serene, thanks to a limit on the number of daily visitors (make reservations). Vashon is more agricultural and low-key. The most popular way to explore either island is by bicycle, though note that Bainbridge has some hills. Both islands have beach strolls, too. Bainbridge also has many shops and good restaurants, so it's easy to grab a bite before heading back into the city. You'll need less time to explore the islands than you'll need to do a hiking excursion, so you can probably see one or two sights Downtown before going to the pier. If you haven't made it to the aquarium yet, its proximity to the ferry makes it a great option.

DAY 4: STEPPING OFF THE TOURIST TRAIL

Since you covered Downtown on Days 1 and 2, today you can sleep in a bit and explore some of the different residential neighborhoods. Check out Capitol Hill for great shopping, strolling, café culture, and people-watching. Or head north of the Lake Washington Ship Canal to Fremont and Ballard. Wherever you end up, you can start your day by having a leisurely breakfast or getting a coffee fix at an independent coffee shop. To stretch your legs, make the rounds at Volunteer Park in Capitol Hill or follow the Burke-Gilman Trail from Fremont Center to Gasworks Park. Both the Woodland Park Zoo (slightly north of Fremont) and the Hiram M. Chittenden Locks ("Ballard" Locks) are captivating. In Capitol Hill or in the northern neighborhoods, you'll have no problem rounding out the day by ducking into shops and grabbing a great meal. If you're looking for late-night entertainment, you'll find plenty of nightlife options in both areas, too.

DAY 5: LAST RAYS OF SUN AND LOOSE ENDS

Spend at least half of your last day in Seattle outdoors, exploring Discovery Park or renting kayaks in the University District, from Agua Verde Café and Paddle Club, for a trip around Portage Bay or into Lake Washington. Linger in your favorite neighborhood (you'll have one by now). Note that you can combine a park visit with kayaking if you head to the Washington Park Arboretum and Japanese Garden first. From there, it's a quick trip to the U-District.

Contacts

 Air

AIRPORTS King County Airport (Boeing Field). ☎ *206/296–7334* 🌐 *https://www.kingcounty.gov/services/airport.aspx.* **Paine Field .** ✉ *3300 100th Street SW, Everett* ☎ *425/622–9040* 🌐 *www.flypainefield.com.* **Seattle–Tacoma International Airport.** ☎ *206/787–5388, 800/544–1965* 🌐 *https://www.portseattle.org/sea-tac.*

AIRLINE CONTACTS Air Canada. ☎ *888/247–2262* 🌐 *www.aircanada.com.* **Alaska Airlines.** ☎ *800/252–7522* 🌐 *www.alaskaair.com.* **American Airlines.** ☎ *800/433–7300* 🌐 *www.aa.com.* **Continental Airlines.** ☎ *800/523–3273 for U.S. and Mexico reservations, 800/231–0856 for international reservations* 🌐 *www.continental.com.* **Delta Airlines.** ☎ *800/221–1212 for U.S. reservations, 800/241–4141 for international reservations* 🌐 *www.delta.com.* **Frontier.** ☎ *800/432–1359* 🌐 *www.frontierairlines.com.* **Hawaiian Airlines.** ☎ *800/367–5320* 🌐 *www.hawaiianair.com.* **jetBlue.** ☎ *800/538–2583* 🌐 *www.jetblue.com.* **Kenmore Air.** ☎ *866/435–9524* 🌐 *www.kenmoreair.com.* **Southwest Airlines.** ☎ *800/435–9792* 🌐 *www.southwest.com.* **United Airlines.** ☎ *800/864–8331 for U.S. reservations, 800/538–2929 for international reservations* 🌐 *www.united.com.*

Taxi

CONTACTS Eastside For Hire. ☎ *206/242–6200* 🌐 *flatrateforhire.com.* **Green Cab.** ☎ *206/575–4040* 🌐 *greencab.me.* **Orange Cab.** ☎ *206/522–8800 Seattle, 425/453–0919 Eastside* 🌐 *www.orangecab.net.* **Yellow Cab.** ☎ *206/622–6500 for Seattle, 425/455–4999 for Eastside* 🌐 *www.seattleyellowcab.com.* **King County Water Taxi.** ☎ *206/477–3979* 🌐 *kingcounty.gov/transportation/kcdot/WaterTaxi.*

 Train

TRAIN CONTACTS Amtrak. ☎ *800/872–7245, 206/382–4125* 🌐 *www.amtrak.com.*

 Bus

CITY BUS CONTACTS Metro Transit. ☎ *206/553–3000 for customer service, schedules, and information,* 🌐 *metro.kingcounty.gov.* **OneBusAway.** 🌐 *www.onebusaway.org.* **ORCA Card.** ☎ *888/988–6722* 🌐 *www.orcacard.com.* **Metro Transit.** ☎ *206/553–3000* 🌐 *metro.kingcounty.gov.* **Shuttle Express.** ☎ *425/981–7000* 🌐 *www.shuttleexpress.com.* **Sound Transit.** ☎ *888/889–6368, 206/398–5000* 🌐 *www.soundtransit.org.*

 Ferry

CONTACTS Washington State Ferries. ☎ *888/808–7977 WA and BC reservations, 206/464–6400* 🌐 *www.wsdot.wa.gov/ferries.*

Visitor Information

CONTACTS Seattle Visitors Center. ✉ *Suite 800, 701 Pike Street* ☎ *866/732–2695 visitor information* 🌐 *www.visitseattle.org.* **State Parks Information Center.** ☎ *800/233–0321* 🌐 *www.parks.wa.gov/winter.* **Washington State Parks.** ✉ *1111 Israel Rd. SW, Olympia* ☎ *360/902–8844 for general information, 888/226–7688 for campsite reservations* 🌐 *www.parks.wa.gov.* **Washington Tourism Alliance.** ☎ *800/544–1800* 🌐 *www.experiencewa.com.*

Chapter 3

DOWNTOWN AND BELLTOWN

Updated by
Anna Maria Stephens

Sights	Restaurants	Hotels	Shopping	Nightlife
★★★★★	★★★★☆	★★★★★	★★★★★	★★★★☆

NEIGHBORHOOD SNAPSHOT

GETTING AROUND

Both Downtown and Belltown are very easy to explore on foot—walking from one neighborhood to the other is easy, too—but if you head down to the waterfront, be prepared for some major hills on the way back up toward your hotel or the main shopping area. Buses are $2.75 (two-hour transfer included, or buy a regional day pass for $8 if you're doing a lot of exploring), a small price to pay when you're hoofing it in a hilly area.

PLANNING YOUR TIME

A Downtown day can take many shapes. All itineraries should include a stop at Pike Place Market. Two other can't-miss sights are the Olympic Sculpture Park in Belltown and the Seattle Art Museum Downtown. If you have children, consider the aquarium, a ride on the Seattle Great Wheel, and the sights along the waterfront.

Try to arrive at Pike Place Market in the morning when it's a bit calmer (before cruise ships have docked). The aquarium gets crowded midday, but it's a happy chaos and preferable to negotiating the midday market crowds.

Even though the shops in both neighborhoods are concentrated in small areas, doing a comprehensive shopping tour will take all day—just plan to hit Belltown when you start to get tired, as there are good cafés along 1st and 2nd avenues.

TOP REASONS TO GO

Find your perfect souvenir—along with yummy breakfast or lunch—at **Pike Place Market.**

Visit the **Seattle Art Museum**—consider doing it on a First Thursday or during a Remix event.

Make time for a stroll in the **Olympic Sculpture Park,** or, if you're traveling with kids, make a beeline for the **Seattle Aquarium** to watch sea otters frolic.

Attend a concert at **Benaroya Hall.** The home of the Seattle Symphony is renowned for its near-perfect acoustics.

QUICK BITES

■ **Cherry Street Coffee House.** A variety of yummy breakfast, lunch, and vegan items are on the menu, including smoothies and breakfast bagels. **Known for:** quick breakfast; vegan options; bagels. ✉ *2621 5th Ave., Belltown* ☏ *206/812–1298* 🌐 *www.cherryst.com* 💳 *No credit cards.*

■ **Macrina.** Macrina, close to the Olympic Sculpture Park, is famous for its delicious breads, sandwiches, cookies, and coffee cakes. **Known for:** baked goods. ✉ *2408 1st Ave., Belltown* ☏ *206/448–4032* 🌐 *www.macrinabakery.com* 💳 *No credit cards* ⏲ *No dinner.*

■ **Storyville Coffee.** In addition to perfectly pulled espresso drinks, Storyville offers fresh pastries, light lunch items, and beer and wine in a welcoming space with ample comfy seating and Elliott Bay views. **Known for:** skilled baristas; housemade ingredients like chocolate syrup; cashew and other alt-milks. ✉ *94 Pike St. #34, Seattle* ☏ *206/780–5777* 🌐 *www.storyville.com.*

Except for the busy areas around the market and the piers, and the always-frenetic shopping district, a lot of Downtown can often seem deserted, especially at night. Still, while it may not be the soul of the city, it's definitely the heart, and there's plenty to do—nearly all of it easily reachable by foot.

There's the city's premier art museum, the eye-popping Rem Koolhaas–designed Central Library, lively Pike Place Market, and a major shopping corridor along 5th Avenue and down Pine Street. And, of course, there's the water: Elliott Bay beckons from every crested hill. Within the core of Downtown—which is bounded on the west by Elliott Bay and on the east by I–5, stretching from Virginia Street to Yesler Way—are several different experiences. The waterfront and much of 1st Avenue are lively and at times quite touristy, thanks to Pike Place Market, the Seattle Art Museum (SAM), and the piers, which have several kid-friendly sights as well as ferries to Bremerton and to Bainbridge Island. As you head east from Pike Place Market, you soon hit Downtown's shopping and entertainment district. The flagship Nordstrom department store is here, and the Westlake Center and Pacific Place shopping centers offer plenty of opportunities to part with your money. In addition to the shopping at Pacific Place, there are multiplex movie theaters, a multistory arcade, and a few popular chain restaurants. Heading south of Pike Street, the Central Business District holds mostly office and municipal buildings. There are a few sights scattered about, including the remarkable Central Library, a handful of art galleries, and a sampling of higher-end shops. There are a few major cultural sights, too, including the Seattle Symphony's elegant concert venue, Benaroya Hall. North of Downtown, Belltown beckons with hip shops, bars, and restaurants, as well as the free waterfront Olympic Sculpture Museum, which has beach access and some of the best views in town.

Downtown

Sights

★ Pike Place Market

MARKET | FAMILY | One of the nation's largest and oldest public markets dates from 1907, when the city issued permits allowing farmers to sell produce from parked wagons. At one time the market was a madhouse of vendors hawking their produce and haggling with customers over prices; now you might find fishmongers engaging in frenzied banter and hilarious antics, but chances are you won't get them to waver on prices. There are many restaurants, bakeries, coffee shops (including the flagship Starbucks), lunch counters, and ethnic eateries. Go

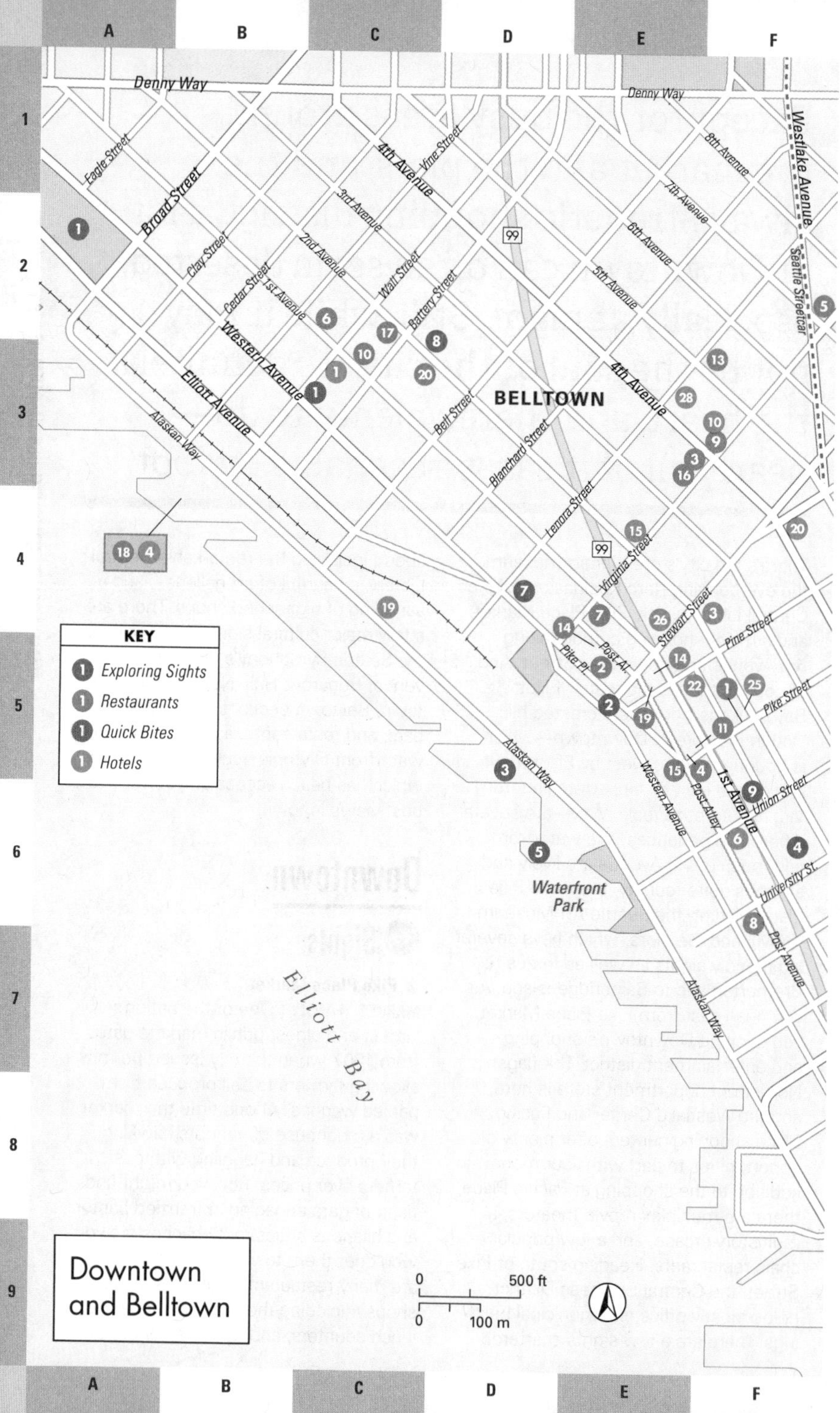
Downtown and Belltown
KEY
Exploring Sights
Restaurants
Quick Bites
Hotels
BELLTOWN
Denny Way
Eagle Street
Broad Street
Clay Street
Cedar Street
Western Avenue
Elliott Avenue
Alaskan Way
1st Avenue
2nd Avenue
3rd Avenue
4th Avenue
Vine Street
Wall Street
Battery Street
Bell Street
Blanchard Street
Lenora Street
Virginia Street
Stewart Street
Pine Street
Pike Street
Pike Pl
Post Al.
Post Alley
Union Street
University St.
Post Avenue
5th Avenue
6th Avenue
7th Avenue
8th Avenue
Westlake Avenue
Seattle Streetcar
Waterfront Park
Elliott Bay
99
0
500 ft
100 m
A
B
C
D
E
F
1
2
3
4
5
6
7
8
9

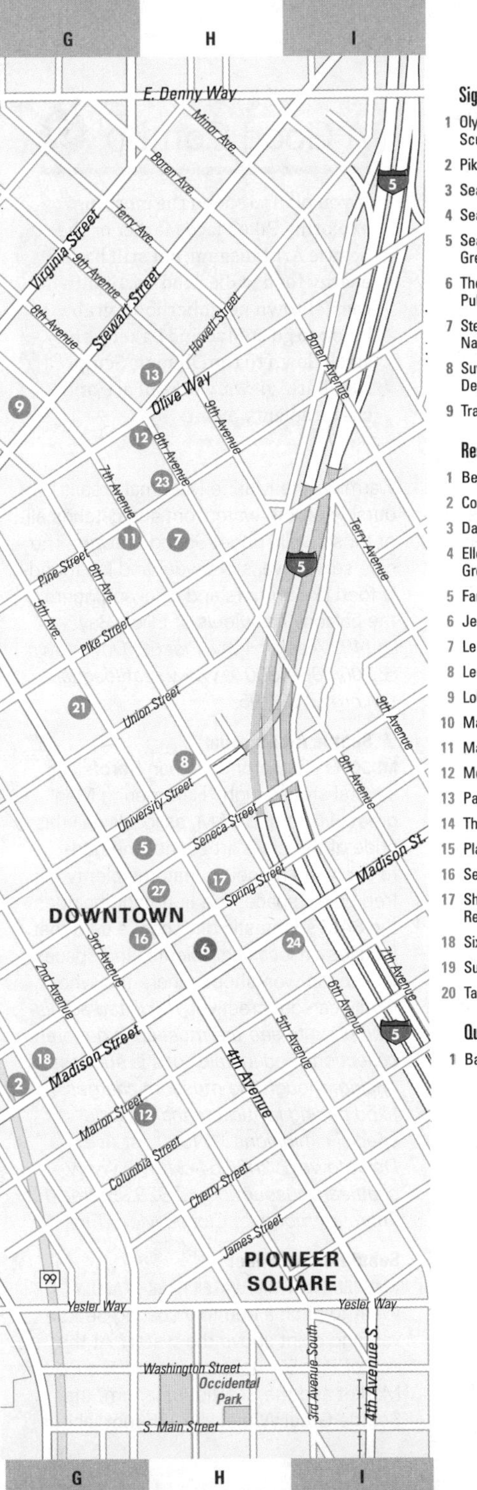

Sights

1 Olympic Sculpture Park **A2**
2 Pike Place Market **E5**
3 Seattle Aquarium **D5**
4 Seattle Art Museum **F6**
5 Seattle Great Wheel **D6**
6 The Seattle Public Library **H6**
7 Steinbrueck Native Gallery **D4**
8 Suyama Peterson Deguchi **C2**
9 Traver Gallery **F6**

Restaurants

1 Ben Paris **F5**
2 Country Dough **E5**
3 Dahlia Lounge **E3**
4 Ellenos Real Greek Yogurt **E5**
5 FareStart **F2**
6 Jerk Shack **C2**
7 Le Pichet **E4**
8 Lecosho **F6**
9 Lola **F3**
10 Macrina Bakery **C3**
11 Matt's in the Market **E5**
12 Metropolitan Grill **G7**
13 Palace Kitchen **F3**
14 The Pink Door **E5**
15 Place Pigalle **E5**
16 Serious Pie **E3**
17 Shiro's Sushi Restaurant **C2**
18 Six Seven **B4**
19 Sushi Kashiba **E5**
20 Tavolàta **C3**

Quick Bites

1 Bang Bang Cafe **C3**

Hotels

1 Ace Hotel **C3**
2 Alexis Hotel **G7**
3 The Charter Hotel **F4**
4 The Edgewater **B4**
5 Fairmont Olympic Hotel - Seattle **G6**
6 Four Seasons Hotel Seattle **F6**
7 Grand Hyatt Seattle **H4**
8 Hilton Seattle **H5**
9 Hotel Max **G3**
10 Hotel Ändra **F3**
11 Hotel Theodore **G4**
12 Hyatt At Olive 8 .... **G3**
13 Hyatt Regency **H2**
14 Inn at the Market **E5**
15 Kimpton Palladian Hotel **E4**
16 Hotel Monaco **G6**
17 Hotel Vintage **H6**
18 Loews Hotel 1000 .... **G7**
19 Marriott Seattle Waterfront **C4**
20 Mayflower Park Hotel ... **F4**
21 Motif Seattle Hotel **G5**
22 Palihotel **E5**
23 The Paramount Hotel ... **H3**
24 Renaissance Seattle Hotel **I6**
25 The State Hotel **F5**
26 Thompson Seattle **E4**
27 W Seattle **H6**
28 Warwick Seattle Hotel **E3**

to Pike Place hungry and you won't be disappointed. The flower market is also a must-see—gigantic fresh arrangements can be found for around $12. It's well worth wading through dense crowds to enjoy the market's many corridors, where you'll find specialty-food items, quirky gift shops, tea, honey, jams, comic books, beads, eclectic crafts, and cookware. In 2017, Pike Place Market debuted a significant expansion, fulfilling a decades-long vision for Seattle's Market Historic District. The market's new digs feature artisanal-food purveyors, an on-site brewery, four public art installations, seasonal pop-up vendors, and a 30,000-square-foot open public space with a plaza and a viewing deck overlooking Elliott Bay and the Seattle waterfront. ■ **TIP→ The famous "flying fish" fishmonger is located at the main entrance on Pike Street. Just be patient and eventually someone will toss a big fish through the air.** ✉ *Pike Pl. at Pike St., west of 1st Ave., Downtown* ☎ *206/682–7453* 🌐 *www.pikeplacemarket.org.*

A Good Combo

If you plan to spend the morning exploring Pike Place Market or the Seattle Art Museum, but still have energy for a walk, head north into the Belltown neighborhood, grab lunch to go at Macrina Bakery, and stroll down to the Olympic Sculpture Park: views, works of art, and chairs aplenty await.

★ Seattle Aquarium

ZOO | **FAMILY** | Located right at the water's edge, the Seattle Aquarium is one of the nation's premier aquariums. Among its most engaging residents are the sea otters—kids, especially, seem able to spend hours watching the delightful antics of these creatures and their river cousins. In the Puget Sound Great Hall, "Window on Washington Waters," a slice of Neah Bay life, is presented in a 20-foot-tall tank holding 120,000 gallons of water. The aquarium's darkened rooms and large, lighted tanks brilliantly display Pacific Northwest marine life, including clever octopuses and translucent jellyfish. The "Life on the Edge" tide pools re-create Washington's rocky coast and sandy beaches—kids can touch the starfish, sea urchins, and sponges. Huge glass windows provide underwater views of the harbor seal exhibit; go up top to watch them play in their pools. If you're visiting in fall or winter, dress warmly—the Marine Mammal area is outside on the waterfront and catches all of those chilly Puget Sound breezes. The café serves Ivar's chowder and kid-friendly food like burgers and chicken fingers; the balcony has views of Elliott Bay. ✉ *1483 Alaskan Way, Pier 59, Downtown* ☎ *206/386–4300* 🌐 *www.seattleaquarium.org* 🎟 *$34.95.*

★ Seattle Art Museum

MUSEUM | Sculptor Jonathan Borofsky's several-stories-high "Hammering Man" greets visitors to SAM, as locals call this pride of the city's art scene. The genre-spanning museum features plenty of free public space. The first floor includes the SAM's fantastic gift shop, a café that focuses on local ingredients, and spaces for drop-in workshops where the whole family can get creative. *The listed admission price to see the museum's general collections and installations is suggested pricing, though the museum charges fixed pricing for tickets that include special exhibitions.* ✉ *1300 1st Ave., Downtown* ☎ *206/654–3100* 🌐 *www.seattleartmuseum.org* 🎟 *$29.95; free 1st Thurs. of month* ⏲ *Closed Mon.-Tues.*

Seattle Great Wheel

AMUSEMENT PARK/WATER PARK | **FAMILY** | Want to hitch a ride to a soaring Seattle vantage point above the water? At the end of Pier 57, just steps from Pike Place Market and the Seattle Aquarium, the Seattle Great Wheel is a 175-foot (about

The stunning Seattle Central Library.

17 stories tall) Ferris wheel. As you round the top, enjoy views of the city skyline, Elliott Bay, the Olympic Mountains, and Mt. Rainier (on a clear day, of course). Rides are slow and smooth, lasting 15 to 20 minutes, with three revolutions total. Each climate-controlled gondola can hold six people (up to eight if some are children) and, generally speaking, parties will be able to sit together. The Seattle Great Wheel also lights up the waterfront after dark with dazzling colors. Advance tickets are recommended—you'll still have to wait in line, but the line is a lot shorter. ■ **TIP→ If you're afraid of heights, you may want to skip this attraction.** ✉ *1301 Alaskan Way (Pier 56), Downtown* ☎ *206/623–8600* 🌐 *www.seattlegreatwheel.com* 🎫 *$15.*

★ The Seattle Public Library

LIBRARY | The hub of Seattle's 26-branch library system is a stunning jewel of a building that stands out against the concrete jungle of Downtown. Designed by renowned Dutch architect Rem Koolhaas and Joshua Ramus, this 11-story structure houses more than 1 million books, a language center, terrific areas for kids and teens—plus hundreds of computers, an auditorium, a "mixing chamber" floor of information desks, and a café. The building's floor plan is anything but simple; stand outside the beveled glass-and-metal facade of the building and you can see the library's floors zigzagging upward. Tours are self-guided via a laminated sheet you can pick up at the information desk; there's also a number you can call on your cell phone for an audio tour. The reading room on the 10th floor has unbeatable views of the city and the water, and the building has Wi-Fi throughout (look for the network "spl-public"). Readings and free film screenings happen on a regular basis; check the website for more information. ✉ *1000 4th Ave., Downtown* ☎ *206/386–4636* 🌐 *www.spl.org/locations/central-library.*

Traver Gallery

MUSEUM | One block north of the Seattle Art Museum, Traver Gallery is like a little slice of SoHo in Seattle, with large picture windows and uneven wood floors. The focus is on contemporary studio glass, paintings, sculpture, and installation art from local and international artists. Pieces are exquisite—never whimsical or gaudy—and the staff is extremely courteous. After you're done tiptoeing around the gallery, head back downstairs and around the corner to **Vetri** (*1404 1st Ave.*), which sells smaller-scale glass art and home objects from emerging artists at reasonable prices. *✉ 110 Union St., Suite 200, Downtown ☎ 206/587–6501 🌐 www.travergallery.com 🎫 Free ⏲ Closed Sun.-Mon.*

Restaurants

After a day of exploring the museums, sights, and shops, what could be better than a perfect meal? Luckily, this area is filled with a wide range of eateries, from the offerings in and around Pike Place Market to happening spots inside hotels. Though Downtown has great options, serious foodies will want to venture outside of this area for something truly spectacular.

Ben Paris

$$ | **AMERICAN** | Located in the hip State Hotel, Ben Paris has become a neighborhood favorite for elevated classic American fare—think shrimp cocktail, wedge salads, fried chicken, and crab Louie—dished up in a stylish space with graphic wallpaper and a bustling bar. Don't miss the outstanding grilled octopus or the creative cocktail list designed by Abigail Gullo, a star bartender from New Orleans (one drink is served in a darling copper bird mug). **Known for:** avocado or tuna confit toast for breakfast/lunch; craft cocktails with unique ingredients; inside one of Seattle's coolest hotels. *$ Average main: $22 ✉ The State Hotel, 130 Pike St., Downtown ☎ 206/513-7303 🌐 www.benparis.com.*

Country Dough

$ | **SICHUAN** | After introducing Seattle to the wonders of Sichuanese cuisine at a variety of restaurants around town in the last few decades, chef Cheng Biao Yang has settled into his smallest space yet, where he serves a pared-down menu of Chinese street foods. The hand-shaved noodles, flatbread sandwiches, and Chinese crepes (known as *jian bing* in Chinese) form the backbone of the menu, each dough-based specialty customizable with various stews, meats, and spicy sauces. **Known for:** flatbread sandwiches; street food. *$ Average main: $8 ✉ 1916 Pike Pl., #14, Downtown ✥ Walk through building entrance and to back, Country Dough is on your right ☎ 206/728–2598 🌐 www.countrydough.com ⏲ No dinner.*

★ Ellenos Real Greek Yogurt

$ | **FAST FOOD** | When people walk by the Pike Place Market booth, they might think they're passing a gelato stand from the artful display, but in fact Ellenos is serving up the best (and best-looking) yogurt in the city—and possibly the country. Thicker and smoother than most commercial Greek yogurts, the Australian-Greek family behind the brand uses local milk and a slow culturing process to create their nearly ice cream-like treat. **Known for:** Greek yogurt with a cult following; fresh fruit toppings. *$ Average main: $4 ✉ 1500 Pike Pl., Downtown ☎ 206/535–7562 🌐 www.ellenos.com ⏲ No dinner.*

FareStart

$$ | **AMERICAN** | A project of the nationally lauded FareStart job-training program, this eatery in a sleek, dramatic space on Virginia Street serves an American-style lunch of sandwiches, burgers, mac-and-cheese, and fries during the week, as well as rotating specials. Reservations

Matt's in the Market is a favorite eatery at Pike Place.

are essential for the three-course, $34.95 Thursday dinners, prepared by a guest chef from an impressive rotating roster of occasionally noteworthy local restaurants from across the city. **Known for:** philanthropic mission and a reliably good lunch; some talented chefs participate in guest night. *Average main: $14 ✉ 700 Virginia St., Downtown ☎ 206/267–7601 🌐 www.farestart.org ⏲ No lunch weekends, no dinner Fri.–Wed.*

Le Pichet

$$ | FRENCH | Slate tabletops, a tile floor, and a rolled-zinc bar will transport you out of Downtown Seattle and into the charming 6th arrondissement. The menu is quintessentially French: at lunch there are rustic pâtés and *jambon et fromage* (ham-and-cheese) sandwiches on crusty baguettes; dinner sees homemade sausages, daily fish specials, and steak tartare. **Known for:** where local chefs go for real French food; a roast chicken for two that's worth the hour-long wait; always bustling and loud with conversation. *Average main: $20 ✉ 1933 1st Ave., Downtown ☎ 206/256–1499 🌐 www.lepichetseattle.com.*

Lecosho

$$$ | AMERICAN | Matt Janke (formerly of Matt's in the Market) doesn't have his name on the marquee here, but he still prepares modern, hearty, soul-satisfying dishes that rely on ingredients from Pike Place Market. Lecosho's motto is "food we like"—they say the name is Chinook for "swine," and that means a menu heavy on the likes of house-made charcuterie and sausage, guanciale with salmon, and a pork chop served with pancetta. **Known for:** seasonal Northwest cooking; lighter fish and veggie dishes measure up; a breezy and fairly quiet outdoor patio. *Average main: $28 ✉ 89 University St., Downtown ☎ 206/623–2101 🌐 www.lecosho.com ⏲ No lunch weekends.*

★ Matt's in the Market

$$$$ | PACIFIC NORTHWEST | One of the most beloved of Pike Place Market's restaurants, Matt's is all about intimate dining, fresh ingredients, and superb service. You can perch at the bar for pints and the signature deviled eggs or be seated at a table—complete with vases filled with flowers from the market—for a seasonal menu that synthesizes the best picks from the restaurant's produce vendors and an excellent wine list. **Known for:** wonderful Market and water views; a fresh catch of the day; daily late-night hours until 1 am. *$ Average main: $40 ✉ 94 Pike St., Downtown ☎ 206/467–7909 🌐 www.mattsinthemarket.com.*

Metropolitan Grill

$$$$ | STEAKHOUSE | This is a favorite lunch spot for the professional crowd but it's not for timid eaters: custom dry-aged mesquite-grilled steaks and chops (note that steaks start at $60 but the meal will end up costing much more than that)—among the best in Seattle—are huge and come with a hearty side option. The Met's take on a steak house is either classic or a caricature, depending on how you take to the cigar-and-cognac vibe: servers wear tuxes and everything is clad in fine wood, brass, and velvet. **Known for:** splurge-worthy steaks; rich sides like lobster mac 'n' cheese; classic service. *$ Average main: $72 ✉ 820 2nd Ave., Downtown ☎ 206/624–3287 🌐 www.themetropolitangrill.com ⏲ No lunch weekends.*

The Pink Door

$$$ | ITALIAN | With its Post Alley entrance and meager signage, the Pink Door's speakeasy vibe draws Pike Place Market regulars almost as much as its savory, seasonal Italian food does. The food is good, and the pappardelle *al ràgu Bolognese* and cioppino are reliably standout entrées, but people come here mostly for the atmosphere (which includes tasteful cabaret acts) and shaded outdoor deck with views of Elliott Bay (reservations are strongly recommended). **Known for:** an entertaining atmosphere; classic Italian dishes; a large patio with an arbor, grapevines, and a view. *$ Average main: $25 ✉ 1919 Post Alley, Downtown ☎ 206/443–3241 🌐 www.thepinkdoor.net ⏲ No lunch Sun.*

Place Pigalle

$$$ | MODERN AMERICAN | Large windows look out on Elliott Bay in this cozy spot tucked behind a meat vendor in Pike Place Market's main arcade. In nice weather, open windows let in the fresh salt breeze. **Known for:** more Pacific Northwest than French; rich oyster stew; local beer on tap. *$ Average main: $35 ✉ 81 Pike St., Downtown ☎ 206/624–1756 🌐 www.placepigalle-seattle.com.*

Six Seven

$$$$ | SEAFOOD | Like the Edgewater Hotel that houses it, Six Seven would be noteworthy for its views of Elliott Bay and the Puget Sound alone, especially if you opt to dine at the café tables lining the deck. Regionally sourced seafood such as planked salmon and miso-glazed black cod take top billing on the menu, which also features dishes like wild boar Bolognese and Roquefort-crusted filet Mignon alongside an award-winning wine list. **Known for:** budget-friendly brunch; classic shareable sides; nice alternative to touristy waterfront seafood restaurants. *$ Average main: $45 ✉ In Edgewater Hotel, 2411 Alaskan Way, Pier 67, Downtown ☎ 206/728–7000 🌐 www.edgewaterhotel.com.*

★ Sushi Kashiba

$$$$ | SUSHI | After decades spent earning a reputation as one of Seattle's top sushi chefs, Shiro Kashiba opened his own spot in a location as notable as his skill with seafood deserves. Diners in the spare-but-elegant Pike Place Market space can opt for the *omakase* (chef's choice) selection of the best fish from around the world and just up the street, or order from the menu of Japanese classics and sashimi. **Known for:** local celebrity chef; omakase is expensive but a memorable tasting experience; outstanding service. *$ Average main: $85 ✉ 86 Pine St., Suite 1, Downtown ✣ Inn at the Market ☎ 206/441–8844 🌐 www.sushikashiba.com ⊗ No lunch.*

Hotels

Downtown has the greatest concentration of hotels, many of which are new or updated high-end high-rises, though there are also several boutique hotels and midrange properties in historic buildings. There aren't many budget properties in the area. All Downtown hotels are convenient (and within walking distance) to many major sights—including the Seattle Art Museum, Pike Place Market, and the Olympic Sculpture Park; sights that aren't a short walk away are easily accessible via public transit, and there are plenty of buses, as well as the light rail and the Monorail in this part of town. Although the waterfront is an integral part of Downtown, there are surprisingly few hotels directly on the water. Many high-rises have water views, but make sure to specify that you want a room with a view. Hotel prices climb significantly during July and August, which are the two most reliably good weather months in Seattle.

★ Alexis Hotel

$$$ | **HOTEL** | The guestrooms received a top-to-bottom redo in 2019 at the boutique Alexis, which occupies a pair of historic buildings (on the National Register of Historic Places, in fact) near the waterfront; the new design features nautical- and Northwest-inspired hues, textures, and furnishings that complement the hotel's exposed brick and walls of windows. **Pros:** a short walk to the waterfront; chic modern rooms that appeal to design lovers; suites aren't prohibitively expensive. **Cons:** small lobby; not entirely soundproofed against old building and city noise; some rooms can be a bit dark. *$ Rooms from: $397 ✉ 1007 1st Ave., Downtown ☎ 206/624–4844, 888/850–1155 🌐 www.alexishotel.com ⇆ 88 rooms 🍽 No meals.*

The Charter Hotel

$$ | **HOTEL** | Part of the Hilton's upscale Curio Collection, the new Charter Hotel features chic, quiet rooms with floor-to-ceiling windows, marbled wallpaper, 50-inch TVs, and spacious bathrooms; don't miss the hotel's 16th-floor Fog Room bar, which has city and water views and outdoor seating. **Pros:** quiet and immensely comfortable rooms; a treat for Hilton Honors loyalists; great location near Pike Place Market. **Cons:** not the best water views considering its location; the on-site restaurant is only so-so; showers only in some bathrooms. *$ Rooms from: $228 ✉ 1610 2nd Ave., Downtown ☎ 206/256-7500 ⇆ 229 rooms 🍽 No meals.*

★ The Fairmont Olympic Hotel

$$$$ | **HOTEL** | **FAMILY** | While the lobby of this glamorous luxury hotel sweeps guests away with Old World marble floors, soaring ceilings, massive chandeliers, and grand staircases, the guest rooms have a decidedly more modern feel, with mid century-inspired furnishings and all-marble bathrooms featuring rain showers and designer toiletries. **Pros:** impeccable service; a top-notch fitness center with an indoor pool; great on-site dining and amenities. **Cons:** not much in the way of views; valet parking is $60; some rooms on the small side. *$ Rooms from: $366 ✉ 411 University St., Downtown ☎ 206/621–1700, 888/363–5022 🌐 www.fairmont.com/seattle ⇆ 450 rooms 🍽 No meals.*

★ Four Seasons Hotel Seattle

$$$$ | **HOTEL** | **FAMILY** | Just south of the Pike Place Market and steps from the Seattle Art Museum, this Downtown gem overlooking Elliott Bay is polished and elegant, with spacious light-filled guest rooms that were renovated in 2019; the fresh new design features serene hues that nod to the hotel's

surroundings, museum-quality art reproductions, and comfortable high-end modern furnishings. **Pros:** fantastic outdoor inifinity pool with views for miles; luxurious marble bathrooms with deep soaking tubs; lovely spa facility offering extensive treatments. **Cons:** Four Seasons regulars might not click with this modern take on the brand; street-side rooms not entirely soundproofed; some water-facing room views are partially obscured by industrial sites. *Rooms from: $720 ✉ 99 Union St., Downtown ☎ 206/749–7000, 800/332–3442 🌐 www.fourseasons.com/seattle 134 rooms No meals.*

Grand Hyatt Seattle

$$ | **HOTEL** | Adjacent to the Washington State Convention Center, this view-centric hotel with spacious rooms appeals to business travelers, conventioneers, or brand loyalists who want a dependable Hyatt-level stay in a central Downtown location. **Pros:** city-and-water views from upper-floor rooms; large bathrooms with ample counter space; on-site brand-name restaurants. **Cons:** not a ton of personality; some traffic and construction noise; no lounge. *Rooms from: $279 ✉ 721 Pine St., Downtown ☎ 206/774–1234 🌐 www.grandseattle.hyatt.com 425 rooms No meals.*

Hilton Seattle

$$ | **HOTEL** | Just west of I–5, the Hilton Seattle is a popular site for meetings, conventions, and the summer cruise set, with newly renovated rooms are tasteful but nondescript—you'll be paying for a brand name here, reliable though it may be. **Pros:** helpful staff; clean rooms, some with city views; comfortable beds. **Cons:** overpriced for what you get; small bathrooms; lacks personality compared to other area hotels. *Rooms from: $230 ✉ 1301 6th Ave., Downtown ☎ 206/624–0500, 800/426–0535 🌐 www.thehiltonseattle.com 237 rooms, 3 suites No meals.*

Hotel Max

$$$ | **HOTEL** | Hip and art-forward, the Hotel Max (for "Maximalism") blends artsy decor with punchy minimalism for an architect-office effect, and though most of the rooms are on the small side, they come with cushy trimmings. **Pros:** hip, youthful vibe; extra pet-friendly (it's OK to leave pets in the room unattended); 4-minute walk from Westlake Center transit hub. **Cons:** tiny rooms and even tinier elevator; traffic noise, thin walls, and late-night revelers; older and larger travelers may not be comfortable here. *Rooms from: $325 ✉ 620 Stewart St., Downtown ☎ 866/833–6299, 866/833–6299 🌐 www.hotelmaxseattle.com 163 rooms No meals.*

Hotel Monaco

$$ | **HOTEL** | **FAMILY** | It only takes one glimpse of the gorgeous global-modern lobby to know that this stylish boutique hotel in the heart of Downtown is a standout, and rooms carry on the eclectic feel, with a palette of soft reds and gunmetal grays, beds topped with Frette linens, floor-to-ceiling drapes in a Turkish motif, and floor lamps that recall telescopes. **Pros:** some rooms feature fabulous deep soaking tubs; welcoming public spaces; daily hosted wine reception with savory snacks. **Cons:** some street-facing rooms can be noisy; small gym; a daily "facilities" fee. *Rooms from: $200 ✉ 1101 4th Ave., Downtown ☎ 206/621–1770, 800/715–6513 🌐 www.monaco-seattle.com 187 rooms No meals.*

Hotel Theodore

$$ | **HOTEL** | The 90-year-old Roosevelt Hotel got a serious makeover before debuting as Hotel Theodore, a stylish boutique hotel with handsome industrial furnishings and artwork, soundproofed guest rooms, and Rider, an upscale restaurant with Pacific Northwest fare and an exhibition kitchen that includes an impressive wood-fired grill. **Pros:** some rooms have Freeman Seattle raincoats

available to borrow; right by freeway and great Downtown shopping; a warm and welcoming bar. **Cons:** standard rooms are small; though interior soundproofing is great, some street/construction noise gets through; lower-floor views can be drab. *Rooms from: $190 1531 7th Ave., Downtown 206/621-1200 hoteltheodore.com 153 rooms No meals.*

Hotel Vintage

$$ | **HOTEL** | Each of the serene, quiet rooms—some of which boast marvelous views of Seattle's iconic public library—feature a vineyard-inspired palette of burgundy, taupe, and green hues, with a focus on unique interior design and comfortable touches. **Pros:** truly pet-friendly (dogs get their own beds and bowls); a wonderful hosted wine hour; on-site Tulio is a nice upscale Italian restaurant. **Cons:** a short-but-steep uphill walk from Downtown could be tough on some travelers; lobby is attractive but small; bathrooms aren't particularly spacious. *Rooms from: $240 1100 5th Ave., Downtown 206/624–8000, 800/853–3914 www.hotelvintage-seattle.com 125 rooms No meals.*

★ Hyatt at Olive 8

$$$$ | **HOTEL** | In a city known for environmental responsibility, being one of the greenest hotels in town is no small feat, and green is rarely this chic—rooms have floor-to-ceiling windows flooding the place with light along with enviro touches like dual-flush toilets, fresh-air vents, and low-flow showerheads. **Pros:** central location; serene indoor pool; one of Seattle's best day spas. **Cons:** standard rooms have showers only; guests complain of hallway and traffic noise; translucent glass bathroom doors offer little privacy. *Rooms from: $339 1635 8th Ave., Downtown 206/695–1234, 800/233–1234 www.olive8.hyatt.com 346 rooms No meals.*

Dog-Friendly Seattle

Seattle ranks as one of the top dog cities in the country, with more canines living here than children. Pooches are pampered with 14 off-leash areas within city boundaries, including 9-acre Magnuson Park, which includes a stretch of beach on Lake Washington and a special area for small dogs. More than 70 hotels allow furry friends to stay for free or a fee, and some go out of their way to make pets feel as welcome as their human pals (Hotel Vintage puts out a special bed and bowls for canine guests and offers pet-sitting services and a list of Fido-friendly attractions).

Hyatt Regency

$$ | **HOTEL** | **FAMILY** | This newcomer to the Downtown hotel scene—which happens to be right next door to the future Convention Center expansion—currently holds the title of the biggest hotel in the Pacific Northwest; the Hyatt's sophisticated 45-story tower practically feels like a small city, with multiple dining options, a large cutting-edge gym, and an especially swanky Regency Club. **Pros:** spacious rooms are brand-new, quiet, and very comfortable; expansive cityscape and water views; an outpost of Seattle steak house Daniel's Broiler. **Cons:** not as close to the waterfront action as many hotels; no single cozy lobby space for gathering; might feel a bit business-y for pleasure travelers. *Rooms from: $246 808 Howell St., Downtown 206/973–1234 www.hyatt.com 1,260 rooms No meals.*

★ **Inn at the Market**

$$$$ | **HOTEL** | From its heart-stopping views to the fabulous location just steps from Pike Place Market, this is a place you'll want to visit again and again. **Pros:** outstanding views from most rooms; deals on rooms that don't have views, even in peak season; guests have access to the fabulous rooftop deck. **Cons:** not much indoor common space; some street and Market noise; not the easiest to get in and out by car. *Rooms from: $390* ✉ *86 Pine St., Downtown* ☎ *206/443–3600, 800/446–4484* 🌐 *www.innatthemarket.com* *70 rooms* *No meals.*

Loews Hotel 1000

$$$ | **HOTEL** | **FAMILY** | Part of the reliably luxurious Loews brand and a short walk from the waterfront, Hotel 1000 features chic, ultra-comfortable rooms with on-trend contemporary design elements and unexpected touches like large soaking tubs that fill from the ceiling. **Pros:** ideal location near Pike Place Market; golf simulator and spa; upper-floor rooms have great city and water views. **Cons:** bar attracts a lot of tourists; a handful of no-view rooms look out to a cement wall; on-site seafood restaurant just so-so. *Rooms from: $302* ✉ *1000 1st Ave., Downtown* ☎ *206/957–1000, 844/244–4973* 🌐 *www.hotel1000seattle.com* *120 rooms* *No meals.*

★ **Mayflower Park Hotel**

$$$ | **HOTEL** | Comfortable, old-world charm comes with sturdy antiques, Asian accents, brass fixtures, and florals, and though the hotel's main draw is its central location close to all the action, street noise isn't much of an issue thanks to the sturdy old construction of the historic 1927 building. **Pros:** close to light rail and Monorail; on-site Spanish restaurant Andaluca is well worth a visit; comfortable beds. **Cons:** some of the rooms are small; old-fashioned for some travelers; not all rooms have mini fridges. *Rooms from: $354* ✉ *405 Olive Way, Downtown* ☎ *206/623–8700, 800/426–5100* 🌐 *www.mayflowerpark.com* *189 rooms* *No meals.*

Motif Seattle Hotel

$$ | **HOTEL** | With a colorful vibe and eye-catching design motifs throughout, this conveniently located urban property has a boutique feel despite its large size, with basic, comfortable guest rooms and a 4,000-square-foot outdoor terrace on the fifth floor with fireplaces, games, and city views. **Pros:** in the heart of Downtown; water-and-mountain views in some upper-floor rooms; several cool communal spaces. **Cons:** rooms near terrace can be loud; small bathrooms; service can be slow and mediocre. *Rooms from: $199* ✉ *1415 5th Ave., Downtown* ☎ *206/971–8015* *329 rooms* *No meals.*

Palihotel

$$ | **HOTEL** | A fabulous shade of dark green coats most of the interior walls and brick surfaces at this eclectic boutique hotel in a historic building (circa 1898) just a block up from Pike Place Market, and other vintage-modern design touches are equally memorable, like bold graphic tile in the bathrooms, chintz headboards and accent pillows, and Smeg tea kettles. **Pros:** the fresh design perfectly suits the old architecture; good coffee shop and cocktail bar; cool, cozy lounge with a fireplace. **Cons:** no free coffee in rooms or the lobby; light sleepers might be disturbed by street noise; bathrooms are small. *Rooms from: $240* ✉ *107 Pine St., Downtown* ☎ *206/596–0600* 🌐 *www.palisociety.com* *96 rooms* *No meals.*

★ **The Paramount Hotel**

$$ | **HOTEL** | Good value meets great location at this comfortable boutique hotel with friendly service and tasteful contemporary furnishings, including a decent-size desk for business travelers. **Pros:** close to the Convention Center; clean, quiet rooms; ice chests instead of machines mean less noise. **Cons:** not much in the way of amenities; tiny fitness center;

small lobby. $ *Rooms from: $240 ✉ 724 Pine St., Downtown ☎ 206/292–9500 ⊕ www.paramounthotelseattle.com ⇆ 146 rooms 🍴 No meals.*

Renaissance Seattle Hotel

$$$ | **HOTEL** | A bit of a walk uphill from Downtown, this high-rise has a calm feel to it, with contemporary decor, inviting common areas, and especially great views of Elliott Bay from rooms above the 20th floor. **Pros:** comfy beds; the pool at the rooftop health club; good deals are often available online. **Cons:** freeway noise; some visitors won't enjoy the walk uphill; not much happening in the area at night. $ *Rooms from: $369 ✉ 515 Madison St., Downtown ☎ 206/583–0300, 800/546–9184 ⊕ www.renaissanceseattle.com ⇆ 553 rooms 🍴 No meals.*

★ **The State Hotel**

$$ | **HOTEL** | From the huge exterior mural by artist Shepard Fairey to the gorgeous graphic wallpaper inspired by nearby Pike Place Market, every inch of this hip new boutique hotel is eye candy, including stylish rooms with sleek, tiled rain showers, an eclectic and welcoming lobby, and vibrant Ben Paris bar and restaurant, where neighborhood locals are as likely to hang out as tourists. **Pros:** minimal but well-appointed guest rooms, some with nice water views; really friendly service; great lobby coffee. **Cons:** some rooms are on the small side; not kid-friendly; rooftop patio only has a few tables. $ *Rooms from: $200 ✉ 1501 2nd Ave., Downtown ☎ 800/827–3900 ⊕ www.statehotel.com ⇆ 91 rooms 🍴 No meals.*

★ **Thompson Seattle**

$$$ | **HOTEL** | Designed by local starchitects Olson Kundig, the 12-story Thompson Seattle (a Hyatt hotel) makes an impression with a contemporary glass exterior and sophisticated guest rooms that feature floor-to-ceiling windows—some framing epic water views—hardwood floors, a crisp white-and-navy palette, and leather and smoked-glass accents. **Pros:** perfect for the style obsessed; very close to Pike Place Market; home to The Nest rooftop bar. **Cons:** blazing afternoon sun in some rooms; some small rooms; floor beneath rooftop bar can be noisy. $ *Rooms from: $279 ✉ 110 Stewart St., Downtown ☎ 206/623–4600 ⊕ www.thompsonhotels.com/hotels/thompson-seattle ⇆ 158 rooms 🍴 No meals.*

W Seattle

$$$ | **HOTEL** | With a club-like atmosphere that starts at the VIP-style lobby check-in, the W Seattle goes for a distinct "urban lodge" vibe, with guest rooms that feature a palette of Seattle-inspired grays and blues accented by bright pops of color, as well as headboards made from floor-to-ceiling backlit wood stacks and Northwest touches like plaid pillows and Pendleton-pattern wallpaper. **Pros:** lively late-night scene in lobby bar; comfortable beds; great city views. **Cons:** self-consciously trendy; a bit too youthful for some visitors; outrageous room service prices. $ *Rooms from: $319 ✉ 1112 4th Ave., Downtown ☎ 206/264–6000, 877/946–8357 ⊕ www.wseattle.com ⇆ 424 rooms, 9 suites 🍴 No meals.*

Nightlife

Downtown is a great place for anyone looking to dress up a bit and hit glam hotel bars, classy lounges, and wine bars where you don't have to be under the age of 30 to fit in. Downtown also has a smattering of pubs popular with the happy-hour crowd. Barhopping Downtown may require several taxi rides, as things can be a bit spread out, but cabs can actually be hailed on the street in this part of town.

COCKTAIL LOUNGES

Alibi Room

BARS/PUBS | Well-dressed locals head to this hard-to-find wood-paneled bar to sip double martinis while taking in views of Elliott Bay or studying the scripts, handbills, and movie posters that line the walls. The lower level is more crowded and casual. Stop by for a drink or a meal, and stay to listen and dance to live music. Happy hour—daily from 11:30 am to 6 pm—is quiet and a good respite from the Market. ✉ *85 Pike St., in Post Alley, at Pike Place Market, Downtown* ☎ *206/623–3180* 🌐 *www.seattlealibi.com.*

The Diller Room

BARS/PUBS | Occupying the former lobby of the historic Diller Hotel, which was built in 1890, the Diller Room is a charming, worn-around-the-edges spot for cocktails in downtown, across the street from the Seattle Art Museum. Exposed brick, mismatched crystal chandeliers, a beat-up white tile floor, and a vintage neon Diller Hotel sign above the wood bar provide the atmosphere. The drink menu includes cocktails and a section devoted to tallboys. Happy hour runs 2–7 pm every day, and the food menu offers various sliders, pizzas, and bar snacks. ✉ *1224 1st Ave., Downtown* ☎ *206/467–4042* 🌐 *www.dillerroom.com.*

Fog Room

BARS/PUBS | Perched on the 16th floor of The Charter Hotel, Fog Room is the latest arrival to Seattle's small rooftop bar scene and it's a classy modern one, from the decor to the cocktails. A chic indoor lounge with expansive windows opens to an outdoor terrace with seating and a fire pit; the city and water views aren't the best of the bunch, but you don't need to reserve outdoor seating. ✉ *The Charter Hotel, 1610 2nd Ave., Downtown* ☎ *206/256–7525* 🌐 *www.fogroomseattle.com.*

Heartwood Provisions

BARS/PUBS | From the arcing bar at Heartwood Provisions, you can look through tall windows onto Spring Street as you sip house cocktails, wine, or beer, and eat upscale bar food in a light-filled room. During the daily happy hour from 3 to 6 pm, specials include discounted cocktails, beer, and wine, and a small menu ranging from snacks to a steak. ✉ *1103 1st Ave., Downtown* ☎ *206/582–3505* 🌐 *www.heartwoodsea.com.*

Oliver's

BARS/PUBS | The most important question here: shaken or stirred? This sophisticated bar in the Mayflower Park Hotel is famous for its martinis. In fact, having a cocktail here is like having afternoon tea in some other parts of the world. Wing chairs, low tables, and lots of natural light make it easy to relax after a hectic day. The likes of Frank Sinatra or Billie Holiday may be playing in the background; expect an unfussy crowd of regulars and hotel guests. ✉ *405 Olive Way, Downtown* ☎ *206/623–8700* 🌐 *oliverstwistseattle.com.*

The Nest at Thompson Seattle

BARS/PUBS | Yes, the Nest has carefully crafted cocktails and tasty snacks, but the real draw is the breathtaking, unobstructed view of Elliot Bay. On a clear evening, the outdoor deck, with ample seating and fireplaces, is the perfect spot to gaze across Puget Sound at the Olympic Mountains. This place gets busy, though, so reservations—available for parties of four to 20 guests—are a good idea. ✉ *110 Stewart St., Downtown* ☎ *206/623–4600* 🌐 *www.thompsonhotels.com.*

★ Zig Zag Café

BARS/PUBS | A mixed crowd of mostly locals hunts out this unique spot at Pike Place Market's Street Hill Climb (walk past the Gum Wall—yes, it really is as disgusting as it sounds—to find a nearly hidden stairwell leading down to the piers). In addition to pouring a perfect martini, Zig Zag features a revolving cast of memorable cocktails. A Mediterranean-inspired food menu offers plenty of tasty bites to accompany the excellent cocktails. A small patio is the place to be on a summery happy-hour evening. Zig Zag is friendly—retro without being obnoxiously ironic—and very Seattle, with the occasional live music show to boot. ✉ *1501 Western Ave., Downtown* ☎ *206/625–1146* 🌐 *zigzagseattle.com.*

WINE BARS

Purple Café and Wine Bar

BARS/PUBS | Wine lovers come for the massive selection—the menu boasts 90 wines by the glass and some 600 bottles—but this place deserves props for its design, too. Despite the cavernous quality of the space and floor-to-ceiling windows, all eyes are immediately drawn to the 20-foot tower ringed by a spiral staircase that showcases thousands of bottles. Full lunch and dinner menus feature American and Pacific Northwest fare—the lobster mac 'n' cheese is especially tasty—and servers know their ideal pairings. ✉ *1225 4th Ave., Downtown* ☎ *206/829–2280* 🌐 *www.thepurplecafe.com.*

BREW PUBS

The Pike Brewing Company

BARS/PUBS | True to its location, you might find more tourists than locals at the Pike Brewing Company, though it is popular with the Downtown after-work crowd. The cavernous bar and restaurant, operated by the brewers of the Pike Place Pale Ale, also houses the Seattle Microbrewery Museum and an excellent shop with home-brewing supplies. Pints of beer are cold and satisfying—the pale ale and the Kilt Lifter Scottish ale have been local favorites for more than two decades. ✉ *1415 1st Ave., Downtown* ☎ *206/622–6044* 🌐 *www.pikebrewing.com.*

Old Stove Brewing Co.

BREWPUBS/BEER GARDENS | **FAMILY** | Part of Pike Place Market's recent expansion, Old Stove Brewing—which is brewed on site—might be the kid-friendliest taproom in town. Choose from 24 drafts at the award-winning brewery and restaurant; try to nab a seat on the patio or by the window (especially at sunset) so you can watch ferries glide across the Puget Sound from the 80-foot west-facing window that frames Elliott Bay and the mountains. ✉ *Pike Place Market, 1901 Western Ave., Downtown* ☎ *206/602–6120* 🌐 *www.oldstove.com.*

COMEDY CLUBS

Unexpected Productions Improv

COMEDY CLUBS | Unexpected Productions Improv, adjacent to Pike Place Market, hosts tons of different improv events; shows may have holiday or seasonal themes or be done in the style of a certain TV or film genre like sci-fi or noir. On Friday and Saturday at 10:30, the troupe presents the long-running "TheatreSports" show, in which the skits are based entirely on audience suggestions. ✉ *Market Theater, 1428 Post Alley, Downtown* ☎ *206/587–2414* 🌐 *www.unexpectedproductions.org.*

LIVE MUSIC

Dimitriou's Jazz Alley

MUSIC CLUBS | Seattleites dress up to see nationally known jazz artists at Dimitriou's. The cabaret-style theater, where intimate tables for two surround the stage, runs shows nightly. Those with reservations for cocktails or dinner, served during the first set, receive priority seating. ✉ *2033 6th Ave., Downtown* ☎ *206/441–9729* 🌐 *www.jazzalley.com.*

Owl N' Thistle Irish Pub

MUSIC CLUBS | This affable pub near Pike Place Market presents acoustic folk music on a small stage in a cavernous room. It's often loaded with regulars, who appreciate the well-drawn pints of Guinness, the talent, and the Tuesday-night jazz jam. ✉ *808 Post Ave., Downtown* ☎ *206/621–7777* 🌐 *www.owlnthistle.com.*

The Triple Door

MUSIC CLUBS | Come here for live world music and jazz. The seating is half-moon booths giving it a cabaret lounge feel. They also host a bawdy burlesque show during the holidays. ✉ *216 Union St., Downtown* ☎ *206/838–4333* 🌐 *www.thetripledoor.net.*

The Grammy-nominated Seattle Symphony performs in Benaroya Hall.

Performing Arts

The high-tech boom created an enthusiastic and philanthropic audience for Seattle's arts community, which continues to grow. The gorgeous Benaroya Hall is a national benchmark for acoustic design.

FILM

Big Picture

FILM | Enjoy the same first-run films that are playing down the street at the multiplex—minus the crowds, screaming kids, and sensory overload—at the Big Picture. This small, elegant theater has a full bar (you can order refills during the screening), and it's 21 and older only. ✉ *2505 1st Ave., Belltown* ☎ *206/256–0572* 🌐 *www.thebigpicture.net.*

★ **Cinerama**

FILM | This 1963 cinema, scooped up and restored by the late Microsoft billionaire Paul Allen, seamlessly blends the luxury of the theater with high technology. Behind a standard-size movie screen sits an enormous, 30-foot by 90-foot restored curved panel—one of only three in the world—used to screen old three-strip films like *How the West Was Won,* as well as 70-millimeter presentations of *2001: A Space Odyssey.* The sight lines throughout are amazing. Rear-window captioning, assisted listening devices, audio narration, wheelchair access, and other amenities ensure that everyone has an outstanding experience. ✉ *2100 4th Ave., Belltown* ☎ *206/448–6680* 🌐 *www.cinerama.com.*

ARTS CENTERS

Benaroya Hall

CONCERTS | The acoustics are good from every one of the main hall's 2,500 seats—great news if you want to check out the Seattle Symphony, which is based here, or any of a number of world-class speakers, musicians, and other performers who appear here throughout the year. The four-story lobby has a curved glass facade that makes intermissions almost as impressive as performances. ✉ *200 University St., Seattle* ☎ *206/215–4800* 🌐 *www.seattlesymphony.org/benaroya.*

CLASSICAL MUSIC

★ Seattle Symphony

MUSIC | The symphony performs under the direction of Ludovic Morlot from September through June in the stunning Benaroya Hall. The group has been nominated for numerous Grammy Awards and is well regarded nationally and internationally. ✉ *Benaroya Hall, 200 University St., Downtown* ☎ *206/215–4747* 🌐 *www.seattlesymphony.org.*

THEATER

A Contemporary Theatre (*ACT*)

THEATER | Dedicated to launching exciting works by emerging dramatists, the Contemporary has four staging areas, including a theater-in-the-round and an intimate downstairs space for small shows. The season runs from April to November. ✉ *700 Union St., Downtown* ☎ *206/292–7676* 🌐 *www.acttheatre.org.*

The 5th Avenue Theatre

THEATER | Even if you don't plan on seeing anything here, this Asian fantasia is worth a peek—it's one of the most beautiful venues in the world. The 5th Avenue Theatre opened in 1926 as a silent-movie house and vaudeville stage, complete with a giant pipe organ and ushers who dressed as cowboys and pirates. Today it has its own theater company, which stages lavish productions October through May. At other times it hosts concerts, lectures, and films. ✉ *1308 5th Ave., Downtown* ☎ *206/625–1900* 🌐 *www.5thavenue.org.*

Shopping

Much of the Downtown core is given over to chains, but shoppers from towns without their own J.Crew and Ann Taylor will be pleased with the ample offering of reliable retail. Louis Vuitton, Gucci, Anthropologie, and Brooks Brothers anchor the area around 5th Avenue. You'll find Nordstrom's lovely flagship store here, and an outdoor urban atmosphere of street musicians, and the bustle of industry, making for an enjoyable, walkable retail experience. Independent gems are scattered throughout, particularly in and around Pike Place Market and along Western Avenue—although for a greater concentration of indie stores, head to Capitol Hill, Belltown, or the northern neighborhoods. Downtown is a great area for wandering, browsing, and people-watching along the way, but we've listed the shops that are worth a special visit.

Best shopping: 4th, 5th, and 6th Avenues between Pine and Spring Streets, and 1st Avenue between Virginia and Madison Streets.

ANTIQUES AND COLLECTIBLES

Seattle Antiques Market

ANTIQUES/COLLECTIBLES | For antiques lovers, this market should not be missed. A funky warehouse offering everything from modern furniture to gemstones and bicycles, there is an unmistakable charm that keeps Seattleites coming back. Parking is tricky, so if you are already shopping in Pike Place Market, we recommend soaking up the fresh salty breeze and walking to this hidden gem. ✉ *1400 Alaskan Way* ☎ *206/623–6115* 🌐 *www.seattleantiquesmarket.com.*

APPAREL

Alhambra

CLOTHING | Sophisticated yet casual, this pricey boutique delivers quality, European-style looks for women of all ages. Pop into the Moorish-inspired shop for a party dress, elegant jewelry, or separates, and be sure to check out the house line, designed by the owners. ✉ *101 Pine St., Downtown* ☎ *206/621–9571* 🌐 *www.alhambrastyle.com.*

Baby & Company

CLOTHING | There's nothing childish about this sophisticated fashion house. A longtime Seattle favorite, Baby and Company dresses women and men in urban-lifestyle looks by independent designers that only the fashion savvy would know. Edgy, asymmetrical frocks; jackets; and sweaters with graphic prints come in butter-soft linens, wool, jersey, and crepe. You'll pay a lot for the privilege of being ahead of the trends. ✉ *1936 1st Ave., Downtown* ☎ *206/448–4077* 🌐 *www.babyandco.us.*

Endless Knot

CLOTHING | An alternative to the high-end designers that are scattered throughout Downtown Seattle's shopping haven, this women's clothing store offers on-trend options that won't break the bank. From dresses to coats to accessories galore, this perfectly manicured boutique is a gold mine. ✉ *2300 1st Ave.* ☎ *206/448–0355* 🌐 *www.endlessknotseattle.com.*

Marios

CLOTHING | Known for fabulous service and designer labels, this high-end boutique treats every client like a superstar. Men shop the ground floor for Armani, Etro, and Zegna; women ascend the ornate staircase for Prada, Emilio Pucci, and Lanvin. A freestanding Hugo Boss boutique sells the sharpest tuxedos in town. ✉ *1513 6th Ave., Downtown* ☎ *206/223–1461* 🌐 *www.marios.com.*

BOOKS

Metsker Maps of Seattle

BOOKS/STATIONERY | Whether you're searching for a laminated pocket map of Seattle or a world map made up of music notes, stop here for a massive selection of books, globes, charts, atlases, antique reproduction maps, and local satellite images. Don't let the store's location in the middle of Pike Place Market fool you: this is a Seattle institution, not a tourist trap. ✉ *1511 1st Ave., Downtown* ☎ *206/623–8747* 🌐 *www.metskers.com.*

DEPARTMENT STORES

★ Nordstrom

DEPARTMENT STORES | Seattle's own retail giant sells quality clothing, accessories, cosmetics, jewelry, and lots of shoes—in keeping with its roots in footwear—including many hard-to-find sizes. Peruse the various floors for anything from trendy jeans to lingerie to goods for the home. A sky bridge on the store's fourth floor will take you to Pacific Place Shopping Center. Deservedly renowned for its impeccable customer service, the busy Downtown flagship has a concierge desk and valet parking. **■ TIP→ The Nordstrom Rack store at 1st Avenue and Spring Street, close to Pike Place Market, has great deals on marked-down items.** ✉ *500 Pine St., Downtown* ☎ *206/628–2111* 🌐 *shop.nordstrom.com.*

Furniture Row

You're probably not planning to browse for armchairs and coffee tables while on vacation, but if you're in the market for such things, Western Avenue between Union and Seneca Streets has several high-end home-furnishings showrooms, which make up an informal and stylish "Furniture Row."

GIFTS AND HOME DECOR

Sur La Table

GIFTS/SOUVENIRS | Need a brass-plated medieval French duck press? You've come to the right place. Culinary artists and foodies have flocked to this popular Pike Place Market destination since 1972. The chain's flagship shop is packed to the rafters with many thousands of kitchen items, including an exclusive line of copper cookware, endless shelves of baking equipment, tabletop accessories, cookbooks, and a formidable display of knives. ✉ *84 Pine St., Downtown* ☎ *206/448–2244* 🌐 *www.surlatable.com.*

Watson Kennedy Fine Living

GIFTS/SOUVENIRS | This small store in the courtyard of the Inn at the Market is worth a visit just for how heavenly it smells. With a lovely line of artisanal jewelry, luxurious bath products, and enticing—and often aromatic—gifts, it makes for a relaxing stop in the Pike Place tour. A standout favorite? Seattle-based fragrance brand Antica Farmacista—you'll want every scent of their luxury reed diffusers. Watson Kennedy's sister store is located on 1st Avenue and Spring Street (Watson Kennedy Fine Home) and includes vintage furniture, tableware, gourmet foods, and its own line of beeswax candles. ✉ *86 Pine St., Downtown* ☎ *206/443–6281* 🌐 *www.watsonkennedy.com.*

JEWELRY

Turgeon Raine Jewelers

JEWELRY/ACCESSORIES | Offering an art-forward take on gems and jewelry in a spacious contemporary gallery, Turgeon Raine employs only staff with a design background—you can work with them to create a one-of-a-kind piece, or pick from house-made items on display. It's also Washington's exclusive representative for Patek Philippe watches. ✉ *1407 5th Ave., Downtown* ☎ *206/447–9488* 🌐 *www.turgeonraine.com.*

Pacific Place Shopping Center

SHOPPING CENTERS/MALLS | While malls across the country are shutting down, Pacific Place just received a multimillion-dollar makeover, which includes a dramatic new entrance and large-scale sculptural art. Stores, restaurants, and an excellent movie multiplex are wrapped around a four-story, light-filled atrium, making this a cheerful destination even on a stormy day. The mostly high-end shops include Tiffany & Co., Coach, and True Religion, and there's also Victoria's Secret, lululemon, and J.Crew. A third-floor sky bridge provides a rainproof route to the neighboring Nordstrom. One of the best things about the mall is its parking garage, which is surprisingly affordable, given its location; valet parking is just a few bucks more. ✉ *600 Pine St., Downtown* ☎ *206/652–1300* 🌐 *www.pacificplaceseattle.com.*

SHOES

A Mano

SHOES/LUGGAGE/LEATHER GOODS | The store's name means "by hand," and that ethos of handmade, high-quality craftsmanship seems soaked into the very (exposed brick) walls of this charming shop. A small selection of shoes from all over the world, along with some jewelry and handbags from local designers can be found here—all of it lovingly selected and much of it unique. ✉ *1115 1st Ave., Downtown* ☎ *206/292–1767* 🌐 *www.shopamano.com.*

John Fluevog Shoes

SHOES/LUGGAGE/LEATHER GOODS | You'll find the store's own brand of fun and funky boots, chunky leather shoes, and urbanized wooden sandals here in men's and women's styles. ✉ *205 Pine St., Downtown* ☎ *206/441–1065* 🌐 *www.fluevog.com.*

SPAS

Gene Juarez Salons & Spas

SPA/BEAUTY | With both a lively hair and nail salon and a more tranquil retreat for massage and skin treatments, Gene Juarez (in Downtown and Bellevue and elsewhere) offers one-stop shopping. The skin-care menu is long and inventive; massage techniques stick to the classics like deep tissue, shiatsu, and reflexology, with Hawaiian healing and hot-stone methods thrown in for good measure. The spa also offers a full menu of men's treatments, including hide-the-gray hair coloring and pedicures. ✉ *607 Pine St., Downtown* ☎ *206/326–6000* 🌐 *www.genejuarez.com.*

Ummelina International Day Spa

SPA/BEAUTY | Hand-carved Japanese doors open into this tranquil and luxurious, Asian-influenced spa. Relax beneath a warm waterfall shower, take a steamy, scented sauna, or submit to a mud wrap or smoothing body scrub. The three-hour Equator package for couples includes all this and more. Linger over the experience with a cup of house-blended tea.

✉ *1525 4th Ave., Downtown* ☎ *206/624–1370* 🌐 *www.ummelina.com.*

WINE AND SPECIALTY FOODS

★ DeLaurenti Specialty Food and Wine

FOOD/CANDY | Attention foodies: clear out your hotel minibars and make room for delectable treats from DeLaurenti. And, if you're planning any picnics, swing by here first. Imported meats and cheeses crowd the deli cases, and packaged delicacies pack the aisles. Stock up on hard-to-find items like truffle-infused olive oil or excellent Italian vintages from the wine shop upstairs. Spring travelers will also want to stop by DeLaurenti's nosh nirvana, called Cheesefest, in May. ✉ *Pike Place Market, 1435 1st Ave., Downtown* ☎ *206/622–0141* 🌐 *www.delaurenti.com.*

★ Fran's Chocolates

FOOD/CANDY | A Seattle institution (helmed by Fran Bigelow) has been making quality chocolates for decades. Its world-famous salted caramels are transcendent—a much-noted favorite of the Obama family, in fact—as are delectable truffles, which are spiked with oolong tea, single-malt whiskey, or raspberry, among other flavors. This shop is housed in the elegant Four Seasons on 1st Avenue. ✉ *1325 1st Ave., Downtown* ☎ *206/682–0168* 🌐 *www.franschocolates.com.*

Pike and Western Wine Shop

FOOD/CANDY | These folks have spent more than four decades carving out a reputation as one of the best wine markets in the city. With more than 1,000 wines personally selected from the Pacific Northwest and around the world, this shop offers expert advice from friendly salespeople. ✉ *1934 Pike Pl., Downtown* ☎ *206/441–1307* 🌐 *www.pikeandwestern.com.*

Sotto Voce Inc

LOCAL SPECIALTIES | This Italian-inspired local company has taken savory infusions to the next level with its assortment of "made from scratch" oils and vinegars. Each bottle is produced by hand, from flavoring to filling and labeling. Tastings are encouraged at the Pike Place Market storefront. The red-chili-and-horseradish-infused olive oil and the lemon- , tarragon- , and dill-infused balsamic vinegar are the perfect Pacific Northwest mementos you can enjoy in your own home for many meals to come. ✉ *1532 Pike Pl.* ☎ *206/624–9998* 🌐 *www.sottovoce.com.*

The Tasting Room

FOOD/CANDY | When you're ready for a break from sightseeing, make a detour into this relaxing tasting room and wine store in the northern end of Post Alley. Several Washington State boutique wineries are represented; most of the bottles are handcrafted and/or reserve vintages. Taste the offerings, then buy a bottle or two—you can sit and enjoy your pick in the wine bar without paying for corkage. ✉ *1924 Post Alley, Downtown* ☎ *206/770–9463* 🌐 *www.winesofwashington.com.*

World Spice Merchants

FOOD/CANDY | Many of the city's best chefs get their herbs, spices, and salts at this aromatic shop under Pike Place Market. Many teas are also available. ✉ *1509 Western Ave., Downtown* ☎ *206/682–7274* 🌐 *www.worldspice.com.*

Belltown

Belltown is Downtown's younger sibling, just north of Virginia Street (up to Denny Way) and stretching from Elliott Bay to 6th Avenue. Not so long ago, Belltown was home to some of the most unwanted real estate in the city. Today, Belltown is increasingly hip, with luxury condos, trendy restaurants, swanky bars, and a number of boutiques. (Most of the action happens between 1st and 4th Avenues and between Bell and Virginia Streets.) You can still find plenty of evidence of its edgy past—including a gallery exhibiting

A steel sculpture by Richard Serra at the Olympic Sculpture Park

urban street art, a punk-rock vinyl shop, and a major indie rock music venue that was a cornerstone of the grunge scene—but today Belltown is almost unrecognizable to long-term residents. Except for the stunning Olympic Sculpture Park—which, especially on a gorgeous day, is not to be missed—the area doesn't have much in terms of traditional sights, but it's an interesting extension of Downtown. Though the number of homeless people in the neighborhood can be off-putting, Belltown is generally safe during the day and is very pleasant to explore.

Sights

Belltown doesn't have much in the way of sights other than the magnificent Olympic Sculpture Park, which is truly a waterfront show-stopper. On the way, be sure to pop into Steinbrueck Gallery, which features artwork from indigenous Northwest Coast artists.

★ Olympic Sculpture Park

PUBLIC ART | An outdoor branch of the Seattle Art Museum is a favorite destination for picnics, strolls, and quiet contemplation. Nestled at the edge of Belltown with views of Elliott Bay, the gently sloping green space features native plants and walking paths that wind past larger-than-life public artwork. On sunny days, the park frames an astounding panorama of the Olympic Mountains, but even the grayest afternoon casts a favorable light on the site's sculptures. The grounds are home to works by such artists as Richard Serra, Louise Bourgeois, and Alexander Calder, whose bright-red steel "Eagle" sculpture is a local favorite (and a nod to the bald eagles that sometimes soar above). "Echo," a 46-foot-tall elongated girl's face by Spanish artist Jaume Plensa, is a beautiful and bold presence on the waterfront. The park's PACCAR Pavilion has a gift shop, café, and information about the artworks. ✉ *2901 Western Ave., between Broad and Bay Sts., Belltown* ☎ *206/654–3100* 🌐 *www.seattleartmuseum.org* *Free.*

Steinbrueck Native Gallery

MUSEUM | Prints, masks, drums, sculptures, baskets, and jewelry by local Native artists fill the space of this elegant Belltown gallery near Pike Place Market. Alaskan and Arctic art is also on display, including beautiful sculptural pieces carved from ivory, wood, and soapstone. ✉ *2030 Western Ave., Belltown* ☎ *206/441–3821* 🌐 *www.steinbruecknativegallery.com* 🎫 *Free.*

Suyama Peterson Deguchi

MUSEUM | The brainchild of art advocate and noted local architect George Suyama, this nonprofit gallery located within the architecture firm of Suyama Peterson Deguchi exhibits large-scale, site-specific contemporary installations three times a year. Unlike many of Seattle's galleries, this is not a commercial venue—its programming is made possible through grants and donations—which is just another reason to stroll through the lofty space. When you visit, ring the bell at 2324 2nd Avenue for entry. ✉ *2324 2nd Ave., Belltown* ☎ *206/256–0809* 🌐 *www.suyamaspace.org* 🎫 *Free.*

Restaurants

Belltown is home to a small empire of restaurants from Seattle restaurateur Tom Douglas, including many of the eateries recommended below. Since Douglas put down roots here, Belltown has continued to expand, with hip new places to eat and drink continually cropping up alongside new luxury condos.

Jerk Shack

$$ | CARIBBEAN | Stepping inside feels like a temporary island getaway, from the cheery yellow walls and rum barrels repurposed as palm planters to the complex aromas wafting through the air. The Caribbean food here is the real deal—the Seattle-born chef Trey Lamont has Jamaican roots—with a menu featuring signature jerk spice-dredged meats and seafood as well Cuban sandwiches, black beans, collard greens, tropical fruit salads, and fried plantains. **Known for:** big flavors and even bigger portions; sun-dappled fenced-in patio; island-style cocktails. 💲 *Average main: $20* ✉ *2510 1st Ave., Belltown* ☎ *206/441–7817* 🌐 *www.jerkshackseattle.com.*

Lola

$$$ | MEDITERRANEAN | Tom Douglas dishes out his signature Northwest style, spiked with Greek and Mediterranean touches—another huge success for the local celebrity chef. Try a sensational tagine of Northwest seafood; a variety of meat kebabs; and scrumptious spreads including hummus, tzatziki, and *harissa* (a red-pepper concoction). **Known for:** Greek flavors; popular brunch; made-to-order pillowy square doughnuts. 💲 *Average main: $24* ✉ *2000 4th Ave., Belltown* ☎ *206/441–1430* 🌐 *www.lolaseattle.com.*

Macrina Bakery

$ | BAKERY | One of Seattle's favorite bakeries is also popular for breakfast and brunch and an excellent place to take a delicious break on your way to or from the Olympic Sculpture Park. With its perfectly executed breads and pastries—from Nutella brioche and ginger cookies to almond croissants and dark-chocolate, sugar-dusted brownies—it's become a true Belltown institution. **Known for:** baguettes; pastries. 💲 *Average main: $7* ✉ *2408 1st Ave., Belltown* ☎ *206/448–4032* 🌐 *www.macrinabakery.com* 🕓 *No dinner.*

Palace Kitchen

$$$ | PACIFIC NORTHWEST | The star of this chic yet convivial Tom Douglas eatery may be the 45-foot bar, but the real show takes place in the giant open kitchen at the back. Wood-grilled chicken wings, olive poppers, Penn Cove mussels, roast-pork ravioli, and a nightly selection of cheeses vie for your attention on the ever-changing menu of small plates. **Known for:** half-pound Palace

Burger Royale; decadent desserts; late-night food offerings. *Average main: $28 2030 5th Ave., Belltown 206/448–2001 www.tomdouglas.com No lunch.*

Serious Pie

$$ | **PIZZA** | Serious artisanal pizzas are worth the wait here—and there will be a wait at this teeny-tiny Belltown restaurant. Famed local restaurateur Tom Douglas delivers chewy, buttery crusts anchored by such toppings as fresh arugula, guanciale (cured pork jowl), and a soft egg; or Meyer lemon, chili, and buffalo mozzarella. **Known for:** fun atmosphere; egg-topped pizza; local wine and beer selections. *Average main: $18 316 Virginia, Belltown 206/838–7388 www.tomdouglas.com.*

★ Shiro's Sushi Restaurant

$$$ | **JAPANESE** | Founder Shiro Kashiba is no longer here (he's now at Downtown's Sushi Kashiba), but this sushi spot is still the best in Belltown, with simple decor, ultra-fresh fish, and an omakase service that's a bit more affordable than at other spots. **Known for:** chef's choice omakase; simple ambience. *Average main: $28 2401 2nd Ave., Belltown 206/443–9844 www.shiros.com No lunch.*

Tavolàta

$$ | **ITALIAN** | This Belltown favorite (there's another location in Capitol Hill) is helmed by superstar-chef Ethan Stowell (also of How to Cook a Wolf and Staple & Fancy), who is known for his way with fresh pasta. Serving up Italian goodness by the plateful in an industrial-chic bi-level space, Tavolàta is a decidedly lively, loud, and delicious night out on the town. **Known for:** community-style dining; housemade pasta; elegant cocktails. *Average main: $25 2323 2nd Ave., Belltown 206/838–8008 www.tavolata.com.*

Coffee and Quick Bites

Bang Bang Cafe

$ | **CAFÉ** | The New Mexican-style breakfast burritos at this cozy counter-service spot have a cult following, thanks to a tasty homemade hatch chili sauce. Bang Bang also serves coffee, bagels, and a handful of lunch options. **Known for:** vegetarian and vegan options, including a vegan mac and cheese; quick service. *Average main: $10 2460 Western Ave., Belltown 206/448–2233 www.bangbangseattle.com.*

Dahlia Lounge

$$$ | **PACIFIC NORTHWEST** | Romantic Dahlia Lounge has valentine-red walls and deep booths, providing a cozy space for Seattle diners since 1989. Chef Tom Douglas's famous crab cakes, served as an appetizer or an entrée, lead a regionally-oriented menu. **Known for:** foraged mushrooms and local seafood; outrageously good triple coconut cream pie; weekend brunch (or pop over to nearby Dahlia Bakery). *Average main: $31 2001 4th Ave., Belltown 206/682–4142 www.tomdouglas.com.*

Hotels

Belltown, slightly north and within walking distance of Downtown, has some of the city's trendiest hotels. It's a great place to stay if you plan to hit the bars and clubs in the neighborhood. Belltown hotels are convenient (and within walking distance) to many major sights—including the Seattle Art Museum, Pike Place Market, and the Olympic Sculpture Park.

★ Ace Hotel

$ | **HOTEL** | The Ace is a dream come true for anyone who appreciates unique minimalist decor, with touches like army-surplus blankets, industrial metal sinks, and street art breaking up any notion of austerity; the cheapest rooms share bathrooms, which have enormous showers. **Pros:** ultratrendy but with some of the most affordable rates in town; good place to meet other travelers; free Wi-Fi. **Cons:** half the rooms have shared bathrooms; not for people who want pampering; lots of stairs to get to lobby. *Rooms from: $149 2423 1st Ave., Belltown 206/448–4721 www.acehotel.com 14 standard rooms, 14 deluxe rooms No meals.*

The Edgewater

$$$$ | **HOTEL** | Literally perched over Elliott Bay, the rustic-chic Edgewater has spectacular west-facing views of ferries and sailboats, seals and seabirds, and the distant Olympic Mountains, so don't even think of booking a city-view room. **Pros:** one of Seattle's most unique properties; stunning public lobby lounge; ; complimentary bikes. **Cons:** overpriced; rooms without views not worth it; visitors complain of spotty service and thin walls. *Rooms from: $399 Pier 67, 2411 Alaskan Way, Belltown 206/728–7000, 800/624–0670 www.edgewaterhotel.com 213 rooms, 10 suites No meals.*

★ Hotel Ändra

$$$ | **HOTEL** | Scandinavian sensibility and clean, modern lines define this sophisticated hotel on the edge of Belltown, where spacious, comfortable rooms have dark fabrics and light woods, with a few bright accents and geometric prints. **Pros:** hangout-worthy lobby lounge; on-trend Scandinavian vibe; very close to transit. **Cons:** some street noise; not family-friendly; small bathroom. *Rooms from: $295 2000 4th Ave., Belltown 206/448–8600, 877/448–8600 www.hotelandra.com 93 rooms, 4 studios, 22 suites No meals.*

★ The Inn at El Gaucho

$$ | **B&B/INN** | Hollywood Rat Pack enthusiasts will want to move right in to these swank, retro-style suites done in dark wood with buttery leather furniture, comfortable beds, and bathrooms featuring antique tile and fixtures. **Pros:** unique old-school aesthetic; city or water view options; warm, helpful staff. **Cons:** steep stairs with no elevator; some rooms only have showers; no on-site fitness center. *Rooms from: $249 2505 1st Ave., Belltown 206/728–1133, 866/354–2824 www.elgaucho.com 17 suites No meals.*

Kimpton Palladian Hotel

$$ | **HOTEL** | At this hip Kimpton hotel in a 1910 Belltown landmark, the unpretentious vibe is masculine-chic, from the tufted-leather front desk to the Napoleonic-style pop-art portraits of local icons like Jimi Hendrix, Bill Gates, and Frasier Crane that hang in the lobby and appear again as pillows in the guest rooms. **Pros:** has tons of bold style; a short walk from Pike Place Market; chic Shaker + Spear restaurant serves fab seafood. **Cons:** rooms are on the small side; awkward bathroom layout; street noise. *Rooms from: $210 2000 2nd Ave., Belltown 206/448–1111 www.palladianhotel.com 97 rooms No meals.*

Marriott Seattle Waterfront

$$$ | **HOTEL** | With views of Elliott Bay from most rooms (half have small Juliet balconies), proximity to the cruise terminals, comfy beds, and a great location near the tourist spots and the financial district, this property is a hot spot for groups and cruise travelers. **Pros:** relaxing lobby invites lounging; elevator takes you directly to Pike Place Market; outdoor pool. **Cons:** train noise; expensive restaurant and bar; it's an uphill walk to most sites. *Rooms from: $349 2100 Alaskan Way, (between Piers 62/63 and Pier 66), Belltown 206/443–5000, 800/455–8254 www.marriott.com/seawf 358 rooms No meals.*

Warwick Seattle Hotel

$$ | **HOTEL** | Space Needle views, vintage charm, and family-friendly service abound at this renovated classic hotel in Belltown, which features contemporary

guest rooms with sliders and patios and Italian marble-clad bathrooms. **Pros:** great location (across from Cinerama); Juliet balconies in most rooms; heated indoor pool and whirlpool. **Cons:** slow Wi-Fi; small fitness room; expensive valet parking. *$ Rooms from: $225 ✉ 401 Lenora St., Belltown ☎ 206/443–4300, 206/443–4300 ⊕ www.warwickwa.com* *230 rooms No meals.*

 Nightlife

Belltown can be an absolute madhouse on weekends. That said, there are some lovely spaces here, a few of which stay relatively low-key even during the Saturday-night crush, as well as some quirky old neighborhood dives left over from Belltown's former life. Belltown can get gritty late at night around the Pike–Pine Corridor, so stick to busy, well-lit areas.

BARS AND LOUNGES

Bathtub Gin & Co.

BARS/PUBS | The speakeasy trend has produced some lovely, intimate bars, including this one, which is reached via a wooden door in an alley next to the Humphrey Apartments (it's actually in the basement of the building). The tiny, shabby-chic bar is a very laid-back spot to settle into a couch for a few drinks. Note that despite being a pain in the neck to find, the bar still attracts the hard-partying Belltown crowd on weekends, so go midweek for maximum serenity. *✉ 2205 2nd Ave., Belltown ☎ 206/728–6069 ⊕ bathtubginseattle.com.*

Black Bottle

BARS/PUBS | This sleek and sexy gastro-tavern makes the northern reaches of Belltown look good. The interior is simple but stylish, with black chairs and tables and shiny wood floors. It gets crowded on nights and weekends with a laid-back but often dressed-up clientele. A small selection of beers on tap and a solid wine list (with Washington, Oregon, California, and beyond well represented) will help you wash down the sustainably sourced and creatively presented snacks and shareable dishes, including house-smoked wild boar ribs, pork belly with kimchi, and oysters on the half shell. Vegan and nut-, dairy-, and gluten-free options are plentiful. *✉ 2600 1st Ave., Belltown ☎ 206/441–1500 ⊕ www.blackbottleseattle.com.*

List

BARS/PUBS | A Belltown favorite for great happy-hour deals, this hip, dimly lit space has a come-hither glow thanks to red and white backlighting. An all-day happy hour on Sunday and Monday (or Tuesday to Saturday from 4–6:30 pm and 9 pm to midnight) means you get half off the yummy food menu (local clams, Angus beef burgers, bacon-wrapped prawns, spicy calamari), plus $19 bottles of wine. *✉ 2226 1st Ave., Belltown ☎ 206/441–1000 ⊕ www.listbelltown.com.*

Mr. Darcy's

BARS/PUBS | Named for the moody hero of "Pride and Prejudice," this intimate cocktail bar has dark walls, wood furnishings, and a few literary touches like shelved hardcover books, deep tufted leather chairs, and an antique piano. The craft cocktail list carries on the theme with drinks like Mrs. Bennett (gin, green chartreuse, and honey) and Pride (rye, smoke, and bitters), along with other cleverly named concoctions. *✉ 2222 2nd Ave., Belltown ☎ 206/441–2491 ⊕ www.mrdarcysbar.com.*

No Anchor

BARS/PUBS | The draft list at this gleaming wood-clad gastropub—a James Beard Award semi-finalist in 2017—features unique selections from mostly local breweries, and the seasonal cocktail list is just as solid, as is a menu of small and large plates, which includes options like vealed sweet breads and corned duck breast. *✉ 2505 2nd Ave., #105, Belltown ☎ 206/448–2610.*

The Rendezvous

BARS/PUBS | It opened in 1926 as an elite screening room for film stars and moguls. Since then, Rendezvous has done time as both a porn theater and a much-loved dive bar, but today it's settled down as a multipurpose "hub" with a small theater, a basement bar, a lounge, and a classic dining room. While maintaining the building's 1920s charm, it's been spruced up just enough to suit the new wave of wealthy locals without alienating everyone else. The Jewelbox Theater (live music, comedy, film, burlesque shows) sets it apart from the neighborhood's string of cookie-cutter trendy spots. ✉ *2322 2nd Ave., Belltown* ☎ *206/441–5823* 🌐 *www.therendezvous.rocks.*

Rob Roy

BARS/PUBS | With its deep selection of dark liquor, low-light ambience, and black leather walls, Rob Roy is a serious-but-inviting cocktail bar. Their original concoctions change four to five times a year, and include drinks like a Saffron Sandalwood Sour. They also feature nonalcoholic cocktails for teetotalers and designated drivers. Meatballs and a breakfast sandwich decorate a limited food menu, which is half-off during a daily 4 to 7 pm happy hour that also features drink specials. They also have Tiki Night every Monday. ✉ *2332 2nd Ave., Belltown* ☎ *206/956–8423* 🌐 *www.robroyseattle.com.*

Shorty's

BARS/PUBS | It may be one of the diviest bars in Belltown, but Shorty's is a bright spot in a neighborhood where most bars serve $14 cocktails (and the bathrooms happen to be spotless). Along with a come-as-you-are atmosphere, the grown-up arcade features pinball machines and video games, cheap beer and gourmet hot dogs, and lots of no-frills fun. ✉ *2316 2nd Ave., Belltown* ☎ *206/441–5449* 🌐 *www.shortydog.com.*

Umi Sake House

BARS/PUBS | Choose from a wide selection of sake and sake-based cocktails in a space designed to look like someone shoehorned a real *izakaya* (a sake house that also serves substantial snacks) into a Belltown building—there's even an enclosed patio, which they refer to as the "porch," and a tatami room that can be reserved for larger parties. The sushi is good, and there's a very long happy hour offered at one of the bar areas. Umi is less of a meat market than some Belltown spots—unless you're here late on a Friday or Saturday night. ✉ *2230 1st Ave., Belltown* ☎ *206/374–8717* 🌐 *www.umisakehouse.com.*

The Whisky Bar

BARS/PUBS | One of Belltown's reigning dive bars, this aptly named spot has a jaw-dropping selection of whisky, bourbon, and rye, as well as weekly bagpipe music. They also have 24 beers on tap, mostly from West Coast brewers, and a bottle list with beers from around the world. The food menu includes sliders, a burger, and a scotch egg among other snacks and small plates. Daily happy hour runs from when they open the doors—noon on weekends, 2 pm weekdays—until 7 pm. ✉ *2122 2nd Ave., Belltown* ☎ *206/443–4490* 🌐 *www.thewhiskybar.com.*

Shopping

Stroll along 1st Avenue to find an eclectic mix of high-end clothing boutiques, custom tailoring shops, artsy gift stores, and gritty standouts. Many local, independent designers are represented here, although the clothing tends to be more upmarket than the crafty, DIY goods offered in Capitol Hill or Ballard.

Best shopping: Along 1st Avenue between Cedar and Virginia Streets.

BOOKS

★ Peter Miller Architectural & Design Books and Supplies

BOOKS/STATIONERY | Aesthetes and architects haunt this shop, which is stocked with all things design. Rare, international architecture, art, and design books (including titles for children) mingle with high-end products from Alessi and Iittala; sleek notebooks, bags, portfolios, and drawing tools round out the collection. This is a great shop for quirky, unforgettable gifts, like a pentagram typography calendar, an Arne Jacobsen wall clock, or an aerodynamic umbrella. ✉ *304 Alaskan Way South, Post Alley, Belltown* ✥ *entrance off alley* ☎ *206/441–4114* 🌐 *www.petermiller.com* ⏲ *Closed Sun.*

CLOTHING

Gian DeCaro Sartoria

CLOTHING | There is nothing quite like a bespoke suit to make a man look like a million bucks, and luckily, Gian DeCaro's offerings don't cost anywhere near that much. The suits may be pricey, but DeCaro is one of the best tailor-designers around, counting local and visiting celebrities among his well-dressed clientele. For the rest of us, his shop is also stocked with elegant ties, cuff links, and other accessories, as well as some ready-to-wear clothing in luxurious fabrics. ✉ *2025 1st Ave., Suite D, Belltown* ☎ *206/448–2812* 🌐 *www.giandecaro.com.*

Kuhlman

CLOTHING | This tiny store on the same hip block as the Ace Hotel has a careful selection of urban street wear that includes hard-to-find designers like Nudie Jeans Co., Barbour, and Fred Perry—it's sophisticated while still maintaining an edge. Kuhlman is best known for creating custom clothing, often from superb European and Japanese fabrics. ✉ *2419 1st Ave., Belltown* ☎ *206/441–1999* 🌐 *www.kuhlmanseattle.com.*

Moorea Seal

CLOTHING | Are accessories your Achilles' heel? Then look no further than the chic, trendy Moorea Seal. With its modern, airy storefront offering everything from booties to boho-chic handbags, Moorea pledges 7% of all proceeds to benefit nonprofits supporting environmental issues and women's causes. Shop till you drop with these great prices, and do some good while you're at it. ✉ *2523 3rd Ave.* ✥ *Between Wall St. and Vine St.* ☎ *206/728–2523* 🌐 *www.mooreaseal.com.*

Patagonia

CLOTHING | If the person next to you on the bus isn't wearing North Face, he or she is probably clad in Patagonia. This popular and durable brand excels at functional outdoor wear—made with earth-friendly materials such as hemp and organic cotton—as well as technical clothing hip enough for mountaineers or urban hikers. The line of whimsically patterned fleece wear for children is particularly cute. ✉ *2100 1st Ave., Belltown* ☎ *206/622–9700* 🌐 *www.patagonia.com.*

Sassafras

CLOTHING | Find locally-made fashions from eight in-house designers and some 60 local designers in this charming Belltown storefront, including a popular obi wrap dress that seems to flatter everybody and stylish jewelry and accessories. ✉ *2307 1st Ave., Belltown* ☎ *206/420–7057* 🌐 *www.sassafras-seattle.com* ⏲ *Closed Sun.*

Continued on page 88

PIKE PLACE MARKET

Nine Acres of History & Quirky Charm

With more than a century of history tucked into every corner and plenty of local personality, the Market is one spot you can't miss. Office workers hustle past cruise-ship crowds to take a seat at lunch counters that serve anything from pizza to piroshkies to German sausage. Local chefs plan the evening's menu over stacks of fresh, colorful produce. At night, couples stroll in to canoodle by candlelight in tucked-away bars and restaurants. Sure, some residents may bemoan the hordes of visitors, and many Seattleites spend their dollars at a growing number of neighborhood farmers' markets. But the Market is still one of Seattle's best-loved attractions.

The Pike Place Market dates from 1907. In response to anger over rising food prices, the city issued permits for farmers to sell produce from wagons parked at Pike Place. The impromptu public market grew steadily, and in 1921 Frank Goodwin, a hotel owner who had been quietly buying up real estate around Pike Place for a decade, proposed to build a permanent space.

More than 250 businesses, including 70 eateries. Breathtaking views of Elliott Bay. A pedestrian-friendly central shopping arcade that buzzes to life each day beginning at 6:30 AM. Strumming street musicians. Cobblestones, flying fish, and the very first Starbucks. Pike Place Market—the oldest continuously operated public market in the United States and a beloved Seattle icon—covers all the bases.

The Market's vitality ebbed after World War II, with the exodus to the suburbs and the rise of large supermarkets. Both it and the surrounding neighborhoods began to deteriorate. But a group of dedicated residents, led by the late architect Victor Steinbrueck, rallied and voted the Market a Historical Asset in the early 1970s. Years of subsequent restoration turned the Market into what you see today.

Pike Place Market is many buildings built around a central arcade (which is distinguished by its huge red neon sign). Shops and restaurants fill buildings on Pike Place and Western Avenue. In the main arcade, dozens of booths sell fresh produce, cheese, spices, coffee, crafts, and seafood—which can be packed in dry ice for flights home. Farmers sell high-quality produce that helps to set Seattle's rigorous dining standards. The shopkeepers who rent store spaces sell art, curios, clothing, beads, and more. Most shops cater to tourists, but there are gems to be found.

EXPLORING THE MARKET

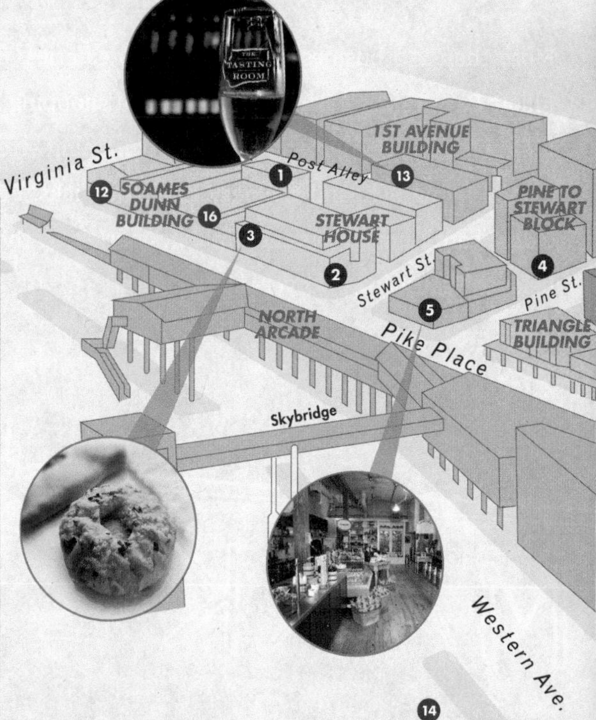

TOP EATS

❶ THE PINK DOOR. This adored (and adorable) Italian eatery is tucked into Post Alley. Whimsical decor, very good Italian food (such as the scrumptious *linguine alla vongole*), and weekend cabaret and burlesque make this gem a must-visit.

❷ LE PANIER. It's a self-proclaimed "Very French Bakery" and another Seattle favorite. The pastries are the main draw, but sandwiches on fresh baguettes and stuffed croissants offer more substantial snacks.

❸ PIROSHKY PIROSHKY. Authentic piroshky come in both standard varieties (beef and cheese) and Seattle-influenced ones (smoked salmon with cream cheese). There are plenty of sweet piroshky, too, if you need a sugar fix.

❹ CAMPAGNE. This French favorite and its charming attached café have you covered, whether you want a quick Croque Madame for lunch, a leisurely and delicious weekend brunch, or a white-tablecloth dinner.

❺ BEECHER'S. Artisanal cheeses—and mac-n-cheese to go—make this a spot Seattleites will brave the crowds for.

❻ THREE GIRLS BAKERY. This tiny bakery turns out piles of pastries and sandwiches on their fresh-baked bread (the baked salmon is a favorite).

❼ MATT'S IN THE MARKET. Matt's is the best restaurant in the Market, and one of the best in the city. Lunch is casual (try the catfish po'boy), and dinner is elegant, with fresh fish and local produce showcased on the small menu. Reservations are essential.

❽ DAILY DOZEN DONUTS. Mini-donuts are made fresh before your eyes and are a great snack to pick up before you venture into the labyrinth.

❾ MARKET GRILL. This no-frills counter serves up the market's best fish sandwiches and a great clam chowder.

❿ CHUKAR CHERRIES. Look for handmade confections featuring—but not restricted to—local cherries dipped in all sorts of sweet, rich coatings.

TOP SHOPS

⓫ MARKET SPICE TEA. For a tin of the Market's signature tea, Market Spice Blend, which is infused with cinnamon and clove oils, seek out Market Spice shop on the south side of the main arcade.

⓬ PIKE & WESTERN WINE SHOP. The Tasting Room in Post Alley may be a lovely place to sample Washington wines, but Pike and Western is the place where serious oenophiles flock.

⓭ THE TASTING ROOM. With one of the top wine selections in town, the Tasting Room offers Washington wines for the casual collector and the experienced connois-

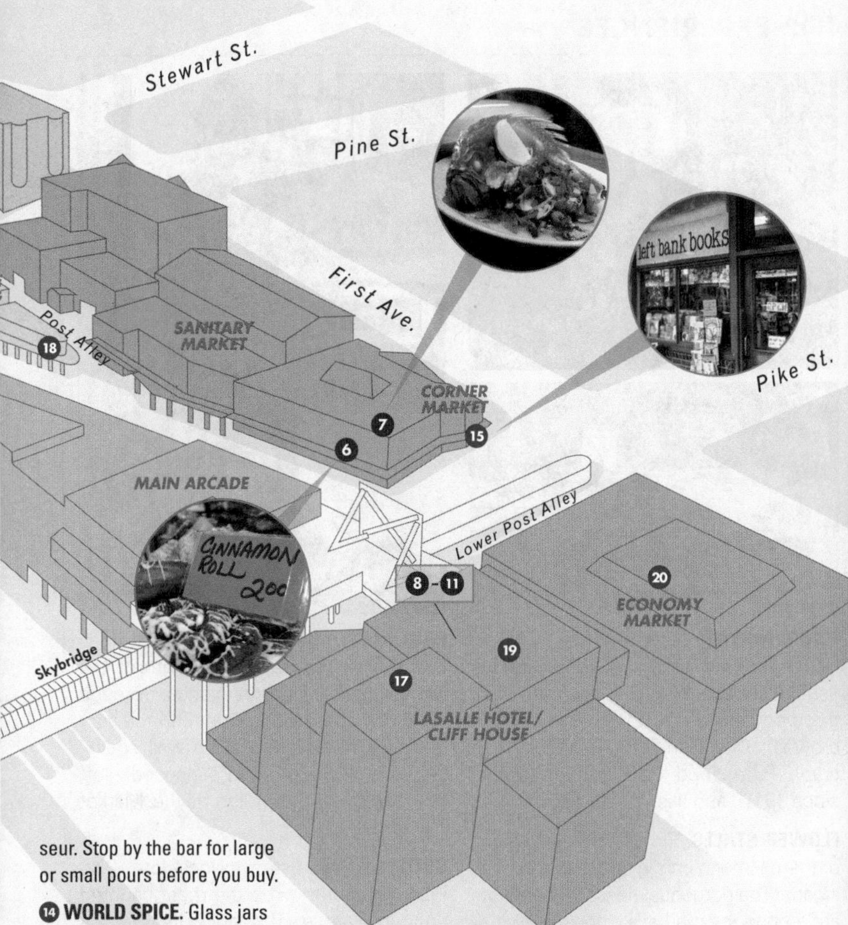

seur. Stop by the bar for large or small pours before you buy.

⓮ **WORLD SPICE.** Glass jars are filled with spices and teas from around the world here: Buy by the ounce or grab a pre-packaged gift set as a souvenir.

⓯ **LEFT BANK BOOKS.** A collective in operation since 1973, this tiny bookshop specializes in political and history titles and alternative literature.

⓰ **THE ORIGINAL STARBUCKS.** At 1912 Pike Place, you'll find the tiny store that opened in 1971 and started an empire. The shop is definitely more quaint and old-timey than its sleek younger siblings, and it features the original, uncensored (read: bare-breasted) version of the mermaid logo.

⓱ **RACHEL'S GINGER BEER.** The flagship store for Seattle's wildly popular ginger beer serves up delicious variations on its homemade brew, including boozy cocktails.

⓲ **PAPPARDELLE'S PASTA.** There's no type of pasta you could dream up that isn't already in a bin at Pappardelle's.

⓳ **DELAURENTI'S.** This amazing Italian grocery has everything from fancy olive oil to digestifs and wine to meats and fine cheeses.

TOP EXPERIENCES

Pike Place Flowers

Pike Place Fish Co.

Market buskers

FISHMONGERS. There are four spots to visit if you want to see some serious fish: Pike Place Fish Co. (where the fish-throwers are—look for the awestruck crowds); City Fish (the place for fresh crab); Pure Food Fish Market (selling since 1911); and Jack's Fish Spot.

FLOWER STALLS. Flower growers, many of them Hmong immigrants, dot the main arcade. The gorgeous, seasonal bouquets are among the market's biggest draws.

PILES OF PRODUCE. The bounty of the agricultural valleys just outside Seattle is endless. In summer, seek out sweet peaches and Rainier cherries. In fall, look for cider made from Yakima Valley apples. There are dozens of produce vendors, but Sosio's and Manzo Brothers have been around the longest.

BUSKERS. The market has more than 240 street entertainers in any given year; the parade of Pacific Northwest hippie quirkitude is entertainment in itself.

POST ALLEY. There are some great finds in the alley that runs the length of the Market, paralleling First Avenue, from the highbrow (The Tasting Room) to the very lowbrow (the Gum Wall, a wall speckled with discarded gum supposedly left by people waiting in line at the Market Theater).

GHOSTS. If you listen to local lore, Pike Place Market may be the most haunted spot in Seattle. The epicenter seems to be 1921 First Avenue, where Butterworths & Sons Undertakers handled most of Seattle's dead in the early 1900s. You might see visitors sliding flowers into the building's old mail slot.

***SLEEPLESS IN SEATTLE* STOP.** Though it's been more than a decade since Rob Reiner and Tom Hanks discussed dating mores at the bar of The Athenian Inn, tourists still snap pictures of the corner they occupied. Look for the bright red plaque declaring: TOM HANKS SAT HERE.

A DAY AT THE MARKET

6:30 AM Delivery vans and trucks start to fill the narrow streets surrounding Pike Place Market. Vendors with permanent stalls arrive to stack produce, arrange flowers, and shovel ice into bins for displaying salmon, crab, octopus, and other delicacies.

7:30 AM Breakfast is served! ■TIP→ **For freshly made pastries head to Three Girls and Le Panier.**

9 AM Craftspeople vying for day stalls sign in and are assigned spots based on seniority.

10 AM Craftspeople set up Down Under —the levels below the main arcade—as the main arcade officially opens. The Heritage Center on Western Avenue opens. Market tours ($10) start at the information booth. ■TIP→ **Make reservations for market tours at least a day in advance; call ☎ 206/774–5249.**

11 AM The Market madness begins. In summer, midday crowds make it nearly impossible to walk through the street-level arcades. ■TIP→ **Head Down Under where things are often a bit quieter.**

12 PM–2 PM Lunch counters at places like the Athenian Inn and the Market Grill fill up.

Pike Place Market

5 PM Down Under shops close and the cobblestones are hosed down. (The Market closes at 6 PM Mon.–Sat. and 5 PM on Sun.)

7 PM–2 AM Patrons fill the tables at the Alibi Room, Zig Zag Café, the Pink Door, Matt's at the Market, and Maximilien's.

RACHEL THE PIG

Rachel, the 550-lb bronze pig that greets marketgoers at the main entrance on Pike and 1st Avenue, is a popular photo stop. But she's also a giant piggy bank that contributes up to $9,000 per year to the Market Foundation. Rachel was sculpted by Georgia Gerber, of Whidbey Island, and was named for the 750-pound pig that won the 1985 Island County Fair.

PARKING

There are numerous garages in the area, including one affiliated with the market itself (the Public Market Parking Garage at 1531 Western Ave.), at which you can get validated parking from many merchants; some restaurants offer free parking at this garage after 5 pm. You'll also find several pay lots farther south on Western Ave. and north on 1st Ave. Street parking is next to impossible to find midday. From Downtown hotels, the Market is easy to reach on foot or on city buses in the "Ride Free Zone."

MUSIC

Singles Going Steady

MUSIC STORES | If punk rock is more to you than anarchy symbols sewn on Target sweatshirts, then stop here. Punk and its myriad subgenres on CD and vinyl are specialties, though they also stock rockabilly, indie rock, and hip-hop. It's a nice foil to the city's indie-rock-dominated record shops, and a good reminder that Belltown is still more eclectic than its rising rents may indicate. ✉ *2219 2nd Ave., Belltown* ☎ *206/441–7396.*

SPAS

Spa Noir

SPA/BEAUTY | If you're not into the new-age earthy vibe found in so many day spas, head to Spa Noir, a hip Belltown spot done up in black, red, and gold. The spa specializes in facials, manicures, pedicures, and other beauty treatments, but it also offers a small menu of reasonably priced massage treatments. ✉ *2120 2nd Ave., Belltown* ☎ *206/448–7600* 🌐 *www.spanoir.net.*

Chapter 4

SOUTH LAKE UNION AND QUEEN ANNE

4

Updated By
Naomi Tomky

 Sights	 Restaurants	 Hotels	Shopping	Nightlife
★★★★☆	★★★★☆	★★★☆☆	★★☆☆☆	★☆☆☆☆

NEIGHBORHOOD SNAPSHOT

GETTING HERE AND AROUND

The monorail runs from Westlake Center (5th Avenue and Pine Street) and makes getting here easy from Downtown. It runs from 7:30 am on weekdays and 8:30 am on weekends to 11 pm (with slightly shorter hours in winter), with departures every 10 minutes. Traffic and parking around the Center can be nightmarish during special events and festivals, so try to walk or take public transportation. Walking to Seattle Center from the Olympic Sculpture Park is a ½-mile (about 15-minute) stroll northeast on Broad Street.

From Downtown, multiple bus lines run up 3rd and 1st avenues to Seattle Center. Buses also climb Queen Anne Avenue, making the commercial districts easy to reach from Downtown or Seattle Center; the rest of that neighborhood will require a car to tour.

From Downtown, South Lake Union is served by the Seattle Streetcar (🌐 *www.seattlestreetcar.org*). The #8 bus connects South Lake Union to Seattle Center and Lower Queen Anne.

TOP REASONS TO GO

Visit (or gaze up at) the **Space Needle** and rock out at **MoPOP**; leave a couple of hours to visit **Chihuly Garden and Glass,** the **Children's Museum** (best for kids ages 10 months to 10 years), or the nearby **Bill & Melinda Gates Visitor Center.**

Kerry Park has outstanding views of the skyline and Elliott Bay. It's an all-time favorite spot for snapshots and public displays of affection.

Seattle Center houses the city's opera and ballet, and the headquarters of **SIFF Cinema**. Don't miss **On the Boards** (🌐 *www.ontheboards.org*), a small but important performing-arts space.

Rent a small boat at the **Center for Wooden Boats** to tour Lake Union, and go back in time with a visit to the **Museum of History and Industry.**

PLANNING YOUR TIME

■ Depending on your endurance, you can combine a visit to the Space Needle with one museum visit before exhaustion sets in. Schedule more time for the Pacific Science Center and MoPOP than other sights—both have a lot of interactive exhibits. The Space Needle is open late in summer.

QUICK BITES

■ **Citizen** A rustic coffee shop in a converted warehouse, this ultrachic spot serves up crepes, breakfast tacos, salads, and wine. **Known for:** former warehouse; excellent coffee. ✉ *706 Taylor Ave. N, Queen Anne* ☎ *206/284–1015* 🌐 *www.citizencoffee.com.*

■ **Dick's Drive In Restaurant** You won't find a quicker or more affordable snack than a few burgers and a milk shake here. **Known for:** Seattle institution; beloved burgers (even if they're not the best in town). ✉ *500 Queen Anne Ave. N, Lower Queen Anne* ☎ *206/285–5155* 🌐 *www.ddir.com/.*

■ **Pho Viet Anh** This popular Vietnamese spot draws a lively local crowd with some of the best banh mi in town. **Known for:** banh mi; local favorite. ✉ *372 Roy St., Lower Queen Anne* ☎ *206/352–1881* 🌐 *www.phovietanh.com.*

South Lake Union

South Lake Union, on the east side of Seattle Center, is a destination in itself. Though it's still in transition (construction is underway in many areas), Amazon's new headquarters here has brought more amenities, such as boutiques and upscale restaurants, including several Tom Douglas eateries. The biggest attractions are Lake Union itself as well as the incredible REI megastore.

Sights

Amazon Spheres

GARDEN | Three giant glass spheres filled with indoor gardens anchor the Amazon campus in South Lake Union. Living walls, 40,000 plants, and acafé exclusively for employees are part of the lounge space at Amazon's headquarters, and the public must admire from afar most of the time. However, on the first and third Saturday of each month, the Spheres open to the public by reservation only. Book online up to 30 days ahead of your visit, and make sure to bring government ID and no large bags. ✉ *2111 7th Ave., South Lake Union* 🌐 *www.seattlespheres.com* 🕑 *Open by reservation only on the 1st and 3rd Sat. each month.*

Lake Union Park

CITY PARK | Before this scenic park at the foot of Lake Union was completed, most people traveled up to Wallingford's Gas Works Park to enjoy Lake Union from a green space. Now the southern shore is more accessible and vibrant than ever—this 12-acre park includes a model boat pond, a boardwalk, a beach where you can launch small craft like kayaks and rowboats to paddle past the houseboats, a spray area for little kids, plus the Museum of History & Industry and the Center for Wooden Boats. Several cruise options also depart from the park. A 45-minute narrated Ice Cream Cruise on the Seattle mini ferry is a family favorite on Sundays (on the hour from 11 to 4; $12, cash only). ✉ *860 Terry Ave. N, South Lake Union* ☎ *206/684–4075* 🌐 *www.atlakeunionpark.org* 🎟 *Free.*

Museum of History & Industry

MUSEUM | **FAMILY** | Located in the Lake Union Park's converted Naval Reserve Building, the 20,000-square-foot MOHAI offers visitors an in-depth slice of regional history with a permanent collection featuring more than 100,000 objects ranging from vintage souvenirs to everyday household items. Permanent exhibitions include the Center for Innovation, which showcases Seattle's role as a place where innovation and entrepreneurship flourish; the exhibit is supported by a $10 million gift from Jeff Bezos, founder and CEO of Amazon (which has its corporate headquarters a few blocks away). Special temporary exhibitions examine everything from chocolate to stories of Jewish merchants in Washington State. ✉ *860 Terry Ave. N, at Lake Union Park, South Lake Union* ☎ *206/324–1126* 🌐 *www.mohai.org* 🎟 *$21.95, free first Thurs. of month (excluding special exhibitions).*

Restaurants

Brave Horse Tavern

$ | **AMERICAN** | When the Amazon offices in South Lake Union empty out for the day, seats at this Tom Douglas eatery fill up fast with techies craving big, fresh, soft pretzels dipped in a selection of house-made mustards, burgers, beer, and shuffleboard. The long wooden tables are quieter at other times, so stop in for eggy brunches made with produce from Douglas's farm in Eastern Washington. **Known for:** long beer list; good for groups; fish and chips. 💲 *Average main: $16* ✉ *310 Terry Ave. N, South Lake Union* ☎ *206/971–0717* 🌐 *www.bravehorsetavern.com.*

Sights	
1 Amazon Spheres	**D5**
2 Bill & Melinda Gates Foundation Visitor Center	**C3**
3 Chihuly Garden and Glass	**B4**
4 Discovery Park	**A1**
5 Kerry Park	**A2**
6 Lake Union Park	**D2**
7 Museum of History & Industry	**D2**
8 Pacific Science Center	**B4**
9 The Children's Museum, Seattle	**B4**
10 Space Needle	**B4**

Restaurants	
1 Brave Horse Tavern	**D4**
2 Canlis Restaurant	**C1**
3 Collections Café	**B4**
4 Eden Hill	**A1**
5 Espresso Vivace	**E4**
6 Great State Burger	**D5**
7 How To Cook A Wolf	**A1**
8 Taylor Shellfish Oyster Bar	**E5**
9 White Swan Public House	**E2**

Quick Bites	
1 La Marzocco Cafe & Showroom	**A4**
2 Seattle Center Armory	**B4**

Hotels	
1 MarQueen Hotel	**A3**
2 The Maxwell Hotel	**B3**
3 Pan Pacific Hotel	**D5**

These giant glass spheres at the Amazon campus are open to the public by reservation.

Espresso Vivace

$ | **CAFÉ** | A cozy and large outpost of the famed Capitol Hill roaster, the Vivace coffee shrine in South Lake Union is right across from the REI megastore and amid a growing number of new apartment buildings and offices. Grab a seat, order an expertly prepared espresso beverage, and munch on a small variety of snacks—this is a perfect stop after an exhausting jaunt through REI and before you head out to the next adventure. **Known for:** café Nicos; espresso. *Average main: $3 227 Yale Ave. N, South Lake Union 206/388–5164 www.espressovivace.com.*

Great State Burger

$ | **BURGER** | **FAMILY** | This new spin on the classic American burger shop manages to be both an ode to the Northwest and an example of how fast food can be done right. Organic, grass-fed beef is broken down and ground in-house, organic milk shakes come in seasonal flavors featuring Washington fruit, and the crinkle-cut french fries feel like a nostalgic nod to childhood. **Known for:** organic burgers; local ingredients. *Average main: $8 2014 7th Ave., South Lake Union 206/775–7880 www.greatstateburger.com Breakfast on weekdays only.*

★ White Swan Public House

$$ | **SEAFOOD** | Weaving local seafood into gastropub-style favorites, this waterfront restaurant makes food as good as the view, which stretches up to the Space Needle to the west and over to Lake Union to the north. Seafood chowder, both on its own and over fries as "Poutine o' the Sea," Dungeness Crab Louie salad, and amazing oysters show off the kitchen's skill with the local treasures. **Known for:** inventive seafood dishes; jaw-dropping views. *Average main: $19 1001 Fairview Ave N., South Lake Union 206/588–2680 www.whiteswanpublichouse.com Brunch on weekends only, closes at 7 pm on Sun.*

Hotels

As a few of the seemingly everlasting construction projects finally start to reach completion, an influx of hotels has begun, but they tend toward the corporate standards catering to business travelers here to meet at Amazon headquarters.

Pan Pacific Hotel

$ | **HOTEL** | In the very heart of South Lake Union, this hotel is conveniently located for tourist attractions and dining, as well as for business. **Pros:** central location; soaking tubs; friendly service. **Cons:** lacks local character; needs updating; small rooms. *Rooms from: $127 2125 Terry Ave, South Lake Union Above Whole Foods 206/264–8111 www.panpacificseattle.com 153 rooms and 22 suites No meals.*

Nightlife

A mix of a few clubs left from the area's previous life as a no-man's land between Downtown and Capitol Hill have long anchored evenings in the neighborhood, but snazzy new cocktail bars have begun to fill in the gaps.

DANCE CLUBS

Kremwerk + Timbre Room Complex

DANCE CLUBS | This "queer-centric" club that combines modern fixtures and an industrial space is known for electronic music and theatrical performances that draw fun crowds. Tickets to shows by local and out-of-town DJs, musicians, and multidisciplinary artists are often available in advance for discounted prices. Upstairs, the Timbre Room hosts smaller, more intimate shows. *1809 Minor Ave., , #10, South Lake Union 206/682–2935 www.kremwerk.com.*

Re-Bar

BARS/PUBS | A loyal following enjoys cabaret shows, weekend stage performances, and great DJs at this combination bar, theater, dance club, and art space. It's extremely friendly to all persuasions and seeks to highlight the queer community. It also has a reputation for playing good house music, but there are lots of different theme nights, including an '80s new wave night. There's also Bawdy Storytelling, staged readings of favorite screenplays, and a monthly burlesque show. *1114 Howell St., South Lake Union 206/233–9873 www.rebarseattle.com.*

BARS AND LOUNGES

Deep Dive

BARS/PUBS | Renowned local chef Renee Erickson opened an enchanting nautical-themed speakeasy inside the Amazon spheres. Aside from the luxurious setting, guests are drawn by creative cocktails with ingredients like yogurt, Cinnamon Toast Crunch coconut cream, and watermelon vinegar. *620 Lenora St., South Lake Union Under the small, barely marked single door on the Lenora side of the spheres. 206/900–9390 www.deepdiveseattle.com.*

Mbar

BARS/PUBS | One of Seattle's few rooftop bars, the colorful, partially covered patio overlooks the entire South Lake Union neighborhood. Guests gaze at the Space Needle as they sip Hemingway Daiquiris or look out at the lake over craft cocktails while swinging in the hanging chairs. In winter, the 14th-floor spot stays open with blankets and the fire pits roaring as guests dig into the Middle Eastern–influenced small plates. *400 Fairview Ave. N, , 14th Floor, South Lake Union Hop on the designated elevator in the lobby, which will whisk you straight up to the bar. 206/457–8287 www.mbarseattle.com.*

Shopping

While there are a few perfunctory shops that fill in the main drag along Westlake, the two biggest shopping destinations here are the flagship stores of Seattle's iconic retail giants.

★ REI

CLOTHING | The enormous flagship for Recreational Equipment, Inc. (REI) has an incredible selection of outdoor gear—polar-fleece jackets, wool socks, down vests, hiking boots, rain gear, and much more—as well as its own 65-foot climbing wall. The staff is extremely knowledgeable; there always seems to be enough help on hand, even when the store is busy. You can test things out on the mountain-bike test trail or in the simulated rain booth. REI also rents gear such as tents, sleeping bags, skis, snowshoes, and backpacks. Bonus: They offer an hour of free parking. ✉ *222 Yale Ave. N, South Lake Union* ☎ *206/223–1944* 🌐 *www.rei.com.*

 Activities

While the land side of the lake is dominated with office buildings and condos, the lakefront holds a little bit of outdoor paradise.

BOATING

The Center for Wooden Boats

BOATING | Located on the southern shore of Lake Union, Seattle's free maritime heritage museum is a bustling community hub. Thousands of Seattleites rent rowboats and small wooden sailboats here every year; the center also offers workshops, demonstrations, and classes. Rentals for nonmembers range from $30 to $65 per hour, and sailboats require a prescheduled sailing checkout test. Free half-hour guided sails and steamboat rides are offered on Sunday from 11 am to 3 pm (arrive an hour early to reserve a spot). ✉ *1010 Valley St., Lake Union* ☎ *206/382–2628* 🌐 *www.cwb.org.*

★ Hot Tub Boats

BOATING | Yes, it's real, and yes it's as cool as it sounds. Grab up to five friends and spend an afternoon or evening motoring (somewhat slowly, it's quite heavy) around Lake Union from the comfort of your own private hot tub. You can bring your own picnic on board and connect the stereo to your phone to play tunes throughout the journey. The custom-made wooden boats can be rented for $350 for the first two hours and $100 after that. ✉ *2520 Westlake Ave. N, South Lake Union* ☎ *206/771–9883* 🌐 *www.hottubboats.com.*

Northwest Outdoor Center

BOATING | This center on Lake Union's west side rents one- or two-person kayaks (it also has a few triples) by the hour or day, including equipment and wetsuits (much needed outside of summer). The hourly rate is $18 for a single and $25 for a double (costs are figured in 10-minute increments after the first hour). For the more vertically inclined, the center also rents out stand-up paddleboards for $20 an hour. NWOC also runs classes, sunset tours near Golden Gardens Park, and full moon moonlight paddles. Reservations recommended in summer. ✉ *2100 Westlake Ave. N, Lake Union* ☎ *206/281–9694* 🌐 *www.nwoc.com.*

Outdoor Nirvana

If you are looking for more outdoor sportswear, or are in the market for a kayak, tent, snowshoes, or hiking boots—including weekend rentals—head to the nearby South Lake Union neighborhood for a visit to the memorable REI flagship store. For serious old-school anglers and mountain men, you can't miss the out-of-the-way Filson flagship store south of Downtown, for plaid vests, rugged pants, and coats that will last a lifetime.

The view from Kerry Park.

Queen Anne

Just west of the Seattle Center is the intersection of Queen Anne Avenue North and Denny Way. This marks the start of the Queen Anne neighborhood, which stretches all the way up formidable Queen Anne Hill to the ship canal on the other side. The neighborhood is split into Upper and Lower Queen Anne, and the two are quite different: Lower Queen Anne is a mixed-income neighborhood that has a small, interesting mix of independent record shops and bookstores, laid-back pubs, and a few upmarket restaurants and bars. Past Aloha Street, the neighborhood starts to look more upscale, with the snazzy Galer Street commercial strip marking the heart of Upper Queen Anne. Queen Anne doesn't have many sights, but the residential streets west of Queen Anne Avenue in Upper Queen Anne are fun to stroll, and sunny days offer gorgeous views. This ribbon of residential turf extends to the Magnolia neighborhood. There's only one sight to see in off-the-beaten-path Magnolia, but it's a terrific one: Discovery Park.

Within Queen Anne, Seattle Center is the home to Seattle's version of the Eiffel Tower—the Space Needle—and is anchored by Frank Gehry's wild MoPOP building, the acclaimed Pacific Science Center, and the dazzling Chihuly Garden and Glass. This area is a key destination for the museums or to catch a show at one of the many performing arts venues.

Seattle Center's 74-acre complex was built for the 1962 World's Fair. A rolling green campus with multiple venues is organized around the massive International Fountain. Among the arts groups based here are the Seattle Repertory Theatre, Intiman Theatre, the Seattle Opera, and the Pacific Northwest Ballet. It's also the site of three of summer's largest festivals—Northwest Folklife Festival, Bite of Seattle, and Bumbershoot. The Pacific Science Center, Seattle Children's Museum, and nearby Bill & Melinda Gates Visitor Center offer engaging activities for visitors of all ages.

Sights

Bill & Melinda Gates Foundation Visitor Center

MUSEUM | FAMILY | The Bill & Melinda Gates Foundation has some lofty goals, and it's here, across the street from Seattle Center, where you get to witness their plans in action. Exhibits are thought provoking and interactive, inviting you to offer up your own solutions to complex global problems like poverty and climate change. Fight disease, design a media campaign, and take part in a featured project to make a difference during your visit. *440 5th Ave. N, South Lake Union* *206/709–3100* *www.discovergates.com* *Free* *Closed Sun.–Mon.*

★ Chihuly Garden and Glass

MUSEUM | Just steps from the base of the Space Needle, fans of Dale Chihuly's glass works will be delighted to trace the artist's early influences—neon art, Native American Northwest Coast trade baskets, and Pendleton blankets, to name a few—to the vibrant chandelier towers and architectural glass installations he is most known for today. There are eight galleries total, plus a 40-foot-tall "Glasshouse," and an outdoor garden that serves as a backdrop for colorful installations that integrate with a dynamic Northwest landscape, including native plants and a 500-year-old western cedar that washed up on the shores of Neah Bay. Chihuly, who was born and raised in Tacoma, was actively involved in the design of the exhibition as well as the whimsical Collections Cafe, where you'll find Chihuly's quirky personal collections on display—everything from tin toys to vintage cameras to antique shaving brushes. Indeed, so many of his personal touches are part of the exhibition space, you can almost feel his presence in every room (look for the guy with the unruly hair and the black eye patch). Chihuly is kid-friendly for all but the littlest ones. **TIP→ If you're also planning to visit the Space Needle, the combination ticket can save you some money.** *305 Harrison St., under Space Needle, Central District* *206/753–4940* *www.chihulygardenandglass.com* *$32* *Discounts for evening tickets.*

The Children's Museum, Seattle

MUSEUM | FAMILY | If you're traveling with kids, you already know that a good children's museum is like gold at the end of a rainbow. This colorful, spacious museum, located on the lower level of The Armory in the heart of Seattle Center, provides hours of exploration and fun. Enter through a Northwest wilderness setting, with winding trails, hollow logs, and a waterfall. From there, you can explore the Global Village where rooms with kid-friendly props show everyday life in Ghana, the Philippines, and Japan. Cog City is a giant game of pipes, pulleys, and balls; kids can also test their talent in a mock recording studio. There's a small play area for toddlers and plenty of crafts to keep everyone engaged. *305 Harrison St., Central District* *206/441–1768* *www.thechildrensmuseum.org* *$12.*

★ Discovery Park

NATIONAL/STATE PARK | FAMILY | You won't find more spectacular views of Puget Sound, the Cascades, and the Olympics. Located on Magnolia Bluff, northwest of Downtown, Seattle's largest park covers 534 acres and has an amazing variety of terrain: shaded, secluded forest trails lead to meadows, saltwater beaches, sand dunes, a lighthouse, and 2 miles of protected beaches. The North Beach Trail, which takes you along the shore to the lighthouse, is a must-see. Head to the South Bluff Trail to get a view of Mt. Rainier. The park has several entrances—if you want to stop at the visitor center to pick up a trail map before exploring, use the main entrance at Government Way. The North Parking Lot is much closer to the North Beach Trail and to Ballard and Fremont, if you're coming from that direction. First-come, first-served beach parking passes for the disabled, elderly,

Did You Know?

You can snap photos of the Space Needle framed by Chihuly sculptures from the Glasshouse, a 40-foot-tall conservatory, at the Chihuly Garden and Glass.

and families with small children are available at the Learning Center. Note that the park is easily reached from Ballard and Fremont. It's easier to combine a park day with an exploration of those neighborhoods than with a busy Downtown itinerary. ✉ *3801 W. Government Way, Magnolia* ⊕ *From Downtown, take Elliot Ave. W (which turns into 15th Ave. W), and get off at Emerson St. exit and turn left onto W Emerson. Make a right onto Gilman Ave. W (which eventually becomes W Government Way). As you enter park, road becomes Washington Ave.; turn left on Utah Ave.* ☎ *206/386–4236* 🌐 *www.seattle.gov/parks/find/parks/discovery-park* 🎟 *Free.*

★ Kerry Park

VIEWPOINT | **FAMILY** | While in Seattle, if the mood strikes you to "pop the question" (any question will do, really), you'll find the answer at Kerry Park. Famous for engagements, sweeping views of the city skyline and, on clear days, Mt. Rainier, camera buffs and romantic types can't help but linger at this 1¼-acre sliver of a city park, which is a short but steep walk up from the shops and restaurants of Lower Queen Anne. The sculpture "Changing Form" by Doris Chase was added in 1971. There's a terrific little park and play area for kiddos at Bayview-Kinnear Park, just below the viewpoint of Kerry Park. ✉ *211 W Highland Dr., Queen Anne* ☎ *206/684–4075* 🌐 *www.seattle.gov/parks.*

★ Pacific Science Center

MUSEUM | **FAMILY** | If you have kids, this nonprofit science center in the heart of Seattle is a must-visit, home to more than 200 indoor and outdoor hands-on exhibits, two IMAX theaters, a Laser Dome, a butterfly house, and a state-of-the-art planetarium. The dinosaur exhibit—complete with moving robotic reproductions—is a favorite, and tots can experiment with water at the ever-popular stream table. Machines analyze human physiology in the *Body Works* exhibit. When you need to warm up, the Tropical Butterfly House is 80°F and home to colorful butterflies from South and Central America, Africa, and Asia; other creatures live in the Insect Village and saltwater tide-pool areas. IMAX movies, planetarium shows, Live Science Shows, and Laser Dome rock shows run daily. Look for the giant white arches near the Space Needle and make a day of the surrounding sights. **■ TIP→ Pacific Science Center offers a number of lectures, forums, and "Science Cafes" for adults, plus a variety of educational programs for kids, including camp-ins, monthly parents' night outs, workshops, and more. See website for schedule information.** ✉ *200 2nd Ave. N, Queen Anne* ☎ *206/443–2001* 🌐 *www.pacsci.org* 🎟 *Center $29.95, IMAX $10.75–$16.95, laser shows $5–$14, combined museum/IMAX $34.95.*

Chief Seattle

At the southeast side of Seattle Center (on the corner of 5th Avenue and Denny Way) stands a statue of Chief Seattle (originally Si'ahl), of the Duwamish tribe. The chief was among the first Native Americans to have contact with the white explorers who came to the region. His fellow tribesmen considered him to be a great leader and peacemaker. The sculpture was created by local artist James Wehn in 1912 and dedicated by the chief's great-great-granddaughter, Myrtle Loughery.

Space Needle

BUILDING | **FAMILY** | Almost 60 years old, Seattle's most iconic building is as quirky and beloved as ever, and a recent remodel has restored and improved it. The distinctive, towering, 605-foot-high structure is visible throughout much of Seattle—but the view from the inside out is even better. A less-than-one-minute ride up to the observation deck yields

360-degree vistas of Downtown Seattle, the Olympic Mountains, Elliott Bay, Queen Anne Hill, Lake Union, and the Cascade Range through floor-to-ceiling windows, the open air observation area, and the rotating glass floor. Built for the 1962 World's Fair, the Needle has an app to guide you around and interactive experiences to leave your own mark, and a virtual reality bungee-jump. If the forecast says you may have a sunny day during your visit, schedule the Needle for that day! If you can't decide whether you want the daytime or nighttime view, for an extra 10 bucks you can buy a ticket that allows you to visit twice in one day. (Also look for package deals with Chihuly Garden and Glass.) ✉ *400 Broad St., Central District* ☎ *206/905–2100* 🌐 *www.spaceneedle.com* 🎫 *From $32.50.*

Restaurants

Canlis Restaurant

$$$$ | PACIFIC NORTHWEST | Canlis has been setting the standard for opulent dining in Seattle since the 1950s, and the food, wine, practically clairvoyant service, and views overlooking Lake Union are still remarkable. Executive chef Brady Williams (formerly of New York's acclaimed Roberta's and Blanca) ensures the finest meat and freshest produce, but he has also refreshed the menu—which now offers a single, simple four-course tasting menu. **Known for:** stunning views; impeccable service; unbeatable entrées. $ *Average main: $135* ✉ *2576 Aurora Ave. N, Queen Anne* ☎ *206/283–3313* 🌐 *www.canlis.com* ⏲ *Closed Sun. No lunch* 🧥 *Jacket required.*

Collections Café

$$ | AMERICAN | While the food is more than passable, the real draw here is the decor: "Collections" refers to that of Dale Chihuly, the inspiration for the café (it's part of the Chihuly Garden and Glass campus). Chihuly is a lifelong collector of everything from bottle openers to radios to vintage accordions and much, much more—and a vast array of his findings are displayed on the walls, suspended from the ceiling, and even encased in the table tops. **Known for:** quirky decor; seasonal menu with local ingredients; burger topped with bacon and red onion jam. $ *Average main: $22* ✉ *305 Harrison St., under Space Needle, Lower Queen Anne* ☎ *206/753–4935* 🌐 *www.chihulygardenandglass.com/visit/collections-cafe* ⏲ *No dinner.*

★ **Eden Hill**

$$$$ | MODERN AMERICAN | This tiny, 24-seat restaurant quietly turns out some of the most exciting and innovative food in the city in the form of visually stunning small plates. Tables are seated beside wide windows overlooking the serene side of Queen Anne. **Known for:** signature dessert "lick the bowl" made with foie gras; grand tasting menu requires reservations; daily changing menus. $ *Average main: $160* ✉ *2209 Queen Anne Ave. N, Queen Anne* ☎ *206/708–6836* 🌐 *www.edenhillrestaurant.com* ⏲ *Closed Mon. No lunch.*

How to Cook a Wolf

$$ | ITALIAN | This sleek eatery features fresh, artisanal ingredients. Starters run the gamut from cured-meat platters to roasted almonds, pork terrine, chicken-liver mousse, and arugula salad, while tasty mains focus on simple handmade pastas—orecchiette with sausage, garlic, and ricotta. **Known for:** small plates; pasta. $ *Average main: $22* ✉ *2208 Queen Anne Ave. N, Queen Anne* ☎ *206/838–8090* 🌐 *www.ethanstowellrestaurants.com* ⏲ *No lunch.*

★ **Taylor Shellfish Oyster Bar**

$ | PACIFIC NORTHWEST | When the family behind a fifth-generation shellfish farm decides to open a restaurant devoted to their signature products, the result is a temple to those oysters, mussels, and clams. Cool colors, a metal bar, and big windows give the urban restaurant a distinctly beachy feel, which seems appropriate for digging into dozens of

La Marzocco Cafe shares its space with Seattle's public radio station, KEXP.

the region's acclaimed bivalves. **Known for:** salish sampler; tide-to-table seafood; chowder. *Average main: $$14* *124 Republican St., South Lake Union* *206/501–4442* *www.taylorshellfishfarms.com.*

Coffee and Quick Bites

★ La Marzocco Cafe & Showroom
$ | **CAFÉ** | Though better known for making espresso machines than espresso, La Marzocco brings a sprawling open café, gorgeous light, and incredible coffee and coffeemakers to Seattle Center. Sharing space with Seattle's cherished public radio station, KEXP, the café brings in a different roaster—their drinks, experts, and style—each month. **Known for:** elevated espresso drinks; monthly rotating roasters; inside KEXP space. *Average main: $3* *KEXP Seattle Center Campus, 472 1st Ave. N, Lower Queen Anne* *206/388–3500* *www.lamarzoccousa.com/locations/* *No dinner.*

Seattle Center Armory
$ | **AMERICAN** | A complete remodel has changed the Seattle Center food court from an only-if-you're-desperate stop into a quick-bite destination. Several high-quality indie restaurants have erected walk-up windows or shops here, from skillet burgers to Montreal-style bagels at Eltana. **Known for:** beautiful space; quick service; variety. *Average main: $8* *305 Harrison St., Queen Anne* *206/684–7200* *www.seattlecenter.com.*

Hotels

Queen Anne is a mostly residential neighborhood spread out over a large hill just to the north of Belltown and close to Seattle Center. Upper Queen Anne is posh, quiet, and scenic. Lower Queen Anne, where all the lodging options lie, is very walkable to Belltown, Downtown, and Seattle Center—but it's considerably less elegant than the top of the hill. You can find better deals here than in most of Downtown—and you'll still be close to everything.

MarQueen Hotel

$ | **HOTEL** | Fans of historic boutique hotels will love this reasonably priced 1918 brick property at the foot of Queen Anne Hill. **Pros:** in-room kitchens and living room areas; free Wi-Fi and complimentary breakfast; speakeasy on property. **Cons:** street-side rooms can be loud; housekeeping not always consistent; no elevator. 💲 *Rooms from: $101* ✉ *600 Queen Anne Ave. N, Queen Anne* ☎ *206/282–7407, 888/445–3076* 🌐 *www.marqueen.com* 🛏 *58 rooms* 🍴 *Free Breakfast.*

The Maxwell Hotel

$ | **HOTEL** | Colorful and funky rooms, with argyle-print chairs and outlines of chandeliers painted on the walls, are *the* choice for visitors frequenting the Seattle Center for opera or the ballet. **Pros:** free parking and shuttle; complimentary bikes; some rooms have great views of the Space Needle. **Cons:** hotel is on a busy street; pool and gym are tiny; guests complain of low water pressure. 💲 *Rooms from: $105* ✉ *300 Roy St., Queen Anne* ☎ *206/286–0629, 866/866–7977* 🌐 *www.themaxwellhotel.com* 🛏 *139 rooms* 🍴 *No meals.*

Nightlife

Queen Anne is a diffuse and mostly residential neighborhood, so while there are a few bars scattered around the formidable hill, most are on the lower reaches, near Seattle Center and Key Arena.

BARS AND LOUNGES

The Masonry

BARS/PUBS | Mostly a beer bar, The Masonry also happens to have great Neapolitan-style pizzas and other brick-oven dishes. Events like brewer dinners, good music, and a bottle list that includes limited releases from top breweries, are other highlights. There are also ciders and wine on draft. ✉ *20 Roy St., Lower Queen Anne* ☎ *206/453–4375* 🌐 *www.themasonryseattle.com.*

The Sitting Room

BARS/PUBS | With its European-café vibe and excellent mixed drinks, the Sitting Room lures residents of both the lower and upper parts of Queen Anne. It's quite an accomplishment to get those two very different demographics to agree on anything, but this sweet, relaxed little spot has done it with its eclectic furniture, zinc bar, sexy lighting, and friendly staff. ✉ *108 W Roy St., Queen Anne* ☎ *206/285–2830* 🌐 *www.the-sitting-room.com.*

Solo

BARS/PUBS | This spot has a lot going on: it's part tapas bar, part art gallery, part screening room, and part music venue, where up-and-coming indie musicians perform on a small stage. ✉ *200 Roy St., Queen Anne* ☎ *206/213–0080* 🌐 *www.solo-bar.com.*

Performing Arts

ARTS CENTERS

Marion Oliver McCaw Hall

ARTS CENTERS | The home of the Seattle Opera and the Pacific Northwest Ballet is an opulent, glass-enclosed structure reflecting the skies and the Space Needle nearby. The facility houses two auditoriums and a four-story main lobby area where several artworks are on display. A programmed light art installation by Leni Schwendinger displays outside McCaw Hall in the Kreielsheimer Promenade. ✉ *321 Mercer St., Lower Queen Anne* ☎ *206/389–7676, 206/733–9725* 🌐 *www.mccawhall.com.*

Seattle Center

ARTS CENTERS | Several of the Seattle Center's halls are used for theater, opera, dance, music, and performance art. Public radio station KEXP frequently hosts concerts in their home on the Seattle Center campus, and the center is also the site of many of Seattle's major cultural festivals. ✉ *305 Harrison St., Queen Anne* ☎ *206/684–7200* 🌐 *www.seattlecenter.org.*

THEATER

Cornish Playhouse at Seattle Center
THEATER | This performance and education venue run by the Cornish College of the Arts hosts public music and theater programs, produced by students and professionals, throughout the year in a 432-seat auditorium on the Seattle Center Campus. ✉ *Seattle Center, 201 Mercer St., Queen Anne* ☎ *206/315–5776* 🌐 *www.cornish.edu/playhouse.*

Seattle Children's Theatre
THEATER | FAMILY | Top-notch productions of new works join adaptations from classic children's literature here. After the show, actors come out to answer questions and explain how the tricks are done. ✉ *201 Thomas St., Lower Queen Anne* ☎ *206/441–3322* 🌐 *www.sct.org.*

Seattle Repertory Theater
THEATER | During its season (September through June), the Seattle Repertory Theater brings new and classic plays to life. Adoring fans flock to new takes on choice classics as well as works fresh from the New York stage. You can pre-order your drinks from the lobby bar to enjoy during intermission. ✉ *155 Mercer St., Lower Queen Anne* ☎ *206/443–2222* 🌐 *www.seattlerep.org.*

DANCE

On the Boards
DANCE | Since 1978, On the Boards has been presenting contemporary dance performances, as well as theater, music, and multimedia events. The main subscription series runs from August through June, but events are scheduled nearly every weekend year-round. ✉ *100 W Roy St., Lower Queen Anne* ☎ *206/217–9886* 🌐 *www.ontheboards.org.*

Pacific Northwest Ballet
DANCE | The lineup of Seattle's resident ballet company and school includes works from celebrated contemporary choreographers as well as a mix of classic and international productions (think *Swan Lake* and *Carmina Burana*). Fans of *Swan Lake* and *The Nutcracker* can rest assured that those timeless productions are still part of the company's repertoire. Its season runs from September through June. ✉ *McCaw Hall at Seattle Center, 301 Mercer St., Lower Queen Anne* ☎ *206/441–2424* 🌐 *www.pnb.org.*

Novel Needle

SpaceBase Gift Shop The SpaceBase Gift Shop has the city's ultimate icon, the Space Needle, rendered in endless ways. Among the officially licensed goods are bags of Space Needle Noodles, towering wooden pepper grinders, and artsy black T-shirts. ✉ *400 Broad St., Queen Anne* ☎ *206/905–2100* 🌐 *www.spaceneedle.com.*

OPERA

Seattle Opera
MUSIC | Housed in the beautiful Marion Oliver McCaw Hall, the opera stages productions from August through May. Evening-event guests are treated to a light show from 30-foot hanging scrims above an outdoor piazza. ✉ *McCaw Hall at Seattle Center, 321 Mercer St., Lower Queen Anne* ☎ *206/389–7676* 🌐 *www.seattleopera.org.*

Shopping

There are actually two shopping areas in this hillside neighborhood—the more urban-feeling Lower Queen Anne, near the large Seattle Center campus, and the more neighborhoody Upper Queen Anne, along Queen Anne Avenue North at the top of the hill. West from the Seattle Center along Queen Anne and Mercer Avenues are tiny cafés, antiques, and music stores. The cluster of businesses at the top of the hill includes a bookshop, gift stores, and a heralded wine shop.

Best shopping: Along Queen Anne Avenue North between West Harrison and Roy Streets, and between West Galer and McGraw Streets.

McCarthy & Schiering Wine Merchants
FOOD/CANDY | One of the oldest wine shops in the city is attitude-free and offers an amazing selection of wines from around the world. Check out the selection of local wines to experience the true flavor of the Northwest. Free tastings are held on Saturday. ✉ *2401B Queen Anne Ave. N, Queen Anne* ☎ *206/282–8500* 🌐 *www.mccarthyand-schiering.com.*

Peridot Boutique
CLOTHING | Animal-print pocket dresses, retro gingham tops, and ruffly skirts abound in this contemporary women's boutique in lower Queen Anne. The prices are reasonable, the accessories are abundant, and local designers are represented as well. ✉ *2135 Queen Anne Ave. N, Queen Anne* ☎ *206/687–7130* 🌐 *www.peridotboutique.wordpress.com.*

Chapter 5

PIONEER SQUARE

Updated by
AnnaMaria Stephens

Sights ★★★☆☆ | Restaurants ★★☆☆☆ | Hotels ★☆☆☆☆ | Shopping ★★★☆☆ | Nightlife ★★☆☆☆

NEIGHBORHOOD SNAPSHOT

GETTING HERE AND AROUND

Pioneer Square is directly south of Downtown, which means you can easily walk here. However, the stretch between the two neighborhoods is not the most scenic trip, so you can also hop on a bus heading south on 1st Avenue.

Pioneer Square is pretty small; you'll easily be able to walk to all the galleries. If you've driven in from a more distant neighborhood, most of the pay parking lots and garages are on South Jackson Street.

Most people combine Pioneer Square with a trip to the International District, which together would make for a full day of sightseeing. Pioneer Square is also the closest neighborhood to CenturyLink Field and T-Mobile Park, so it also makes sense to end a touring day here before heading to a game.

TOP REASONS TO GO

Leave the Space Needle to the masses and check out the observation deck and speakeasy-style bar at 38-story **Smith Tower** at 506 2nd Avenue and Yesler Way.

Gallery hop on First Thursday art walks—perhaps the best time to see Pioneer Square, when animated crowds walk from gallery to gallery. Or tour on your own: Greg Kucera, James Harris, and the Tashiro-Kaplan Building are must-sees, as is the Arctic Club Hotel Seattle, which features terra cotta walruses on the exterior, a chic lobby bar, and a gold rush-era vibe.

Soak up some weird and wonderful historic Seattle tidbits on the zany **Bill Speidel's Underground Tour.**

Catch your reflection in the hood of an antique fire truck at **Last Resort Fire Department Museum.**

Cheer for one of the home teams at **CenturyLink or T-Mobile Park**.

TOURS

■ At a kiosk on Occidental between Main and Jackson Streets, you can pick up a booklet that outlines three walking tours around the historic buildings of Pioneer Square.

■ The Underground Tour shows you the remnants of passageways and buildings buried when the city regraded the streets in the 1880s. The tour is fun and full of Seattle-history tidbits, though younger kids might be bored as there's not much to see.

QUICK BITES

■ **Grand Central Bakery.** This bakery serves hearth-baked breads, artisanal pastries, panini, soups, and salads. ✉ *214 1st Ave. S, Pioneer Square* ☎ *206/622–3644* 🌐 *www.grandcentralbakery.com* ⏲ *Closed Sun.*

■ **Salumi Artisan Cured Meats.** Salumi serves artisanal cured meats in heavenly sandwiches. ✉ *404 Occidental Ave. S, Pioneer Square* ☎ *206/621–8772* 🌐 *www.salumicuredmeats.com* ⏲ *Closed Sun.*

■ **Zeitgeist.** The best-loved coffee shop in the neighborhood. ✉ *171 S Jackson St., Pioneer Square* ☎ *206/583–0497* 🌐 *zeitgeistcoffee.com.*

The Pioneer Square district, directly south of Downtown, is Seattle's oldest neighborhood. It attracts visitors for elegantly renovated (or in some cases replica) turn-of-the-20th-century redbrick buildings and art galleries. It's the center of Seattle's arts scene, and the galleries in this small neighborhood make up the majority of its sights.

Today's Yesler Way was the original "Skid Road," where, in the 1880s, timber was sent to the sawmill on a skid of small logs laid crossways and greased so that the cut trees would slide down to the mill. The area later grew into Seattle's first center of commerce. Many of the buildings you see today are replicas of the wood-frame structures destroyed by fire in 1889.

The rôle Pioneer Square plays in the city today is harder to define. Despite the concentration of galleries, the neighborhood is no longer a center for artists per se, as rents have risen considerably; only established gallery owners can rent loft-like spaces in heavily trafficked areas.

By day, you'll see a mix of Downtown workers and tourists strolling the area. The neighborhood also has one of the highest concentrations of homeless people in Seattle, and though they don't typically aggressively panhandle, they do tend to congregate at public parks. Pioneer Square has a well-known nightlife scene, but these days it's a much-derided one, thanks to the meat-market vibe of many of the clubs. If you want classier venues, you'll be smart to head north up 1st Avenue to Belltown or to select spots on Capitol Hill.

When Seattleites speak of Pioneer Square, they usually speak of the love they have for certain neighborhood spots—the original Grand Central Bakery in the historic Grand Central Arcade, Zeitgeist coffeehouse, a beloved art gallery, a friend's loft apartment, a great store—than the love they have for the neighborhood as a whole. Pioneer Square is always worth a visit, but reactions do vary. Anyone seriously interested in doing the gallery circuit will be impressed, and foodies will find a few buzzworthy options. The recently renovated Smith Tower, once the tallest building on the West Coast, beckons with an observation deck and a speakeasy on the 35th floor. That said, those looking for a vibrant, picture-perfect historic district will be underwhelmed.

Pioneer Square is a gateway of sorts to the stadium district, which segues into SoDo (South of Downtown). First comes CenturyLink Field, where the Seahawks and the Sounders play. Directly south of that is Safeco Field, where the Mariners play. There's not much to see in this industrial area, but if you're a sports fan you can easily make a run from Pioneer Square to one of the stadiums' pro shops. There are also a few good brewpubs close to the stadiums.

 Sights

AXIS Pioneer Square

MUSEUM | Soaring 18-foot ceilings, classic brick arches, and antique wood floors make a dramatic backdrop for monthly rotating exhibits with a contemporary bent. Part of a multitasking, 6,000-square-foot studio space, the gallery features a roster of local, national, and international artists and photographers. AXIS hosts new shows with entertainment during First Thursday Art Walk. ✉ *308 1st Ave. S, Pioneer Square* ☎ *206/681–9316* 🌐 *www.axispioneersquare.com* 🎟 *Free.*

Bill Speidel's Underground Tour

TOUR—SIGHT | Present-day Pioneer Square is actually one story higher than it used to be. After the Great Seattle Fire of 1889, Seattle's planners regraded the neighborhood's streets, which had been built on filled-in tide lands and regularly flooded. The result? There is now an intricate and expansive array of subterranean passageways and basements beneath Pioneer Square, and Bill Speidel's Underground Tour is the only way to explore them. Speidel was an irreverent historian, PR man, and former *Seattle Times* reporter who took it upon himself to preserve historic Seattle, and this 75-minute tour is packed with his sardonic wit and playful humor. It's very informative, too—if you're interested in the general history of the city or salty anecdotes about Seattle's early denizens, you'll appreciate it that much more. Younger kids will almost certainly be bored, as there's not much to see at the specific sites, which are more used as launching points for the stories. Comfortable shoes, a love for quirky historical yarns, and an appreciation of bad puns are musts. Several tours are offered daily, and schedules change month to month: call or visit the website for a full list of tour times. ✉ *608 1st Ave., Pioneer Square* ☎ *206/682–4646* 🌐 *www.undergroundtour.com* 🎟 *$22.*

CenturyLink Field

SPORTS VENUE | Located directly south of Pioneer Square, CenturyLink Field hosts two professional teams, the Seattle Seahawks (football) and the Seattle Sounders FC (soccer). The open-air stadium has 67,000 seats; sightlines are excellent thanks to a cantilevered design and the close placement of lower sections. Tours start at the pro shop (be sure to arrive at least 30 minutes prior to purchase tickets) and last an hour and a half. You'll get a personal look at behind-the-scenes areas as well as the famous 12th Man Flag Pole, and have a chance to sink your feet into the same playing surface as your favorite Seahawks and Sounders stars. ✉ *800 Occidental Ave. S, SoDo* ☎ *206/381–7582* 🌐 *www.centurylinkfield.com* 🎟 *$14.*

Davidson Galleries

MUSEUM | Davidson has several different departments in one building: the Contemporary Print & Drawing Center, which holds the portfolios of 50 print artists; the Antique Print Department; and the Painting and Sculpture Department. Though the Antique Print Department is more of a specialized interest, the contemporary-print exhibits are always interesting and worth a look. ✉ *313 Occidental Ave. S, Pioneer Square* ☎ *206/624–7684 contemporary prints, 206/624–6700 antique prints, 206/624–7684 painting and sculpture* 🌐 *www.davidsongalleries.com* 🎟 *Free* ⏲ *Closed Sun.–Mon.*

Flury & Co.

MUSEUM | One of the largest collections of vintage photographs by Edward Curtis, along with Native American antiques, traditional carvings, baskets, masks, jewelry, and tools are showcased in a historic space that's as interesting as the store's wares. ✉ *322 1st*

Ave. S, Pioneer Square ☎ *206/587–0260* 🌐 *www.fluryco.com* ⏲ *Closed Sun.*

Foster/White Gallery

MUSEUM | One of the Seattle art scene's heaviest hitters has digs as impressive as the works it shows: a century-old building with high ceilings and 7,000 square feet of exhibition space. Works by internationally acclaimed Northwest masters Kenneth Callahan, Mark Tobey, Alden Mason, and George Tsutakawa are on permanent display. ✉ *220 3rd Ave. S, Pioneer Square* ☎ *206/622–2833* 🌐 *www.fosterwhite.com* 🎫 *Free* ⏲ *Closed Sun.–Mon.*

Gallery 110

MUSEUM | Gallery 110 works with a collective of 30 contemporary artists (primarily Northwest-based) showing pieces in its small space that are energetic, challenging, and fresh. On-site exhibitions change monthly, and once a year the gallery hosts a juried exhibition. ✉ *110 3rd Ave. S, Pioneer Square* ☎ *206/624–9336* 🌐 *www.gallery110.com* 🎫 *Free* ⏲ *Closed Sun.–Wed.*

★ **Greg Kucera Gallery**

MUSEUM | One of the most important destinations on the First Thursday gallery walk, this gorgeous space is a top venue for national and regional artists. Be sure to check out the outdoor sculpture deck on the second level. If you have time for only one gallery visit, this is the place to go. You'll see big names that you might recognize—along with newer artists—and the thematic group shows are always thoughtful and well presented. ✉ *212 3rd Ave. S, Pioneer Square* ☎ *206/624–0770* 🌐 *www.gregkucera.com* 🎫 *Free* ⏲ *Closed Sun.–Mon.*

James Harris Gallery

MUSEUM | One of Seattle's oldest and most respected galleries, James Harris Gallery is known for creating small shows that selectively and impeccably survey both local and international work. Three exhibition rooms provide intimacy and connectivity to tightly curated shows, including work from artists like Steve Davis, Squeak Carnwath, Claire Cowie, Karin Davie, Richard Rezac, and Akio Takamori. ✉ *312 2nd Ave. S, Pioneer Square* ☎ *206/903–6220* 🌐 *www.jamesharrisgallery.com* 🎫 *Free* ⏲ *Closed Sun.–Tues.*

Klondike Gold Rush National Historical Park

MUSEUM | A tiny yet delightful free museum illustrating Seattle's role in the 1897–98 Gold Rush in the Klondike region, this gem is located inside a historic redbrick building with wooden floors and soaring ceilings. Walls are lined with photos of gold miners, explorers, and the hopeful families who followed them. Film presentations, gold-panning demonstrations (daily in summer, at 10 and 3), and rotating exhibits are scheduled throughout the year. Other sectors of this park are in southeast Alaska. ✉ *319 2nd Ave. S, Pioneer Square* ☎ *206/220–4240* 🌐 *nps.gov/klse/index.htm* 🎫 *Free.*

Last Resort Fire Department Museum

MUSEUM | Occupying the bottom floor of the Seattle Fire Department's headquarters, the museum includes eight historic rigs from Seattle dating from the 19th and early 20th centuries, as well as artifacts (vintage helmets and uniforms, hose nozzles, and other equipment) and photos, logs, and newspaper clippings recording historic fires. ✉ *301 2nd Ave. S, Pioneer Square* ☎ *206/783–4474* 🌐 *www.lastresortfd.org* 🎫 *Free.*

Occidental Park

PLAZA | This shady, picturesque cobblestone park is the geographical heart of the historic neighborhood—on first Thursdays it's home to a variety of local artisans setting up makeshift booths. Grab a sandwich or pastry at the Grand Central Bakery (arguably the city's finest artisanal bakery) and get in some good people-watching at the outdoor patio. Note that this square is a spot where homeless people congregate; you're likely to encounter more than a few oddballs. The square is best avoided at night. ✉ *Occidental Ave. S and S Main St., Pioneer Square.*

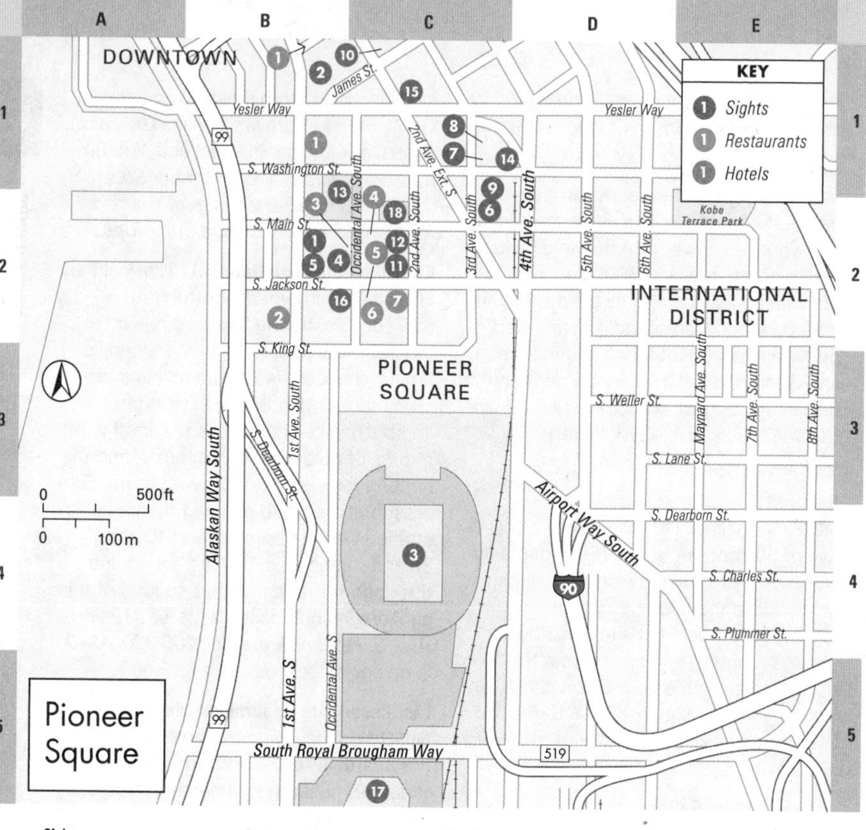

Sights

1 AXIS Pioneer Square... **B2**
2 Bill Speidel's Underground Tour **B1**
3 CenturyLink Field **C4**
4 Davidson Galleries **B2**
5 Flury & Co................ **B2**
6 Foster/White Gallery **C2**
7 G. Gibson Gallery **C1**
8 Gallery 110................ **C1**
9 Greg Kucera Gallery..... **C2**
10 James Harris Gallery.... **C1**
11 Klondike Gold Rush National Historical Park **C2**
12 Last Resort Fire Department Museum ... **C2**
13 Occidental Park......... **B2**
14 Punch Gallery **C1**
15 Smith Tower.............. **C1**
16 Stonington Gallery...... **B2**
17 T-Mobile Park **C5**
18 Waterfall Garden **C2**

Restaurants

1 Damn the Weather **B1**
2 Il Terrazzo Carmine..... **B2**
3 Locus Wines **B2**
4 The London Plane **C2**
5 Salumi Cured Meats..... **C2**
6 Taylor Shellfish Oyster Bar **C2**
7 Zeitgeist Coffee **C2**

Hotels

1 The Arctic Club Seattle **B1**

Smith Tower

BUILDING | When this iconic landmark opened in 1914, it was the tallest office building outside New York City and the fourth-tallest building in the world. (It remained the tallest building west of the Mississippi for nearly 50 years.) The Smith Tower Observatory on the 35th floor is an open-air wraparound deck providing panoramic views of the surrounding historic neighborhood, ball fields, the city skyline, and the mountains on clear days. It's also a superb spot to take in a sunset. The top floor includes the speakeasy-themed Observatory Bar, which features striking original architectural details and a cocktail and nibbles menu that pays homage to the Prohibition era. Smith Tower's ground-floor Provisions General Store, where you'll find a nostalgic soda fountain and locally inspired gifts, is also worth a visit. *Smith Tower hosts an outdoor pop-up bar with beer and wine called The Lookout on the 22nd floor during the warm summer months. Admission is $5. Check the website for details.* ✉ *506 2nd Ave. S, Pioneer Square* ☎ *206/622–4004* 🌐 *www.smithtower.com* 🎫 *$12 before 6pm; $14 after.*

Stonington Gallery

MUSEUM | You'll see plenty of cheesy tribal art knockoffs in tourist-trap shops, but this elegant gallery will give you a real look at the best contemporary work of Northwest Coast and Alaska tribal members (and artists from these regions working in the Native style). Three floors exhibit wood carvings, paintings, sculpture, and mixed-media pieces from the likes of Robert Davidson, Joe David, Preston Singeltary, Susan Point, and Rick Barto. ✉ *119 S Jackson St., Pioneer Square* ☎ *206/405–4040* 🌐 *www.stoningtongallery.com* 🎫 *Free.*

T-Mobile Park

SPORTS VENUE | This 47,000-seat, open-air baseball stadium with a state-of-the-art retractable roof is the home of the Seattle Mariners. If you want to see the stadium in all its glory, take the one-hour tour, which brings you onto the field, into the dugouts, back to the press and locker rooms, and up to the posh box seats. Tours depart from the Team Store on 1st Avenue, and you purchase your tickets there, too (at least 15 minutes prior to the scheduled tour). Afterward, head across the street to the Pyramid Alehouse for a local brew. ✉ *1250 1st Ave. S, SoDo* ☎ *866/800–1275* 🌐 *www.mlb.com/mariners/ballpark/tours* 🎫 *$12.*

Gallery Walks

It's fun to simply walk around Pioneer Square and pop into galleries. South Jackson Street to Yesler between Western and 4th Avenue South is a good area. The first Thursday of every month, galleries stay open late for First Thursday Art Walk, a neighborhood highlight. Visit 🌐 *www.firstthursdayseattle.com.*

Waterfall Garden

GARDEN | A tranquil spot to take a break, this small garden surrounds a 22-foot (artificial) waterfall that cascades over large granite stones. There are a few café tables; it's a great place to rest for a few minutes and seek out your next destination in the guidebook. ✉ *219 2nd Ave. South, Pioneer Square* ☎ *206/624–6096.*

Restaurants

Damn the Weather

$$ | **AMERICAN** | In addition to the navy-blue exterior and cheeky name of this small, upscale gastropub, they're also known for simple craft cocktails made by devoted mixologists and a small but spot-on menu of comfort foods. The bar offers several snacks (olives, nuts, fries) and small plates ideal for sharing as well as heartier options including a shrimp po'boy and classic burger with

The popular Foster/White Gallery has 7,000 square feet of exhibition space.

fries at lunch. **Known for:** chicken-fat fries; booze expertise; cool historic building. *Average main: $20 116 1st Ave. S, Pioneer Square 206/9461283 www.damntheweather.com.*

Il Terrazzo Carmine

$$$ | ITALIAN | Ceiling-to-floor draperies lend the dining room understated dignity, and intoxicating aromas waft from the kitchen all the way to the restaurant's small outdoor patio that sits beneath a canopy of lights. The chef blends Tuscan-style and regional southern Italian cooking to create soul-satisfying dishes such as veal osso buco, homemade ravioli, linguine *alle vongole*, and eggplant Parmesan. **Known for:** elegant space; classic Italian fare. *Average main: $32 411 1st Ave. S, Pioneer Square 206/467–7797 www.ilterrazzocarmine.com Closed Sun., no lunch Sat.*

Locus Wines

$ | WINE BAR | Already a familiar name in the Seattle wine scene, Locus Wines recently debuted a bright, modern tasting room that showcases food-and-wine pairings. The small menu features flights served with a small bite that perfectly complements each pour—like a carmelized onion and lamb pastry square matched with the signature Locus Red—although Locus also offers wine by the glass and a few light snacks, including a kale salad and pillowy meatballs. **Known for:** Rhône-style wines; food-focused flights; friendly, knowledgeable service. *Average main: $12 307 Occidental Ave. S, Pioneer Square 206/682–1760 www.locuswines.com Closed Tues.*

The London Plane

$ | BAKERY | In an airy building right on the corner of Occidental Square, the London Plane is a gorgeous multipurpose space that also includes a small artisanal shop, florist, and bakery. The "daytime" menu (until 3 pm) features mostly vegetarian light bites, many with Mediterranean-inspired flavors, from classic pastries and quiches to grain-enriched salads and seared albacore. **Known for:** fresh coffee

Continued on page 120

SEATTLE'S SIPPING CULTURE

ARTISAN COFFEES, CRAFT MICROBREWS, AND BOUTIQUE WINES

by Carissa Bluestone

Seattle's beverage obsession only begins with coffee. Whether you're into hoppy microbrews, premium wines, or expertly crafted cappuccinos, prepare to devote much of your visit to sipping the best Seattle and Washington State have to offer.

Seattle may forever be known as the birthplace of Starbucks, but nowadays foodies are just as likely to talk about Washington state's wine industry as the city's coffeehouses. Not to pronounce coffee dead, however. After a few years of inertia, the coffee scene is growing again with more independent roasters and shops than ever.

In fact, in the past few years the city's seen a profusion of potables: New microbreweries and wineries are opening, and hip new bars, taprooms, and tasting rooms are thriving more than ever. Like its sister city, Portland, Seattle is a hotspot for entrepreneurial spirit—it's this energy, mixed with a passion for local and organic ingredients, that has raised the bar on everything artisan.

COFFEE

Although Seattle owes much of its coffee legacy to Starbucks, the city's independent coffee shops rule the roast here. Their ardent commitment to creating premium artisanal blends from small batches of beans is what truly defines the scene. The moment you take your first sip of an expertly executed cappuccino at a coffeehouse such as **Caffé Vita** or **Espresso Vivace** you realize that the drink is never an afterthought here. Perfectly roasted beans ground to specification and pulled into espresso shots using dual-boiler machines and velvety steamed milk are de rigueur. In most restaurants, your coffee is likely to be a personal French press filled with a brew roasted just a few blocks away.

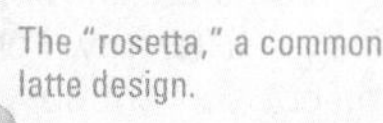
The "rosetta," a common latte design.

LATTE ART

Latte art is a given in Seattle. Designs vary by barista, but the most common flourish is the rosetta, which resembles a delicate fern. Here's how it's done:

1. THE BASE. A latte consists of a shot (or two) of espresso and hot, frothy milk.

2. THE POUR. First the shot is poured. The milk pitcher gets a few gentle swirls and taps (to burst the largest bubbles), then the milk is poured at a steady pace into the center of the tilted cup.

3. THE SHAKE. When the cup's about three-quarters full, the milk is streamed with tiny side-to-side strokes up and down the cup's center line. The "leaves" will start to fan out.

4. THE TOP. When the cup's almost full, the milk is drawn towards the bottom. With the last stroke the "stem" is drawn through the center of the leaves.

BEST COFFEEHOUSES

Many Seattle roasters obtain their beans through Direct Trade, sourcing directly from growers rather than brokers. They travel across the globe to meet with farmers, often paying them well above Fair Trade prices to ensure the highest-quality beans. Local roasters are also intensely community-minded: Caffé Vita, for example, recently partnered with the much-loved local chocolate factory Theo to produce sublime espresso-flavored chocolate bars.

CAFFÉ VITA. Though now a mini-chain (with locations in Fremont, Queen Anne, Pioneer Square, and Seward Park), Vita's roasting operations (and heart and soul) are in Capitol Hill. ✉ *1005 E. Pike St., Capitol Hill* ☎ *206/709–4440* 🌐 *www.caffevita.com*

Caffé Vita

ESPRESSO VIVACE. A top roaster, Vivace has two tidy coffee shops (the other's by REI in South Lake Union), and a sidewalk espresso stand at Broadway and Harrison. ✉ *532 Broadway Ave E, Capitol Hill* ☎ *206/860–2722* 🌐 *www.espresso-vivace.com*

FREMONT COFFEE COMPANY. Known for its awesome wraparound porch and exceptional brews, this friendly shop is the city's latest small-batch roaster. ✉ *459 N. 36th St., Fremont* ☎ *206/632–3633* 🌐 *www.fremontcoffee.net*

Stumptown

HERKIMER. This cheerful small-batch roaster is a northern neighborhoods favorite. ✉ *7320 Greenwood Ave. N, Phinney Ridge* ☎ *206/784–0202* 🌐 *www.herkimer-coffee.com*

STUMPTOWN. This hip Portland powerhouse has two branches (the other is on Pine and Boylston). The 12th Ave. branch has the roasting facility. ✉ *1115 12th Ave., Capitol Hill* ☎ *206/860–2937* 🌐 *www.stumptowncoffee.com*

VICTROLA COFFEE. The original branch on 15th Avenue is a favorite standby, but the newer branch at 310 E. Pike St. in the Pike-Pine Corridor has a great view of the roasting room from its cafe tables. ✉ *411 15th Ave. E, Capitol Hill* ☎ *206/462–6259* 🌐 *www.victrolacoffee.com*

Victrola Coffee

BEER

Craft brews have fewer ingredients than you might think.

Next time you drink a beer, thank the state of Washington. More than 70% of the nation's hops is grown in the Yakima Valley, and Washington is the fourth-largest producer of malting barley. The state's 80-plus breweries combine top-notch ingredients with crystal-clear snowpack waters to make high-quality craft beers. Seattle has at least a dozen breweries within its city limits, plus many fine gastropubs with standout locals on tap.

GREAT BREWERIES

ELLIOTT BAY BREWING. A dozen of Elliott Bay's beers are certified organic. The pub is a neighborhood favorite for its good, locally sourced food. ✉ *4720 California Ave NW, West Seattle* ☎ *206/932–8695* 🌐 *www.elliottbaybrewing.com*

PIKE PUB. The most touristy of the local breweries, Pike Pub also has a small microbrewery museum. The pale ale and the Kilt Lifter Scottish ale have been local favorites for two decades. There's a full pub menu. ✉ *1415 1st Ave, Downtown* ☎ *206/622–6044* 🌐 *www.pikebrewing.com*

ELYSIAN BREWING COMPANY. Known for its Immortal IPA and good seasonal brews and pub grub, Elysian has three branches, in Capitol Hill, Green Lake, and across from Qwest Field. ✉ *1221 E. Pike St., Capitol Hill* ☎ *206/860–1920* 🌐 *www.elysianbrewing.com*

FREMONT BREWING. This brewery makes small-batch pale ales using organic hops. The Urban Beer Garden is open Thurs.–Sat. 4–8:30. ✉ *1050 N 34th St, Seattle* ☎ *206/420-2407* 🌐 *www.fremontbrewing.com*

Elysian Brewing Company

Hale's beer

GEORGETOWN BREWING CO. This brewery offers a very small list, including Manny's Pale Ale and a special namesake porter for neighborhood bar the Nine Pound Hammer. Visit the store to pick up souvenirs or a growler of beer. Open weekdays 10–6 and Sat. 9–noon. ✉ *5200 Denver Ave. S., Georgetown* ☎ *206/766–8055* 🌐 *www.georgetownbeer.com*

HALE'S ALES. One of the city's oldest craft breweries (1983), Hale's does cask-conditioned ales and nitrogen-conditioned cream ales. The Mongoose IPA is also popular. The pub serves a full menu and has a great view of the fermenting room. ✉ *4301 Leary Way NW, Fremont* ☎ *206/706–1544* 🌐 *www.halesbrewery.com*

Pike Pub

REDHOOK. This brewery specializes in amber ales—their ESB is an award-winner. The Redhook Brewlab in the Pike Motorworks building is open daily. It's open Mon.–Thurs. 11–10, Fri. and Sat. 11–midnight, and Sun. 11–9. ✉ *714 E Pike St.* ☎ *206/823-3026* 🌐 *www.redhook.com.*

TWO BEERS BREWING CO. A small list of ales and IPAs, and interesting seasonal experiments—such as a summer ale with coriander and sweet orange peel. Tasting room open Thurs. and Fri. 3–7. No food. ✉ *4700 Ohio Ave. S., SoDo* ☎ *206/762-0490* 🌐 *www.twobeersbrewery.com*

BEER FESTIVALS

Washington Brewers Festival (🌐 washingtonbeer.com; June/Father's Day weekend).

Fremont Oktoberfest (🌐 www.fremontoktoberfest.com; September).

Washington Cask Beer Festival (🌐 www.washingtonbrewersguild.org, end of March).

Fremont Oktoberfest

WASHINGTON STATE WINE REGIONS

Second only to California in U.S. wine production, Washington has more than 500 wineries and 11 official American Viticultural Areas. The state is increasingly becoming known for its fine cabernet sauvignons after decades-strong on its crisp chardonnays and complex merlots. Here's a sampling of some of the state's best grape varieties.

Orchards and vineyard near Wishram, WA

WHITE WINES

CHARDONNAY. The French grape widely planted in eastern Washington, where the wines range from light to big and complex.

GEWÜRZTRAMINER. A German-Alsatian grape in the Columbia Gorge and the Yakima Valley that produces a spicy, aromatic wine.

RIESLING. A German grape that makes a delicate, floral wine.

Chateau Ste. Michelle

SAUVIGNON BLANC. Herbal, dry wine from this Bordeaux grape, fermented in oak, is sold as fumé blanc.

VIOGNIER. A Rhône Valley grape that in eastern Washington makes fragrant wine with a good acid content.

WINERY SAMPLING

Amavi Cellars (www.amavicellars.com)

Chateau Ste. Michelle (www.ste-michelle.com)

Columbia Crest (www.columbiacrest.com)

Cote Bonneville (www.cotebonneville.com)

DeLille (www.delillecellars.com)

Gramercy Cellars (www.gramercycellars.com)

L'Ecole no. 41 (www.lecole.com)

Long Shadows (www.longshadows.com)

Mark Ryan (www.markryanwinery.com)

Maryhill (www.maryhillwinery.com)

àMaurice (www.amaurice.com)

RED WINES

CABERNET FRANC. A Bordeaux grape that produces well-balanced wine in the Walla Walla and Yakima Valleys and Columbia Gorge.

CABERNET SAUVIGNON. The famed Bordeaux grape grows well in the Columbia Valley and makes deeply tannic wines in Walla Walla and Yakima.

MERLOT. A black grape yielding a softer, more supple wine than cabernet sauvignon, merlot has recently experienced a boom, especially in the Walla Walla Valley.

Columbia Crest

SYRAH. A Rhône grape that produces complex, big-bodied wines; increasingly planted in the Yakima and Walla Walla Valleys.

ZINFANDEL. A hot-climate grape that in the Yakima Valley and the Columbia Gorge makes big, powerful wines.

BEST TASTING ROOMS AND WINE BARS

Almost every wine list in Seattle includes at least some regional choices, even when the cuisine has origins far from the Pacific Northwest.

BRICCO DELLA REGINA ANNA. Less comprehensive on the Northwest selections than some of its peers, Bricco compensates with a good list of Italian wines. *1525 Queen Anne Ave N, Queen Anne* *206/285–4900* *www.briccoseattle.com*

PIKE & WESTERN. This well-respected wine shop holds weekly tastings—limited-production bottles are sampled Wed. 4–6 PM ($5); new arrivals are tested Fri. 3–6 PM. *1934 Pike Pl., Downtown* *www.pike-andwestern.com*

POCO WINE ROOM. Feels like both a date spot and a friendly neighborhood hangout. Reasonably priced Pacific Northwest wines are the focus. *1408 E. Pine St., Capitol Hill* *206/322–9463* *www.pocowineroom.com*

PORTALIS. A cozy wine bar and well-stocked shop, Portalis has happy hours, prix-fixe dinners, and regular thematic tastings. *5205 Ballard Ave NW, Ballard* *www.portaliswines.com*

PURPLE CAFE AND WINE BAR. Rumor has it that the imposing tower at this lofty wine bar contains more than 5,000 bottles. It should be no surprise, then, that this sprawling downtown spot has one of the largest local wine selections in the city, with more than 50 choices from Washington state alone and hundreds from around the globe. Try the wines on their own or with snacks like Gorgonzola-stuffed dates, beef tartare, or meat and cheese plates. *1225 4th Ave., Downtown* *206/829-2280* *www.purplecafe.com*

THE TASTING ROOM. Wine shop and tasting bar with hard-to-find boutique Washington wines. Tastings range from $2 to $6. *1924 Post Alley, Downtown* *www.tastingroomseattle.com*

Cabernet Sauvignon, Chateau Ste. Michelle

and pastries; focus on fresh vegetables; a lovely space to explore. *$ Average main: $12 ✉ 300 Occidental Ave. S, Pioneer Square ☎ 206/624–1374 🌐 www.thelondonplaneseattle.com.*

★ Salumi Cured Meats

$ | ITALIAN | The lines are long for hearty, unforgettable sandwiches filled with superior house-cured meats and more at this shop, originally founded by famed New York chef Mario Batali's father Armandino. The oxtail sandwich special is unbeatable, but if it's unavailable or sold out (as specials often are by the lunchtime peak) order a salami, bresaola, porchetta, meatball, sausage, or lamb prosciutto sandwich with onions, peppers, cheese, and olive oil. **Known for:** cured meats; long lines; famous chef. *$ Average main: $10 ✉ 404 Occidental Ave. S, Pioneer Square ☎ 206/621–8772 🌐 www.salumicuredmeats.com ⏲ Closed Sat.–Sun.*

★ Taylor Shellfish Oyster Bar

$ | PACIFIC NORTHWEST | Oysters don't get any fresher than this: Taylor, a fifth-generation, family-owned company, opened its own restaurant in order to serve their products in the manner most befitting such pristine shellfish. The simple preparations—raw, cooked, and chilled—are all designed to best show off the seafood with light broths and sauces and a few accoutrements. **Known for:** popular with locals; expert shucking; unlikely pre-stadium tailgating stop. *$ Average main: $15 ✉ 410 Occidental Ave., Pioneer Square ☎ 206/501–4060 🌐 www.taylorshellfishfarms.com.*

Zeitgeist Cafe

$ | CAFÉ | A colorful local favorite among coffee shops: even Seattleites who don't haunt Pioneer Square will happily hunt for parking to spend a few hours here. In one of Pioneer Square's great brick buildings, with high ceilings and a few artfully exposed ducts and pipes, Zeitgeist has a simple, classy look that's the perfect backdrop for the frequent art shows held in this space. **Known for:** great place to work; art. *$ Average main: $6 ✉ 171 S Jackson St., Pioneer Square ☎ 206/583–0497 🌐 www.zeitgeistcoffee.com.*

Hotels

★ The Arctic Club Seattle

$$$ | HOTEL | From the building's famous antique terra cotta walrus heads and Alaskan-marble-sheathed foyer to guest rooms with vintage bathroom tile and explorer-chic touches like steamer trunks for bedside tables, the Arctic Club pays homage to an era of gold-rush opulence (the early 1900s building was once a gentlemen's club). **Pros:** feels boutique but has Doubletree by Hilton level standards; a truly beautiful lobby, which includes the Polar Bar; light-rail and bus lines just outside the door. **Cons:** much closer to Pioneer Square than the heart of Downtown; rooms are a bit dark; style may be off-putting for travelers who like modern hotels. *$ Rooms from: $304 ✉ 700 3rd Ave., Downtown ☎ 206/340–0340, 800/445–8667 🌐 thearcticclubseattle.com 🛏 120 rooms 🍽 No meals.*

Nightlife

Pioneer Square is changing. The area is still home to dance clubs that attract a very young crowd, many of whom come in from the suburbs. But with new offices opening, and new bars, restaurants, and coffee shops catering to after-work and sports crowds, Pioneer Square is a place worth visiting. As always, First Thursdays attracts a more varied crowd participating in the art walk. Galleries provide another focal point, and an additional reason to spend the evening here.

Despite the development, transients and drug use remain a part of the Pioneer Square scene, and it can feel unsafe at times. On weekends, disturbances from the hard-partying crowd make this a less-attractive neighborhood for some.

BARS AND LOUNGES

Collins Pub

BARS/PUBS | The best beer bar in Pioneer Square features 22 rotating taps of Northwest (including Boundary Bay, Chuckanut, and Anacortes) and California beers and a long list of bottles from the region. Its upscale pub menu features local and seasonal ingredients. ✉ *526 2nd Ave., Pioneer Square* ☎ *206/623–1016* 🌐 *www.collinspubseattle.com.*

Good Bar

BARS/PUBS | This bright, high-ceilinged space in a historic building in Pioneer Square still features the safe doors of the former Japanese Commercial Bank that once occupied the building. Postwork crowds and some pregaming sports fans mix at the U-shape marble bar and few small tables during a daily 4–7 pm happy hour. There's a rotating list of classic cocktails, newly developed libations featuring house-made infusions, and a beer and wine list. Small plates like pork terrine, wings, and sardines come out of an open kitchen. ✉ *240 2nd Ave. S, Pioneer Square* ☎ *206/624–2337* 🌐 *www.goodbarseattle.com.*

Pyramid Alehouse

BARS/PUBS | The loud and festive Pyramid brews a top-notch Hefeweizen and an apricot ale that tastes much better than it sounds. Madhouse doesn't even begin to describe this place when it hosts concerts or during games at Safeco Field or CenturyLink Field, so if you're looking for quiet and immediate seating, make sure your visit doesn't coincide with either. The brewery, which is just south of Pioneer Square, offers tours daily at 4 pm. ✉ *1201 1st Ave. S, SoDo* ☎ *206/682–3377* 🌐 *www.pyramidbrew.com.*

Sake Nomi

BARS/PUBS | Whether you're a novice or expert, you'll appreciate the authentic offerings here. The shop and tasting bar is open until 10 pm Tuesday through Saturday and from noon to 6 on Sunday. Don't be shy—have a seat, try a few of the rotating samples, and ask a lot of questions. Sake can be served up in a variety of temperatures and styles. ✉ *76 S. Washington St., Pioneer Square* ☎ *206/467–7253* 🌐 *www.sakenomi.us.*

COMEDY CLUBS

The Comedy Underground

COMEDY CLUBS | Beneath Swannie's Sports Bar & Grill, this club puts on stand-up comedy, open-mike sessions, and comedy competitions nightly at 8:30. ✉ *109 S. Washington St., Pioneer Square* ☎ *206/628–0303* 🌐 *www.comedyunderground.com.*

DANCE CLUBS

Club Contour

DANCE CLUBS | If you're not ready to quit partying when Seattle's bars shut at 2, then head here; this small club is famous for after-hours events that keep the doors open until 7 am. There are regular nights for deep house and Nu Disco; '80s industrial and goth; Top 40 and throwback hits; and reggae on Sunday. ✉ *807 1st Ave., Pioneer Square* ☎ *206/447–7704* 🌐 *www.clubcontour.com.*

Trinity

DANCE CLUBS | This multilevel, multiroom club plays hip-hop, reggae, disco, and Top 40. It gets packed on weekends—arrive early to avoid lines or to snag a table for some late-night snacks. This is the most appealing and interesting of the Pioneer Square megaclubs—in terms of decor, anyway. ✉ *107 Occidental Ave S., Pioneer Square* ☎ *206/697-7702* 🌐 *www.trinitynightclub.com.*

Shopping

Gritty, eccentric, artsy, and fabulous, Pioneer Square is an eclectic blend of what makes Seattle … Seattle. Although this neighborhood has more than a few tourist traps hiding in its attractive brick buildings, it also has some wonderful shops with unique wares that range from

The Seattle Seahawks play at the state-of-the-art CenturyLink Field.

antiques to heritage clothing. As Pioneer Square has been redeveloped over the recent years, many of the area's longtime antique and furniture shops have shuttered, but you'll still find old classics like the flagship Filson store.

Best shopping: 1st Avenue South between Yesler Way and South Jackson Street, and Occidental Avenue South between South Main and Jackson Streets.

Agate Designs

GIFTS/SOUVENIRS | Amateur geologists, curious kids, and anyone fascinated by fossils and gems should make a trip to this store that's almost like a museum (but a lot more fun). Between the 500-million-year-old fossils and the 250-pound amethyst geodes, there's no shortage of eye-popping items on display. ✉ *120 1st Ave. S, Pioneer Square* ☎ *206/621–3063* 🌐 *www.agatedesigns.com.*

Arundel Books

BOOKS/STATIONERY | Since 1984, this bastion of bibliophilia has offered new, used, and collectible titles to discerning shoppers. Its shelves are especially strong in art, photography, and graphic design. This eclectic assortment will satisfy both the avid reader and discriminating collector. ✉ *212 1st Ave. S, Pioneer Square* ☎ *206/624–4442* 🌐 *www.arundelbookstores.com.*

Chidori Antiques

ANTIQUES/COLLECTIBLES | So packed full of stuff it looks more like a curio shop than a high-end antiques seller, Chidori deals in high-quality Asian antiques, pre-Columbian and primitive art, Japanese paintings, and antiquities from all over the world. ✉ *108 S Jackson St., Pioneer Square* ☎ *206/343–7736* 🌐 *www.chidori-antiques.com* ⏲ *Closed Sun.*

Clementines

CLOTHING | This tiny boutique provides a unique collection of shoes, clothing, and accessories from designer brands like Coclico and Arama. The sales personnel create an inviting shopping experience that will leave no room for buyer's remorse. ✉ *310 Occidental Ave. S* ☎ *206/935–9400* 🌐 *www.clementines.com.*

Division Road, Inc.

CLOTHING | Luxury heritage menswear made in North America, Western Europe, and Japan looks right at home in this handsome space with distressed floors, black subway tile, and reclaimed wood. The shop, which stocks some 30 brands, focuses on craftsmanship and classic, casually rugged men's clothing and accessories that never go out of style: high-end denim, flannel shirts, sweaters, and leather boots. ✉ *536 1st Ave. S, Pioneer Square* ☎ 🌐 *www.divisionroad-inc.com.*

Filson

CLOTHING | Seattle's 6,000-square-foot flagship Filson store is a shrine to meticulously well-made outdoor wear for men and women. The hunting-lodge-like decor of the space, paired with interesting memorabilia and pricey, made-on-site clothing, makes the drive south of Pioneer Square worth it (we recommend catching a cab, not hoofing it). The attention to detail paid to the plaid vests, oil-treated rain slickers, and fishing outfits borders on the fetishistic. ✉ *1741 1st Ave. S, Pioneer Square* ☎ *206/622–3147* 🌐 *www.filson.com.*

Glass House Studio

GIFTS/SOUVENIRS | Seattle's oldest glass-blowing studio and gallery lets you watch fearless artisans at work in the "hot shop." Some of the best glass artists in the country work out of this shop, and many of their impressive studio pieces are for sale, along with around 40 other Northwest artists represented by the shop. ✉ *311 Occidental Ave. S, Pioneer Square* ☎ *206/682–9939* 🌐 *www.glass-house-studio.com.*

Magic Mouse Toys

TOYS | FAMILY | Since 1977, this two-story, 7,000-square-foot shop in the heart of Pioneer Square has been supplying families with games, toys, puzzles, tricks, candy, and figurines. They claim a professional child runs this friendly store—and it shows. ✉ *603 1st Ave., Pioneer Square* ☎ *206/682–8097* 🌐 *www.magicmousetoys.com.*

Utilikilts

CLOTHING | The flagship Utilikilts store stocks their own brand of utility-style kilts, which you'll see out and about often in Seattle, often paired with rugged combat boots—especially at outdoor events. Pick up a workman's kilt, made from thick duck cloth, with a hammer loop and plenty of pockets for nails and screws; or snag a tuxedo kilt, for those formal occasions when you really want to make a statement. ✉ *620 1st Ave., Pioneer Square* ☎ *206/282–4226* 🌐 *www.utilikilts.com.*

Velouria

CLOTHING | The ultimate antidote to mass-produced, unimaginative women's clothes can be found in this exquisitely feminine shop where independent West Coast designers rule. Much on offer is one of a kind: handmade, '70s-inspired jumpsuits; romantic, demure eyelet dresses; and clever screen-printed tees. Superb bags, delicate jewelry, and fun cards and gifts are also on display. It's worth a look just to check out all the wearable art. ✉ *145 S King St., Pioneer Square* ☎ *206/788–0330* 🌐 *shopvelouria.com* 🕓 *Closed Sun.–Mon.*

FOOTBALL

Seattle Seahawks

FOOTBALL | If you heard the earth rumbling on February 2, 2014, it was probably just Seattle. The entire city went nuts when their beloved team trounced the Denver Broncos and won the Super Bowl. They haven't reclaimed the glory since, but it's still near-impossible to get tickets to see the Seattle Seahawks play in their $430 million arena, the state-of-the-art **CenturyLink Field.** Single-game tix go on sale in late July or early August, and all home games sell out quickly. They're expensive, too, leading the NFL in starting prices at $150 for the cheap seats. The average ticket ask-price averages more like $400. Note that traffic and parking are both nightmares on game days; try to take public transportation—or walk the mile from Downtown. **Fun local trivia:** The number 12—look around and you'll see it everywhere—refers to Seattle's "12th Man" phenomenon. The squad consists of 11 players and the fans are the 12th man. Just how serious are the Seahawks fans to earn such a title? The stadium gets so loud that it literally generates earthquakes. ✉ *800 Occidental Ave. S, SoDo* ☎ *425/203–8000* 🌐 *www.seahawks.com.*

Chapter 6

INTERNATIONAL DISTRICT

Updated by
Naomi Tomky

Sights	Restaurants	Hotels	Shopping	Nightlife
★★☆☆☆	★★★★☆	★☆☆☆☆	★★★☆☆	★☆☆☆☆

NEIGHBORHOOD SNAPSHOT

GETTING AROUND

The I.D. is southeast of Pioneer Square, and the neighborhoods are often combined in one visit—you may find yourself wandering into the I.D. anyway, along South Jackson Street, which is the main thoroughfare connecting the two neighborhoods.

From the center of Downtown, walking to the I.D. takes about 20 minutes. However, it's not a scenic route, so unless you need the leg stretch, take the light rail, a bus, or hail a cab or Uber. Buses 7, 14, and 36 pick up along 3rd Avenue throughout Downtown.

TOP REASONS TO GO

Browse for unique gifts, souvenirs, and trinkets at **Uwajimaya** and **Kobo at Higo.** Uwajimaya has an amazing selection of Asian foods, plus a great bookstore and home section. Kobo, a gallery for local artists, is the spot for classy mementos.

Get a history lesson with your tea at the **Panama Hotel.** Although not one of our top choices for lodging, this hotel is a must-see for its lovely ground-floor teahouse and window into the lives of Japanese Americans shipped to internment camps during World War II.

Tour the neighborhood with docents from the **Wing Luke Museum of the Asian Pacific American Experience.** The museum casts a no-nonsense eye on the story of Asian and Pacific Islander communities, and guided tours point out the living history in the neighborhood.

Sample something from **every major Asian cuisine.**

PLANNING YOUR TIME

■ The I.D. is a very popular lunchtime spot with Downtown office workers and a popular dinner spot with many Seattleites. You should definitely make a meal here part of your visit. You'll need at least an hour at the Wing Luke Museum. A stop at Uwajimaya is essential. Don't plan on spending a full day here—a morning or an afternoon will suffice. And be forewarned that, as in adjacent Pioneer Square, Seattle's homelessness problem is quite visible here.

QUICK BITES

■ **Jade Garden** The go-to place for dim sum. ✉ *424 7th Ave. S, International District* ☎ *206/622–8181* 🌐 *www.jadegardenseattle.com.*

■ **KauKau BBQ Restaurant** This simple spot serves the best Chinese barbecue in the I.D. ✉ *656 S King St., International District* ☎ *206/682–4006* 🌐 *www.kaukaubbq.com* 💳 *No credit cards.*

■ **Saigon Deli** One of the best banh mi in the neighborhood. ✉ *1237 S Jackson St., International District* ☎ *206/322–3700* 💳 *No credit cards.*

Bright welcome banners, 12-foot fiberglass dragons clinging to lampposts, and a traditional Chinese gate confirm you're in the International District. The I.D., as it's locally known, is synonymous with delectable dining—it has many inexpensive Chinese restaurants (this is the neighborhood for barbecued duck and dumplings), but the best eateries reflect its Pan-Asian spirit: Vietnamese, Japanese, Filipino, and Korean.

With the endlessly fun Uwajimaya shopping center, the gorgeously redesigned Wing Luke Museum, and several walking tours to choose from, you now have something to do in-between bites.

The I.D. used to be called Chinatown; it began as a haven for Chinese workers who came to the United States to work on the transcontinental railroad. It was later a hub for Seattle's growing Japanese population, and now one of the biggest presences is Vietnamese, both in the center of the I.D. and in "Little Saigon," directly east of the neighborhood. Though the neighborhood has weathered the anti-Chinese riots and the forced eviction of Chinese residents during the 1880s and the internment of Japanese-Americans during World War II, it's become increasingly less vital to its communities. Many of the people who actually live in the neighborhood are older—the northern and southern suburbs of the city are where the newer generations are being raised (though everyone still often makes the I.D. an obligatory snack stop before heading home after a night out in Seattle).

The I.D. stretches from 4th Avenue to 12th Avenue and between Yesler Way and S Dearborn Street. The main business anchor is the Uwajimaya superstore, and there are other small businesses scattered among the restaurants, including herbalists, acupuncturists, antiques shops, and private clubs. Note that the area is more diffuse than similar communities in larger cities like San Francisco and New York. You won't find the densely packed streets chockablock with tiny storefronts and markets that spill out onto the sidewalk—scenes that have become synonymous with the word "Chinatown."

When the Wing Luke Museum of the Asian Pacific American Experience moved from its tiny cluttered home to a refurbished historic building on one of the main drags here, it refocused the city's attention on the I.D. as more than a collection of restaurants. There are indeed signs of further improvement, which the neighborhood sorely needs. The I.D. does have more energy these days: students crowd bubble tea parlors, and the community has been holding more special events like parades and periodic night markets and movie nights in Hing Hay Park.

Sights

Kobe Terrace Park

CITY PARK | Follow pathways adorned by Mt. Fuji trees at this lovely hillside pocket park. The trees and a 200-year-old stone lantern were donated by Seattle's sister city of Kobe, Japan. Despite being so close to I–5, the terrace is a peaceful place to stroll and enjoy views of the city, the water, and, if you're lucky, Mt. Rainier; a few benches line the gravel paths. The herb gardens you see are part of the Danny Woo Community Gardens, tended to by the neighborhood's residents. Across the street from the park is the historic Panama Hotel, featured in the novel *Hotel on the Corner of Bitter and Sweet* by Jamie Ford. Artifacts from the days of Japanese internment are on display, including a window on the floor showing a basement storage space that still contains a time capsule of unclaimed belongings. ✉ *Main St. between 6th Ave. S and 7th Ave. S, International District* ☎ *206/684–4075* 🎟 *Free.*

↗ Kubota Garden

About 20 minutes south of the International District by car, these serene 20 acres of streams, waterfalls, ponds, and rock outcroppings were created by Fujitaro Kubota, a 1907 emigrant from Japan. The gardens on the Seattle University campus, and the Japanese Garden at the Bloedel Reserve on Bainbridge Island are other examples of his work. The garden, a designated historical landmark of the city of Seattle, is free to visitors and tours are self-guided, though you can go on a docent-led tour on the fourth Saturday of every month, April through October, at 10 am. ✉ *9817 55th Ave. S, Mt. Baker* ✥ *From I–5, take Exit 158 and turn left toward Martin Luther King Jr. Way; continue up hill on Ryan Way. Turn left on 51st Ave. S, then right on Renton Ave. S, and right on 55th Ave. S to parking lot.* ☎ *206/684–4584* 🌐 *www.seattle.gov/parks/find/parks/kubota-garden* 🎟 *Free.*

Seattle Pinball Museum

MUSEUM | FAMILY | More arcade than museum, this space puts a collector's life work in play: more than 50 of the games are lined up on the two floors, all included in the price of admission. The games rotate out frequently, and the collection includes pinball machines as old as 1934 right up to recent releases. Entrance includes unlimited games, so take a break to chat with the staff, who can point out interesting features like the cigarette holders on the older machines. **■ TIP→ For $5 extra you can get a multientry pass, which means you can head out for lunch or for a walk before coming back to play more.** **⚠ Children under 7 not permitted to play.** ✉ *508 Maynard Ave. S, International District* ☎ *206/623–0759* 🌐 *www.seattlepinballmuseum.com* 🎟 *$18* ⏲ *Closed Tues.–Wed.*

★ Uwajimaya

STORE/MALL | FAMILY | This huge, fascinating Japanese supermarket is a feast for the senses. A 30-foot-long red Chinese dragon stretches above colorful mounds of fresh produce and aisles of delicious packaged goods—colorful sweets and unique savory treats from countries throughout Asia. A busy food court serves sushi, Japanese bento-box meals, Chinese stir-fry combos, Korean barbecue, Hawaiian dishes, Vietnamese spring rolls, and an assortment of teas and tapioca drinks. You'll also find authentic housewares, cosmetics (Japanese-edition Shiseido), toys (Hello Kitty), and more. There's also a fantastic branch of the famous Kinokuniya bookstore chain, selling many Asian-language books. The large parking lot is free for one hour with a minimum $10 purchase or two hours with a minimum $20 purchase—don't forget to have your ticket validated by the cashiers. ✉ *600 5th Ave. S, International District* ☎ *206/624–6248* 🌐 *www.uwajimaya.com.*

★ **Wing Luke Museum of the Asian Pacific American Experience**

MUSEUM | FAMILY | One of the only museums in the United States devoted to the Asian Pacific American experience provides a sophisticated and often somber look at how immigrants and their descendants have transformed (and been transformed by) American culture. The evolution of the museum has been driven by community participation—the museum's library has an oral history lab, and many of the rotating exhibits are focused around stories from longtime residents and their descendants. Museum admission includes a guided walk-and-talk tour through the East Kong Yick building, where scores of immigrant workers from China, Japan, and the Philippines first found refuge in Seattle. ✉ *719 S King St., International District* ☎ *206/623–5124* 🌐 *www.wingluke.org* 🎫 *$17.*

Restaurants

A favorite culinary destination for its many varied Asian restaurants—from dim sum palaces to hole-in-the-wall noodle shops, the International District (I.D.) is a cultural destination. Along Main Street, the restaurants hold Nihonmachi's, or Japantown's, history (sometimes literally, in the case of the Panama Hotel). Moving east along Jackson, the old Chinatown fades into what's now called Little Saigon, and the signs for Chinese barbecue become ones for banh mi. Around the neighborhood, the latest trendy food imports pop up sporting spiffy signs for the hottest boba teas or coolest shave ice desserts.

Dong Thap Noodles

$ | VIETNAMESE | While this humble little noodle shop once went viral on the Internet for its giant "Super Bowl" challenge (supposedly the world's biggest bowl of pho), what people really come for is the house-made rice noodles. It's one of the only places outside of Vietnam making them fresh daily, and the difference is easy to taste. **Known for:** rice noodles; vermicelli bowls; great intro to pho. [$] *Average main: $$12* ✉ *303 12th Ave S, International District* ☎ *206/325–1122.*

Dough Zone

$ | CHINESE | What started as a small dumpling restaurant has grown into a juggernaut local chain, with this location as their flagship. Crowds pack in for the juicy pork dumplings, crisp-bottomed q-bao, and artfully arranged noodles and vegetables. **Known for:** pork soup dumplings; join the waitlist via Yelp; friendly and efficient service. [$] *Average main: $12* ✉ *504 5th Ave. S, Suite 109, International District* ☎ *206/285–9999* 🌐 *www.doughzonedumplinghouse.com.*

Green Leaf Vietnamese Restaurant

$ | VIETNAMESE | Locals pack this friendly café for the expansive menu of fresh, well-prepared Vietnamese staples. The quality of the food—the spring rolls, *báhn xèo* (the Vietnamese version of an omelet), and lemongrass chicken are just a few standouts—and reasonable prices would be enough to make it an instant I.D. favorite. **Known for:** báhn xèo; spring rolls. [$] *Average main: $11* ✉ *418 8th Ave. S, International District* ☎ *206/340–1388* 🌐 *www.greenleaftaste.com.*

Little Sheep Mongolian Hot Pot

$$$ | CHINESE | This Chinese chain brings their cook-it-yourself soup to Seattle with all of the choice that experienced hot-pot eaters want and all of the introduction newcomers might need. The steaming pots of soup filled with herbs and spices (available in both spicy and plain) provide the perfect antidote to Seattle's gray winter weather. **Known for:** all-you-can-eat

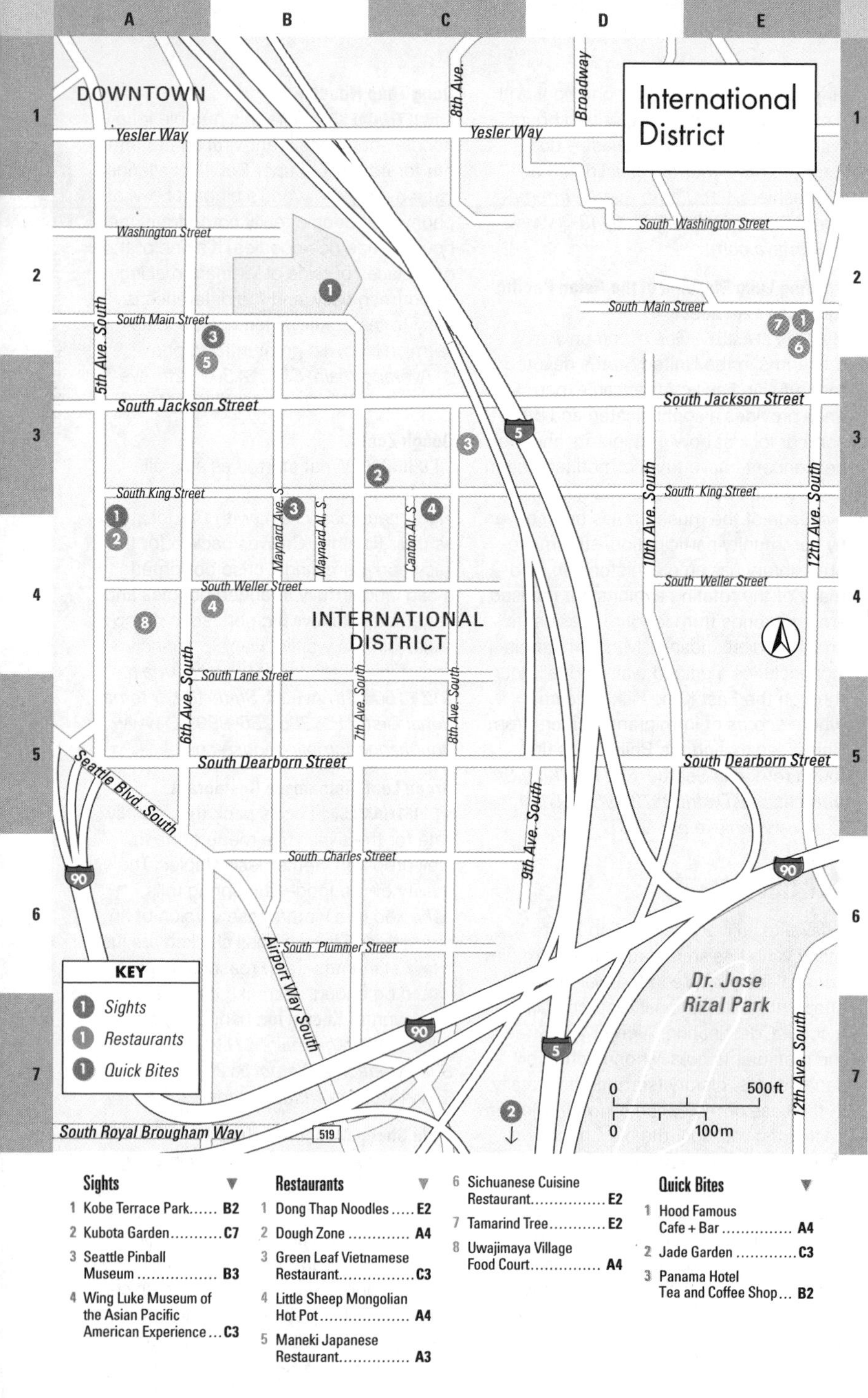

Sights

1 Kobe Terrace Park...... **B2**
2 Kubota Garden........... **C7**
3 Seattle Pinball Museum.................. **B3**
4 Wing Luke Museum of the Asian Pacific American Experience... **C3**

Restaurants

1 Dong Thap Noodles..... **E2**
2 Dough Zone............. **A4**
3 Green Leaf Vietnamese Restaurant.............. **C3**
4 Little Sheep Mongolian Hot Pot.................... **A4**
5 Maneki Japanese Restaurant.............. **A3**
6 Sichuanese Cuisine Restaurant............... **E2**
7 Tamarind Tree........... **E2**
8 Uwajimaya Village Food Court.............. **A4**

Quick Bites

1 Hood Famous Cafe + Bar................ **A4**
2 Jade Garden............. **C3**
3 Panama Hotel Tea and Coffee Shop... **B2**

Kubota Garden was created by Fujitaro Kubota and is free to visit.

options; customizable dishes; cook-it-yourself. *Average main: $29* *609 S Weller St., International District* *206/623–6700* *www.littlesheephot-pot.com* *No credit cards.*

Maneki Japanese Restaurant

$ | JAPANESE | The oldest Japanese restaurant in Seattle, Maneki is no longer a hidden gem that caters to in-the-know locals and chefs, but that doesn't mean the food is any less authentic. Though the James Beard American Classic winner serves good sushi, it's better known for the home-style Japanese dishes, which can be ordered as small plates and accompanied with sake. **Known for:** oldest Japanese restaurant in Seattle; authentic Japanese dishes; tatami rooms reservable for parties of 4 to 10. *Average main: $14* *304 6th Ave. S, International District* *206/622–2631* *www.manekirestaurant.com* *Closed Mon. No lunch.*

Sichuanese Cuisine Restaurant

$ | CHINESE | For cheap but oh-so-good Sichuan cooking, head to this hole-in-the-wall in the Asian Plaza strip mall east of I–5. The atmosphere is forgettable, but the service is friendly and the food here is just about as traditional as it gets. **Known for:** housemade noodles; spicy Sichuanese ravioli; ma po tofu. *Average main: $12* *1048 S Jackson St., International District* *206/399–8242* *www.sichuan-cuisine.com.*

Tamarind Tree

$$ | VIETNAMESE | Wildly popular with savvy diners from all across the city, this Vietnamese haunt on the eastern side of the I.D. *really* doesn't look like much from the outside, especially because the entrance is through a cramped parking lot (which it shares with Sichuanese Cuisine restaurant), but once you're inside, the elegantly simple, large, and warm space is extremely welcoming. The food is the main draw—try the spring rolls, which are stuffed with fresh herbs, fried tofu, peanuts, coconut, jicama, and

The Seattle Pinball Museum has at least 50 games from all different eras.

carrots; authentic bánh xèo; spicy pho; the signature "seven courses of beef"; and, to finish, grilled banana cake with warm coconut milk. **Known for:** great service; delicious cocktails; reservations recommended. *Average main: $21* *1036 S Jackson St., International District* *206/860–1404* *www.tamarindtreerestaurant.com.*

Uwajimaya Village Food Court
$ | ASIAN | Aside from being an outstanding grocery and gift shop, Uwajimaya also has a lively food court offering a quick tour of Asian cuisines at lunch-counter prices. Everyone can find their own perfect bowl of noodles or congee from Samurai Noodle, Noodle Zen, or Congeez, while the deli offers sushi, teriyaki, and barbecued duck; for Vietnamese food, try the fresh spring rolls, served with hot chili sauce, at Saigon Bistro; Shilla has Korean grilled beef and kimchi stew. **Known for:** Japanese, Korean, and Vietnamese cuisine; prepared lunch at reasonable prices. *Average main: $8* *600 5th Ave. S, International District* *206/624–6248* *www.uwajimaya.com/.*

Coffee and Quick Bites

★ Hood Famous Cafe + Bar
$ | PHILIPPINE | Starting out small and growing on word of mouth, as the name implies, Chera Amlag's bakery and bar sprouted from the popularity of the desserts she would make for her musician husband's Filipino pop-up dinners. Now in a cozy but elegant I.D. space, she serves the same dazzling purple ube cheesecake that got her here, alongside breakfast foods with Filipino touches, like longanisa (sausage) quiche, and butter mochi waffles with calamansi demerara syrup. **Known for:** ube cheesecake; innovative pastries. *Average main: $5* *504 5th Ave S, Suite 107A, International District* *206/485–7049* *www.hoodfamousbakeshop.com.*

Jade Garden

$ | **CHINESE** | This is a longtime favorite for dim sum enthusiasts, who also come for fluffy barbecue pork buns, walnut shrimp, chive dumplings, congee, and sticky rice. There's no doubt that the waits are long and the atmosphere is lacking, but when you're craving dim sum (served 9 am to 3 pm daily) this is the place to go. **Known for:** dim sum; dumplings; long wait times. *Average main: $9 ✉ 424 7th Ave. S, , at King St., International District ☎ 206/622–8181.*

Panama Hotel Tea and Coffee Shop

$ | **ASIAN** | On the ground floor of the historic Panama Hotel is a serene teahouse with tons of personality and a subtle Asian flair that reflects its former life as a Japanese bathhouse. The space is lovely, with exposed-brick walls, shiny hardwood floors, and black-and-white photos of old Seattle (many of them relating to the history of the city's Japanese immigrants). **Known for:** historic ambience; tea. *Average main: $3 ✉ 607 S Main St., International District ☎ 206/515–4000 🌐 www.panamahotelseattle.com.*

Shopping

Seattle's primarily Asian neighborhood is meant to be explored for its edible delicacies. Sample tea at Seattle Best Tea, leaf through books at Kinokuniya, check out Asian antiques, and stop for dim sum along the way. Megamarket Uwajimaya *(Sights)* is the major shopping attraction of the International District, but the rest of the neighborhood is packed with shops worth visiting, too. Wander the neighborhood for bubble tea (milky tea with tapioca pearls), Chinese pastries, jade and gold jewelry, Asian produce, and Eastern herbs and tinctures. Little souvenir shops, dusty and deep, sell plants, Japanese kites, Vietnamese bowls, Chinese slippers, Korean art, and tea or dish sets.

A Good Combo 

For a great day of walking and exploring, start your day with breakfast at Pike Place Market, then bus, cab, or stroll down 1st Avenue to Pioneer Square (you'll pass SAM along the way). After visiting some art galleries, which generally open between 10:30 and noon, and stopping at any of the neighborhood's coffee shops such as Zeitgeist or Grand Central Bakery, walk southeast to the International District for some retail therapy at Uwajimaya and a visit to the Wing Luke Museum. Then cab it back to your hotel.

Best shopping: South Jackson Street to South Lane Street, between 5th and 8th Avenues South.

Kinokuniya Book Stores of America

BOOKS/STATIONERY | Japanamaniacs, get thee to this Tokyo-based chain for a huge collection of books, magazines, office supplies, collectibles, clothes, and gifts. Their manga selection is particularly impressive—nearly every title you could want is represented, and they'll happily order anything you don't find in the store. *✉ 525 S Weller St., International District ☎ 206/587–2477 🌐 www.kinokuniya.com.*

Kobo at Higo

GIFTS/SOUVENIRS | Housed in what used to be a 75-year-old five-and-dime store, this distinctive gallery has fine ceramics, textiles, and exquisite crafts by Japanese and Northwest artists; you can also see artifacts from the old store, a part of the original Nihonmachi (Japantown). Items range from something as simple as incense from Kyoto to an enormous painted antique chest. *✉ 602 S Jackson St., International District ☎ 206/381–3000 🌐 www.koboseattle.com.*

Moksha

CLOTHING | Local designers, international finds, and the store's own silk-screened streetwear fill the racks at this bright clothing and accessory shop. From banh mi (Vietnamese sandwich) earrings to "Break the Cycle" hoodies, colorful jackets to statement hats, the vibrant space embodies the message of the neighborhood and its welcoming, forward-thinking nature. Fittingly, the space also serves as a gallery and sometimes an event space. ✉ *670 S King St, International District* 🌐 *www.mokshaseattle.org* 🕒 *Closed Mon.*

Momo

GIFTS/SOUVENIRS | Right next door to the Kobo gallery is a perky little shop with great gift options, including unique clothing, vials of perfume, plastic sushi magnets, coin purses with personality, canvas bags, quirky jewelry (such as a long chain necklace dangling a wee enamel cupcake at the end), and more. The owner is friendly and fun, and that comes through in this adorable store, where it's fun to shop if you need nothing, and you're still likely to end up with something. ✉ *600 S Jackson St., International District* ☎ *206/329–4736* 🌐 *www.momoseattle.com.*

Seattle Best Tea Corporation

FOOD/CANDY | If you haven't been introduced to the wonders of Asian tea, you need to make a trip here, where the experience is as enriching as the tea itself. Helpful staff will walk you through the selection of oolong, pouchong, jasmine, and green teas. All the teas are available to try, and you can pick up a cute teapot while you're at it. ✉ *506 S King St., International District* ☎ *206/749–9855* 🌐 *www.seattlebesttea.com* 🕒 *seattlebesttea@gmail.com.*

Chapter 7

FIRST HILL AND THE CENTRAL DISTRICT

Updated by
AnnaMaria Stephens

Sights	Restaurants	Hotels	Shopping	Nightlife
★★☆☆☆	★★☆☆☆	★☆☆☆☆	★☆☆☆☆	★☆☆☆☆

NEIGHBORHOOD SNAPSHOT

GETTING AROUND

Because the sights are so spread out here, having a car is essential. This is especially true if you want to tool around the Central District to see the landmark buildings and houses, or if you want to visit the Northwest African American Museum, which is far south of everything else, in the Rainier Valley area. If you're busing it to the Northwest African American Museum from Downtown, take Bus 7 to Rainier Avenue South and South State Street. From Capitol Hill take Bus 48 from 23rd Avenue and East Madison Street to 23rd Avenue and South Massachusetts Street, which is right in front of the museum. If you're just visiting the Frye and the Sorrento Hotel, you can walk from either Downtown or Capitol Hill. By bus, take the 2, 10, 11, or 14 from Downtown (some run on weekdays only). Another option for the Frye is the First Hill Streetcar; the closest stop for the museum is at Broadway and Marion (see Getting Around).

TOP REASONS TO GO

Spend a quiet, art-filled afternoon at the free **Frye Art Museum,** the only real attraction in First Hill and one of Seattle's best museums. The Frye mixes representational art with rotating exhibits of folk and pop art, so there's something for everyone.

Settle into an overstuffed chair for a drink at the Sorrento Hotel's delightfully fussy **Fireside Room.** This is an especially pleasant stop on a chilly, rainy day—a few leather easy chairs are parked in front of a crackling fireplace.

Redefine dinner theater at **Central Cinema.** This off-the-beaten-path movie house serves beer, wine, burgers, pizzas, and salads. Screenings are a mix of classics (*The Shining, Animal House*) and small independent films.

QUICK BITES

■ **Broadcast Coffee** Grab Stumptown coffee, pastries from Macrina Bakery, bagels, and salads here. ✉ *1918 E Yesler Way, Central District* ☎ *206/322–0807* 🌐 *www.broadcastcoffee.com.*

■ **Katy's Corner Café** A tiny, unpretentious neighborhood espresso bar with homemade pastries, quiches, and sandwiches. ✉ *2000 E Union St., Central District* ☎ *206/329–0121.*

■ **Union Coffee** Locally roasted beans, fresh pastries, and yogurt bowls get your morning started right at this bright coffee shop filled with comfy couches, laptop-friendly tables, and houseplants. ✉ *2407 E Union St., , Suite B, Central District* ☎ *206/577–7953.*

PLANNING YOUR TIME

■ Both of these neighborhoods are best as detours from other itineraries. First Hill is adjacent to Downtown, and the C.D. is close to the International District. The Northwest African American Museum requires at least an hour. A visit to the small but captivating Frye Art Museum could take anywhere from one to three hours.

The little-visited neighborhoods of First Hill and the Central District are nonetheless important pieces of the city's fabric. First Hill is an eastern extension of Downtown, and one tree-lined street has something truly spectacular: the Frye Art Museum. The Central District, mostly residential and off the beaten path, is the historic hub of Seattle's African American community, though to the dismay of many, the neighborhood is rapidly gentrifying.

First Hill

First Hill earned its unimaginative moniker because it's the first big hill that you encounter while heading east from downtown toward Lake Washington. Starting in the early 1890s, many of Seattle's wealthiest residents built homes atop the steep hill, which was close to downtown but still offered some distance from the bustling urban core. Today the neighborhood is a mix of stately old mansions, dense high-rises, and modern hospitals (which explains the nickname "Pill Hill"). There isn't much for tourists to see in First Hill with a couple of notable exceptions: The Frye Art Museum and Hotel Sorrento, which features lovely Italianate architecture and a fabulous outdoor patio with black-and-white-striped umbrellas.

Sights

Frye Art Museum

MUSEUM | In addition to its beloved permanent collection—predominately 19th- and 20th-century pastoral paintings—the Frye hosts eclectic and often avant-garde exhibits, putting this elegant museum on par with the Henry in the U-District. No matter what's going on in the stark, brightly lighted back galleries, it always seems to blend well with the permanent collection, which is rotated regularly. Thanks to the legacy of Charles and Emma Frye, the museum is always free, and parking is free as well. ✉ *704 Terry Ave., First Hill* ☎ *206/622–9250* 🌐 *www.fryemuseum.org* 🎫 *Free.*

Town Hall

READINGS/LECTURES | Town Hall, which unveiled a $35-million renovation in 2019, hosts scores of events in its spacious yet intimate Great Hall, chief among them talks and panel discussions with leading

Sights

1 Crespinel Martin Luther King Jr. Mural **E3**
2 Douglass-Truth Neighborhood Library.. **D4**
3 First African Methodist Episcopal Church........ **C1**
4 Frye Art Museum **A3**
5 Jimi Hendrix Park........ **E7**
6 Mount Zion Baptist Church **D1**
7 Northwest African American Museum..... **D7**
8 Seward Park **D7**
9 Town Hall **A2**

Restaurants

1 Ba Bar.................... **B3**
2 Cafe Selam **E3**
3 Ezell's Fried Chicken.... **D3**
4 Fat's Chicken and Waffles **E3**
5 Reckless Noodle House............ **E5**

Quick Bites

1 George's Sausages and Delicatessen **A3**
2 Italian Family Pizza **A3**
3 Sugar Bakery & Cafe... **A3**

Hotels

1 Hotel Sorrento **A3**

The Frye Art Museum has permanent and rotating collections and is always free to visit.

politicians, authors, scientists, and academics.

Christian Scientists occupied the Roman-revival-style Town Hall for decades, and attending lectures here can still make you feel a little starchy. ✉ *1119 8th Ave., Downtown* ☎ *206/652–4255* 🌐 *www.townhallseattle.org.*

Coffee and Quick Bites

Most of the restaurants in First Hill cater to the neighborhood's working crowd, so you'll find plenty of budget-friendly places to grab a coffee or quick bite if you're visiting the museum or staying at Hotel Sorrento. For more dining options, head north to Capitol Hill, a 7-minute drive or 20-minute bus or streetcar ride.

George's Sausage and Delicatessen

$ | **DELI** | For nearly 40 years, George's has sold delicious deli sandwiches in a small market filled with Polish and Eastern European groceries. **Known for:** potato salad; housemade sausages. [$] *Average main: $8* ✉ *907 Madison St., First Hill* ☎ *206/622–1491* 🕒 *Closed Sun.*

Italian Family Pizza

$ | **PIZZA** | New Yorkers always say this family-owned place comes close to the pizza they know and love with thin crusts and just the right proportions of red sauce and cheese. **Known for:** real-deal NYC-style pizza; huge family-size pies. [$] *Average main: $16* ✉ *1028 Madison St., First Hill* ☎ *206/538–0040* 🌐 *italianfamilypizza.juisyfood.com.*

Sugar Bakery & Cafe

$ | **BAKERY** | An early-morning crowd lines up here for flaky pastries, bagels, coffee, and sweet treats; the freshly made soups and sandwiches are also tasty. **Known for:** gluten-free-friendly; nondairy choices; cookies and cakes. [$] *Average main: $7* ✉ *1014 Madison St., First Hill* ☎ *206/749–4105* 🌐 *www.sugarbakerycafe.com.*

Hotels

★ Hotel Sorrento
$$$$ | HOTEL | Built in 1906, the historic and serene Hotel Sorrento hits the perfect note between traditional and modern, with lovely Italianate architecture, carved wood moldings, white marble bathrooms, antique furnishings in sumptuous fabrics, and chic original contemporary artwork in the common spaces, including the Sorrento's stylish Dunbar Room restaurant. **Pros:** the elegant wood-paneled Fireside Room is perfect for cocktail hour; courteous guest service; comfortable beds. **Cons:** not central; rooms are a bit small (though corner suites are commodious); ho-hum views. *Rooms from: $424* ✉ *900 Madison St., First Hill* ☎ *206/622–6400, 800/426–1265* 🌐 *www.hotelsorrento.com* *76 rooms* *No meals.*

Central District

The predominantly residential Central District, or the "C.D.," lies south of Capitol Hill and northeast of the International District. Its boundaries are roughly 12th Avenue on the west, Martin Luther King Jr. Boulevard on the east, East Madison to the north, and South Jackson Street to the south. As Downtown Seattle rapidly develops, the C.D. is facing a transitional period. Community groups are working hard to ensure that the "revitalization" of the area doesn't come at the expense of stripping the city's oldest residential neighborhood of its history or breaking up and pricing out the community that's hung in there during years of economic blight. It has a few monuments honoring the city's African American community, as well as some good restaurants and a few landmarks that provide a fairly good survey of architectural trends throughout the decades. ■ **TIP→ Several pop-culture icons hail from the C.D., including Jimi Hendrix, Quincy Jones, Bruce Lee, and Sir Mix-a-Lot.**

Sights

Crespinel Martin Luther King Jr. Mural
PUBLIC ART | Heading west on Cherry Street in the Central District, you'll see a 17-foot-tall mural of Dr. Martin Luther King Jr. on the side of Fat's Chicken and Waffles restaurant. Pacific Northwest artist James Crespinel painted the mural in the summer of 1995 on the eastern face of the building and touched up his faded work in 2016 while the community gathered to watch. ✉ *Corner of Martin Luther King Jr. Way and Cherry St., Central District.*

Douglass-Truth Neighborhood Library
LIBRARY | A city landmark that offers a little something for history buffs, architecture fans, and public-art lovers alike, this 1914 library was the first to be funded entirely by Seattle. After a lauded remodel and expansion a decade ago that followed strict historic preservation guidelines, Douglass-Truth remains a cherished community gathering spot. It also houses one of the largest collections of African American literature and history on the West Coast. Local artists Marita Dingus and Vivian Linder created sculptures and three-dimensional relief panels for the branch, which can be seen in the spacious corridor connecting the two buildings. Paintings of former slaves and abolitionists Frederick Douglass and Sojourner Truth by artist Eddie Ray Walker are also on display. Don't miss the Soul Pole, a totem pole depicting African American history, located outside on the grassy area on the corner of 23rd Avenue and E Yesler Way. ✉ *2300 E Yesler Way, Central District* ☎ *206/684–4704* 🌐 *www.spl.org/locations/douglass-truth-branch.*

First African Methodist Episcopal Church
RELIGIOUS SITE | Founded in 1886, the state's oldest African American church and the community's nexus has operated out of this historic building since 1912. Their gospel choirs are among the city's best, and discussions with and among

intellectuals, authors, artists, and the community are regularly scheduled. ✉ *1522 14th Ave., Central District* ☎ *206/324–3664* 🌐 *www.fameseattle.org.*

Jimi Hendrix Park

LOCAL INTEREST | Adjacent to the Northwest African American Museum, Jimi Hendrix Park pays homage to one of the Central District's most famous sons. In the final stages of development after a six-year project, the 2.3-acre park features walking paths, landscaping, interpretative signs about Hendrix's legacy, and a colorful 100-foot-long outdoor public art piece called the Shadow Wave Wall. Unveiled in late 2019, the sculpture, which consists of undulating pieces of gray and purple metal with cut-out designs, has a huge mural of the musical icon engraved at the center. Jimi Hendrix Park will serve as an outdoor community gathering space in warmer months. **■ TIP→ Hendrix fans should find the Shadow Wave Wall one of the most selfie-friendly new spots in Seattle.** ✉ *2400 S Massachusetts St., Central District* ☎ *206/684-4075* 🌐 *www.seattle.gov/parks/find/parks/jimi-hendrix-park.*

Mount Zion Baptist Church

RELIGIOUS SITE | Gospel-music fans are drawn to the home of the state's largest African American congregation. The church's first gatherings began in 1889; back then its prayer meetings were held in homes and in a store. The church, which was recently designated an official Seattle landmark, was incorporated in 1903, and after a number of moves, settled in its current simple but sturdy brick building. Eighteen stained-glass windows, each with an original design that honors a key African American figure, glow within the sanctuary. Beneath the bell tower, James Washington's sculpture *The Oracle of Truth,* a gray boulder carved with the image of a lamb, is dedicated to children struggling to find truth. ✉ *1634 19th Ave., Central District* ☎ *206/322–6500* 🌐 *www.mountzion.net.*

Jazzy School

Garfield High School (400 23rd Avenue) is one of the Central District's historic landmarks. Alumni include Quincy Jones and Jimi Hendrix; today the school enjoys national attention for its jazz program. The 30-piece ensemble often performs at local festivals, including Earshot Jazz Festival in October and Folk Life in May. 🌐 *www.garfieldjazz.org*

Northwest African American Museum

MUSEUM | Focusing on the history of African Americans in the Northwest, this museum housed in an old school building tells stories through a diverse collection of well-curated and insightful photos, artifacts, and compelling narratives. Past exhibits have included "Xenobia Bailey: The Aesthetics of Funk," and "The Test: The Tuskegee Project," focusing on the first African American aviation units in the U.S. military to serve in combat. One gallery is dedicated to the work of local artists. NAAM also hosts film screening, talks, and other community events. **■ TIP→ Don't miss the small-but-strollable Jimi Hendrix Park adjacent to the museum.** ✉ *2300 S Massachusetts St., Leschi* ☎ *206/518–6000* 🌐 *www.naamnw.org* 🎟 *$7* ⏲ *Closed Mon.–Tues.*

Seward Park

NATIONAL/STATE PARK | Seward Park, about 10 minutes southeast of Downtown, is a relatively undiscovered gem on the shores of Lake Washington. The 300-acre park includes trails through old-growth forest, mountain views, eagles' nests, a 2½-mile biking and walking path, a native plant garden, art studio, and a small swimming beach. Free walking tours are offered by Friends of Seward Park at 11

Did You Know?

Seward Park offers free walking tours on the first Saturday of the month; more than just a park, here you'll also find an art studio and beach.

am on most first Saturdays (check the website to confirm), departing from the Seward Park Environmental and Audubon Center. ■ **TIP→ Turn your park visit into a bike tour on select summer Sundays for Bicycle Sunday, when Lake Washington Boulevard (south of Mount Baker Beach to the entrance of Seward Park) is closed to motorized traffic, 10 am–6 pm. Check www.seattle.gov/parks/bicyclesunday.** ✉ *5895 Lake Washington Blvd. S, , Columbia City–Seward Park, Mt. Baker* 🌐 *www.sewardpark.org, www.seattle.gov/parks/bicyclesunday.*

Restaurants

The C.D. isn't a culinary destination, partially because it's incredibly spread out and residential, but the authentic Ethiopian restaurants are noteworthy (there are several on E Cherry Street), and you'll also find some of Seattle's best fried chicken here, as well as a growing list of new spots that are opening as the neighborhood continues to gentrify.

Ba Bar

$ | VIETNAMESE | From the sibling chefs behind Monsoon, Ba Bar celebrates Saigon street food with dishes like dumplings, rice bowls, pork belly, and fish-sauce wings. It's on the pricey side for Vietnamese food, but the space is lively and it's open all day—and until 4 am on the weekend in case you're craving a late-night nosh. **Known for:** Vietnamese street food; classic cocktails; late-night hours. *$ Average main: $12* ✉ *550 12th Ave., Central District* ☎ *206/328–2030* 🌐 *www.babarseattle.com.*

Cafe Selam

$ | ETHIOPIAN | Don't let the modest digs dissuade you from sitting down: the Ethiopian fare here is delicious. Open all day, Cafe Selam serves various specialties like beef or lamb *tibs* (cubed meat sautéed with onions and spices) and *ketfo* (steak tartare) but is particularly known for its *foul*, a spicy breakfast dish of pureed fava beans topped with eggs, onions, peppers, and feta cheese, served with two fluffy French loaves. **Known for:** butter-brushed injera bread; a deliciously complex berbere sauce. *$ Average main: $15* ✉ *2715 E Cherry St, Central District* ☎ *206/328–0404* 🌐 *www.cafeselam.com.*

Ezell's Fried Chicken

$ | AMERICAN | Though slammed at lunchtime thanks to the high school across the street, this fast-food restaurant serves up some of the best fried chicken in Seattle. Both original and spicy flavors are terrific, but be warned that the spicy is exactly that. **Known for:** fluffy rolls; classic sides like coleslaw. *$ Average main: $* ✉ *501 23rd Ave., Central District* ☎ *206/324–4141.*

Fat's Chicken and Waffles

$ | SOUTHERN | Offering a taste of New Orleans in the Central District, relative neighborhood newcomer Fat's Chicken and Waffles serves authentic Southern cuisine in a hip spot filled with furniture and murals made by local artists. Helmed by a chef with deep Louisiana roots, Fat's serves shrimp and grits, fried okra, red beans and rice, and other soul food classics in addition to the namesake chicken and waffles. **Known for:** New Orleans–style fare; trendy space; filling comfort food. *$ Average main: $15* ✉ *2726 Cherry St., Central District* ⏲ *Closed Mon.*

Reckless Noodle House

$$ | VIETNAMESE | Traveling around Vietnam together led two friends to open Reckless, which taps Vietnamese and other Asian flavors for its inventive street food–style noodle and rice bowls, salads, and crispy rolls. The craft cocktail list is just as creative as the culinary offerings at this cozy spot with dark walls, rustic wood booths, and eclectic artwork. **Known for:** sustainable ingredients; hip ambience; authentic pan-Asian flavors. *$ Average main: $18* ✉ *2519 S Jackson St., Central District* ☎ *206/329–5499* 🌐 *www.recklessnoodles.com.*

FILM

Central Cinema

FILM | If you're tired of 40-ounce Cokes and $10 popcorn with neon-yellow butter and wish that moviegoing could be a little more elegant, check out Central Cinema. The first few rows of this charming, friendly, little theater—which shows second-run films—consist of diner-style booths where you can order food and adult beverages before the movie starts. A server takes orders for delicious pizzas, salads, and snacks (including popcorn with inventive toppings like curry or brewer's yeast), and your food is delivered unobtrusively during the first few minutes of the movie. Wash it down with a normal-size soda, a cup of coffee, or better yet a cocktail or a glass of wine or beer. You won't find new films here, but the theater shows a great mix of favorites (*Hairspray* and *E.T.*) and local indie and experimental films. ✉ *1411 21st Ave., Central District* ☎ *206/328–3230* 🌐 *www.central-cinema.com.*

NEIGHBORHOOD SNAPSHOT

TOP REASONS TO GO

Browse the stacks at **Elliott Bay Book Company,** Seattle's biggest independent bookstore. Then find a sunny reading spot in **Cal Anderson Park,** a block away.

After you've stocked up on books, visit the surrounding shops, ice cream shops, coffeehouses, and restaurants that make the **Pike–Pine Corridor** so hip and happening.

Browse the art collection at the **Seattle Asian Art Museum,** then relax in the surrounding **Volunteer Park.**

Rock out at **Neumos,** to anything from indie music to national touring acts.

Sample fantastic restaurants and coffeehouses, including **Altura, Dacha Diner,** and **Cascina Spinasse** for food; and **Stumptown, Espresso Vivace,** and **Caffé Vita** for caffeine.

See the season's colors at nearby **Washington Park Arboretum.**

QUICK BITES

Oddfellows Cafe + Bar Scones, fluffy eggs, and Stumptown coffee in the morning, rustic sandwiches and salads midday, and pan-seared salmon and tasty quinoa cakes in the evening—the ever-hip Oddfellows is a Capitol Hill hot spot. **Known for:** healthy breakfast options; trendy; Stumptown coffee ✉ *1525 10th Ave., Capitol Hill* ☎ *206/325–0807* 🌐 *www.oddfellowscafe.com* 💳 *No credit cards.*

Salt and Straw Though the Portland-based ice cream chain has since opened stores up and down the West Coast, it found a welcoming home on Capitol Hill, where its "farm-to-cone" style of ice cream is respected, and the creative, sometimes a little out-there monthly specials don't scare anyone. **Known for:** creative flavors; long lines in summer. ✉ *7414 Pike St., Suite A, Capitol Hill* ☎ *206/258–4574* 🌐 *www.saltandstraw.com.*

GETTING HERE AND AROUND

■ You can walk from Downtown, taking Pine or Pike Street across I–5 to Melrose Avenue, but keep in mind that touring the neighborhood itself will require a lot of walking, and it's uphill from Downtown.

■ Light-rail runs from Westlake Center to Capitol Hill. The First Hill Streetcar connects the International District, and First Hill to Capitol Hill. Buses 10, 11, 43, and 49 all pick up on Pike Street Downtown and head to various parts of Capitol Hill. This is the easiest crosstown route to Capitol Hill's Pike–Pine Corridor. The 10 and the 49 continue up toward Volunteer Park. The 8 connects Seattle Center to Capitol Hill via Denny Way. The 11 will get you to Madison Park and the Washington Park Arboretum, which is technically several neighborhoods out of Capitol Hill (most people usually drive or bike there).

■ Street parking here is difficult. Keep an eye out for pay lots, which are numerous.

PLANNING YOUR TIME

■ Spend the morning at the Seattle Asian Art Museum or at Washington Park Arboretum, or visit in the afternoon, then stay for dinner and barhopping.

Chapter 8

CAPITOL HILL AND MADISON PARK

8

Updated by
Naomi Tomky

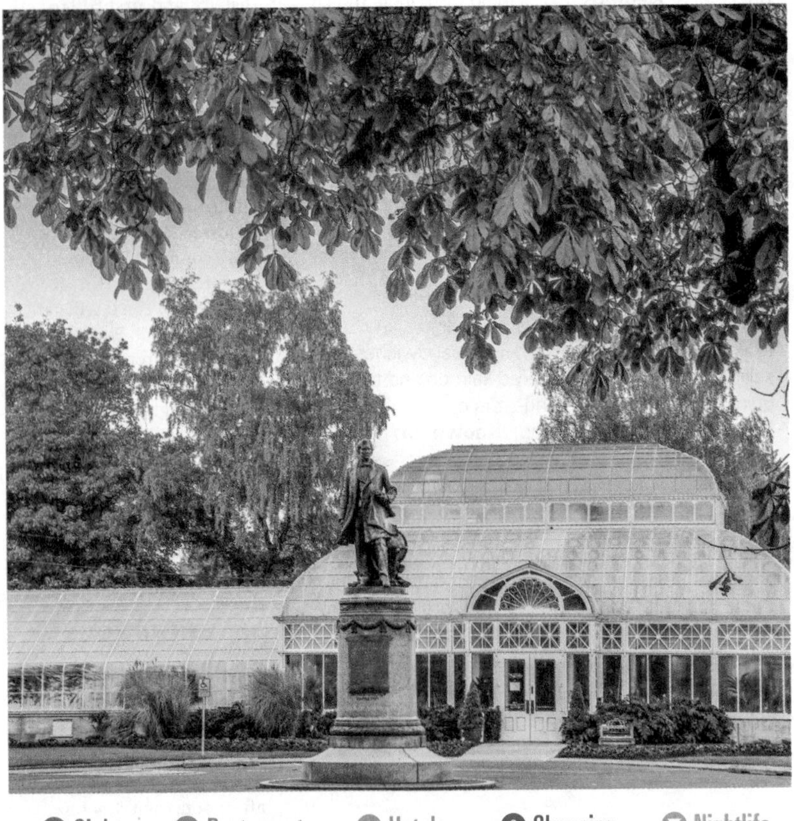

Sights ★★★☆☆ | Restaurants ★★★★★ | Hotels ★★★☆☆ | Shopping ★★★★☆ | Nightlife ★★★★★

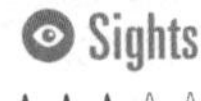

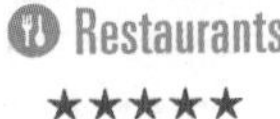

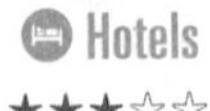

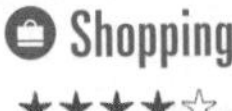

The Hill has two faces: on one side, it's young and edgy, full of artists, musicians, and students. Tattoo parlors and coffeehouses abound, as well as thumping music venues and bars. On the other side, it's elegant and upscale, with tree-lined streets, 19th-century mansions, and John Charles Olmsted's Volunteer Park and the Seattle Asian Art Museum.

Converted warehouses, modern high-rises, colorfully painted two-story homes, and brick mansions all occupy the same neighborhood. There are parks aplenty and cute, quirky shops to browse, including one of the best bookstores in the city.

The Pike–Pine Corridor (Pike and Pine Streets running from Melrose Avenue to 15th Avenue) is the heart of the Hill. Pine Street is a slightly more pleasant walk, but Pike Street has more stores—and unless you're here in the evening (when the area's restaurants come to life), it's the stores and coffee shops that will be the main draw. The architecture along both streets is a mix of older buildings with small storefronts, a few taller buildings that have lofts and office spaces, and garages and warehouses (some converted, some not). Pine skirts Cal Anderson Park—a small, pleasant park with an unusual conic fountain and reflecting pool—a lovely place to take a break after walking and shopping. Depending on weather, the park can be either very quiet or filled with all kinds of activities from softball games to impromptu concerts.

The Hill's other main drag is Broadway East (a north–south avenue that crosses both Pike and Pine). Seattle's youth culture, old money, gay scene, and everything in between all converge on Broadway's lively if somewhat seedy stretch between East Denny Way and East Roy Street. Broadway is undergoing a renaissance, thanks to a few new high-profile condo buildings and a light-rail station. Although it's got a few spots of note (Nathan Lockwood's ode to Northwestern ingredients, Altura, for one), it's still mostly a cluttered stretch of cheap restaurants, even cheaper clothing stores, and a few bars. Many people still find the area compelling for its people-watching. If you really want to see Seattle in all its quirky glory, head to Dick's Drive-In around midnight on a weekend.

The neighborhood's reputation as one of the city's hippest and most vibrant is bringing some good developments, too—Seattle's beloved Elliott Bay Book Company relocated here in the hopes that the constant street traffic and focus on the arts would revitalize its business. It's within walking distance of several great pizzerias, ice cream shops, and coffeehouses.

Capitol Hill

Sights

★ Washington Park Arboretum

GARDEN | **FAMILY** | As far as Seattle's green spaces go, this 230-acre arboretum is arguably the most beautiful. On calm weekdays, the place feels really secluded. The seasons are always on full display: in warm winters, flowering cherries and plums bloom in its protected valleys as early as late February, while the flowering shrubs in Rhododendron Glen and Azalea Way bloom March through June. In autumn, trees and shrubs glow in hues of crimson, pumpkin, and lemon; in winter, plantings chosen specially for their stark and colorful branches dominate the landscape. In 2018, as part of a 20-year master plan, the arboretum completed a 1¼ mile trail that connects to an existing path to create a 2½-mile accessible loop, giving all guests access to areas that were previously hard to reach. March through October, visit the peaceful **Japanese Garden,** a compressed world of mountains, forests, rivers, lakes, and tablelands. The pond, lined with blooming water irises in spring, has turtles and brightly colored koi. An authentic Japanese tea house is reserved for tea ceremonies and instruction on the art of serving tea (visitors who would like to enjoy a bowl of tea and sweets can purchase a $10 "Chado" tea ticket at the Garden ticket booth). The Graham Visitors Center at the park's north end has descriptions of the arboretum's flora and fauna (which include 130 endangered plants), as well as brochures, a garden gift shop, and walking-tour maps. Free tours are offered most of the year; see website for schedule. There is a pleasant playground at the ball fields on the south end of the park. ✉ *2300 Arboretum Dr. E, Capitol Hill* ☎ *206/543–8800 arboretum, 206/684–4725 Japanese garden* 🌐 *botanicgardens.uw.edu/washington-park-arboretum/* 🎫 *Free, Japanese garden $8.*

Lakeview Cemetery

CEMETERY | One of the area's most beautiful cemeteries, dating back to 1872, looks east toward Lake Washington from its elevated hillside directly north of Volunteer Park. Several of Seattle's founding families are interred here (names you will likely recognize from street names and public places), and Bruce Lee's grave and that of his son Brandon are the most visited sites. Maps are available at the cemetery office. ✉ *1554 15th Ave. E, Capitol Hill* ☎ *206/322–1582* 🌐 *www.lakeviewcemeteryassociation.com* 🎫 *Free.*

Photographic Center Northwest

MUSEUM | A small, starkly attractive gallery space occupies the front of this photo education center. Curated shows often feature well-respected photographers, ranging from journalistic to fantastical, and "crash course" workshops are open to the public. The gallery is convenient to the Pike–Pine Corridor—it's a few blocks south of Pike. ✉ *900 12th Ave., Capitol Hill* ☎ *206/720–7222* 🌐 *www.pcnw.org* 🎫 *Free.*

Restaurants

Capitol Hill has become Seattle's major culinary destination. The greatest concentration of restaurants is in and around the Pike–Pine Corridor—Pike and Pine Streets running from Melrose Avenue to 15th Avenue. All-day cafés like Oddfellows are all the rage, as are smaller, posh new American and Italian-inspired eateries like Lark, Altura, and Cascina Spinasse. On the west edge of the hill, smaller shops like Dino's Tomato Pie, Yalla, and Dacha Diner have created a more casual restaurant corridor.

★ Altura

$$$$ | **ITALIAN** | A hand-carved cedar angel statue watches over diners at this lively spot, where chef-owner Nathan Lockwood lends a Northwest focus to Italian cuisine. The set tasting menu weaves rare, intriguing, and fascinating local and global ingredients into classic Italian techniques. **Known for:** tasting menu; interesting ingredients. *Average main: $157 617 Broadway E, Capitol Hill 206/402–6749 www.alturarestaurant.com Closed Sun.-Mon. No lunch.*

Bar Melusine

$$$ | **SEAFOOD** | Renee Erickson, 2016 James Beard Award winner for best chef in the Northwest, takes inspiration from France's Atlantic coast and transforms it into a cool, marble-topped ode to Northwest seafood. The menu offers seafood both raw and cooked, like the fried oysters with vadouvan curry aioli, as well as meaty continental classics like steak tartare and a burger. **Known for:** oysters; delightful interior. *Average main: $24 1060 E Union St., Capitol Hill 206/900–8808 www.barmelusine.com No lunch.*

By Tae

$$$$ | **JAPANESE** | At the eight seats that surround his kitchen, chef Sun Hong serves his mini tasting menu just two or three times each weekday. Most of the seats, then, have been claimed by 9 or 10 am by people filling in their name on the sheet of paper hung on a nearby pillar. **Known for:** delicious hand rolls; mini omakase lunch; limited seating. *Average main: $35 Chophouse Row, 1424 11th Ave, Suite E, Capitol Hill.*

Café Presse

$$ | **FRENCH** | Two distinct rooms create plenty of space at this French bistro just off the Pike–Pine Corridor, where you can get such Parisian fare as pressed chicken with greens; a *croque madame*; mussels with french fries; roasted chicken; and simple cheese platters with slices of baguette. This is the spot to order some red table wine and people-watch. **Known for:** Parisian cuisine; relaxed atmosphere; magazine rack. *Average main: $20 1117 12th Ave., Capitol Hill 206/709–7674 www.cafepresseseattle.com.*

★ Cascina Spinasse

$$$ | **ITALIAN** | Wth cream-colored lace curtains and true Italian soul, Spinasse brings the cuisine of Piedmont to Seattle. Chef Stuart Lane makes the pasta fresh daily and with such sauces and fillings as short rib ragu, eggplant and anchovies, or simply, as in their signature dish, dressed in butter and sage. *Secondi* options can range from braised pork belly with cabbage to stewed venison served over polenta. **Known for:** handmade pasta; amaro. *Average main: $27 1531 14th Ave., Capitol Hill 206/251–7673 www.spinasse.com No lunch.*

Dick's

$ | **BURGER** | This local chain of hamburger drive-ins with iconic orange signage has changed little since the 1950s. The fries are hand-cut, the shakes are hand-dipped (made with hard ice cream), and the burgers hit the spot. **Known for:** classic burgers; iconic local staple. *Average main: $3 115 Broadway E, Capitol Hill 206/323–1300 www.ddir.com.*

★ Dino's Tomato Pie

$ | **PIZZA** | Long hailed as the creator of Seattle's best pizza at his first shop, Delancey, Brandon Petit perhaps even improves on his previous recipe as he re-creates the neighborhood joints of his New Jersey childhood. The thick, crisp corners of the square Sicilian pies caramelize in the hot oven into what is practically pizza candy, while lovers of traditional round pizza will enjoy the char on the classics. **Known for:** square pizza; creative cocktails; children are not allowed to dine. *Average main: $15 1524 E Olive Way, Capitol Hill 206/403–1742 www.dinostomatopie.com No lunch.*

Kurt Farm Shop

$ | **AMERICAN** | Few ice creams in the world go as directly from cow to cone as those of Kurt Farm Shop: Kurt Timmermeister milks his Jersey cows each morning for a smooth, rich, and incredibly fresh scoop. His Jersey cream base flavor combines with both traditional and

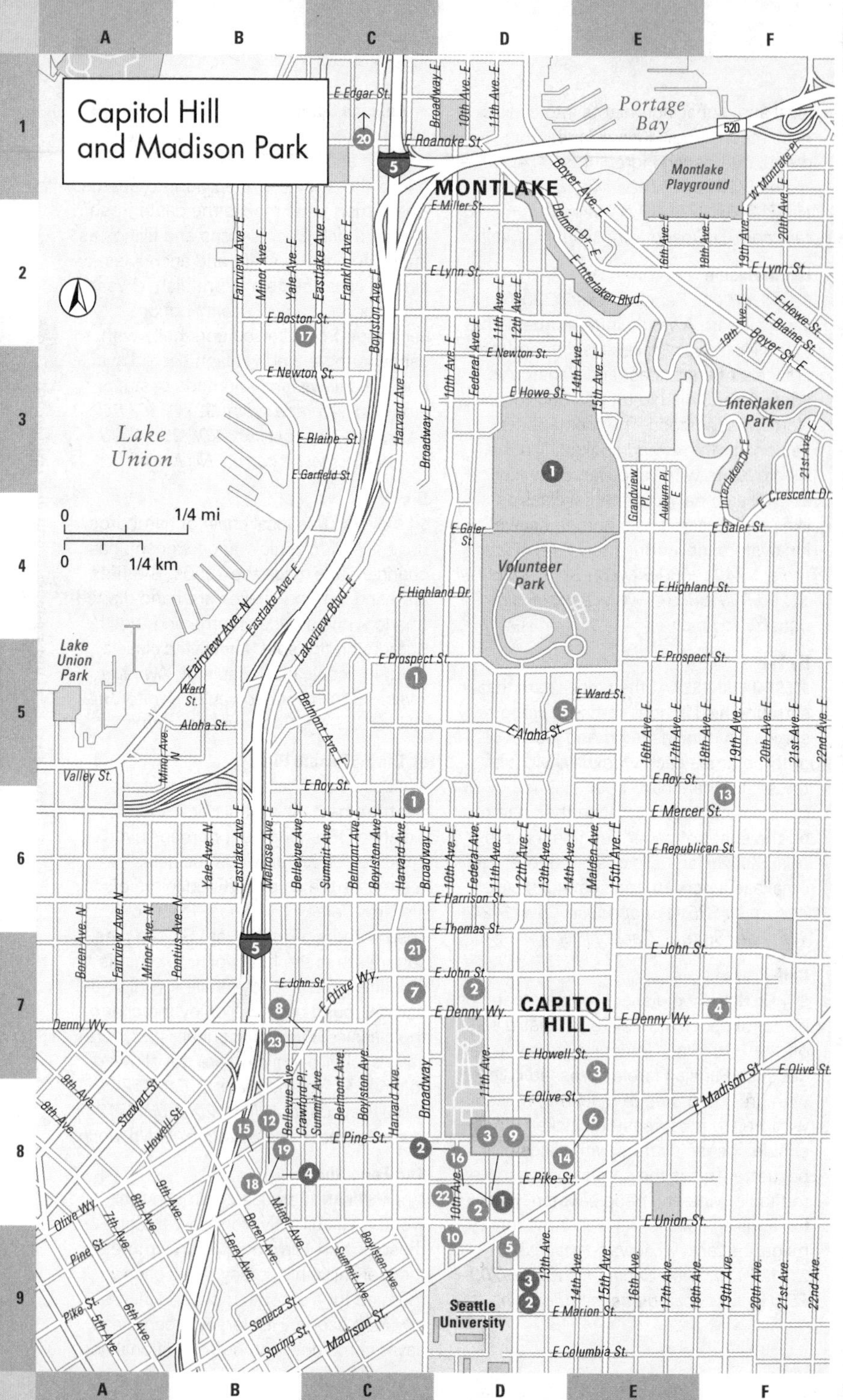
Capitol Hill and Madison Park
MONTLAKE
CAPITOL HILL
Portage Bay
Lake Union
Lake Union Park
Montlake Playground
Interlaken Park
Volunteer Park
Seattle University
0 1/4 mi
0 1/4 km

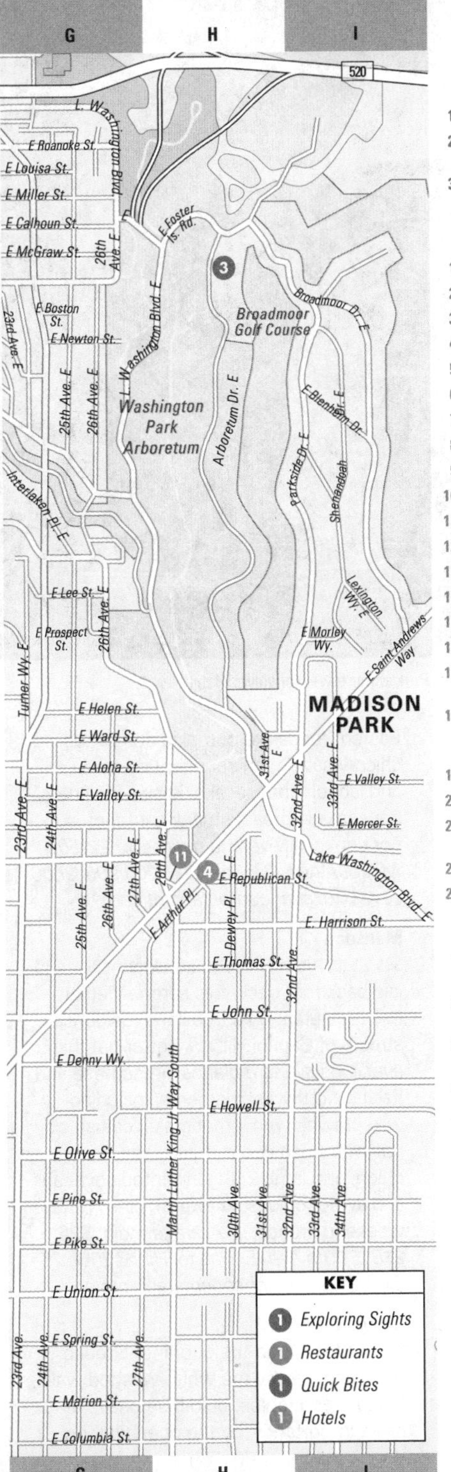

Sights

1 Lakeview Cemetery **D3**

2 Photographic Center Northwest **D9**

3 Washington Park Arboretum **H2**

Restaurants

1 Altura........................ **C6**

2 Bar Melusine............ **D8**

3 By Tae.................... **D8**

4 Café Flora................ **H6**

5 Café Presse **D9**

6 Cascina Spinasse........ **E8**

7 Dick's...................... **C7**

8 Dino's Tomato Pie........ **C7**

9 Kurt Farm Shop **D8**

10 Lark....................... **D9**

11 Luc........................ **H6**

12 Mamnoon................ **B8**

13 Monsoon **F6**

14 Omega Ouzeri............ **E8**

15 Qin Xi'an Noodles....... **B8**

16 Quinn's **D8**

17 Serafina osteria & enoteca **C2**

18 Starbucks Reserve Roastery & Tasting Room............ **B8**

19 Stateside................. **B8**

20 Sushi Kappo Tamura **C1**

21 Taneda Sushi in Kaiseki **C7**

22 Via Tribunali **D8**

23 Yalla **C7**

Quick Bites

1 Caffé Vita Coffee Roasting **D8**

2 Oddfellows Café + Bar **D8**

3 Stumptown Coffee Roasters **D9**

4 Victrola Coffee Roasters **B8**

Hotels

1 The Bacon Mansion Bed and Breakfast....... **C5**

2 11th Avenue Inn Seattle Bed & Breakfast........ **D7**

3 Gaslight Inn............... **E7**

4 Inn Seattle **F7**

5 Shafer Baillie Mansion Bed & Breakfast........ **D5**

Climb the spiral staircase to the top of the Volunteer Park water tower for views of the city.

innovative flavors from his own farm, including nocino, Sichuan peppercorn, and carrot. **Known for:** creative flavors; farm-fresh ingredients. *Average main: $5 1424 11th Ave., Capitol Hill www.kurtwoodfarms.com/kurt-farm-shop.*

Lark

$$$ | **MODERN AMERICAN** | The Central Agency Building, a converted 1917 warehouse with 25-foot ceilings, is the setting for mouthwateringly delicious small plates to share and seasonally inspired main dishes—you'll want to sample as much as possible. The expert servers can help you choose from an impressive wine list, and will happily help you decide from the list of starters, secondi, and mains. **Known for:** small plates; local ingredients. *Average main: $32 952 E Seneca St., Capitol Hill 206/323–5275 www.larkseattle.com Closed Mon. No lunch.*

Mamnoon

$$$ | **MIDDLE EASTERN** | The sophistication, elegance, and excitement of Mamnoon are rare in Seattle's excessively casual restaurant culture. Try inventive Middle Eastern foods like pumpkin dumplings, chicory salad with sour mint dressing, and labneh cheesecake. **Known for:** fluffy housemade bread; stunning interior; superior drinks. *Average main: $30 1508 Melrose Ave, Capitol Hill 206/906–9606 www.mamnoonrestaurant.com.*

Monsoon

$$$ | **VIETNAMESE** | With an elegant bar and laid-back roof deck, this serene Vietnamese restaurant on a tree-lined residential stretch of Capitol Hill is a better bet than ever. Upscale fare blends Vietnamese and Pacific Northwest elements, including wild prawns with lemongrass, catfish clay pot with fresh coconut juice and green onion, and lamb with fermented soybeans and sweet onions. **Known for:** crab; wine; weekend brunch. *Average main: $25 615 19th Ave. E, Capitol Hill 206/325–2111 www.monsoonrestaurants.com.*

Omega Ouzeri

$$ | **GREEK** | Open the door into Greece, be welcomed by the white-washed walls, blond-wood tables, bold-blue chairs, and most importantly, by the open kitchen

full of grilling and olive oil. Greek classics dominate here, with lots of seafood. **Known for:** seafood; Greek spirits. *Average main: $22 ✉ 1529 14th Ave., Capitol Hill ☎ 206/257–4515 🌐 www.omegaouzeri.com ⏲ No lunch ▭ No credit cards.*

Qin Xi'an Noodles

$ | **CHINESE** | Silky, chewy noodles, named biang biang for the noise made when they're slapped on a counter as they're stretched by hand, are the specialty at this tiny spot serving up big flavors—and you can watch them being prepared while you eat. Aside from the signature hot oil–seared biang biang noodles, the shop serves Xi'an delicacies such as stewed pork sandwiches and cold spicy appetizers. **Known for:** hot oil–seared biang biang noodles; Xi'an delicacies. *Average main: $9 ✉ 1203 Pine St., Capitol Hill ☎ 206/332–0220 🌐 https://miahskitchen.weebly.com.*

Quinn's

$$ | |**BREWPUBS/BEER GARDENS** | Capitol Hill's original gastropub has friendly bartenders, an extensive selection of beers on tap (with the West Coast and Belgium heavily represented), an extensive list of whiskey, and a menu of rib-sticking food to soak it up, which you can enjoy at the long bar or at a table on either of the two floors of the industrial-chic space. A pretzel and some foie gras poutine are good ways to start—then you can choose from Painted Hills beef tartare with pumpernickel crisps, perfect marrow bones with baguette and citrus jam, or a cheese plate. Heartier mains, like the signature wild boar sloppy Joe are available at dinnertime. A pared-down pub menu is also available from 4 pm to midnight or later. The folks here take their libations seriously, so feel free to chat up the bartenders about their favorites. *✉ 1001 E Pike St., Capitol Hill ☎ 206/325–7711 🌐 www.quinnspubseattle.com ⏲ No lunch ✍ Reservations not accepted.*

Serafina osteria & enoteca

$$$ | **ITALIAN** | To many loyal patrons, Serafina is *the* perfect neighborhood restaurant: burnt-sienna walls topped by a forest-green ceiling convey the feeling of a lush garden villa—a sense heightened by the small sheltered courtyard out back. Menu highlights include grilled eggplant rolled with ricotta and basil; asparagus with an egg and truffle oil; and gnocchi with rotating ingredients such as mushrooms, nettle, or beef cheeks. **Known for:** live music on some nights; eggplant rolls; gnocchi. *Average main: $29 ✉ 2043 Eastlake Ave. E, Capitol Hill ☎ 206/323–0807 🌐 www.serafinaseattle.com ⏲ No lunch Sat.*

Starbucks Reserve Roastery & Tasting Room

$ | **CAFÉ** | You could call it a coffee amusement park for its many ways to keep audiences entertained, but the sprawling combination café and showroom is deadly serious about its beans. Fans of the chain, and the coffee curious, will find lots to taste and explore here in 15,000 square feet of coffee culture. **Known for:** personalized attention; brewing and roasting methods on display. *Average main: $3 ✉ 1124 Pike St., Capitol Hill ☎ 206/624–0173 🌐 www.roastery.starbucks.com.*

Stateside

$$ | **VIETNAMESE** | Low lights, ceiling fans, and palm-patterned wallpaper combine with weathered gold fixtures to evoke a sense of Vietnam with nearly the same precision as the chef's rendition of *bun cha Hanoi.* The setting transports, while the food impresses: great Vietnamese food isn't hard to find around town, but chef Eric Johnson brings an outsider's playfulness to the cuisine—as well as a pedigree at Michelin-starred restaurants. Vietnamese coffee finds its way into popsicles and tropical cocktails find their way into coconuts, but what's most impressive is the sheer amount of flavor—through technique, herbs, and spices—that Johnson packs into each of

his dishes. **Known for:** great ambience; bun cha Hanoi. *Average main: $24 ✉ 300 E Pike St., Suite 1200, Capitol Hill ☎ 206/557–7273 🌐 www.statesideseattle.com ⏲ No lunch weekdays.*

Sushi Kappo Tamura

$$$$ | **SEAFOOD** | The seafood is as blindingly fresh as one would hope for at a Seattle sushi bar, but chef Taichi Kitamura ups the ante by adding seasonal and Northwest touches to the meals at his sophisticated restaurant—such as pork loin from sustainable Skagit River Ranch with organic watercress. Order a series of small plates at the blond-wood tables, like oysters from nearby Totten Inlet in ponzu sauce, or impeccable spot prawns in soy-butter sauce—or put yourself in Kitamura's more-than-capable hands for omakase (chef's choice) at the 13-seat bar. **Known for:** high-quality fish; creative sushi. *Average main: $39 ✉ 2968 Eastlake Ave. E, Capitol Hill ☎ 206/547–0937 🌐 www.sushikappotamura.com.*

Taneda Sushi in Kaiseki

$$$$ | **JAPANESE** | While this is more a hallway hidden inside an aging mall than a traditional restaurant, the space is modern and lovely and the food is transportive. Reserve far in advance for one of the nine coveted spots at Hideki Taneda's counter where each diner receives a progression of dishes, built from seasonal ingredients transformed into elaborate flavors and stunning presentations. **Known for:** Kaiseki; see the food as it's prepared; limited seating. *Average main: $124 ✉ 219 E Broadway, Suite 14, Capitol Hill ✣ Enter through the center of the building, between American and Hana, and it will be on your left on the first floor. ☎ 206/457–8921 🌐 www.tanedaseattle.com ⏲ Closed Mon.*

Via Tribunali

$$ | **PIZZA** | This atmospheric and happening pizza spot on Pike Street is a reliable place for a fun pizza feast—they churn Neapolitan-style pizzas from the wood-burning stove so quickly that it may take you by surprise. Fresh, large salads—such as the di Parma, with arugula and Parmigiano-Reggiano, and the Tonno, with mozzarella, cherry tomatoes, tuna, and olives—and a vast variety of pizza toppings make this a crowd-pleaser. **Known for:** pizza margherita; lively scene. *Average main: $17 ✉ 913 Pike St., Capitol Hill ☎ 206/322–9234 🌐 www.viatribunali.com ⏲ No lunch.*

Yalla

$ | **MIDDLE EASTERN** | Conveniently located in the heart of the Olive Way bar scene, this walk-up window caters to the drinking crowd with its late-night hours but serves its Middle Eastern sandwiches and sides all day. The menu centers on saj, a thin bread that wraps around eggplant, meat, cheese, or falafel like a burrito, or comes with dips like muhummara, baba ghanouj, or hummus. **Known for:** Saj sandwiches; late night eats; takeout only. *Average main: $9 ✉ 1510 E Olive Way, Capitol Hill.*

Coffee and Quick Bites

Caffé Vita

$ | **CAFÉ** | Though it's now a certifiable mini-empire with locations throughout Seattle and in other cities, Caffé Vita's roasting operations, and indeed its heart and soul, are located right in Capitol Hill's Pike–Pine Corridor. The super-savvy owner also owns Via Tribunali pizzeria and several other local hot spots—and there's no doubt he knows how to tap into the gritty Seattle energy. **Known for:** good place to work; coffee. *Average main: $3 ✉ 1005 E Pike St., Capitol Hill ☎ 206/709–4440 🌐 www.caffevita.com.*

Oddfellows Cafe + Bar

$$ | **MODERN AMERICAN** | Right in the center of the Pike–Pine universe, this huge, ultrahip space anchoring the Oddfellows Building, across from Cal Anderson Park, serves inspired American food from morning coffee to late-night drinks. The day might start with breakfast

Lakeside Beaches Nearby

Madison Park In the late 19th century, Madison Park was the most popular beach in the city, with a promenade, floating bandstands, gambling halls, and ship piers. Now it's a lakefront park with sloping lawns, a swimming area, playgrounds, and tennis courts. The whole area is usually bustling with activity—there are a number of upscale coffee shops, restaurants, and boutiques nearby. As the closest beach to densely populated Capitol Hill, it serves a wide audience. The beach has picnic tables, restrooms, and showers, and lifeguards on duty in summer, and a children's playground across the street. From Downtown, go east on Madison Street; it'll take you straight down to the lake. ✉ *Madison St. and 43rd Ave., Madison Park.*

Madrona Park Several beach parks and green spaces front the lake along Lake Washington Boulevard; Madrona Park is one of the largest. Lifeguards are on duty in the summer, and young swimmers have their own roped-in area, while teens and adults can swim out to a floating raft with a diving board. The trail along the shore is a great jogging spot. Grassy areas encourage picnicking; there are grills, picnic tables, phones, restrooms, and showers. From Downtown, go east on Yesler Way about 2 miles to 32nd Avenue. Turn left onto Lake Dell Avenue and then right; go to Lake Washington Boulevard and take a left. ✉ *853 Lake Washington Blvd., Madrona.*

biscuits and thick brioche French toast; later on you can order the "Oddball" sandwich of meatballs in marinara sauce with provolone and Parmesan and roasted free-range chicken. **Known for:** baked goods; coffee and late-night drinks; dependable cuisine. $ *Average main: $20* ✉ *1525 10th Ave., Capitol Hill* ☎ *206/325–0807* 🌐 *www.oddfellowscafe.com.*

Stumptown Coffee Roasters

$ | CAFÉ | This hip Portland powerhouse is one of the West Coast's most well-known coffee-roasting operations and Seattle simply loves the stuff. There's good reason: the coffee is divine, and the vibe, while überhip, isn't too cool for school. **Known for:** good coffee; laid-back vibe. $ *Average main: $3* ✉ *1115 12th Ave., Capitol Hill* ☎ *206/860–2937* 🌐 *www.stumptowncoffee.com.*

Victrola Coffee Roasters

$ | CAFÉ | Victrola is one of the most loved of Capitol Hill's many coffeehouses, and it's easy to see why: the sizable space is lovely—the walls are hung with artwork by local painters and photographers—the coffee and pastries are fantastic, the baristas are skillful, and everyone, from soccer moms to indie rockers, is made to feel like this neighborhood spot exists just for them. If 15th Avenue East is too far off the beaten path for you, there are also branches at 310 East Pike Street (*206/462–6259*), between Melrose and Bellevue, as well as in Beacon Hill and Downtown. **Known for:** espresso; fresh-roasted beans. $ *Average main: $3* ✉ *411 15th Ave. E, Capitol Hill* ☎ *206/462–6259* 🌐 *www.victrolacoffee.com.*

Hotels

To experience a true Seattle neighborhood, stay in Capitol Hill. Close to Downtown but with its own distinct scene, "the Hill" offers character-rich bed-and-breakfasts in old mansions and oversized Craftsmans run by thoughtful proprietors. Airbnb also has a wealth of offerings in this hip neighborhood. Though many of the Hill's residents appear to be hipsters and intellectual dilettantes, anyone with an open mind is welcome. Seattle's historically LGBTQ neighborhood is chock-full of live-music venues, true foodie establishments, and little retail gems. While the Pike–Pine Corridor and much of Broadway are alive until the wee hours, most of the neighborhood's lodging spots are set in quiet, tree-lined side streets off the main drags. Most B&Bs require multinight stays.

The Bacon Mansion Bed and Breakfast
$ | **B&B/INN** | **FAMILY** | Serene and traditional, this 1909 Tudor home is surrounded by opulent gardens and is near both Volunteer Park and Broadway—and it also has two suites that welcome children and/or pets. **Pros:** quiet, relaxing retreat; knowledgeable owner; lovely patio and porch; great for families. **Cons:** no a/c; rooms could use updating; breakfasts are on the light side. *Rooms from: $184 959 Broadway E, at E Prospect St., Capitol Hill 206/329–1864, 800/240–1864 www.baconmansion.com 22 rooms Free Breakfast.*

★ 11th Avenue Inn Seattle Bed & Breakfast
$ | **B&B/INN** | The closest B&B to Downtown offers all the charm of a classic bed-and-breakfast (exquisitely styled with antique beds and Oriental rugs) with the convenience of being near the action. **Pros:** free on-site parking; oozes vintage charm; wonderful owner and staff. **Cons:** although most guests are courteous, sound does carry in old houses; no kids under 12; minimum three-night stay. *Rooms from: $169 121 11th Ave. E, Capitol Hill 206/720–7161 www.11thavenueinn.com 9 rooms Free Breakfast.*

Gaslight Inn
$ | **B&B/INN** | Rooms here range from a crow's nest with peeled-log furniture and Navajo-print fabrics to a more traditional suite with Arts and Crafts–style furnishings, a fireplace, and stained-glass windows. **Pros:** great art collection; in-ground heated pool; free Wi-Fi. **Cons:** breakfast is unimpressive; street parking not always easy to find; minimum two-night stay. *Rooms from: $168 1727 15th Ave., Capitol Hill 206/325–3654 www.gaslight-inn.com 6 rooms with private bath; 2 rooms with shared bath Free Breakfast.*

Inn Seattle
$ | **HOTEL** | With fewer of the cutesy trappings of many B&Bs, this modern, elegant inn housed in a three-story Capitol Hill mansion welcomes guests as if it were their own house. **Pros:** allows legal marijuana use; comfortable beds; modern decor. **Cons:** shared bathrooms; continental breakfast; residential neighborhood. *Rooms from: $155 1808 E Denny Way, Capitol Hill 206/412–7378 www.seattlebednbreakfast.com 15 rooms Free Breakfast.*

★ Shafer Baillie Mansion Bed & Breakfast
$$ | **B&B/INN** | The opulent guest rooms and suites on the second floor are large, with private baths, antique furnishings, Oriental rugs, huge windows, and lush details like ornate four-poster beds; third-floor rooms, while lovely, have a more contemporary country feel, but still have private baths and large windows. **Pros:** wonderful staff; great interior and exterior common spaces; free Wi-Fi. **Cons:** no elevator and the walk to the third floor might be hard for some guests; while children are allowed, some guests say the mansion isn't kid-friendly; three-night minimum stay during summer weekends. *Rooms from: $199 907 14th Ave. E, Capitol Hill 800/985–4654 www.sbmansion.com 6 rooms, 2 suites Free Breakfast.*

Nightlife

Capitol Hill has a lot of music venues and interesting watering holes—it's one of the city's best areas for nightlife. The Pike–Pine Corridor was always base camp for hipsters drinking Pabst out of the can, but the changing face of the neighborhood has brought some edgy, upscale gastropubs and appearance-conscious lounges. The Hill is also the center of the city's LGBTQ+ community, with the majority of gay bars and dance clubs along Pike, Pine, and Broadway. A short stretch of East Olive Way from Denny to Melrose is another mini–nightlife district, which is a bit more subdued.

As with Downtown, most of the neighborhood's restaurants double as nightspots. Quinn's (on Pike Street) and Smith (on 15th Avenue), for example, both get kudos for tasty food but are also notable as drinking spots (in Quinn's case for its excellent beer list).

BARS AND LOUNGES

Artusi

BARS/PUBS | Sit at the white tile bar—or on the patio on a sunny day—of this Italian cocktail bar and order delicious antipasti and desserts to go with expertly prepared drinks. Beer selection is limited, but Artusi has great wine options. Make it to the 5–7 pm happy hour Monday through Thursday, or the 10 pm–close late-night happy hour on Friday if you can. ✉ *1535 14th Ave., Capitol Hill* ☎ *206/678–2516* 🌐 *www.artusibar.com.*

Barca

BARS/PUBS | A large space with velvet-lined booths and dark lighting, Barca has mood to spare. There is plenty of bar space early on in the evening and a mezzanine with ample seating, too. Because they can tout the largest vodka selection in the state at their Vodka Bar, as well as a renowned menu of mixed drinks, the bar fills up relatively early with young patrons. As the evening unfolds, it becomes a frenzy of drinking, merrymaking, and people-watching. Check the website for weekly and monthly events like drag burlesque and live jazz. ✉ *1510 11th Ave., Capitol Hill* ☎ *206/325–8263* 🌐 *www.barcaseattle.com.*

Hopvine Pub

BARS/PUBS | A neighborhood institution, Hopvine is a no-frills pub with solid pub grub and local beers on tap. This is a favorite spot for locals in this slightly out-of-the-way neighborhood—it's not Pike–Pine central, but instead it's on 15th, closer to Volunteer Park. There's an open-mike night on Wednesday and trivia night on most Tuesdays. Note that it serves beer and wine only. ✉ *507 15th Ave. E, Capitol Hill* ☎ *206/328–3120* 🌐 *www.3pubs.com/Hopvine.html.*

Knee High Stocking Co

BARS/PUBS | Though it came of age in the height of the speakeasy trend, this little bar has since evolved (and grown) with the times. You'll still feel the thrill of ringing the doorbell at your reservation time, but those reservations are far easier to come by. It retains the cozy, throwback feel, but now with more space, a kitchen serving excellent Filipino food, and cocktails that continue to intrigue and improve. The menu makes choosing a drink fun, with descriptions like "crisp, fall, spices, bubbles," but the bartenders are always up for a good custom drink if you tell them what you want. ✉ *1356 E Olive Way, Capitol Hill* ☎ *206/979–7049 Text for reservations* 🌐 *kneehighstocking.com.*

Linda's Tavern

BARS/PUBS | Welcome to one of the Hill's iconic dives—and not just because it was allegedly the last place Kurt Cobain was seen alive. The interior has a vaguely Western theme, but the patrons are pure Capitol Hill indie-rockers and hipsters. The bartenders are friendly, the burgers are good (brunch is even better), and the always-packed patio is one of the liveliest places to grab a happy-hour drink. ✉ *707 E. Pine St., Capitol Hill* ☎ *206/325–1220* 🌐 *www.lindastavern.com.*

★ Montana

BARS/PUBS | Lived-in booths and a welcoming atmosphere keep this place packed with everyone from couples on a first date to groups of old friends. As an

The Pine Box beer hall is housed in a former funeral home.

anchor to the E Olive bar strip, it makes for excellent people-watching, either from the inside looking out or from the co-opted piece of sidewalk called a "parklet" that serves as the patio. ✉ *1506 E Olive Way, Capitol Hill* ☎ *206/327–9362* 🌐 *www.montanainseattle.com.*

Oddfellows

BARS/PUBS | Oddfellows anchors a 19th-century building, a former Oddfellows Lodge, that also houses the Century Ballroom, Tin Table, and Elliott Bay Books. It doubles as a bar on weekends, and there's a pleasant, small outdoor space, too. The vibe is hipster-chic; grab a seat at one of the large communal tables and hit up the small but quirky cocktail list. Steak, porchetta sandwiches, soups, salads, bread pudding, and more are on offer, as well. ✉ *1525 10th Ave., Capitol Hill* ☎ *206/325–0807* 🌐 *www.oddfellowscafe.com.*

The Pine Box

BARS/PUBS | The clever name is just one reason to visit this beer hall housed in a former funeral home on the corner of Pine Street. The churchlike interior is stately, with soaring ceilings, dark woodwork, and custom furniture made from huge Douglas fir timbers found in the basement—they were supposedly used to shelve coffins many years ago. The place is rumored to be haunted, but that doesn't stop a trendy crowd from congregating to sample from 30-plus taps of craft beer and a menu of wood-fired pizza and meatballs and pulled-pork tacos. Or get your morning drink on at the weekend brunch. ✉ *1600 Melrose Ave., Capitol Hill* ☎ *206/588–0375* 🌐 *www.pineboxbar.com.*

Poco Wine + Spirits

BARS/PUBS | Poco Wine + Spirits deserves accolades just for taking one of the least interesting architectural spaces out there—the oddly proportioned retail space of a condo complex—and making it into a sophisticated parallel universe where a friendly crowd lounges on couches and huddles around two small bars to enjoy a competent menu of artisanal Northwest wines, cocktails, and tapas. A selection of subtle fruit wines is a nice surprise. Happy hour runs 4–6:30 pm, and again 10–midnight, Sunday–Thursday. ✉ *1408 E. Pine St., Capitol Hill* ☎ *206/322–9463* 🌐 *www.pocowineand-spirits.com.*

Revolver

BARS/PUBS | Revolver stands out from a row of bars on this crowded block of Capitol Hill with a vinyl-only music policy, classic cocktails, draft beer, and boozy snow cones. ✉ *1514 E. Olive Way, Capitol Hill* ☎ *206/860–7000* 🌐 *www.revolverbarseattle.com.*

★ **Rumba**

BARS/PUBS | A spot of Caribbean sunshine in the Northwest, Rumba stocks hundreds of different rums which they offer in a half-dozen styles of daiquiri, various punches, and other assorted cocktails. Staffed by many of the best bartenders in town, this is a place for serious spirit aficionados to dig deep, but even rum rookies will feel welcome in the bright, friendly space with its turquoise bar stools and banquettes. ✉ *1112 Pike St, Capitol Hill* ☎ *206/583–7177* 🌐 *www.rumbaonpike.com.*

Smith

BARS/PUBS | Great for people-watching and very Capitol Hill, Smith is a large, dark space with portraits of ex-presidents and taxidermied birds all over the walls, plus a mixture of booth seating and large communal tables. A bit outside the Pike-Pine heart, and filled to brimming with tattooed hipsters on weekends, this is a super-friendly and inviting space with a very solid menu of food (including a top-notch burger and sweet-potato fries) and a full bar. Beer selection is small but good, and the cocktail list is decent. ✉ *332 15th Ave. E, Capitol Hill* ☎ *206/709–1099* 🌐 *www.smithseattle.com.*

Tavern Law

BARS/PUBS | Take a trip back in time to the golden age of cocktails before Prohibition and the speakeasies that followed it. Tavern Law is dark and tucked away, and houses a "secret" upstairs area (accessed, if there's room available, by picking up the phone next to the old bank-vault door). And the drinks are impeccably made, often with surprising ingredients. ✉ *1406 12th Ave., Capitol Hill* ☎ *206/322–9734* 🌐 *www.tavernlaw.com.*

The Tin Table

BARS/PUBS | Upstairs from Oddfellows and across from Cal Anderson Park, the Tin Table is a welcoming little lounge with lots of exposed brick and a long, glossy bar. Its happy hour (5 to 6 daily, and 10 pm to 1 am Wednesday through Saturday), is very popular, and so is the Chimay that's on tap. It's also beloved for its good food, like dynamite steak frites. Try the "floozy burger" (with caramelized onion, bacon, cheese, and shoestring fries) and a creative cocktail. ✉ *915 E. Pine St., Capitol Hill* ☎ *206/320–8458* 🌐 *www.thetintable.com.*

BILLIARDS

Garage Billiards

BARS/PUBS | Built in 1928, this former auto-repair shop is now a large, happening, chrome-and-vinyl pool hall, restaurant, and bar. The large garage doors are thrown wide open on warm evenings, making it a pleasurable alternative to other, more cramped places. There are 25 tournament pool tables and a small bowling alley, and you must be 21 to enter the bowling and billiards areas. ✉ *1130 Broadway Ave., Capitol Hill* ☎ *206/322–2296* 🌐 *www.garagebilliards.com.*

BREWPUBS

Elysian Brewing Company

BARS/PUBS | Worn booths and tables are scattered across the bi-level warehouse space of this Capitol Hill mainstay, where the beers are a good representation of the thriving brewing scene in the Northwest. Always on tap are the hop-heavy Immortal IPA, the rich Perseus Porter, and the crisp Elysian Fields Pale Ale. The food (burgers, fish tacos, sandwiches, salads) is decent, too. This is a favorite of Seattleites and Capitol Hill residents and a laid-back alternative to the more trendy haunts and lounges in the area. ✉ *1221 E. Pike St., Capitol Hill* ☎ *206/860–1920* 🌐 *www.elysianbrewing.com.*

Optimism Brewing Company

BREWPUBS/BEER GARDENS | Optimism, like so many of the city's breweries acts as a multifunctional third place for locals. What sets it apart is how deftly it serves as beer nerd haven, gathering space for parties and events, bar, and even indoor play space for kids and dogs. There are 16 beers on tap in a variety of styles (and one of sparkling water) to keep drinkers happy, while food trucks keep them fed. ⚠ **Optimism is a cash-free establishment, so payment is accepted only with credit cards or apps.** ✉ *1158 Broadway, Capitol Hill* 🌐 *www.optimismbrewing.com.*

Quinn's

$$ | |**BREWPUBS/BEER GARDENS** | Capitol Hill's original gastropub has friendly bartenders, an extensive selection of beers on tap (with the West Coast and Belgium heavily represented), an extensive list of whiskey, and a menu of rib-sticking food to soak it up, which you can enjoy at the long bar or at a table on either of the two floors of the industrial-chic space. A pretzel and some foie gras poutine are good ways to start—then you can choose from Painted Hills beef tartare with pumpernickel crisps, perfect marrow bones with baguette and citrus jam, or a cheese plate. Heartier mains, like the signature wild boar sloppy Joe are available at dinnertime. A pared-down pub menu is also available from 4 pm to midnight or later. The folks here take their libations seriously, so feel free to chat up the bartenders about their favorites. ✉ *1001 E Pike St., Capitol Hill* ☎ *206/325–7711* 🌐 *www.quinnspubseattle.com* ⏲ *No lunch* ✍ *Reservations not accepted.*

DANCE CLUBS

The Baltic Room

DANCE CLUBS | It's the little dance club that could: a classy piano bar–turned–art deco cocktail lounge that's still popular after quite a few years on the scene—and that still manages to get Seattleites of all stripes to take a few turns on the dance floor. Dress up a bit, but keep it comfortable. Along with top-notch DJs, skillful rock and blues acts entertain from a small stage. The compact dance floor gets crowded—a little too crowded—on weekends. ✉ *1207 E. Pine St., Capitol Hill* ☎ *206/625–4444* 🌐 *balticroom.com.*

Century Ballroom

DANCE CLUBS | This is an elegant place for dinner and dancing, with a polished, 2,000-square-foot dance floor. Salsa and swing events often include lessons in the cover charge. The Tin Table, the restaurant-bar across the hall, is excellent. There's a bachata social on Wednesday, salsa on Thursday, Friday, and Saturday, and swing on Sunday. ✉ *915 E. Pine St., 2nd fl., Capitol Hill* ☎ *206/324–7263* 🌐 *www.centuryballroom.com.*

LGBTQ+ SPOTS

Gay City

GATHERING PLACES | An inclusive gathering space for Seattle's LGBTQ community, Gay City hosts regular parties, variety shows, and music and theater events at this space that also tests for HIV and sexually transmitted diseases as part of its mission to promote health and wellness. ✉ *517 E. Pike St., Capitol Hill* ☎ *206/860–6969* 🌐 *www.gaycity.org.*

Madison Pub

BARS/PUBS | Regulars shoot pool, hang out with groups of friends, and chat up the friendly bartenders at this laid-back, anti-scenester joint. ✉ *1315 E. Madison St., Capitol Hill* ☎ *206/325–6537* 🌐 *www.madisonpub.com.*

Neighbours

BARS/PUBS | In business since 1983, Neighbours is an institution thanks in part to its drag shows, great theme DJ nights, and relaxed atmosphere (everyone, including the straightest of the straights, seems to feel welcome here). It's no longer the center of the gay and lesbian scene, but the dance floor and the rest of this large club is still usually packed Thursday through Saturday. ✉ *1509 Broadway, Capitol Hill* ☎ *206/324–5358* 🌐 *www.neighboursnightclub.com.*

Pony

DANCE CLUBS | The original and short-lived Pony, which got bulldozed along with the rest of the 500 block of Pine Street, was notorious for wild fun. The current incarnation, just a bit more polished and with an amazing patio, retains some of the former space's decorating touches (vintage nude photos). There's a small dance floor and a mix of gays, lesbians, and their friends. ✉ *1221 E. Madison St., Central District* ☎ *206/324–2854* 🌐 *www.ponyseattle.com.*

Wildrose

BARS/PUBS | Seattle's only dedicated lesbian bar draws a mob nearly every night. The crowd at weeknight karaoke is fun and good-natured, cheering for pretty much anyone. Weekends are raucous, so grab a window table early and settle in for perpetual ladies' night. ✉ *1021 E. Pike St., Capitol Hill* ☎ *206/324–9210* 🌐 *www.thewildrosebar.com.*

MUSIC CLUBS

Neumos

MUSIC CLUBS | One of the grunge era's iconic clubs (when it was Moe's) has managed to reclaim its status as a staple of the Seattle rock scene, despite being closed for a six-year stretch. And it is a great rock venue: acoustics are excellent, and the roster of cutting-edge indie rock bands is one of the best in the city. Other genres of music are also represented among the acts coming through Neumos. Their intimate downstairs venue, Barboza, often brings in great, lesser-known acts. ✉ *925 E. Pike St., Capitol Hill* ☎ *206/709–9467* 🌐 *www.neumos.com.*

Performing Arts

Capitol Hill is a rabbit warren of small theaters and arts organizations, many of which make for a nice night out but few of which warrant a rearranging of schedules. The best way to navigate them is to check event listings in The Stranger 🌐 *www.thestranger.com* or on the local blog Capitol Hill Seattle 🌐 *www.capitolhillseattle.com* for what is happening while you're there. If you're in town on the second Thursday of a month, the Capitol Hill Art Walk (5–8 pm) is worth the hike up the hill and features all types of art and performances. 🌐 *www.capitolhillartwalk.com*

ARTS CENTERS

12th Avenue Arts

NIGHTLIFE OVERVIEW | Developed by Capitol Hill Housing, 12th Avenue Arts is designed to keep the arts in the neighborhood. It plays host to two theaters with rotating shows from various local troupes, including the excellent Strawberry Theatre Workshop and Washington Ensemble Theatre. The building itself also provides low-cost housing, office space for nonprofits, and has a restaurant, ✉ *1620 12th Ave. #101, Capitol Hill* 🌐 *12avearts.org.*

FILM

Siff Cinema Egyptian

FILM | Head to this art deco movie palace, a former Masonic temple, for first-run films. ✉ *805 E. Pine St., at Broadway, Capitol Hill* ☎ *206/324–9996* 🌐 *siff.net/year-round-cinema/cinema-venues/siff-cinema-egyptian.*

Northwest Film Forum

FILM | A cornerstone of the city's independent film scene, its two screening rooms screen classic repertory, cult hits, experimental films, and documentaries. ✉ *1515 12th Ave., Capitol Hill* ☎ *206/329–2629* 🌐 *www.nwfilmforum.org.*

Madison Park is a quaint residential neighborhood.

READINGS AND LECTURES

Elliott Bay Book Company Reading Series

READINGS/LECTURES | The famed bookstore presents a popular series of renowned local, national, and international author readings in a cozy, basement room next to a café. Events are free, but tickets are often required. ✉ *1521 10th Ave., Capitol Hill* ☎ *206/624–6600* 🌐 *www.elliottbaybook.com.*

Shopping

If you always make sure that your clothes are on trend, subscribe to *Dwell* magazine, embody the DIY ethos, or just like to people-watch, head to Capitol Hill for some of the best shopping in town. Broadway is popular among college students because of its cheap clothing stores, including standbys Urban Outfitters and American Apparel. The Pike–Pine Corridor holds the majority of the neighborhood's most interesting shops.

Best shopping: East Pike and East Pine Streets between Bellevue Avenue and Madison Avenue East, East Olive Way between Bellevue Avenue East and Broadway East, and Broadway East between East Denny Way and East Roy Street.

CLOTHING

Le Frock

CLOTHING | It may look like just another overcrowded consignment shop, but among the racks of Seattle's classiest vintage and consignment store you'll find classic steals for men and women from Burberry, Fendi, Dior, Missoni, and the like. Contemporary looks from Prada, Gucci, and Chanel round out the collection. ✉ *613 E Pike St., Capitol Hill* ☎ *206/623–5339* 🌐 *instagram.com/lefrockconsignment.*

LIKELIHOOD

SHOES/LUGGAGE/LEATHER GOODS | With designers ranging from Golden Goose to Nike this store has an extensive brand selection that's perfect for the eclectic Capitol Hill neighborhood. With its emphasis on "less is more," the clean white space creates the illusion of art gallery rather than shoe retailer. They also have a wide variety of apparel and bags. ✉ *1101 E Union St.* ☎ *206/257–0577* 🌐 *www.likelihood.us.*

Revival Shop

CLOTHING | Vintage shopping meets modern style in this consignment shop. Mixing used women's clothing with a collection of jewelery and art from local designers and other miscellaneous items, the store winds up with just the kind of eclectic collection that feels curated enough not to be slogging through junk, but haphazard enough to feel like your next treasure could be right in front of you. ✉ *233 Broadway E, Seattle* ☎ *206/395–6414* 🌐 *www.revivalshopseattle.com.*

★ **Standard Goods**

CLOTHING | If you want to get a true sense of Pacific Northwest style, this men's and women's clothing shop embodies it all, from casual plaid button-down shirts to wood-framed sunglasses. Carrying local brands like Filson, Shwood, and Capitol Hill Candles, this trendy local shop sources only quality goods. ✉ *701 E Pike St., Capitol Hill* ☎ *206/323–0207* 🌐 *www.thestandardgoods.com.*

Totokaelo

CLOTHING | Not many luxury clothing brands come from Seattle—things tend to be more REI than Gucci in the Northwest—but Totokaelo bucks plenty of trends within its sparse, modern store. With monochromatic T-shirts and handmade ceramics, the shop is stunningly beautiful, and the goods inside—women's and men's clothing, shoes, and household objects—are impeccably merchandized. While you might prefer to window shop rather than actually buy, there are plenty of affordable knick-knacks and housewares. ✉ *1523 10th Ave, Capitol Hill* ☎ *844/868–6523* 🌐 *totokaelo.com.*

BOOKS

★ **Elliott Bay Book Company**

BOOKS/STATIONERY | A major reason to visit this landmark bookstore—formerly a longtime haunt in Pioneer Square, hence the name—is the great selection of Pacific Northwest history books and fiction titles by local authors, complete with handwritten recommendation cards from the knowledgeable staff. A big selection of bargain books, lovely skylights, and an appealing café all sweeten the deal—and the hundreds of author events held every year mean that nearly every day is an exciting one for dropping by. ✉ *1521 10th Ave., Capitol Hill* ☎ *206/624–6600* 🌐 *www.elliottbaybook.com.*

Twice Sold Tales

BOOKS/STATIONERY | It's hard to miss this excellent used-book store—simply look for the six-foot neon cat sign—he'll be waving his Cheshire tail. Inside, you'll find plenty more kitties winding their way through the maze of stacks. Pick up a few tales and take advantage of the 25% discount offered the last two hours of the evening. Be sure to grab a map of all the used bookstores in the city if you're hungry for more. ✉ *1833 Harvard Ave., at Denny, Capitol Hill* ☎ *206/324–2421* 🌐 *www.twicesoldtales.com.*

HOME AND GIFTS

Kobo

GIFTS/SOUVENIRS | This lovely store sells artisan crafts from studios in Japan and in the Northwest. What's here is similar to what's stocked at the International District branch: tasteful home wares, cute but functional gifts, and quirky pieces of furniture. After a long day of looking at retro and ironic items, this place will cleanse your palate. ✉ *814 E Roy St., Capitol Hill* ☎ *206/726–0704* 🌐 *www.koboseattle.com.*

MARKETS

★ **Broadway Farmers Market**

OUTDOOR/FLEA/GREEN MARKETS | One of the city's liveliest and most interesting farmers' markets fills a plaza and spills onto the sidewalk of Broadway. There's fresh produce galore, prepared foods including Dutch pancakes and doughnuts, plus music, samples, and plenty of cut flowers. The market is open Sunday from 11 am to 3 pm. ✉ *Seattle Central, 1601 Broadway, Capitol Hill* 🌐 *www.seattlefarmersmarkets.org.*

Melrose Market

FOOD/CANDY | Seattle is famously foodie-friendly, and this historic triangular building packs several of the city's best culinary shops under one roof. Browse and sample artisanal meats, cheeses, shellfish, and liquor, all with locavore leanings. Unlike Pike Place, the relatively pint-size Melrose is more a hipster haunt than a tourist trap: Anthony Bourdain and the Seattle *Top Chef* contestants have been spotted here. ✉ *1501–1535 Melrose Ave., Capitol Hill* 🌐 *melrosemarketseattle.com.*

MUSIC

Everyday Music

MUSIC STORES | For a huge selection of used CDs and vinyl, wander over to Everyday Music, where you'll find more than 100,000 titles in stock. The local mini-chain is one of the few remaining places that carry such a wide selection, which makes it as good a spot for picking up used vinyl as the latest pop CD. Despite the size, they maintain the old-school coziness essential to complete the record store vibe. ✉ *1520 10th Ave., Capitol Hill* ☎ *206/568–3321* 🌐 *www.everydaymusic.com.*

Wall of Sound

MUSIC STORES | If you're on the hunt for Japanese avant-rock on LP, antiwar spoken word, spiritual reggae with Afro-jazz undertones, or old screen-printed show posters, you've found the place. ✉ *315 E Pine St., Capitol Hill* ☎ *206/441–9880* 🌐 *www.wosound.com.*

Madison Park

Restaurants

Café Flora

$ | VEGETARIAN | FAMILY | The vegetarian and vegan menu changes frequently at Café Flora, but the chefs tend to keep things simple, with dishes like black-bean burgers topped with spicy aioli, polenta with leeks and spinach, and the popular "Oaxaca tacos" (corn tortillas filled with potatoes and four types of cheese). You can eat in the Atrium, which has a stone fountain, skylight, and garden-style café tables and chairs, or try the weekday happy hour in the bar or on the garden patio. **Known for:** vegan fare; brunch. *Average main: $15* ✉ *2901 E Madison St., Madison Park* ☎ *206/325–9100* 🌐 *www.cafeflora.com.*

Luc

$$$$ | FRENCH | Thierry Rautureau (aka the Chef in the Hat) opened one of Seattle's first modern French restaurants, bringing the art of precise sourcing and fine-dining to the city in the late '80s with Rover's. Now, just blocks from where that once stood, he puts the same care and skill into classic French bistro–style food. **Known for:** live accordion music and other entertainment; elegant atmosphere; chef is a Seattle favorite. *Average main: $35* ✉ *2800 E Madison, Madison Valley* ☎ *206/328–6645* 🌐 *https://thechefinthehat.com/luc.*

Chapter 9

FREMONT, PHINNEY RIDGE, AND GREENWOOD

Updated by
AnnaMaria Stephens

Sights ★★☆☆☆

Restaurants ★★★★☆

Hotels ★☆☆☆☆

Shopping ★★★★★

Nightlife ★★★☆☆

NEIGHBORHOOD SNAPSHOT

FREMONT SOLSTICE PARADE

If you want to know where all of Fremont's legendary weirdness has retreated, look no further than the Fremont Arts Council's warehouse on Fremont Avenue North. For months leading up to the Fremont Solstice Parade (held on the summer solstice weekend in June), half-finished parade floats spill out of the workshop. The parade is Seattle's most notorious summer event—some of the floats and costumes are political and/or wacky, and the "highlight" is a stream of naked bicyclists, only some of whom don elaborate body paint. And the professionally built floats and puppets are truly spectacular: past participants have included giant robots and a papier-mâché Flying Spaghetti Monster.

QUICK BITES

Flying Apron "I can't believe this is vegan!" is a common reaction to the delicious pastries, cookies, and muffins made by the Flying Apron. All items are also gluten- and wheat-free. ✉ *3510 Fremont Ave. N, Fremont* ☎ *206/442–1115* 🌐 *www.flyingapron.com* 💳 *No credit cards.*

PCC Community Markets PCC Community Markets, an upscale food co-op, has all the fixings you need for a picnic along the canal, including sandwiches and salads. ✉ *600 N 34th St., Fremont* ☎ *206/632–6811* 🌐 *www.pccmarkets.com* 💳 *No credit cards.*

Red Mill People line up out the door at Red Mill for juicy burgers and milk shakes in yummy flavors like mandarin-chocolate and butterscotch. ✉ *312 N 67th St., Greenwood* ☎ *206/783–6362* 🌐 *www.redmillburgers.com* 💳 *No credit cards* ⏲ *Closed Mon.*

Royal Grinders Royal Grinders serves hearty hot subs on soft crusty rolls. The Crown and the Italian are the best. ✉ *3526 Fremont Pl. N, behind Lenin statue, Fremont* ☎ *206/545–7560* 🌐 *www.royalgrinders.com* 💳 *No credit cards* ⏲ *Closed Mon.-Tues.*

GETTING HERE AND AROUND

■ Buses 26, 28, and 5 will drop you in Fremont center. Driving, take either Aurora Avenue North (Route 99) and exit right after you cross the bridge, or take Westlake Avenue North and cross the Fremont Bridge into the neighborhood's core. Phinney is at the top of a big hill. If you want to walk it, the best strategy is to thread your way up through the charming residential streets. If not, take Bus 5 bus up Fremont Avenue.

TOP REASONS TO GO

■ Follow the **Burke-Gilman Trail** along the Fremont section of the Lake Washington Ship Canal.

■ Indulge in retail therapy at the area's **boutiques.** Mandatory stops on the shopping tour include Les Amis and Burnt Sugar in Fremont and the Frock boutique in Phinney Ridge.

■ Sip some brews at a **neighborhood tap house.**

■ Take a spin on a historic wooden carousel, then hang out with snow leopards at **Woodland Park Zoo.**

■ Tour an artisanal-chocolate factory: **Theo Chocolate**'s confections are best sampled after seeing chocolate makers at work.

The charming neighborhoods of Fremont and Phinney Ridge are great side trips when you've done your major Seattle sightseeing and are in the mood for shopping, strolling along the canal, or sampling artisanal goodies.

Fremont

Sights

For many years, Fremont enjoyed its reputation as Seattle's weirdest neighborhood, home to hippies, artists, bikers, and rat-race dropouts. But Fremont has lost most of its artist cachet as the stores along its main strip turned more upscale, luxury condos and town houses appeared above the neighborhood's warren of small houses, and rising rents sent many longtime residents reluctantly packing (many to nearby Ballard). On weekend nights, the Downtown strip sometimes looks like one big party, as a bunch of bars draw in a young crowd from Downtown, the University District, and the city's suburbs.

The mixed bag of "quintessential sights" in this neighborhood reflects the intersection of past and present. Most of them, like Seattle's favorite photo stop, the Fremont Troll, are works of public art created in the 1980s and '90s. Others, like Theo Chocolate and Fremont Brewing, celebrate the independent spirit of the neighborhood but suggest a much different lifestyle than the founders of the "republic of Fremont" espoused. Still others are neutral and timeless, like a particularly lovely section of the Burke Gilman Trail along the Lake Washington Ship Canal.

Theo Chocolate Factory Tour
STORE/MALL | FAMILY | If it weren't for a small sign on the sidewalk pointing the way and the faint whiff of cocoa in the air, you'd never know that Fremont has its own artisanal chocolate factory with daily tours. Since it opened in 2005, Theo has become one of the Northwest's most familiar chocolate brands, sold in shops across the city. Theo uses only organic, fair-trade cocoa beans, usually in high percentages—yielding darker, less sweet, and more complex flavors than some of their competitors. Stop by the factory to buy exquisite "confection" truffles—made daily in small batches—with unusual flavors like basil-ganache, lemon, fig-fennel, and burnt sugar. The friendly staff is known to be generous with samples. You can go behind the scenes as well, with informative, hour-long tours; reservations are highly recommended, especially on weekends and during peak tourist season. ✉ *3400 Phinney Ave. N, Fremont* ☎ *206/632–5100* 🌐 *www.theochocolate.com* 🎫 *Tour $12.*

Restaurants

Friendly neighborhood joints, Thai restaurants, good pubs, and a few swankier eateries worth making the trek to the northern part of the city round out the options in these quirky adjacent neighborhoods.

Fremont Like a Local

Wacky Public Art

Kick-start your tour under the north end of the Aurora Bridge at N 36th Street, where you'll find the **Fremont Troll**, a 2-ton, 18-foot-tall concrete troll clutching a real Volkswagen beetle in his massive hand. The troll appeared in 1991, commissioned by the Fremont Arts Council. Pose for a shot atop his head or pretending to pull his beard.

Next head west down the hill to the statue of **Lenin** (✉ *N 36th St. at Fremont Place and Evanston Ave. N*). Constructed by Bulgarian sculptor Emil Venkov for the Soviets in 1988, the 16-foot, 7-ton statue was removed shortly after the Velvet Revolution and eventually made its way to Seattle. Visitors here during Gay Pride Week might catch a glimpse of him in drag. The annual Lenin lighting, part of the Fremont Festivus in early December, is also a popular tradition.

A few blocks away you'll find the **Fremont Rocket** (✉ *N 35th St. and Evanston Ave. N*), a 53-foot Cold War–era rocket nonchalantly strapped to the side of a retail store—which just may mark the official "center of the universe." This Seattle landmark was rescued from a surplus store in 1991 and successfully erected on its current locale in '94, when neon lights were added, along with the crest "De Libertas Quirkas," meaning "Freedom to Be Peculiar."

Walk along the water toward the Fremont Bridge, past the offices of Adobe, Getty Images, and Google (among others) to visit the cast-aluminum sculpture **Waiting for the Interurban** (✉ *N 34th St. and Fremont Ave. N*). Artist Richard Beyer created this depiction of six people and a dog waiting for a trolley in 1979. Observe that the dog's face is actually that of a man—story goes this is the face of recycling pioneer (and onetime honorary mayor of Fremont) Armen Stepanian, who made disparaging remarks about the statue. It's been a long local tradition to "vandalize" the sculpture with anything from brightly colored umbrellas to signs congratulating newlyweds.

Thai Food and Chocolates and T-Shirts, Oh My!

If the comrades are hungry, opt for Thai food. On sunny days, choose **Kaosamai** (🌐 *www.kaosamai.com*), a crowd-pleasing eatery with a large deck. On rainy days, you might prefer cozy **Kwanjai Thai** (✉ *469 N 36th St.* ☎ *206/632–3656*), where you can dive into home-style Thai curries.

After you've had your fill of spicy food, peruse nearby **Destee-Nation** (🌐 *www.desteenation.com*), a cool little shop that sells vintage-looking T-shirts from independent restaurants and establishments across Seattle.

Next stop is **Theo Chocolate Factory** (🌐 *www.theochocolate.com*), an organic and fair-trade chocolate factory offering tours. You'll learn all about the chocolate-making process and get to sample some of Theo's favorites. Be sure to try the coconut-curry bar!

Check out the neighborhood's website (🌐 *www.fremontuniverse.com*) for more information.

Joule

$$$ | KOREAN | Married chef-owners Rachel Yang and Seif Chirchi have wowed Seattle diners with their French-fusion spins on Asian cuisine. Joule's nouvelle take on a Korean steak house serves meat options like Wagyu bavette steak with truffled pine nuts and short rib with Kalbi and grilled kimchi. Nonmeat menu items include Chinese broccoli with walnut pesto and mackerel with green curry cilantro crust and black currant, while a weekend brunch buffet goes slightly more mainstream with a fruit and pastry buffet, as well as entrées like oatmeal-stuffed porchetta. **Known for:** classic brunch buffet; Korean-inflected flavors; lively vibe. *Average main: $28 ✉ 3506 Stone Way N, Fremont ☎ 206/632–1913 🌐 www.joulerestaurant.com ⏲ No lunch.*

★ Manolin

$$$ | SEAFOOD | Walking into the light-filled dining room of Manolin, with its horseshoe-shape bar framing the open kitchen, transports you straight to the sea. Blue tiles, the wood-fired oven in the center, the cool marble bar, and the seafood-laden menu all bring diners to the ambiguous maritime destination, where ceviches are inspired by coastal Mexico, plantain chips come from the Caribbean, smoked salmon has vaguely Scandinavian flavors, and the squid with black rice and ginger is as if from Asia, all mingling on the menu. **Known for:** a celebration of ceviche; creative cocktails; global flavors. *Average main: $30 ✉ 3621 Stone Way N, Fremont ☎ 206/294–3331 🌐 www.manolinseattle.com ⏲ No lunch. Closed Mon. No credit cards.*

Milstead & Co.

$ | CAFÉ | Seattle's premier multiroaster café would be a parody of coffee culture if it weren't so good at what it does: curate a lineup of the country's best coffees and pour them expertly in a variety of methods. Baristas here coach customers through the process of picking a bean (origin, type, and roast) and method, so this is not the place to come for a quick caffeine hit. **Known for:** "snobby" in the best way; lots of choices. *Average main: $5 ✉ 754 N 34th St., Fremont ☎ 206/659–4814 🌐 www.milsteadandco.com.*

★ Revel

$ | ASIAN FUSION | Adventurous enough for the most committed gourmands but accessible enough to be a neighborhood lunchtime favorite, Revel starts with Korean street food and shakes it up with a variety of influences, from French to Americana. Noodle dishes at this popular, sleek spot (try for a counter seat overlooking the open kitchen) might feature smoked tea noodles with roast duck or seaweed noodles with Dungeness crab, while irresistibly spicy dumplings might be stuffed with bites of short ribs, shallots, and scallions, or perhaps chickpeas, roasted cauliflower, and mustard yogurt. **Known for:** fusion flavors that work; Quoin bar with fun cocktails; creative rice bowls. *Average main: $18 ✉ 401 N. 36th St., Fremont ☎ 206/547–2040 Reservations 🌐 www.revelseattle.com.*

Paseo

$ | CUBAN | The centerpiece of this Cuban-influenced menu is the mouth-watering Famous Caribbean Roast sandwich: marinated pork topped with sautéed onions and served on a chewy baguette. It's doused with an amazing top-secret sauce that keeps folks coming back for more. **Known for:** baguette sandwiches; Cuban-style entrées; takeout if you can't score a table. *Average main: $13 ✉ 4225 Fremont Ave. N, Fremont ☎ 206/545–7440 🌐 www.paseoseattle.com ⏲ Closed Mon.*

RockCreek

$$$ | SEAFOOD | A temple to uniquely prepared seafood, this is the restaurant that locals want to bring visitors to: an example of the casual way seafood weaves into all sorts of dishes when you live so close to such bounty. The mix of appetizers, oyster shooters, small plates, and full entrées makes the long menu

Sights

1 Theo Chocolate Factory Tour B7
2 Woodland Park Zoo B3

Restaurants

1 The Cookie Counter A1
2 FlintCreek Cattle Co..... A1
3 Joule C7
4 Ken's Market A1
5 Manolin C6
6 Milstead & Co. C7
7 Paseo B5
8 Revel B6
9 RockCreek B5
10 Uneeda Burger.......... B5
11 Vif.......................... B4
12 Westward E6

Quick Bites

1 Coyle's Bakeshop A1
2 Herkimer Coffee A1

Hotels

1 Chelsea Station Inn Bed & Breakfast........ B4

Tour the Theo Chocolate factory and sample Seattle's signature artisanal treat.

something of an epic adventure filled with fresh local, domestic, and global fish—from local oysters to Hawaiian tuna, Norwegian mackerel, back to black cod from Washington's own Neah Bay. **Known for:** unexpected but spot-on flavors; fun atmosphere; craft cocktails. *$ Average main: $30 ✉ 4300 Fremont Ave. N, Fremont ☎ 206/557–7732 ⊕ www.rockcreekseattle.com ⏲ No lunch weekdays.*

Uneeda Burger

$ | **BURGER** | **FAMILY** | A casual burger shack from a fine-dining chef means flavor and execution that are always on point. The controlled chaos of this family-friendly joint can make it hard to get an outdoor table on sunny days, but the lines and wait are worth it for the perfectly cooked burgers that range from a classic beef patty to a house-made vegetarian option. **Known for:** perfect for hungry kids; a place to sit outside. *$ Average main: $9 ✉ 4302 Fremont Ave. N, Fremont ☎ 206/547–2600 ⊕ www.uneedaburger.com.*

★ Vif

$ | **BISTRO** | Part coffee shop, part casual snack restaurant, and part wine retailer, Vif is all magic. The brainchild of a former pastry chef and wine director of one of Seattle's bygone restaurants, the menu brings the kind of nuance and skill that you'd expect from a pastry chef but the elegance of a wine expert. **Known for:** expertly prepared coffee; curated wine selection; light fare and "snackettes". *$ Average main: $9 ✉ 4401 Fremont Ave. N, Fremont ☎ 206/557–7357 ⊕ www.vifseattle.com ⏲ No dinner.*

Westward

$$$ | **SEAFOOD** | It's hard to beat the view from the Adirondack chairs around the oyster-shell-lined fire pit that sits on Westward's private lakefront, though tables with large windows framing the water and city skyline also abound inside the spacious restaurant, which serves Northwest seafood with Mediterranean flavors. But unlike so many restaurants with a view, Westward's menu actually matches the scenery, both in style and

quality. **Known for:** some of the most covetable outdoor seating in town; exquisitely prepared seafood; wood-fired dishes. *Average main: $28* *2501 N Northlake Way, Fremont* *206/552–8215* *www.westwardseattle.com* *No lunch weekdays.*

This charming north-end neighborhood is a short drive from Downtown. If you don't mind being in a self-contained spot far away from most attractions, this is a good bet, because there are restaurants, shops, and lovely walking galore. Fremont is close to Ballard, Phinney Ridge, and Green Lake; the closest attractions are the Ballard Locks, the Woodland Park Zoo, and Green Lake's lively park.

★ Chelsea Station Inn Bed & Breakfast

$$$ | **B&B/INN** | The four 900-square-foot suites in this 1920s brick colonial have distressed hardwood floors with colorful rugs, decorative fireplaces, sleeper sofas, contemporary furnishings, and a soft, modern color palette, and are a convenient and luxurious jumping-off point for all the north end has to offer. **Pros:** great, unobtrusive host; huge rooms and 1½ bathrooms per suite; fabulous breakfasts and complimentary snacks. **Cons:** far from Downtown; no TVs; no elevator. *Rooms from: $287* *4915 Linden Ave. N, Fremont* *206/547–6077* *www.chelseastationinn.com* *4 suites* *Free Breakfast.*

Fremont has quite a few bars lining its main commercial drag of North 36th Street, including a few spots for live music. Unfortunately, Fremont suffers from Dr. Jekyll and Mr. Hyde syndrome. During the week, almost any of its simple bars is a fine place to grab a quiet drink with a friend. Come Friday night, however, the neighborhood can transform into an extended frat party—so consider yourself warned.

BARS AND LOUNGES

Brouwer's

BARS/PUBS | It may look like a trendy Gothic castle, but in fact this is heaven for Belgian-beer lovers. A converted warehouse is home to a top selection of suds, which are provided by the owners of Seattle's best specialty-beer shop, Bottleworks. Brouwer's serves plenty of German and American/Northwest beers, too, as well as English, Czech, and Polish selections. Surprisingly good sandwiches, frites, and Belgian specialties help to lay a pre-imbibing foundation (remember that most Belgian beers have a higher alcohol content). Before settling on a seat downstairs, check out the balcony and the cozy parlor room. *400 N. 35th St., Fremont* *206/267–2437* *www.brouwerscafe.com.*

Chuck's Hop Shop

BREWPUBS/BEER GARDENS | Were it not for the picnic tables and rotating food trucks routinely parked outside, this place might look like just another corner convenience store. In fact, that's precisely what it used to be before owner Chuck transformed it into one of North Seattle's favorite spots for sampling craft beer and hanging out for hours. With nearly 40 taps, Chuck's features an especially good selection of IPAs and ciders on draft, many of local origin. Families love this extremely kid-friendly spot—there's an ice-cream counter, ample seating, and a stack of board games inside—and so do the dogs that get plenty of head pats and a big cookie, if you ask. Chuck's also offers a huge selection of bottled beers from all over the world, including gluten- and alcohol-free options. Sticking to the Capitol Hill area? Chuck's also has a second location (2001 East Union Street). *656 N.W. 85th St., Greenwood* *206/297–6212* *www.chuckshopshop.com.*

Fremont Brewing

BREWPUBS/BEER GARDENS | Founded in 2008, Fremont Brewing makes small-batch pale ales using organic hops. Locals (including their kids and dogs) crowd into the communal tables at the Urban Beer Garden, which includes both indoor and outdoor space, and a fireplace. Lines for beer move quickly, and visitors are encouraged to order or bring in outside food, though the brewery provides free pretzels and apples to snack on. ✉ *1050 N. 34th St., Fremont* ☎ *206/420–2407* 🌐 *www.fremontbrewing.com.*

The George & Dragon Pub

BARS/PUBS | Beloved by locals, this divey English pub attracts grizzled old Brits watching soccer, hipsters looking for cheap beer and whiskey, a frat crowd that clogs up the front patio area on weekends, and know-it-alls hoping to crush the competition at the popular Tuesday quiz night. Major soccer events like the World Cup bring in huge crowds. ✉ *206 N. 36th St., Fremont* ☎ *206/545–6864* 🌐 *www.theegeorge.com.*

BREWPUBS

Hale's Ales

BREWPUBS/BEER GARDENS | One of the city's oldest craft breweries, opened in 1983, produces unique English-style ales, cask-conditioned ales, and nitrogen-conditioned cream ales. The pub serves a full menu and has a great view of the fermenting room. Order a taster's flight if you want to try everything. ✉ *4301 Leary Way NW, Fremont* ☎ *206/706–1544* 🌐 *www.halesbrewery.com.*

Shopping

Fremont is full of the sort of stores perfectly suited to browsing and window-shopping—lots of pretty, pricey nonessentials and fun junk shops, in a cute and quirky north-end neighborhood. The weekly summer Sunday market along the waterfront (with free parking nearby) is hit or miss, but worth a look if you're in the area.

Best shopping: Blocks bound by Fremont Place North and Evanston Avenue North to North 34th Street and Aurora Avenue North.

Burnt Sugar

GIFTS/SOUVENIRS | If there's a rocket on the roof, then you've found Burnt Sugar—or you've gone too far and are in Cape Canaveral. This hip and funky shop focuses on cool shoes but also offers a mélange of handbags, greeting cards, soaps, candles, jewelry, toys, children's gifts, makeup, and other eclectic baubles you never knew you needed. ✉ *601 N 35th St., Fremont* ☎ *888/545–0699* 🌐 *www.burntsugarfrankie.com.*

Dusty Strings

MUSIC STORES | A Seattle institution since 1979, Dusty Strings has long been delighting folk and roots music lovers with beautifully crafted hammered dulcimers, harps, guitars of all stripes, banjos, ukuleles, and mandolins. The relaxed shop invites hands-on browsing, and the lilting strains of traditional melodies often fill the space. The nonprofit group Victory Music frequently hosts acoustic concerts and workshops in the store—check *www.victorymusic.org* for showtimes. ✉ *3406 Fremont Ave. N, Fremont* ☎ *206/634–1662* 🌐 *www.dustystrings.com.*

Essenza

GIFTS/SOUVENIRS | A gurgling stone fountain stands in the center of this light-filled boutique, where airy displays showcase delicately scented European bath products by Santa Maria Novella, Tocca, and Cote Bastide. You'll find the complete line of Fresh cosmetics, handmade bed linens, women's loungewear and lingerie, delicate jewelry, and exquisitely detailed children's clothing. ✉ *615 N 35th St., Fremont* ☎ *206/547–4895* 🌐 *www.essenza-inc.com.*

evo

CLOTHING | For outdoor gear with an edgy vibe, locals head to evo, which specializes in snow-sports gear and also carries a solid selection of hip street clothes for men and women. You'll find everything you need to shred Washington's big mountains in style, from fat powder skis and snowboards with wild graphics to flashy ski jackets and thick woolen beanies. Occupying a two-level space at the Fremont Collective building, evo also has a gallery space that hosts art shows. Traveling with skateboarders? Seattle's only indoor skate park, All Together Skate Park, is right next door. ✉ *3500 Stone Way N, Fremont* ☎ *206/973–4470* 🌐 *www.evo.com.*

Fremont Vintage Mall

ANTIQUES/COLLECTIBLES | Goods from about 25 vendors are crammed into every conceivable corner of this bi-level space, so you'll likely score at least something to take home. Clothing, furniture, and collectible art are among the finds, and the dishes, toys, and other cool stuff are fun to look through whether you're a serious collector or just an innocent bystander. The Jive Time Records Annex is also a tenant. It's easy to walk right past this place—look carefully for the door and then proceed down the flight of stairs. ✉ *3419 Fremont Pl. N, Fremont* ☎ *206/548–9140* 🌐 *www.fremontvintagemall.com.*

Les Amis

CLOTHING | Women whose sartorial leanings go beyond basic will adore the sophisticated dresses, gorgeous handknits, and the makings of great work outfits here, much of it from Europe and Japan. Younger fashionistas come here, too, for unique summer skirts and ultrasoft T-shirts. Everyone seems to love the whimsical lingerie collection. Les Amis carries some top designers, such as Dosa, Isabel Marant, and Nanette Lepore. ✉ *3420 Evanston Ave. N, Fremont* ☎ *206/632–2877* 🌐 *www.lesamis-inc.com.*

Ophelia's Books

BOOKS/STATIONERY | With a tiny spiral staircase leading to the basement, and resident cats wandering through the tightly packed aisles, Ophelia's offers a classic used-bookstore experience in an age when so many are disappearing. The owner is well known for her excellent taste, and it shows—you'll find major titles from well-known authors as well as obscure works and poetry books. Be sure to ask for recommendations—she'll be happy to help. ✉ *3504 Fremont Ave. N, Fremont* ☎ *206/632–3759* 🌐 *www.opheliasbooks.com.*

Show Pony

CLOTHING | With a mix of new, used, and locally designed clothing, Show Pony is a great spot to grab reasonably priced girly frocks and fabulous accessories. Especially good is the used/vintage section upstairs, which mostly stocks designer labels. Jewelry, perfume, gifts, and home-decorating items round out the collection. ✉ *702 N 35th St., Fremont* ☎ *206/706–4188* 🌐 *www.showponyseattle.com.*

Phinney Ridge

Sights

Mostly residential Phinney Ridge and its nearby sister neighborhood of Greenwood are just north of Fremont and east of Ballard. Though most visitors come to "PhinneyWood" for the Woodland Park Zoo, located on the main street of Phinney Avenue (which turns into Greenwood Avenue North), the area around the zoo is worth exploring if you have time. Phinney Ridge is the quieter of the two neighborhoods with a few coffee shops, eateries, and boutiques; on a clear day, you'll glimpse gorgeous views of the Cascade Mountains to the east and the Olympics to the west as you walk along Phinney Avenue. Farther north on Greenwood Avenue, the denser

Greenwood neighborhood features a bustling commercial district with a range of dining options and a few interesting shops. It's easy to get from downtown Seattle to the PhinneyWood neighborhoods; the No. 5 bus travels all along Phinney Avenue and Greenwood Avenue North, with stops at the zoo and beyond.

Woodland Park Zoo

ZOO | FAMILY | Ninety-two acres are divided into bioclimatic zones here, allowing many animals to roam freely in habitat areas. A jaguar exhibit is the center of the Tropical Rain Forest area, where rare cats, frogs, and birds evoke South American jungles. The Humboldt penguin exhibit is environmentally sound—it uses geothermal heating and cooling to mimic the climes of the penguins' native home, the coastal areas of Peru. With authentic thatch-roof buildings, the African Village has a replica schoolroom overlooking animals roaming the savanna; the Trail of Vines takes you through tropical Asia; and the Northern Trail winds past rocky habitats where brown bears, wolves, mountain goats, and otters scramble and play. The Reserve Zoomazium is a nature-themed indoor play space for toddlers and young kids, and the Woodland Park Rose Garden (free; located near the zoo's south entrance) is always a hit. ✉ *5500 Phinney Ave. N, Phinney Ridge* ☎ *206/548–2000* 🌐 *www.zoo.org* 🎫 *Oct.–Apr. $15.50, May–Sept. $22.95.*

Restaurants

The Cookie Counter

$ | BAKERY | Vegans flock to this tiny dessert shop that serves entirely dairy- and egg-free baked goods and ice cream, though you don't have to be vegan to appreciate the delicious flavor. The cozy spot, which also offers coffee and espresso, has only a few tables but it's worth the wait (or take your treats to-go and stroll the neighborhood). **Known for:** all-vegan menu; cozy spot for a coffee fix;. $ *Average main: $5* ✉ *7415 Greenwood Ave. N, Greenwood* 🌐 *www.seattlecookiecounter.com.*

★ **FlintCreek Cattle Co.**

$$$ | STEAKHOUSE | Ethically sourced meats, from steak cuts to gamier dishes such as bison, wild boar, and duck, headline the menu at FlintCreek, where floor-to-ceiling windows overlook a busy corner of Greenwood. A small-plates section features a cumin-dusted lamb tartare as well as mussels bathed in charred jalapeño-lime butter, while main-dish standouts include a brined pork chop on grits and a hanger steak topped with onion marmalade. **Known for:** sustainable ingredients; fancy chops and à la carte sides; hip vibe. $ *Average main: $30* ✉ *8421 Greenwood Ave N., Greenwood* ☎ *206/457–5656.*

Ken's Market

$ | DELI | The deli counter at Ken's turns out surprisingly good sandwiches, like an Italian stuffed with cured meats and a chicken banh mi loaded with pickles, all made on fresh bakery rolls. The small, nicely stocked neighborhood grocery store also offers a good selection of local baked goods (doughnuts, muffins), coffee, and beer and wine. **Known for:** to-go lunches; sidewalk seating;. $ *Average main: $9* ✉ *7231 Greenwood Ave. N* ☎ *206/784–3470* 🌐 *www.kensmarkets.com.*

Coffee and Quick Bites

★ **Coyle's Bakeshop**

$ | BAKERY | One of the city's neighborhood charmers, this beloved bakery churns out the best of French, British, and American pastry traditions, as well as their own unique treats. Mornings mean the espresso bar is busy and the croissants are flying off the shelves, while midday offers light salads, quiches, and their savory signature, the cretzel—a buttery, crisp, pretzel-knotted treat. **Known**

Did You Know?

The Northern Trail exhibit at the Woodland Park Zoo is modeled after Alaska's tundra and taiga region. In addition to brown bears, you'll see otters, owls, mountain goats, and sea eagles.

for: cretzels; cake. *Average main: $4 ✉ 8300 Greenwood Ave. N, Greenwood ☎ 206/257–4736 🌐 www.coylesbakeshop.com ⊗ No dinner.*

Herkimer Coffee

$ | **CAFÉ** | Herkimer Coffee's Greenwood outpost is a favorite of coffee connoisseurs, with baristas who know their stuff but won't give you side eye for dumping sweetener in their creations. The coffee shop has some seating, but it's also a great spot to grab a cup to go. **Known for:** perfectly pulled espresso; locally roasted beans. *Average main: $4 ✉ 7320 Greenwood Ave N, ☎ 206/784–0202 🌐 www.herkimercoffee.com.*

Nightlife

Phinney Ridge is a predominantly residential neighborhood with a few nightlife options if you're in the area.

BARS AND LOUNGES

Oliver's Twist

BARS/PUBS | Down the street from the Woodland Park Zoo, Oliver's Twist is a welcoming spot with cozy leather booths and tons of local art on the walls. Drinks are expertly poured with house-made shrubs and syrups, and the tapas menu includes tasty snacks (garlic truffle popcorn, grilled cheese and tomato soup). It makes for a fun evening slightly off the beaten path, especially during the happy hour, 5–7 Monday through Thursday and 4–6 on Friday and Saturday. There's a second location in Magnolia, as well. *✉ 6822 Greenwood Ave. N, Phinney Ridge ☎ 206/706–6673 🌐 www.oliverstwistseattle.com.*

BREWPUBS

Naked City Taphouse

BREWPUBS/BEER GARDENS | This bar has its own small brewery, so expect to see a few of its ales and stouts. The rest of the 48 taps are dedicated to their peers. Pub grub is simple, local, and organic. The beer garden is decorated with murals, and there's also a screening room where they host occasional events. *✉ 8564 Greenwood Ave. N, Phinney Ridge ☎ 206/838–6299 🌐 drink.nakedcity.beer.*

Greenwood

Sip & Ship If you really fall in love with Greenwood, head to this shop where T-shirts, hoodies, coffee mugs, and other accessories are emblazoned with the neighborhood's name and stocked alongside chic little gifts and handmade cards. It's a unique one-stop shop where you can buy a gift and have it wrapped, packed, and shipped while you sip espresso. *✉ 7511 Greenwood Ave. N, Greenwood ☎ 206/783–4299 🌐 www.sipandship.com.*

Shopping

Few of the shops in this area are destination-worthy for out-of-towners, but there are plenty of cute little places to browse if you're out strolling. Just stick to Phinney Avenue and Greenwood Avenue North and you'll find the best offerings.

Greenwood Space Travel Supply Co.

GIFTS/SOUVENIRS | **FAMILY** | The name of this tiny Greenwood shop draws in many curious passersby, who quickly learn that it's part of 826 Seattle, the amazing national creative-writing program for kids that was founded by novelist Dave Eggers and educator Nínive Calegari in 2002. Proceeds from the store's small selection go to the writing center, from kooky items purported to be space-travel essentials (freeze-dried meals, toy "ray guns") to 826-branded clothing. **■ TIP→ While you're here, check the bulletin board for notices about upcoming events and single-session workshops.** Note that this is not a full-blown toy store: go in with a sense of humor and an imagination because much of the cleverness is literary—standard toys and items given ridiculous new names to sound like important instruments of space travel. Everyone will enjoy filling out the hilarious space-traveler screening questionnaires and spaceship accident reports. ✉ *8414 Greenwood Ave. N, Greenwood* ☎ *206/725–2625* 🌐 *www.greenwoodspacetravelsupply.com* ⏲ *Closed Sun.–Mon., Weds., and Fri.–Sat.*

Johnson & Johnson Antiques

ANTIQUES/COLLECTIBLES | This family-owned shop provides 1900s American oak furniture in Craftsman and Mission styles, as well as plenty of other decorating knickknacks. French art deco pieces from the 1930s and 1860s American walnut make their collection distinctive and impressive. Stop in to browse and if something catches your eye; they make shipping easy. ✉ *6820 Greenwood Ave. N* ☎ *206/789–6489* 🌐 *johnsonandjohnsonantiques.com.*

Phinney Books

BOOKS/STATIONERY | A gem of an independent bookstore, Phinney Books is owned by local eight-time "Jeopardy!" champ and reading enthusiast Tom Nissley, who's stocked his charming shop with an expertly curated selection of books, including many titles by local authors and a whimsical section for kids. ✉ *7405 Greenwood Ave. N, Seattle* ☎ *206/297–2665* 🌐 *www.phinneybooks.com.*

Chapter 10

BALLARD

Updated by
Naomi Tomky

Sights ★★☆☆☆ | Restaurants ★★★★★ | Hotels ★☆☆☆☆ | Shopping ★★★★★ | Nightlife ★★★★☆

NEIGHBORHOOD SNAPSHOT

TOP REASONS TO GO

The **Ballard Farmers' Market,** on Ballard Avenue every Sunday from 10 to 3 (rain or shine, year-round), is one of the city's finest farmers' markets.

See a show at the **Sunset Tavern.** Ballard has its own music scene, with several small clubs on Ballard Avenue; the Tractor Tavern is a small venue with a big reputation.

Explore Ballard's **booming beer scene** at one or a few of the kid- and dog-friendly breweries in the area. Among the best: Reuben's, Stoup, and Populuxe.

Get some **retail therapy,** Ballard-style: the area's artsy galleries, many boutiques, and shoe and clothing stores offer tempting reasons to drop some dough.

Dip your toes in the water at **Golden Gardens Park.**

GETTING HERE AND AROUND

Ballard's main drags are NW Market Street and Ballard Avenue. If you're driving from Downtown, the easiest way to reach Ballard's center is to take Western Avenue and follow it as it turns into Elliott Avenue West and then 15th Avenue NW. Cross the bridge and make a left onto NW Market Street.

By bus, the Rapid Ride D, 15, 17, 18, and 40 will get you from Downtown to NW Market Street. Ballard is connected to Phinney Ridge, Wallingford, and the U-District by the 44 bus, which picks up passengers on NW Market Street and make its way to the other northern neighborhoods. Bus 28 connects Fremont's center to NW Market Street.

Note that the neighborhood is more spread out than it appears on a map. For example, walking west from the heart of Market Street to the Locks is almost a mile. Golden Gardens Park is best reached by car, bike, or bus.

PLANNING YOUR TIME

■ Set aside an hour or two to visit the Hiram M. Chittenden Locks. After that, you can spend your afternoon one of three ways before having dinner in the neighborhood: stroll and shop on Ballard Avenue; relax on the sand at Golden Gardens Park; or visit the Nordic Heritage Museum and area art galleries.

QUICK BITES

■ **Ballard Pizza Company** Order a fat slice or a whole pie at this popular family-friendly NYC-style pizza spot. ✉ *5107 Ballard Ave. NW, Ballard* ☎ *206/946–9960* 🌐 *www.ballardpizzacompany.com.*

■ **Cafe Besalu** Cafe Besalu is one of best French bakeries in the city. ✉ *5909 24th Ave. NW, Ballard* ☎ *206/789–1463* 🌐 *www.cafebesalu.com* ▭ *No credit cards.*

■ **La Carta de Oaxaca** Outstanding margaritas and traditional Mexican favorites are served in this lively space on Ballard Avenue. ✉ *5431 Ballard Ave. NW, Ballard* ☎ *206/782–8722* 🌐 *www.lacartadeoaxaca.com* ⏲ *Closed Sun.*

■ **Miro Tea** Modern, hip Miro Tea is the place to go for exotic teas and sweet or savory crepes. ✉ *5405 Ballard Ave. NW, Ballard* ☎ *206/782–6832* 🌐 *www.mirotea.com* ▭ *No credit cards.*

Ballard is Seattle's sweetheart. This historically Scandinavian neighborhood doesn't have many sights outside the Hiram M. Chittenden Locks; you'll spend more time strolling, shopping, and hanging out than crossing attractions off your list. It's got a great little nightlife, shopping, and restaurant scene on Ballard Avenue, and an outstanding farmers' market every Sunday.

Ballard used to be almost exclusively Scandinavian and working-class; it was the logical home for the Swedish and Norwegian immigrants who worked in the area's fishing, shipbuilding, and lumber industries. Reminders of its origins still exist—most literally in the Nordic Heritage Museum—but the neighborhood is undergoing inevitable changes as the number of artists, hipsters, and young professionals (many of whom have been priced out of Fremont and Capitol Hill) increases. Trendy restaurants, upscale furniture stores, and quirky boutiques abound along NW Market Street and Ballard Avenue, the neighborhood's main commercial strips. But no matter how tidy it gets, or how high the condos rise, there's a little bit of fishing village left behind, coursing through the streets.

Ballard used to be its own city: it wasn't a part of Seattle until 1907, when Ballard residents voted to be "annexed" by the city. The citizens of Ballard were responding to a water crisis—which would be solved by becoming part of Seattle—as well as to myriad promises of new and better public services made by Seattle's mayor. While the "Free Ballard" slogan has fallen out of use in recent years, there's still an attitude of pride in being outside of the core of the city. Ballard's unique heritage and way of life are preserved despite being one of the city's hippest neighborhoods.

Sights

★ Hiram M. Chittenden Locks

LIGHTHOUSE | FAMILY | There's no doubt—there's something intriguing and eerie about seeing two bodies of water, right next to each other, at different levels. The Hiram M. Chittenden Locks (also known as "Ballard Locks") are an important passage in the 8-mile Lake Washington Ship Canal that connects Puget Sound to freshwater Lake Washington and Lake Union. In addition to boat traffic, the locks see an estimated half-million salmon and trout make the journey from saltwater to fresh each summer, with the help of a fish ladder.

Families picnic beneath oak trees in the adjacent 7-acre Carl S. English Botanical Gardens; various musical performances

Sights

1 Golden Gardens Park **A1**

2 Hiram M Chittenden Locks..................... **B5**

3 Nordic Heritage Museum **B4**

Restaurants

1 Bastille.................. **D4**

2 Cafe Munir................**C1**

3 Delancey..................**E1**

4 The Fat Hen..............**E1**

5 Hot Cakes.................**C4**

6 Pestle Rock...............**C4**

7 Ray's Boathouse........ **A3**

8 Sawyer................... **D4**

9 Staple & Fancy.......... **D5**

10 Stoneburner............. **D4**

11 The Walrus and the Carpenter................ **D5**

Quick Bites

1 Cafe Besalu **C3**

2 La Carta De Oaxaca.....**C4**

3 Slate Coffee Bar................**E3**

Hotels

1 Ballard Inn............... **D4**

2 Hotel Ballard **D4**

(from jazz bands to chamber music) serenade visitors on summer weekends; and steel-tinted salmon awe spectators as they climb a 21-step fish ladder en route to their freshwater spawning grounds—a heroic journey from the Pacific to the base of the Cascade Mountains.

In the 1850s, when Seattle was founded, Lake Washington and Lake Union were inaccessible from the tantalizingly close Puget Sound. The city's founding fathers—most notably, Thomas Mercer in 1854—began dreaming of a canal that would connect the freshwater lakes and the sound. The lure of freshwater moorage and easier transport of timber and coal proved powerful, but it wasn't until 1917 that General Hiram M. Chittenden and the Army Corps of Engineers completed the Lake Washington Ship Canal and the Locks that officially bear his name. More than 90 years later, the locks are still going strong. Tens of thousands of boaters pass through the locks each year, carrying more than a million tons of commercial products—including seafood, fuel, and building materials.

Free guided tours of the locks depart from the visitor center and will give you far more information than the plaques by the locks. ✉ *3015 NW 54th St., Ballard* ✣ *From Fremont, head north on Leary Way NW, west on NW Market St., and south on 54th St.* ☎ *206/783–7059* 🌐 *www.ballardlocks.org* 🎫 *Free* 🕑 *No tours in Jan. or Feb.*

Golden Gardens Park

BEACH—SIGHT | The waters of Puget Sound may be bone-chillingly cold, but that doesn't stop folks from jumping in to cool off. Besides brave swimmers, who congregate on the small strip of sand between the parking lot and the canteen, this Ballard-area park is packed with sunbathers and walkers in summer. In other seasons, beachcombers explore during low tide, and groups gather around bonfires to socialize and watch the glorious Seattle sunsets. The park has drinking water, grills, picnic tables, phones, restrooms, and a snack shop. It also has two wetlands, a short loop trail, and unbelievable views of the Olympic Mountains. *The park has two dedicated parking lots, but they fill up quickly on weekends.* ✉ *8498 Seaview Pl. NW, , near NW 85th St., Ballard* ✣ *From Downtown, take Elliott Avenue North, which becomes 15th Avenue West, and cross the Ballard Bridge. Turn left to head west on Market Street and follow signs to the Ballard Locks; continue about another mile via Seaview Avenue NW to the park.* ☎ *206/684–4075* 🎫 *Free.*

Nordic Heritage Museum

MUSEUM | Celebrating the five Nordic cultures of Sweden, Finland, Norway, Iceland, and Denmark (of which there are many descendants in Ballard), this museum, once housed in a 1900s schoolhouse, opened in its spacious and modern new building in 2018. Exhibits trace Scandinavian art, artifacts, and heritage all the way from Viking times. Galleries give an in-depth look at how immigrants came to America and settled in the Pacific Northwest (and the rest of America), as well as how Scandinavian culture contributes to and influences various fields around the world. There's also a relaxing "Sense of Place" area, where visitors can immerse themselves in the scenery and sounds of the Nordic region while getting comfortable on plush stuffed rocks. Models of boats lead the way to the back door, which leads to the garden containing both a century-old functional sauna and a Viking ship. ✉ *2655 NW Market Street, Ballard* ☎ *206/789–5707* 🌐 *www.nordicmuseum.org* 🎫 *$15; 1st Thurs. free* 🕑 *Closed Mon.*

Restaurants

Ballard is the north end's answer to Capitol Hill when it comes to edgy, innovative, and delicious dining. Restaurants have taken a cue from the beloved

Golden Gardens Park is one of the best places to see the sun set in Seattle.

year-round farmers' market (held every Sunday, rain or shine, from 10 to 3 along historic Ballard Avenue NW), and fresh produce, local ingredients, and top-notch quality are de rigueur here. Savor anything from chewy slices at local pizza darling Delancey to pristine Northwest oysters at the Walrus and the Carpenter.

Bastille

$$ | **FRENCH** | A trendy, high-design French brasserie mecca for hip folks seeking out reliably delicious French cuisine, Bastille is one of the more popular spots in Ballard. Snazzy diners sip simple house cocktails and munch on delicious steak frites, local oysters, and well-executed daily fish specials such as Washington-caught salmon. **Known for:** steak frites; boisterous atmosphere; cocktails. *Average main: $22* *5307 Ballard Ave. NW, Ballard* *206/453–5014* *www.bastilleseattle.com* *No lunch.*

Cafe Besalu

$ | **BAKERY** | A slice of France here in Ballard, this small, casual bakery gets patrons from across the entire city, thanks to its *I-swear-I'm-in-Paris* croissants—they are buttery, flaky perfection. Weekend lines are long, but if you score a table, you'll be in heaven. **Known for:** croissants; jam. *Average main: $6* *5909 24th Ave. NW, Ballard* *206/789–1463* *www.cafebesalu.com.*

★ Cafe Munir

$$ | **LEBANESE** | Perhaps the best-kept secret in the city, this neighborhood Lebanese joint is adorable and affordable. Whitewashed walls sparsely populated by old-world art match the white tablecloths, which are topped with intricate metal candleholders. **Known for:** hummus with lamb; whiskey. *Average main: $17* *2408 NW 80th St., Ballard* *206/783–4190* *www.cafemunir.blogspot.com* *Closed Mon. No lunch.*

★ Delancey

$ | **PIZZA** | Brandon Pettit spent years developing his thin-but-chewy pizza crust, and the final product has made him a contender for the city's best pies. Pettit himself is occasionally manning the wood-fired oven at this sweetly sophisticated little spot north of downtown Ballard that he owns with partner Molly Wizenberg (author of the popular "Orangette" food blog). **Known for:** quality pizza toppings; desserts. *Average main: $16 1415 NW 70th St., Ballard 206/838–1960 www.delanceyseattle.com Closed Mon. No lunch.*

★ The Fat Hen

$ | CONTEMPORARY | An Instagram-perfect brunch spot, this Ballard charmer deals in trends like thick ricotta toast, and classic comforts like Benedicts and cheesy egg bakes. The light-filled café offers house-made baked goods and coffee to start—and for diners waiting in the sometimes epic lines—from the marble countertop. **Known for:** brunch; egg bakes; ricotta toast. *Average main: $13 1418 NW 70th St., Ballard 206/782–5422 www.thefathenseattle.com No dinner.*

Hot Cakes

$ | CAFÉ | A few savory dishes are available at this Ballard "cakery," but consider passing on the chicken potpie in favor of the grilled chocolate sandwich. Autumn Martin, formerly head chocolatier at Theo Chocolate, specializes in creative, high-quality desserts (including vegan options) such as a "s'mores" molten chocolate cake with house-made marshmallows and caramel, and cookies with house-smoked chocolate chips. **Known for:** molten chocolate cakes; extravagant shakes. *Average main: $11 5427 Ballard Ave. NW, Ballard 206/420–3431 www.getyourhotcakes.com.*

La Carta de Oaxaca

$ | MEXICAN | True to its name, this low-key, bustling Ballard favorite serves traditional Mexican cooking with Oaxacan accents. The *mole negro* is a must, served with chicken or pork; another standout is the *albóndigas* (a spicy vegetable soup with meatballs). **Known for:** margaritas; albóndigas; mole. *Average main: $16 5431 Ballard Ave. NW, Ballard 206/782–8722 www.seattlemeetsoaxaca.com Closed Sun. No lunch Mon.*

Pestle Rock

$$ | THAI | Convincing Seattleites to forgo their pad Thai in favor of the spicy, herb-filled Isan cuisine of northern Thailand was a tough battle, but with a sleek, modern restaurant, skillful cooking, and plenty of peppers, Pestle Rock succeeded handily. Today, the tables are filled with locals knowingly ordering the house-made sausage, the coconut-milk curry noodles called *kao soi,* and pungent papaya salads, all filled with local ingredients such as wild salmon, Dungeness crab, and thoughtfully sourced meats. **Known for:** chicken wings; kao soi. *Average main: $17 2305 NW Market St., Ballard 206/466–6671 www.pestlerock.com Closed Tues.*

Ray's Boathouse

$$$$ | SEAFOOD | The view of Shilshole Bay might be the main draw here, but the seafood is also fresh and well prepared. Perennial favorites include grilled salmon, Kasu sake–marinated sablefish, Dungeness crab, and regional oysters on the half shell. **Known for:** seafood; view. *Average main: $48 6049 Seaview Ave. NW, Ballard 206/789–3770 www.rays.com.*

Sawyer

$$$$ | MODERN AMERICAN | For a taste of creativity with Northwest cuisine, pop into this sprawling but cute spot for a meal that might start with pimento cheesy bread and end with a house-made choco taco. The bright space and covered patio make a casual setting for a meal (kids welcome, they'll even get a lunchbox of toys to occupy them), while the menu balances playful and refined with dishes like a Dungeness crab scallion pancake, and a pho broth matzoh ball soup. **Known for:** matzoh balls in pho broth; desserts. *Average main: $35 5309 22nd Ave. NW,, Suite A, Ballard 206/420–7225 www.sawyerseattle.com No lunch Mon.-Sat.*

Slate Coffee Bar

$ | **CAFÉ** | In a city full of amazing coffee shops, Slate elevates the arts of roasting, brewing, and serving. With a focus on flavor, they roast beans lightly enough to highlight unique characteristics (if you love your Starbucks dark roast, this is not the place for you). **Known for:** deconstructed espresso; light-roasted beans. *Average main: $4* *5413 6th Ave. NW, Ballard* *www.slatecoffee.com.*

Staple & Fancy

$$$$ | **MODERN ITALIAN** | The "Staple" side of this Ethan Stowell restaurant at the south end of Ballard Avenue might mean gnocchi served with corn and chanterelles or a whole grilled branzino. But visitors to the glam, remodeled, historic brick building are best served by going "fancy," meaning the chef's menu dinner where diners are asked about allergies and food preferences, then presented with several courses (technically four, but the appetizer usually consists of a few different plates) of whatever the cooks are playing with on the line that night—cured meats, salads made with exotic greens, handmade pastas, seasonal desserts. **Known for:** multicourse menu; pasta. *Average main: $33* *4739 Ballard Ave. NW, Ballard* *206/789–1200* *www.ethanstowellrestaurants.com* *No lunch.*

Stoneburner

$$$ | **ITALIAN** | Stylish and swimming in light, the oak paneling, dark accents, and wide windows onto bustling Ballard Avenue give this quasi-Italian joint an exciting vibe. The menu keeps one foot firmly rooted in Italy, with sections for pizza and pasta on the menu full of Mediterranean sensibilities. **Known for:** family-friendly; brunch; pizzas. *Average main: $29* *5214 Ballard Ave. NW, Ballard* *206/695–2051* *www.stoneburnerseattle.com* *No lunch weekdays.*

The Walrus and the Carpenter

$$$ | **SEAFOOD** | Chef-owner Renee Erickson was inspired by the casual oyster bars of Paris to open this bustling shoebox of a restaurant on the south end of Ballard Avenue (in the rear of a historic brick building, behind Staple & Fancy). Seats fill fast at the zinc bar and the scattered tall tables where seafood fans slurp on fresh-shucked Olympias and Blue Pools and other local oysters, but the menu also offers refined small plates like grilled sardines with shallots and walnuts or roasted greengage plums in cream. **Known for:** oysters; small plates; very popular (long wait times). *Average main: $27* *4743 Ballard Ave. NW, Ballard* *206/395–9227* *www.thewalrusbar.com.*

Hotels

Ballard has a real neighborhood vibe, so staying here is a good way to feel like a local. You'll be farther from some of the tourist locations, but public transportation to Downtown is fast and frequent, and the excellent restaurant and nightlife scene in this part of town will more than make up for it. While there are only two hotels in the area, home rentals abound in the neighborhood's many old craftsman-style houses and their assorted accessory dwellings. Make sure to double-check the actual location, though, as Ballard is a huge neighborhood and spots farther north will put you out of walking distance from the fun and buses.

Ballard Inn

$ | **B&B/INN** | Travelers seeking an authentic Seattle neighborhood experience will fall hard for this charming budget-friendly inn right in the heart of Ballard, tucked between coffee shops, trendy boutiques, and restaurants. **Pros:** friendly staff; free Wi-Fi; comfy beds. **Cons:** no elevator (ask for a room on main floor if stairs are an issue); no in-room phone; thin walls and street noise; no air conditioning. *Rooms from: $129* *5300 Ballard Ave. NW, Ballard* *206/789–5011* *www.ballardinnseattle.com* *16 rooms* *No meals.*

★ Hotel Ballard

$$$ | **HOTEL** | In the heart of historic Ballard, surrounded by shops and restaurants, this chic boutique hotel features a modern take on baroque style, with gilded mirrors and sumptuous carpeting and furnishings in every room. **Pros:** close to Ballard attractions; friendly service; inexpensive parking by Seattle standards; free access to one of the city's best gyms. **Cons:** a bit isolated from Downtown; some street noise at night, especially on weekends; rooftop event space can be disruptive for guests. *Rooms from: $349 ✉ 5216 Ballard Ave. NW, Ballard ☎ 206/789–5012 ⊕ www.hotelballardseattle.com 18 rooms, 11 suites No meals.*

Nightlife

On weekends, Ballard rivals Capitol Hill in popularity. There are at least a dozen bars and restaurants on Ballard Avenue alone. The neighborhood has quickly evolved from a few pubs full of old salts to a bustling nightlife district that has equal parts average-Joe bars, trendy haunts, music spots, wine bars, and Belltown-style lounges.

BARS AND LOUNGES

The Ballard Smoke Shop Restaurant and Lounge

BARS/PUBS | One of the last of the classic Ballard dives still standing. It once seemed fishermen started drinking here before the day dawned, though now it's just as likely to be hipsters drinking cold cans of Rainier beer and asking for pull tabs. But it's still the same old servers with the same studied nonchalance bringing the drinks and preserving the quintessential dive bar ambience. *✉ 5439 Ballard Ave. NW, Ballard ☎ 206/784–6611 ⊕ www.ballardsmokeshop.com.*

Barnacle

BARS/PUBS | Part of the Sea Creatures mini-empire led by chef Renee Erickson, Barnacle is a narrow bar adjacent to the popular Walrus and Carpenter restaurant. It invariably collects people waiting for tables, but with a beautiful copper-topped bar, tiled walls, and plates of oysters, cured meats, and fish to go with the apertivos, it's a great place to drink and snack even if you aren't planning to dine next door. *✉ 4743 Ballard Ave. NW, Ballard ☎ 206/706–3379 ⊕ www.thebarnaclebar.com.*

Bastille

BARS/PUBS | This French bistro is one of the neighborhood's most attractive spots to sip. First, there's the 45-foot zinc bar in the main dining room. Then there's the Back Bar, which is cozy, dimly lighted, with salvaged antique wood paneling and prints. On warm evenings, there's also the partially enclosed patio that looks out onto Ballard Avenue. Specialty cocktails are popular, and the wine list is extensive (though a bit overpriced). The bar menu lets you sample favorites like the lamb burger and *moules frites*. *✉ 5307 Ballard Ave. NW, Ballard ☎ 206/453–5014 ⊕ www.bastilleseattle.com.*

Essex

BARS/PUBS | Removed from bustling Ballard on a quiet street, Essex boasts craft cocktails, a handful of which are served on tap. The rotating cocktails often include house-made ingredients or are barrel aged. A solid wine list and local beer selections are also available, as are charcuterie plates, salads, snacks, desserts, and a burger. *✉ 1421 N.W. 70th St., Ballard ☎ 206/724–0471 ⊕ www.essexbarseattle.com.*

King's Hardware

BARS/PUBS | Brought to you by the owner of Linda's Tavern in Capitol Hill, King's Hardware has the same ironic rustic decor, the same great patio space, and the same cachet with hipsters. It also has great burgers. This place gets packed to the rafters on weekends—if you want the same scene with fewer crowds, go two doors down to Hattie's Hat, which was the reigning spot until King's showed up. *✉ 5225 Ballard Ave. NW, Ballard ☎ 206/782–0027 ⊕ www.kingsballard.com.*

The Noble Fir

BARS/PUBS | A rotating selection of great beer, cider, and wine and a truly varied crowd are just part of the appeal of this popular bar. Like many (most?) Seattleites, the husband-and-wife owners are outdoorsy—and it shows in the rustic-modern interior, which includes a library-like seating area stocked with large trail maps, as well as hundreds of travel books. The Noble Fir serves a few simple snacks, like cheese, charcuterie, fish, and vegan and vegetarian options, in case you feel like settling in and planning your next big adventure. ✉ *5316 Ballard Ave., Ballard* ☎ *206/420–7425* 🌐 *www.thenoblefir.com* ☞ *Closed Mon.-Tues.*

Ocho

BARS/PUBS | Blink and you'll miss it, and that would be a shame, because this tiny corner hot spot crafts some of the finest cocktails in town. Dimly lit and loud, Ocho only has a few tables and bar seats, and it fills up fast with a mixed crowd that flocks here for the drinks and top-notch Spanish tapas. Come summer, the slender sidewalk patio is an ideal spot for soaking up the sun and people-watching. ✉ *2325 N.W. Market St., Ballard* ☎ *206/784–0699.*

Rupee

BARS/PUBS | A short ride from the heart of Ballard's nightlife, Rupee offers an elegant, upscale drinking experience. Inspired by the owners' travels in Sri Lanka and India, the drinks are spice heavy and employ tropical fruit without the cloying sweetness of tiki (the food is also excellent). Rich colors and dark wood give the narrow space a transportive feel, but don't take too many people on the journey with you: there's no room for groups of more than about four, and waits can get long. ✉ *6307 24th Ave NW, Ballard* ☎ *206/397–3263* 🌐 *www.rupeeseattle.com.*

Stoneburner

BARS/PUBS | Settle into a leather, high-backed stool at the beautiful, wood bar at Stoneburner, the Mediterranean restaurant at Hotel Ballard, and enjoy classic cocktails, fizzes, sours, craft beer, and the full restaurant menu. Happy hour, 3–5 pm daily, is a great time to visit for great prices on the delicious pizzas coming out of the stone oven, but the bar stays open after the kitchen closes. ✉ *5214 Ballard Ave. NW, Seattle* ☎ *206/695–2051* 🌐 *www.stoneburnerseattle.com.*

Stoup

BREWPUBS/BEER GARDENS | Stoup is a great starting point for exploring Ballard's excellent craft-beer scene. A good-size tap room and patio area are family-friendly, and a rotating roster of food trucks provide eats to beer enthusiasts sipping staples like the Citra IPA and Mosaic Pale Ale, as well as new and experimental brews. Reuben's Brews, Peddler Brewing Company, and other brewery taprooms are close by for those looking to sample a variety. ✉ *1108 N.W. 52nd St., Ballard* ☎ *206/457–5524.*

MUSIC CLUBS

Conor Byrne Pub

MUSIC CLUBS | You might actually hear an Irish accent or two at Conor Byrne Pub, along with live folk, roots, alt-country, bluegrass, and traditional Irish music. There's live music almost every night of the week and great beer (including the obligatory Guinness on tap) at this laid-back pub. ✉ *1540 Ballard Ave. NW, Ballard* ☎ *206/784–3640* 🌐 *www.conorbyrnepub.com.*

Egan's Ballard Jam House

MUSIC CLUBS | A neighborhood spot rather than an overpriced tourist trap, this small jazz club and restaurant is devoted to music education for local high schoolers during the day and performances from local and touring acts in the evenings. ✉ *1707 N.W. Market St., Ballard* ☎ *206/789–1621* 🌐 *www.ballardjamhouse.com.*

Suds Appeal

Seattle loves its beer, and for good reason. America's ever-burgeoning craft-beer scene owes this city a big debt. In 1981, RedHook Ale Brewery became one of the country's first microbreweries, and Seattle's love affair with the good stuff hasn't faltered since.

Craft beer aficionados will find plenty of spots for sampling local brews as well as the best imports from around the country and the world; nearly every neighborhood worth its weight boasts a great beer bar or two, and brewery taprooms abound.

People here take beer every drop as seriously as oenophiles at a wine bar. If you have any questions, your bartender—or the person on the barstool next to you—is sure to have plenty of suggestions. Every May brings Seattle Beer Week (🌐 *seattlebeerweek.com*), with events all over town.

Sunset Tavern

MUSIC CLUBS | A Chinese restaurant-turned-bar, Sunset Tavern attracts just about everyone: punks, college students, postgrad nomads, neighborhood old-timers. They come for the ever-changing eclectic music acts. There's also a bar in front, Betty's Room, where you can grab a drink before the show. ✉ *5433 Ballard Ave. NW, Ballard* ☎ *206/784–4880* 🌐 *www.sunsettavern.com.*

Tractor Tavern

MUSIC CLUBS | Seattle's top spot for roots music and alt-country has a large, dimly lighted hall with all the right touches—wagon-wheel fixtures, exposed-brick walls, and a cheery staff. The sound system is outstanding. ✉ *5213 Ballard Ave. NW, Ballard* ☎ *206/789–3599* 🌐 *www.tractortavern.com.*

Shopping

Ballard is the shining star of the north end when it comes to shopping. Packed with cute home stores, great clothing boutiques, locally made gifts, and just about every genre of store imaginable, this neighborhood is a must-visit locale. The Sunday Farmers' Market is one of the best in the city, and it operates year-round for a dependably fun outing. Pick up smoked salmon, artisanal cheese, and vegan baked goods, and pop into the shops listed here if the rain starts.

Best shopping: Ballard Avenue between 22nd Avenue NW and 20th Avenue NW; N.E. Market Street between 20th and 24th Avenues.

APPAREL

Horseshoe

CLOTHING | "A little bit country, a little bit rock and roll," Horseshoe offers girlie Western wear and hipster styles in its Ballard digs. Comfy, sassy shirts and dresses are available from designers like Sanctuary, Trina Turk, and Amuse Society. Premium denim, cowboy boots, unique jewelry, and Little Barn Apothecary beauty products are among the wares. ✉ *5344 Ballard Ave. NW, Ballard* ☎ *206/547–9639* 🌐 *www.horseshoeseattle.com.*

KAVU

CLOTHING | Founded in the Pacific Northwest, KAVU's flagship store in Ballard is an outdoor shopping staple. Loudly printed fleece pullovers, thermal vests, and sturdy duffel bags are just a few items you'll find in this funky shop that feels like REI's cooler kid brother. ✉ *5419 Ballard Ave. NW, Ballard* ☎ *206/783–0060* 🌐 *www.kavu.com.*

Market Street Shoes

SHOES/LUGGAGE/LEATHER GOODS | One of the best all-around shoe stores in town, Market Street stocks so many styles from so many brands that you're likely to find something. Shoes for men, women, and children prioritize comfort, so you'll see sensible picks from Dansko, Born, Camper, Clarks, and Dr. Martens, but there are plenty of fun options by Fluevog, Tsubo, Think!, and Frye, as well. ✉ *2232 NW Market St., Ballard* ☎ *206/783–1670* 🌐 *www.marketstreetshoes.com.*

re-souL

SHOES/LUGGAGE/LEATHER GOODS | Stocking cool but comfortable shoes from Karhu, MOMA, Clae, Miz Mooz, and the like, this hip space offers a small selection of crazy fashionable boots, shoes, sneaks, and high heels. In keeping with the "little bit of everything" trend so popular with Seattle boutiques, re-souL also sells great jewelry pieces. They carry both men's and women's shoes and accessories. Everything is a bit pricey, but not excessively so. ✉ *5319 Ballard Ave. NW, Ballard* ☎ *206/789–7312* 🌐 *www.resoul.com.*

BOOKS AND MUSIC

Secret Garden Bookshop

BOOKS/STATIONERY | **FAMILY** | Named after the Francis Hodgson Burnett classic, this cozy shop has been delighting readers for more than four decades. A favorite of teachers, librarians, and parents, the store stocks a wide array of imaginative literature and thoughtful nonfiction for all ages; their children's section is particularly noteworthy. ✉ *2214 NW Market St., Ballard* ☎ *206/789–5006* 🌐 *www.secretgardenbooks.com.*

★ Sonic Boom

MUSIC STORES | An independent record store that is just the kind of place you would want to find on a Seattle street corner: clean, helpful, and organized, but just a little bit time-worn and too cool. You can count on them to have music from the latest indie darlings alongside the classics, which are on vinyl, CD, or even cassette tape. If they have one of their free in-store events when you're in the neighborhood, stop in for a listen and a unique musical experience. ✉ *2209 NW Market St., Ballard* ☎ *206/297–2666.*

HEALTH AND BEAUTY

Dandelion Botanical Company

GIFTS/SOUVENIRS | This high-end but down-to-earth boutique is one of the top apothecaries in the country. Its brick walls are lined with hundreds of jars of botanicals—bulk Chinese and ayurvedic herbs, teas, and cooking spices among them. Essential oils, bath salts, and aromatherapy products are also on hand, and most of the items they sell are organic or made of all-natural materials. ✉ *5424 Ballard Ave. NW, Ballard* ☎ *206/545–8892* 🌐 *www.dandelionbotanical.com.*

Habitude Salon, Day Spa and Gallery

SPA/BEAUTY | Plush furnishings and tropical scents relax you the moment you enter Habitude (in Ballard and Fremont). Indulge in a single treatment or in such packages as Beneath the Spring Thaw Falls (hydrating glow, massage, scalp treatment, and sauna). Other offerings include the Hot Rocks detox sauna, Rainforest steam shower, and canna-treatments with CBD. ✉ *2801 NW Market St., Ballard* ☎ *206/782–2898* 🌐 *www.habitude.com.*

MARKETS

Ballard Farmers Market

OUTDOOR/FLEA/GREEN MARKETS | Every Sunday, rain or shine, loads of vendors come to Ballard Avenue to set up colorful, welcoming tents and stands to sell produce and all types of local, artisanal foods, as well as gift items like candles and hats. Meanwhile, local buskers entertain foodies and families. ✉ *Ballard Ave., between 20th Ave. NW and 22nd Ave. NW, Ballard* 🌐 *www.sfmamarkets.com.*

The lively Ballard Farmers' Market happens every Sunday.

TOYS AND GIFTS

★ Baleen

JEWELRY/ACCESSORIES | This little independent studio makes some of the most stunning and yet affordable jewelery you can find. Impressively simple, each design still manages to be unique, giving them an elegant and modern edge. While the business has outgrown using the same space as both production and store, you can still stop by to shop all the hand-crafted, locally made necklaces, earrings, and bracelets in the light-filled corner shop. ✉ *6418 20th Ave. NW, Ballard* 🌐 *www.shopbaleen.com* ⏲ *Closed Mon.*

Clover

TOYS | **FAMILY** | What's easily the cutest children's store in town carries wonderful handcrafted wooden toys, European figurines, works by local artists, and a variety of swoon-worthy, perfectly crafted little clothes. Even shoppers without children will be smitten—it's hard to resist the vintage French Tintin posters, knit-wool cow dolls, and classic figurines. ✉ *5333 Ballard Ave. NW, Ballard* ☎ *206/782–0715* 🌐 *www.clovertoys.com.*

Venue

GIFTS/SOUVENIRS | Venue is the chic version of the Made In Washington stores: it stocks only goods made by local artists (some of whom have their studios in the sleek bilevel space), but you won't find any tacky souvenirs here. Watch the designers at work, chat with the staff (most are artists taking shifts), or just browse through artisanal chocolates, custom handbags, handmade soaps, baby wear, and colorful prints and mosaics. ✉ *5408 22nd Ave. NW, Ballard* ☎ *206/789–3335* 🌐 *www.venueballard.com.*

Activities

Ballard's waterfront location makes it a destination for active locals and visitors wanting to soak in the scenery while they play. Though the Burke-Gilman, a popular rail trail for bikes and pedestrians, has a "missing link" from Ballard to the east toward Fremont, the final section to the west runs from the Locks up to Golden Gardens Park. Grabbing one of Seattle's many bike share options, the ride out to the beach is quite pleasant. But for folks looking for something more organized, the neighborhood has plenty of options indoors and out to keep you occupied.

FISHING

Fish Finders Private Charters

FISHING | Fish Finders Private Charters takes small groups of two or more out on Puget Sound for guided salmon and ling cod fishing trips. The cost is $230 per person (excluding a fishing license). Morning trips last about six hours; afternoon trips are about four hours. All gear, bait, cleaning, and bags are included in the fee. ✉ *7001 Seaview Ave. NW, Ballard* ☎ *206/632–2611* 🌐 *www.fishingseattle.com.*

Seattle Fishing Charters

FISHING | Seattle Fishing Charters takes private groups out on six-person trolling boats to fish for salmon, bottom fish, and crab—depending on the season. The guided trips from Shilshole Bay Marina or Edmonds Marina last for six or seven hours. The price per person is $220. ✉ *7001 Seaview Ave., Ballard* ☎ *206/789–8245* 🌐 *www.seattle-fishing-charters.com.*

Seattle Architecture Foundation

WALKING TOURS | Seattle Architecture Foundation tours give fascinating history and context that build out a picture of how Seattle became the city that it now is. Tours cover specialized styles or neighborhoods, including Art Deco skyscrapers, hidden places, and Ballard's maritime history. ☎ *206/667–9184* 🌐 *seattlearchitecture.org/tours.*

ROCK CLIMBING

Stone Gardens Rock Gym

CLIMBING/MOUNTAINEERING | Beyond the trying-it-out phase? Head here and take a stab at the bouldering routes and top-rope faces. Although there's plenty to challenge the advanced climber, the mellow vibe is a big plus for families, part-timers, and the aspiring novice-to-intermediate crowd. The cost is $19; renting a full equipment package of shoes, harness, and chalk bag costs $13. Day passes include a free 5- to 10-minute orientation to bouldering and "Climbing 101" classes most evenings for $55 (includes a two-week pass). ✉ *2839 NW Market St., Ballard* ☎ *206/781–9828* 🌐 *www.stonegardens.com.*

WATER SPORTS

Ballard Kayak

KAYAKING | Get a new perspective on Seattle by exploring from the water with Ballard Kayak's kayak and paddleboard tours. They'll rent you a board or boat on your own, but it's worth joining one of their tours of Puget Sound, the nearby Locks, or the best bowls of clam chowder in the area for a fun, active experience (they also offer sea kayak lessons for folks in need of a bit more instruction). ✉ *Shilshole Bay Marina, W-dock, 7901 Seaview Ave. NW, Ballard* ✣ *Near the Corinthian Yacht Club* ☎ *206/494–3353* 🌐 *www.ballardkayak.com* ☞ *Open Spring to early Fall.*

Surf Ballard

KAYAKING | While nobody is doing any actual surfing on Shilshole Bay, this quaint surf shack carries everything you might need to surf, and also offers rentals for more appropriate water sports like kayaking and stand-up paddleboarding. They offer SUP lessons and even have an on-site stand-up paddleboard yoga school. They also have an outdoor shower to clean off and warm up after your paddle. You can (and should) book ahead on their website. ✉ *6300 Seaview Ave. NW, Ballard* ☎ *206/726–7878* 🌐 *www.surfballard.com.*

Chapter 11

WALLINGFORD AND GREEN LAKE

Updated by
Naomi Tomky

Sights	Restaurants	Hotels	Shopping	Nightlife
★★☆☆☆	★★★★☆	★☆☆☆☆	★★☆☆☆	★★★☆☆

NEIGHBORHOOD SNAPSHOT

GETTING HERE AND AROUND

Bus 62 connects Downtown to North 45th Street in Wallingford (the neighborhood's main drag) and continues north to the east (and main) entrance of Green Lake Park (get out at NE Ravenna Boulevard and Woodlawn Avenue NE). From Downtown it takes about a half hour to reach the lake; the trip between the lake and North 45th Street takes about 10 minutes. Route 44 connects Wallingford to the University District to the east and to Ballard to the west. Bus 45 skirts the northeast side of the lake and connects to Greenwood and the Husky Stadium light rail stop, while the Rapid Ride E runs on the west side, along Aurora Avenue North.

To reach Green Lake by car, take either Aurora Avenue North (Route 99) to West Green Lake Way or I–5 to 50th Street (go west back over the highway at that exit). There are parking lots at both Green Lake Park and Woodland Park; lots at the latter are generally less full. Wallingford is a five-minute drive from Green Lake—if there's no traffic.

QUICK BITES

Fainting Goat Gelato Sample gelato in seasonal flavors like honey lavender and fig vanilla. ✉ *1903 N 45th St., Wallingford* ☎ *206/327–9459* 🌐 *www.nuttysquirrel.com.*

Hiroki Hiroki makes wonderful Japanese desserts along with some standards like tiramisu. ✉ *2224 N 56th St., Seattle* ☎ *206/547–4128* 💳 *No credit cards.*

Molly Moon's Homemade Ice Cream Molly Moon's makes rich, delicious ice creams with local ingredients in flavors like balsamic strawberry and salted caramel. ✉ *1622 N 45th St., Wallingford* ☎ *206/547–5105* 🌐 *www.mollymoon.com* 💳 *No credit cards.*

Rancho Bravo Tacos Pork tacos are the favorite at this humble taco truck that has also now taken over a neighboring doughnut shop. ✉ *211 NE 45th St., between N Thackeray Pl. and N 2nd Ave., Seattle* ☎ *206/466–1693* 🌐 *www.ranchobravotacos.com* 💳 *No credit cards.*

PLANNING YOUR TIME

■ Green Lake is adjacent to Woodland Park Zoo. In summer, you could spend an entire day outdoors, touring the zoo, then strolling around the lake—or floating in a rented rowboat or paddleboat. The Tangletown area of Green Lake can be reached on foot (follow North 55th Street east to the "K" streets of Kenwood, Keystone, Kirkwood, and Kensington) and has a few great casual eateries. Some of the city's best chefs have put down roots in Wallingford, making the neighborhood a good place to end the day.

TOP REASONS TO GO

■ Go souvenir hunting at **Archie McPhee**, a shrine to irreverence. You'll find great Seattle-themed items here, like Tofu Mints and librarian and barista action figures, amid tons of assorted weirdness and fun *(See the Shopping listing)*.

■ Visit the "poem emporium"—**Open Books** is one of two poetry-only bookstores in the country.

■ Stroll or jog around **Green Lake's** loop. If your running shoes are a little ragged, stop at Super Jock 'n' Jill (7210 E Green Lake Drive N, 206/522–7711) for a new pair.

Wallingford and Green Lake are low-profile neighborhoods without much in the way of sights to see, but these are great spots for strolling, especially around the eponymous lake.

Wallingford

Sights

The laid-back neighborhood of Wallingford is directly east of Fremont—the boundaries actually blur quite a bit. There are several lovely parks, and residential streets are brimming with colorful Craftsman houses. The main drag, 45th Street NW, has an eclectic group of shops, from a gourmet beer store to a Hawaiian merchant, along with a few great coffeehouses and several notable restaurants.

In the 1920s, Wallingford was one of the city's most important neighborhoods. It went from forest and cow pasture (one of which, incidentally, hosted Seattle's first golf course for a very short time) to a densely populated neighborhood of 50,000 in less than two decades. The game changer was a trolley line from the University District to Fremont—once the tracks were laid, the bungalow-building frenzy started. Although the initial hoopla died down after a major commercial district on Stone Way never materialized, the neighborhood grew steadily, if quietly. It still holds the same sort of off-radar charm, with low-key restaurants from great chefs and an oddly impressive collection of Japanese restaurants. While it isn't on track to be anybody's culinary hot spot, it has plenty of places ready to pull out a chair and serve a good meal. That's basically Wallingford in a nutshell: welcoming, wonderful, and humble.

★ Gas Works Park

NATIONAL/STATE PARK | FAMILY | Far from being an eyesore, the hulking remains of an old 1907 gas plant actually lends quirky character to the otherwise open, hilly, 20-acre park. Get a great view of Downtown Seattle while seaplanes rise up from the south shore of Lake Union; the best vantage point is from the zodiac sculpture at the top of a very steep hill, so be sure to wear appropriate walking shoes. This is a great spot for couples and families alike; the enormous and recently remodeled playground has rope climbing structures, a variety of swings, and a padded floor. Crowds throng to picnic and enjoy outdoor summer concerts, movies, and the July 4th fireworks display over Lake Union. **■ TIP→ Gas Works can easily be reached on foot from Fremont Center, via the waterfront Burke-Gilman Trail.** ✉ *2101 N Northlake Way, at Meridian Ave. N (the north end of Lake Union), Wallingford.*

Restaurants

With everything from taco shops to ice cream, Trinidadian cuisine to prix-fixe dining, Wallingford has blossomed into a dining destination. James Beard (and *Iron Chef*) winner Maria Hines owns Tilth on 45th, a standout higher-end spot. With Kisaku as the anchor, this part of town has become something of a Japanese

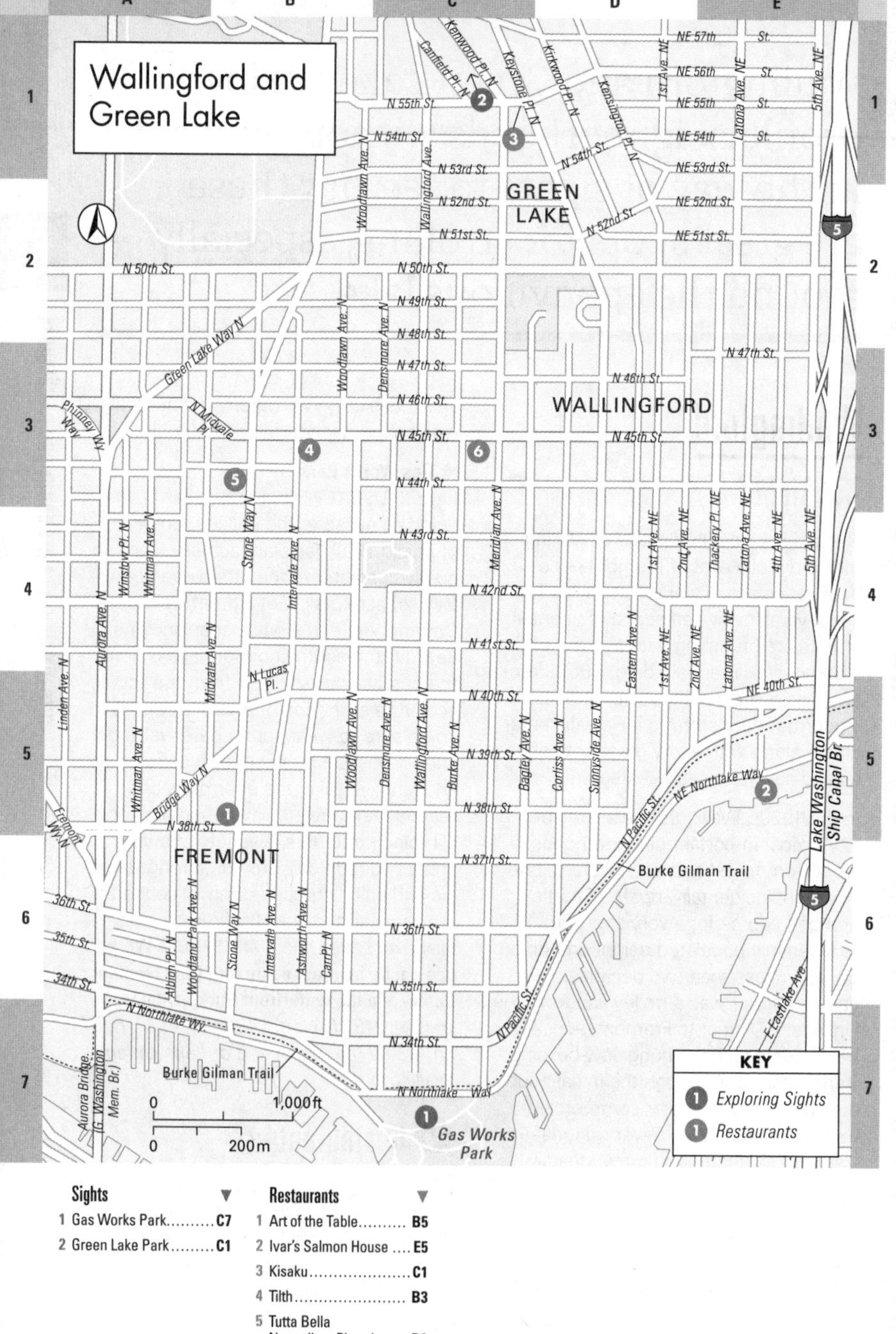

Sights

1 Gas Works Park.......... C7

2 Green Lake Park......... C1

Restaurants

1 Art of the Table.......... B5

2 Ivar's Salmon House E5

3 Kisaku..................... C1

4 Tilth........................ B3

5 Tutta Bella Neapolitan Pizzeria..... B3

6 Yoroshiku C3

Dining with Kids

Seattle is just as serious about its food as it is about ensuring that no visiting parent leaves town without knowing why. Here are some picks you and your kids will enjoy.

Café Flora, Capitol Hill. Local families love this vegetarian spot a short drive from the top of Capitol Hill—brunches are particularly fun.

Cafe Munir, Ballard. Later, this intimate, gorgeous spot turns romantic, but until about 7:30 pm, kids rule the roost, squealing with joy as they're allowed to eat hummus with their hands.

Delancey, Ballard. What kind of kid could turn down pizza this good? None, and neither can their parents, which is why this place stays packed with families.

Dough Zone Dumpling House, various locations. Consider the in-house dumpling makers live entertainment, and the oodles of noodles the perfect meal to keep kids happy.

Kidd Valley. Burgers, fries, shakes, and more in an indestructible fast-food restaurant that has branches in Queen Anne (on Queen Anne Avenue), Greenlake, and the University District.

Marination Ma Kai, West Seattle. Bright colors, fun food, and endless flavors of Hawaiian shave ice should keep the wee ones grinning.

Uneeda Burger, Fremont. A classic, casual burger joint that has as many options for grown-up tastes as it does for the little ones.

restaurant row. Look for sushi spots from cheap and decent to spectacular and ramen shops with deep, savory broths.

Art of the Table

$$$$ | MODERN AMERICAN | Small, pricey, but utterly unforgettable, the Art of the Table is a constantly changing tour de force where you're sure to experience an inspired meal. Fresh farmers' market finds are an absolute obsession here, and on any given night, diners might enjoy offerings from caramelized Brussels sprouts with pistachios, braised oxtail, and rockfish ceviche to manila clams with cauliflower over pasta, and rhubarb soup with crème fraîche. **Known for:** tasting menu; local ingredients. *Average main: $125 ✉ 3801 Stone Way N, Wallingford ☎ 206/282–0942 🌐 www.artofthetable.net ⏲ Closed Mon.–Tues. No lunch.*

Ivar's Salmon House

$$$$ | SEAFOOD | FAMILY | This long dining room facing Lake Union has original Northwest Indian artwork collected by the restaurant's namesake founder. It's touristy, often gimmicky, and always packed, but it's also great Seattle fun—a real institution in a building designed as a loose replica of a traditional longhouse. **Known for:** views; brunch buffet; salmon. *Average main: $36 ✉ 401 NE Northlake Way, Wallingford ☎ 206/632–0767 🌐 www.ivars.com.*

Tilth

$$$ | MODERN AMERICAN | A certified organic restaurant by the much-lauded Maria Hines, Tilth serves up wonderful, inventive dishes that can be had as small plates or full entrées—the mini–duck burgers, seasonally inspired risottos, and wild salmon deserve special mention, and there's a vegan menu as well. The Craftsman house on Wallingford's busy

Runners and bikers take in the views along the 2½-mile paved Green Lake Trail.

commercial strip has been lovingly spruced up with leaf-green paint and local artwork. **Known for:** small plates; organic ingredients; brunch. *$ Average main: $30 ✉ 1411 N 45th St., Wallingford ☎ 206/633–0801 🌐 www.chefmariahines.com ⏲ No lunch.*

Tutta Bella Neapolitan Pizzeria

$ | PIZZA | FAMILY | The Tutta Bella mini-chain serves authentic Neapolitan-style pizzas that are made with organic local and imported ingredients and baked in a wood-fired oven. Crusts are thin but wonderfully chewy, and sauces are light and tangy. **Known for:** Neapolitan pizzas; busy on weekends; family-friendly. *$ Average main: $15 ✉ 4411 Stone Way N, Wallingford ☎ 206/722–6400 🌐 www.tuttabella.com.*

★ Yoroshiku

$$ | JAPANESE | Wallingford's strip of Japanese food (for little rhyme or reason) holds sushi, grilled meats, and ramen for every budget, but for the best and most comprehensive experience head to this izakaya for drinks and snacks. Fresh local seafood meets Japanese technique and creative twists in dishes like sea urchin bruschetta with Parmesan cheese. **Known for:** ramen; drinking snacks; okonomiyaki (savory pancakes). *$ Average main: $18 ✉ 1911 N 45th St, Wallingford ☎ 206/547-4649 🌐 www.yoroshikuseattle.com ⏲ Closed Mon. No lunch.*

Nightlife

MUSIC CLUBS

SeaMonster Lounge

MUSIC CLUBS | With its low lighting and wall of very secluded booths, Sea-Monster makes the tame Wallingford neighborhood just a little bit sexier. The space is tiny—the "stage" is more like a holding pen sandwiched between the bar and a few tables—but that just makes it all the more intimate and friendly. The bar presents high-quality local acts, mainly of the jazz and funk variety. *✉ 2202 N. 45th St., Wallingford ☎ 206/992–1120 🌐 www.seamonsterlounge.com.*

Shopping

Wallingford offers a more grown-up selection of shopping than Fremont or Ballard. You won't find trendy clothing boutiques here, but with a great selection of independent shops, specialty bookstores, fabulous gift-buying opportunities, and one of the best beer stores in the city, you're likely to have a fun afternoon poking through this neighborhood.

Best shopping: 45th Street between Stone Way and Meridian Avenue.

★ Archie McPhee
GIFTS/SOUVENIRS | If your life is missing a punching-nun puppet, an Edgar Allen Poe action figure, or a bacon-scented air freshener, there's hope. Leave your cares and woes at the door and step into a warehouse of the weird and wonderful. It's nearly impossible to feel bad while perusing stacks of armadillo handbags, demon rubber duckies, handerpants (don't ask), and homicidal unicorn play sets. Grab a cat-in-a-can to keep you company or leave with a dramatic chipmunk oil painting. You'll feel better. Trust us. ✉ *1300 N 45th St., Wallingford* ☎ *206/297–0240* 🌐 *www.archiemcphee-seattle.com.*

Bottleworks
WINE/SPIRITS | If you love microbrews, then make a pilgrimage to Bottleworks to peruse its massive collection. With 16 taps plus around 950 chilled varieties of malty goodness available, including seasonal varieties, vintage bottles, and global rarities, there's a beer for everyone here—as well as a good sampling of mead and cider. Try a few beers from the taps or bottles (with corkage fee) in their sit-down area, too. ✉ *1710 N 45th St., Wallingford* ☎ *206/633–2437* 🌐 *www.bottleworks.com.*

Wallingford Center
SHOPPING CENTERS/MALLS | In this quirky shopping center, a converted 1904 schoolhouse, there are 15 resident shops—most of them independent with the exception of Pharmaca, an integrative pharmacy with on-site naturopaths. From cupcakes to contemporary crafts and clothing, there's a lot on offer here. ✉ *1815 N 45th St., Wallingford* ☎ *206/547–7246* 🌐 *www.wallingford-center.com.*

Green Lake

The neighborhood of Green Lake surrounds the eponymous lake, which is 50,000 years old. It was formed by the Vashon Glacial Ice Sheet, which also gave Seattle, among other things, Puget Sound. Green Lake (the neighborhood) is a pleasant stroll. It has a few shops and eateries along the lake, and one standout B&B, if you're looking to be far from Downtown's busy streets.

Sights

Green Lake Park
BODY OF WATER | FAMILY | This beautiful 342-acre park is a favorite of Seattleites, who jog, bike, and walk their dogs along the 2½-mile paved path that surrounds the lake. Beaches on both the east and west sides (around 72nd Street) have lifeguards and swimming rafts. Canoes, kayaks, and paddleboats can be rented (seasonally) at Green Lake Boat Rental on the eastern side of the lake. There are also basketball and tennis courts and baseball and soccer fields. A first-rate play area includes a giant sandbox, swings, slides, and all the climbing equipment a child could ever dream of—and the wading pool is a perfect spot for tots to cool off (in summer, when the temp is above 70 degrees.) The park is generally packed, especially on weekends. And you'd better love dogs: the canine-to-human ratio here is just about even. Surrounding the park are lovely homes, plus a compact commercial district where you can grab snacks or

Native American Culture and Crafts

Looking at a map of the Seattle area, you're bound to encounter some Native American names. Enumclaw, for instance. Or Mukilteo, Puyallup, Snohomish, and Tukwila. They're legacies of the dozens of Native American tribes and nations that first occupied the region.

Seattle, in fact, is named after Chief Si'ahl, a leader of the Suquamish and Duwamish tribes. For many thousands of years, Native American tribes have called the Pacific Northwest home—from the salmon-packed waters of the Skagit River to the high country of the Cascade Mountains. The majority of these tribes were subgroups of the Coast Salish peoples, who historically inhabited the entire Puget Sound region from Olympia north to British Columbia.

Tribes residing in and around the Seattle area included Duwamish, Suquamish, Tulalip, Muckleshoot, and Snoqualmie. Each tribe developed complex cultural and artistic traditions, and a regional language—Lushootseed—allowed tribes to trade resources. Today, members of many Seattle-area tribes are keeping their traditions alive: basketry, weaving, and sculpture—including totems—are traditional artistic media of the Coast Salish, and all three arts are still vibrant today. Contemporary Salish artists work in several modern media as well, including painting, studio glass, and printmaking.

Two top activities for experiencing Native culture up close and personal are:

Burke Museum of Natural History and Culture On the campus of the University of Washington, the recently remodeled Burke Museum of Natural History and Culture houses thousands of Coast Salish artifacts and artworks. The museum's exhibits also feature artwork from farther-flung native tribes, including the Tlingit and Haida of British Columbia and southeast Alaska. ✉ *4300 15th Ave. NE, University District* ☎ *206/543–5590* 🌐 *www.burkemuseum.org.*

Tillicum Village Located on Blake Island, 8 miles west of Seattle in Puget Sound, Tillicum Village offers a combination salmon bake and Native American stage show. Most visitors to the island travel aboard an Argosy Cruise ship; the 4½-hour tours are offered on Saturdays from April through September and more days in the heart of summer. Tours depart from Pier 54 on the Seattle waterfront. ✉ *Seattle* ☎ *206/622–8687* 🌐 *www.argosycruises.com/tillicum-village* 🎫 *$79.95.*

Coast Salish arts and crafts can be found in many museums and galleries around Seattle. Some favorite sites for shopping include:

Seattle Art Museum Store (✉ *1300 1st Ave., Downtown* ☎ *206/654–3100* 🌐 *www.seattleartmuseum.org*)

Steinbrueck Native Gallery (✉ *2030 Western Ave., Belltown* ☎ *206/441–3821* 🌐 *www.steinbruecknativegallery.com*)

Stonington Gallery (✉ *119 S Jackson St., Pioneer Square* ☎ *206/405–4040* 🌐 *www.stoningtongallery.com*)

Eighth Generation (✉ *93 Pike St, #103* ☎ *206/430–6233* 🌐 *www.eighthgeneration.com*)

dinner after your walk. ✉ *7201 E Green Lake Dr. N, Green Lake* ☎ *206/684–4075 general info, 206/527–0171 Greenlake Boat Rental* 🌐 *www.seattle.gov/parks/find/parks/green-lake-park.*

A Good Combo

A trip to Woodland Park Zoo (on the border of Phinney Ridge and Green Lake), a stroll around (or boat ride on) adjacent Green Lake, and then exploring Wallingford's main drag (45th Avenue NW) is a great way to spend a sunny day. Or instead of Wallingford, you could drive to Ballard and peruse its many shops and restaurants.

Restaurants

Kisaku

$$$ | JAPANESE | An outstanding sushi restaurant quietly nestled in Green Lake brings diners in droves. Fresh sushi is the mainstay, along with signature rolls such as the Green Lake variety, with salmon, flying fish eggs, asparagus, avocado, and marinated seaweed, or the Wallingford, with yellowtail, green onion, cucumber, radish, sprouts, and flying fish eggs. **Known for:** omakase (chef's menu); family-friendly; reservations highly recommended. *Average main: $28* ✉ *2101 N 55th St., Green Lake* ☎ *206/545–9050* 🌐 *www.kisaku.com* *No lunch Sun.*

Nightlife

Green Lake is mostly residential neighborhood with a few worth-a-visit options if you happen to be in the vicinity.

BARS AND LOUNGES

Über Tavern

BARS/PUBS | At what many serious aficionados claim may be one of the best beer bars on the planet, there's a constantly changing lineup of drafts—everything from Belgian imports to hop-heavy California DIPAs (double IPAs)—as well as a big list of bottles from around the globe. A digital menu shows what's on tap (and what's almost out) and there are Scrabble and checkerboards built into the bar tables—perfect for lazy afternoons. Über doesn't offer food, but you're free to order from a stack of takeout menus. ✉ *7517 Aurora Ave. N, Green Lake* ☎ *206/782–2337* 🌐 *www.uberbier.com.*

MUSIC CLUBS

The Little Red Hen

MUSIC CLUBS | Bring your cowboy boots and hats to this honky-tonk, which is inexplicably located in one of Seattle's most gentrified and generic neighborhoods. Live country bands take the stage most nights; there are free country- and line-dancing classes on Sunday, Monday, and Tuesday nights. Don't expect anything fancy—this place has not been sanitized for tourists. ✉ *7115 Woodlawn Ave. NE, Green Lake* ☎ *206/522–1168* 🌐 *www.littleredhen.com.*

Performing Arts

★ Seattle Public Theater

THEATER | In a 1927 bathhouse built for swimmers to change in, Seattle Public Theater brings five shows a year to an intimate stage. Beloved by locals for its humorous, ground-breaking, and unique choices, this tiny company puts on performances worth scheduling a day around. ✉ *7312 West Green Lake Dr N, Green Lake* ☎ *206/524–1300* 🌐 *www.seattlepublictheater.org.*

★ Green Lake Boathouse

BOATING | This shop is the source for canoes, paddleboats, sailboats, kayaks, stand-up paddleboards, and rowboats to take out on Green Lake's calm waters. On beautiful summer afternoons, however, be prepared to spend most of your time dealing with traffic, both in the parking lot and on the water. Fees are $24 an hour for paddleboats, single kayaks, rowboats, and stand-up paddleboards, $30 an hour for sailboats. Don't confuse this place with the Green Lake Small Craft Center, which offers sailing programs but no rentals. Golfing is available in the summer as well. ■ **TIP→ Rent before noon to get the "Happy Hour" rate of $16.** ✉ *7351 E Green Lake Dr. N, Green Lake* ☎ *206/527–0171* 🌐 *www.greenlakeboatrentals.net.*

Chapter 12

UNIVERSITY DISTRICT

Updated by
Naomi Tomky

Sights ★★☆☆☆ | Restaurants ★★★☆☆ | Hotels ★★★☆☆ | Shopping ★☆☆☆☆ | Nightlife ★★☆☆☆

NEIGHBORHOOD SNAPSHOT

GETTING HERE AND AROUND

A quick light-rail ride takes you from Downtown or Capitol Hill to the Link light-rail underground station next to Husky Stadium. From there it's a 25-minute walk to the heart of the area, or a quick ride on the 73 bus. Driving is the easiest solution; unless you hit traffic, taking I–5 north to 45th Street takes only 10 minutes from Downtown.

Bus 43, which you can catch Downtown along Pike Street, takes a pleasant route through Capitol Hill, over the Montlake Bridge, and stops on the western side of the campus in front of the Henry Art Gallery.

Getting around the U-District is fairly easy. The major action happens on "The Ave" (University Way NE), between 42nd and 50th Streets. Getting to the other northern neighborhoods of Wallingford, Fremont, and Ballard is easy, too. The only thing not convenient is the University Village shopping center, which is a long walk.

TOP REASONS TO GO

See the **Red Square,** UW's main plaza, named for its brick paving. Stop here for views of college life and, on sunny days, Mt. Rainier (it's also one of the best places to spot spring's fleeting cherry-blossom bloom). Then check out the well-curated exhibits at the **Henry Art Gallery.**

Paddle around **Portage Bay** from Agua Verde Café & Paddle Club. They can set you up with a kayak—and a margarita and Mexican grub when you return.

Make a detour to the **Center for Urban Horticulture,** which is across the street from outdoor shopping center **University Village,** on the shores of Lake Washington, for a relaxing stroll, bird-watching, or an evening picnic.

QUICK BITES

■ **Aladdin Falafel Corner** Lamb gyros, falafel sandwiches, and hummus platters are all excellent here. ✉ *4541 University Way NE, University District* ☎ *206/548–9539.*

■ **Café Allegro** This rustic, brick-walled cafe is Seattle's oldest espresso bar. ✉ *4214 University Way NE, University District* ☎ *206/633–3030* 🌐 *www.seattleallegro.com.*

■ **Guanaco's Tacos Pupusería** Try the fried plantains and *pupusas* (corn pancakes stuffed with meats, veggies, or beans). ✉ *4106 Brooklyn Ave. NE, Suite 102, University District* ☎ *206/547–2369* 🌐 *guanacostacos.weebly.com.*

■ **Portage Bay Cafe** Portage Bay Cafe serves organic and sustainable breakfast, brunch, and lunch. ✉ *4130 Roosevelt Way NE, University District* ☎ *206/547–8230* 🌐 *www.portagebaycafe.com.*

The U-District, as everyone calls it, is the neighborhood surrounding the University of Washington (UW or "U-Dub" to locals). The campus is extraordinarily beautiful (especially in springtime, when the cherry blossoms are flowering), and the Henry Art Gallery, on its western edge, is one of the city's best small museums. Beyond that, the appeal of the neighborhood lies in its variety of cheap, delicious international cuisine, its proximity to the waters of Portage and Union Bays and Lake Washington, and its youthful energy.

The U-District isn't everyone's cup of chai. Almost all businesses are geared toward students, and the area has its own transient population. The area often feels like it's separate from the city—and that's no accident. The university was founded in 1861 and was constructed on newly clear-cut land long before there were any convenient ways to get to the city that was growing Downtown. More so than any other northern neighborhood, the U-District had to be self-sufficient, even though the light rail now links the neighborhood with Capitol Hill and Downtown. Residents don't even have to travel to Downtown to get their shopping done: they have their own upscale megamall, University Village ("U Village"), an elegant outdoor shopping center with an Apple store, chain stores (including H&M, Gap, Eddie Bauer, Crate & Barrel, Room & Board, and Banana Republic), as well as restaurants, boutiques, and two large grocery stores. The Burke-Gilman Trail, Magnuson Park, and the UW Botanic Gardens Center for Urban Horticulture offer scenic detours.

Sights

Burke Museum of Natural History and Culture

MUSEUM | FAMILY | Founded in 1885, the Burke is the state's oldest museum but just underwent a huge redesign and got a new building in 2019. It features exhibits that survey the natural history of the Pacific Northwest, but also a behind-the-scenes look at how museums work, with its open doors and windows.

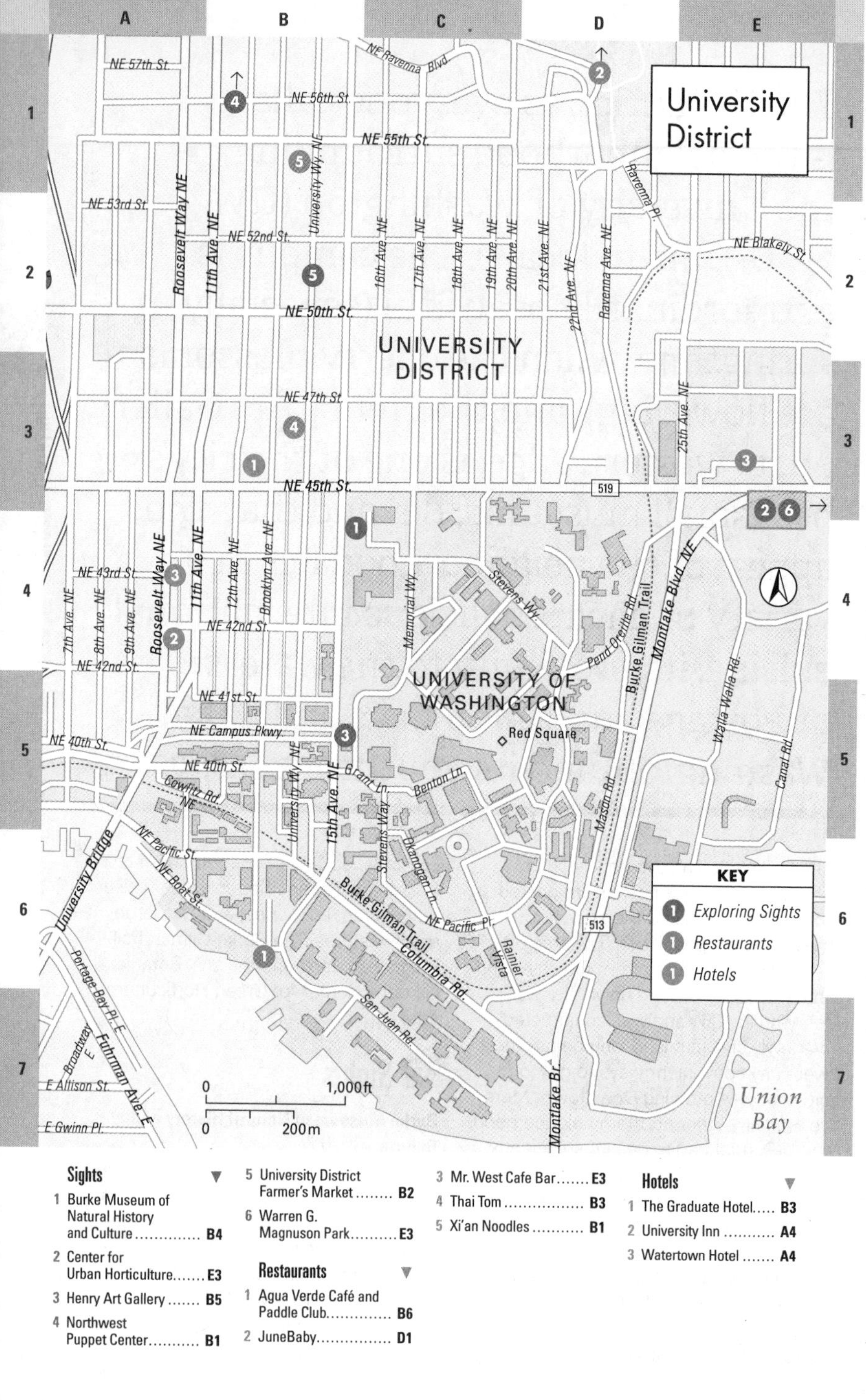

Sights ▼

1 Burke Museum of Natural History and Culture **B4**

2 Center for Urban Horticulture....... **E3**

3 Henry Art Gallery **B5**

4 Northwest Puppet Center........... **B1**

5 University District Farmer's Market **B2**

6 Warren G. Magnuson Park.......... **E3**

Restaurants ▼

1 Agua Verde Café and Paddle Club............. **B6**

2 JuneBaby................. **D1**

3 Mr. West Cafe Bar....... **E3**

4 Thai Tom **B3**

5 Xi'an Noodles **B1**

Hotels ▼

1 The Graduate Hotel..... **B3**

2 University Inn **A4**

3 Watertown Hotel **A4**

Fascinating exhibits fill the Burke Museum of Natural History and Culture.

Highlights include artifacts from Washington's 35 Native American tribes, dinosaur skeletons, and dioramas depicting the traditions of Pacific Rim cultures. An adjacent ethnobotanical garden is planted with species that were important to the region's Native American communities, and the Native-owned cafe serves fry bread and indigenous foods. Check out the schedule for family events and adult classes. ✉ *University of Washington campus, 17th Ave. NE and NE 45th St., University District* ☎ *206/543–5590* 🌐 *www.burkemuseum.org* 🎟 *$22, free 1st Thurs. of month.*

Center for Urban Horticulture

GARDEN | Nestled between a residential lakefront neighborhood to the east and the University of Washington campus to the west are the 16-acre landscaped gardens of the Center for Urban Horticulture and the 74-acre Union Bay Natural Area, part of the University of Washington Botanic Gardens. Inside the Center is the Elisabeth C. Miller Library, open to the public and home to 15,000 books and 500 periodicals on gardening techniques. The Union Bay Natural Area serves as an outdoor laboratory for UW research with some of the best bird-watching in the city. With a ¾-mile loop gravel trail, it's also a terrific place for a walk or a jog, and on a nice day, the views of Mt. Rainier and the surrounding waterfront are simply divine. From the U-District, head east on NE 45th Street and take a right onto Mary Gates Drive. ✉ *3501 NE 41st St., University District* ☎ *206/543–8616* 🌐 *www.botanicgardens.uw.edu/center-for-urban-horticulture* 🕓 *Closed Sun.*

★ Henry Art Gallery

MUSEUM | This large gallery is perhaps the best reason to take a side trip to the U-District and consistently presents sophisticated and thought-provoking contemporary work. Exhibits pull from many different genres and include mixed media, photography, and paintings. Richard C. Elliott used more than 21,500 bicycle and truck reflectors of different colors and sizes in his paintings that fit into the sculpture alcoves on the exterior walls of the museum; in another permanent installation, *Light Reign*, a "Skyspace" from artist James Turrell, an elliptical chamber allows visitors to view the sky. More than a few people have used this as a meditation spot; at night the chamber is illuminated by thousands of LED lights. ✉ *University of Washington campus, 15th Ave. NE and NE 41st St., University District* ☎ *206/543–2280* 🌐 *www.henryart.org* 🎟 *$10* ⏲ *Closed Mon. and Tues.*

Northwest Puppet Center
MUSEUM | FAMILY | In a renovated church in the Maple Leaf neighborhood, the only puppet center in the Northwest highlights the renowned marionettes of the Carter family, professional puppeteers trained by masters from Italy, Romania, and China. For their talents they have received a Fulbright Award and a UNIMA/USA Citation of Excellence, the highest award in American puppet theater. New museum exhibits are curated about every six months and may focus on a particular tradition, technique, or historic period. Past exhibits have included "Puppetry from Around the World" and "Cheering up the Great Depression: Puppetry & the WPA." Performances are open to the public on weekends. Recent shows include *Rapunzel, Puss in Boots,* and *Aladdin and the Wonderful Lamp.* The museum is open before and after shows, or by appointment. ✉ *9123 15th Ave. NE, University District* ✣ *Take I-5 north, Exit 171 to Lake City Way, turn left on 15th Ave. NE and continue to 92nd St.* ☎ *206/523–2579* 🌐 *www.nwpuppet.org* 🎟 *Museum is free, performance ticket prices vary; call ahead to reserve.*

★ **University District Farmers' Market**
MARKET | Seattle's largest "farmers only" market (no crafts, imports, or flea-market finds) operates year-round on Saturday from 9 am to 2 pm in the heart of the U-District, rain or shine. With more than 50 Washington State farmers participating, you'll find a great selection of produce, baked goods, preserves, flowers, cheese, soups, pies, wines, pasta, and handmade chocolates. ✉ *University Way NE between NE 50th and 52nd Sts., University District* 🌐 *seattlefarmersmarkets.org/markets/u-district.*

A Good Combo 

The Henry Art Gallery is well worth the trip. Stroll around the UW campus in the morning, especially if you happen to visit during the spring when the school's many cherry blossom trees are blooming. Then pay a visit to the Henry when it opens at 11 am, followed by spicy Xi'an noodles or Thai curry for lunch on The Ave—the U-District's main drag. If you still have energy, stroll from there to the Montlake Bridge; part of your walk can be along the Burke Gilman Trail. The bridge is a fun place to watch passing boats and kayakers in summer.

Warren G. Magnuson Park
NATIONAL/STATE PARK | FAMILY | Also called Sand Point–Magnuson Park and, most often, simply Magnuson Park, this 350-acre park northeast of the University District was once an active naval air base. Evidence of the park's roots are on full (if somewhat decrepit) display, with barracks and hangars in various stages of use and upkeep. Keep your focus on the areas toward the lake, as the paved trails are wonderful for cycling, jogging, or pushing a stroller. Leashed dogs are welcome on the trails; a gigantic off-leash area includes one of the few public beaches where pooches can swim. Farther south, on the mile-long shore, there's a swimming beach, a seasonal wading pool, and a boat launch. Innovative art is threaded through the grounds, including *Fin Art* (made from submarine

Mr. West serves both fancy coffee and fancy cocktails.

fins, on Kite Hill) and "Straight Shot," allowing visitors to experience what a surveyor does. A fabulous playground engages little ones near the north end. To get here from the U-District, you can follow 45th Street northeast past the University Village shopping center until it turns into Sand Point Way, and then follow Sand Point until you reach the park. If you're coming from Downtown, take I–5 to the 65th Street exit and head east on 65th until you reach the park. Note that traffic around University Village is usually pretty slow, especially on weekends. ✉ *Park entrance, 6500 Sand Point Way NE, Sand Point* ☎ *206/684–4946* 🌐 *www.seattle.gov/parks/magnuson.*

Restaurants

The "U-District" is great for cheap eats from around the world but falls short on fine dining. It's worth strolling up and down The Ave (University Way NE) to see if anything beckons to you before settling on a spot. There are some popular brunch spots scattered about, too.

Agua Verde Café and Paddle Club

$ | MEXICAN | Baja California Mexican cuisine and a laid-back vibe define this casual spot that's done up in bright, beachy colors and has a lively deck come summertime. Regulars swear by the fresh fish tacos and *mangodillas* (quesadillas with mango and poblano chilies). **Known for:** views; fish tacos; margaritas. 💲 *Average main: $14* ✉ *1303 N.E. Boat St., University District* ☎ *206/545–8570* 🌐 *www.aguaverdecafe.com.*

★ JuneBaby

$$$ | SOUTHERN | Southern-born chef Edouardo Jordan deftly translates the traditions of his homeland into the ingredients of his hometown using his fine-dining training. Fried pig ears come with anise hyssop honey, and charred okra with sorghum-chili vinaigrette. **Known for:** biscuits; Southern cuisine; smoked carrots. 💲 *Average main: $25* ✉ *2122 NE 65th St, University District* ☎ *206/257–4470* 🌐 *www.junebabysseattle.com* 🕒 *Closed Mon.–Tues. No lunch Wed.-Fri.*

Mr. West Cafe Bar

$ | **AMERICAN** | An elegant but ultimately casual all-day café suits the needs of upscale U-Village perfectly. Whether you're looking to recharge with a fancy coffee drink, bubbles, or a cocktail, this spot has just the thing. **Known for:** avocado toast; good wine list; cereal milk cappuccino. *Ⓢ Average main: $12 ✉ 2685 NE Village Lane, University District ☎ 206/900–9378 🌐 www.mrwestcafebar.com.*

Thai Tom

$ | **THAI** | This might be the cheapest Thai restaurant in town, but rock-bottom prices aren't the only reason this place is always packed—the food is delicious, authentic, and spicy (two stars is usually pretty hot). But be forewarned: the is a hole-in-the-wall if there ever was one. *Ⓢ Average main: $10 ✉ 4543 University Ave., University District ☎ 206/548–9548.*

Xi'an Noodles

$ | **CHINESE** | Diners here sometimes find their meal interrupted by the soft thumping noise for which the chewy, ropy noodles the restaurant specializes in are named. *Biang biang* noodles are made by slapping strands of dough against the hard counter, which elongates them without toughening the dough. The wide strands come in a number of dishes, along with other preparations from the eponymous city. **Known for:** hand-pulled noodles; spicy food. *Ⓢ Average main: $10 ✉ 5259 University Way NE, University District ☎ 206/522–8888 🌐 www.xiannoodles.com.*

Hotels

Seattleites have a love-hate relationship with the University District. On one hand, you'll find some reasonably priced, decent accommodations here, thanks to the many parents visiting their kids at the University of Washington (UW). On the other hand, the areas closest to the main drag, University Avenue (the Ave) can feel both college-y and gritty. One plus of staying close to the Ave is the plethora of cheap ethnic restaurants. You'll also enjoy access to the city's largest farmers' market on Saturdays as well as the UW's Henry Art Gallery and the Burke Museum. The area on the other side of the campus, closest to the upscale open-air mall University Village, is nicer and more residential but inconvenient to the rest of the city. In terms of location, the U-District hotels listed offer fairly quick commutes to both Downtown and Capitol Hill.

The Graduate Hotel

$$ | **HOTEL** | The 1931 building that began as the Edmond Meany Hotel finally got the upgrade it needed, reopening in late 2018 as the Graduate, designed to appeal to friends and family of students at the nearby University of Washington. **Pros:** modern decor; rooftop bar; large rooms. **Cons:** far from tourist sights; expensive parking; streetside rooms can be noisy. *Ⓢ Rooms from: $189 ✉ 4507 Brooklyn Avenue NE, University District ☎ 206/634–2000 🌐 www.graduateseattle.com ⇆ 154 rooms 🍴 No meals.*

University Inn

$$ | **HOTEL** | **FAMILY** | This impeccably maintained inn (a sister property to the Watertown Hotel) has earned its popularity by steadfastly offering clean, friendly lodging in a city where the price for a room is liable to cause sticker shock. **Pros:** great value; free shuttle and parking; friendly staff. **Cons:** not as nice as the Watertown next door; pool is a little cold; not close to many tourist attractions. *Ⓢ Rooms from: $199 ✉ 4140 Roosevelt Way NE, University District ☎ 206/632–5055, 800/733–3855 🌐 www.universityinnseattle.com ⇆ 102 rooms 🍴 Free Breakfast.*

Watertown Hotel

$$ | **HOTEL** | **FAMILY** | Assorted amenities make this University District hotel a great deal, including inexpensive parking ($20), free Wi-Fi, an afternoon reception with coffee and treats, and complimentary

shuttle service to Downtown, area attractions, and hospitals. **Pros:** free shuttle service; complimentary bikes and laundry; on-site café; pool access. **Cons:** street noise in some rooms; panhandlers in the area; not as close to attractions as other hotels. *Rooms from: $209* ✉ *4242 Roosevelt Way NE, University District* ☎ *206/826–4242* 🌐 *www.watertownseattle.com* *100 rooms* *No meals.*

The U-District doesn't offer much of interest unless you're taking your new fake ID out for a spin. With the exception of the Mountaineering Club at the Graduate Hotel, most U-District haunts fall firmly in the pub category and are filled with students on weekends. If you don't want to drink, you'll have better luck: the neighborhood has a comedy club, a few theater troupes, and several good movie theaters, including beloved art house Grand Illusion Cinema *(Film)*.

BARS AND LOUNGES

Big Time Brewery

BARS/PUBS | With its neat brick walls, polished wood floors, and vintage memorabilia, Big Time Brewery is one of the best places in the U-District for a quiet beer away from the frenetic college scene. The brewery offers more than a dozen beers on tap, including cask ales. Skip the mediocre pub grub. ✉ *4133 University Way NE, University District* ☎ *206/545–4509* 🌐 *www.bigtimebrewery.com.*

Mountaineering Club

BARS/PUBS | It's all about the amazing view at this rooftop bar that crowns the art deco Graduate Hotel. Windows that stretch to the ceiling surround the exploration-themed inside, while the patio space extends the view from the 16th floor outside. In a neighborhood with few tall buildings, this spot feels truly on top of the world. The drinks and food menus are concise and locally themed, but the bartenders can mix a good classic cocktail upon request. ✉ *4507 Brooklyn Ave NE, University District* ☎ *206/634–2000* 🌐 *www.themountaineeringclub.com.*

Supreme Bar

BARS/PUBS | This dimly lit pizza joint serves tasty frozen cocktails like the Cherry Coke slushie with spiced rum, amaretto, and amaro, or cocktails from the draft like the Husky-themed Long Island iced tea called the "Dawg Island." With cocktails that are a step above dive bar levels, and a much cleaner setting than the classic college pub, this spot is a sort of ironic take on the classic New York pizza joint bar. The pizza is very good and worth ordering, too. ✉ *4529 University Way, University District* 🌐 *www.supreme.bar.*

COMEDY CLUBS

Jet City Improv

COMEDY CLUBS | Seattle's best improv group fuses quick wit with music and games, and the audience often provides input on what the skits should be. Shows, which are all ages, are Thursday through Saturday at 7:30 pm, and Friday and Saturday at 10 pm. ✉ *5510 University Way, University District* ☎ *206/352–8291* 🌐 *www.jetcityimprov.com.*

Performing Arts

DANCE

Meany Hall for the Performing Arts

DANCE | National and international companies perform October through May at the University of Washington's Meany Hall. The emphasis is on modern and jazz dance. ✉ *4040 George Washington Lane NE, University District* ☎ *206/543–4880* 🌐 *www.meanycenter.org.*

FILM

The Grand Illusion Cinema

FILM | Seattle's longest-running independent movie house opened in a former dental office in 1968. Now it's an outstanding and unique home for independent and art film that feels as comfortable as a home theater. ✉ *1403 NE 50th St., University District* ☎ *206/523–3935* 🌐 *www.grandillusioncinema.org.*

READINGS AND LECTURES

University Book Store

READINGS/LECTURES | Free readings by best-selling authors and academics are the attraction here. The second-floor space is rich with book stacks, perfect for browsing afterward. Tickets are sometimes required, even for free events, but can go quickly. ✉ *4326 University Way NE, University District* ☎ *206/634–3400* 🌐 *www.ubookstore.com.*

THEATER

The Neptune Theatre

MUSIC | A cultural hub for the nearby University of Washington since opening in 1921, this striking Renaissance-revival theater is operated by STG Presents, which also runs the Paramount and Moore. The lineup—mostly music with a smattering of performing arts—includes a mix of emerging and well-established acts. ✉ *1303 NE 45th St., University District* ☎ *206/682–1414* 🌐 *www.stgpresents.org.*

Shopping

The "U-District" is packed with predictably college-friendly shopping—lots of used clothing, books, trendy footwear, and coffee. Meander down University Way (known to locals as "the Ave") to find the standout shops listed here, and stop at any of the numerous ethnic restaurants to refuel with cheap, decent eats.

Best shopping: University Way NE between NE 42nd and 47th streets, and University Village at 25th Avenue NE and NE 45th Street.

APPAREL

Buffalo Exchange

CLOTHING | This big, bright shop of new and recycled fashions is always crowded, and it takes time to browse the stuffed racks—but the rewards are great: the latest looks from all the trend-heavy outfitters along with one-of-a-kind leather jackets and vintage dresses. As with all thrift stores, the selection can be hit or miss, but you can find some pretty great deals on high-quality clothing. Check out their smaller store in Ballard on NW Market Street. ✉ *4530 University Way NE, University District* ☎ *206/545–0175* 🌐 *www.buffaloexchange.com.*

Crossroads Trading Co.

CLOTHING | Another spot on the used-clothing-store offerings on the Ave, Crossroads Trading Co. carries dependably cute and trendy clothes, bags, and accessories. Their buyers screen each item, so you won't be stuck poring over a rack of stained T-shirts. It's all clean, bright, and fun. A second location can be found on Broadway in Capitol Hill. ✉ *4300 University Way NE, University District* ☎ *206/632–3111* 🌐 *www.crossroadstrading.com.*

Red Light Vintage and Costume

CLOTHING | Nostalgia rules in this cavernous space filled with well-organized, good-quality (and sometimes pricey) vintage and new clothing. Fantasy outfits from decades past—complete with accessories—adorn the dressing rooms. It's a go-to spot for stylists and thrifters. Fun fact: this funky shop was one of the locations in Macklemore's "Thrift Shop" video. ✉ *4560 University Way NE, University District* ☎ *206/545–4044* 🌐 *www.redlightvintage.com.*

Woolly Mammoth

SHOES/LUGGAGE/LEATHER GOODS | A conservative take on Pacific Northwest footwear, this cozy shop offers brands like Birkenstock, Blundstone, Keens, and Toms. The friendly and knowledgeable staff will happily help customers with hard-to-fit feet and help find the perfect shoe. ✉ *4303 University Way NE, Seattle* ☎ *206/632–3254* 🌐 *www.woollymammothshoes.com.*

BOOKS, MOVIES, AND MUSIC

Pink Gorilla Games

BOOKS/STATIONERY | Primarily a video game store, here you'll find a huge variety of new and used classics and rare games for all consoles. They also carry toys and their own branded merchandise, which is pretty snazzy. The original location is in the International District. ✉ *4341 University Way NE, University District* ☎ *206/547–5790* 🌐 *www.pinkgorillagames.com.*

Scarecrow Video

BOOKS/STATIONERY | One of the biggest and best independent film shops in the country can be found on Roosevelt Way, where 100,000 rare, out-of-production, foreign, and mainstream films are available to rent and buy. Scarecrow's friendly staff are bona fide film geeks—pick their brains for suggestions, or stop by for one the shop's many in-store events. ✉ *5030 Roosevelt Way NE, University District* ☎ *206/524–8554* 🌐 *www.scarecrow.com.*

University Book Store

BOOKS/STATIONERY | Campus bookstores are usually rip-offs to be endured only by students clutching syllabi, but the University of Washington's store is a big exception to that rule. This enormous resource has a well-stocked general book department in addition to the requisite textbooks. Author events are scheduled all year long. Check out the bargain-book tables and the basement crammed with every art supply imaginable. They also carry a good selection of UW Husky gear if you need a souvenir and plenty of local gifts. ✉ *4326 University Way NE, University District* ☎ *206/634–3400* 🌐 *www.ubookstore.com.*

MALLS

University Village

SHOPPING CENTERS/MALLS | Make a beeline here for fabulous upscale shopping and good restaurants in a pretty, outdoor, tree- and fountain-laden shopping "village." You can have your fill of chains like Williams-Sonoma, Banana Republic, L'Occitane, Hanna Andersson, Crate & Barrel, Sephora, Aveda, Warby Parker, H&M, Madewell, Apple, Anthropologie, and Kiehl's. If you get enough of that at home, however, there are a few unique gems among the batch, including the excellent Village Maternity Store, candy wonderland the Confectionery, and local artsy chain Fireworks. Note that parking here can be tough, especially in the holiday season, and the atmosphere is slightly snobby. **■ TIP→ If you're in the mood to brave it, go immediately to one of the free parking garages, even if it means you have to walk farther.** ✉ *2623 NE University Village St., University District* ☎ *206/523–0622* 🌐 *www.uvillage.com.*

MARKETS

★ University District Market Farmers Market

OUTDOOR/FLEA/GREEN MARKETS | An understated elegance pervades this farmers' market, one of the oldest and biggest neighborhood markets in the city (and country). Come not just for the local fruits and vegetables, but also the loads of flowers and fine cheeses and meats, as well as a diverse food court with a wide selection of ready-to-eat foods from Salvadorean pupusas to Hungarian pastries. The market is held every Saturday, rain or shine, year-round, with more than 60 farmers and vendors setting up their goods along the closed-off street. ✉ *University Way between NE 50th and 52nd Sts., University District* 🌐 *www.seattlefarmersmarkets.org.*

 Activities

SPORTS

As you might imagine, in the University District, the University of Washington Huskies are a big deal. The Huskies are often at the top of the national rankings in football and both men's and women's soccer, basketball, rowing, volleyball, and much more. Other than football and men's basketball, these events are an affordable way to see future professional or Olympic athletes.

UW Huskies Basketball
BASKETBALL | Representing Seattle basketball in the Pac-12 Conference, the UW Huskies have been a consistent force for many years now. Along with several conference titles, the team has advanced to the NCAA tournament four times in a decade. The always-tough women's team—which also enjoys a very loyal (and loud) fan base—has advanced to the NCAA tournament several times in recent years as well. **Alaska Airlines Arena at Hec Edmundson Pavilion**, known locally as "Hec Ed," is where the UW's men's and women's basketball teams play. Tickets start at $15 ✉ *3870 Montlake Blvd. NE, University District* ☎ *206/543–2200* 🌐 *gohuskies.com.*

UW Huskies
FOOTBALL | The UW Huskies are almost as popular as the Seahawks. The Dawgs host some of the best teams in the nation at the U-shape Husky Stadium, which overlooks Lake Washington and the snow-capped Cascades mountains beyond it. For all but the biggest events, tickets can be found right up until game time for reasonable prices. ✉ *University of Washington, 3800 Montlake Blvd. NE, University District* ☎ *206/543–2200* 🌐 *gohuskies.com.*

WATER SPORTS

★ Agua Verde Cafe & Paddle Club
BOATING | Start out by renting a kayak and paddling along either the Lake Union shoreline, with its hodgepodge of funky-to-fabulous houseboats and dramatic Downtown vistas, or Union Bay on Lake Washington, with its marshes and cattails. Afterward, take in the lakefront as you wash down some Mexican food (halibut tacos, anyone?) with a margarita. Kayaks and stand-up paddleboards are available March through October and are rented by the hour—$20 for single kayaks, $26 for doubles, and $23 for SUPs. It pays to paddle midweek: if you go before early afternoon they offer weekday discounts. Email for winter paddling options or for a tour (tours@aguaverde.com). ✉ *1303 NE Boat St., University District* ☎ *206/545–8570* 🌐 *www.aguaverde.com.*

★ Waterfront Activities Center
BOATING | FAMILY | This center, located behind UW's Husky Stadium on Union Bay, rents three-person canoes and four-person rowboats for $12 an hour from May through October. You can tour the Lake Washington shoreline or take the Montlake Cut portion of the ship canal and explore Lake Union. You can also row to nearby Foster Island and visit the Washington Park Arboretum. They also rent kayaks for $16 an hour. ✉ *3710 Montlake Blvd. NE, University District* ☎ *206/543–9433* 🌐 *depts.washington.edu/ima.*

Chapter 13

WEST SEATTLE

Updated by
Naomi Tomky

Sights	Restaurants	Hotels	Shopping	Nightlife
★★☆☆☆	★★★☆☆	★☆☆☆☆	★★☆☆☆	★☆☆☆☆

NEIGHBORHOOD SNAPSHOT

GETTING HERE AND AROUND

Driving north or south on I–5 or south on Highway 99, take the West Seattle Bridge exit. The Harbor Avenue SW exit will take you to Alki Beach; SW Admiral Way will get you to California Avenue. By bus, take Rapid Ride C or bus 21, 55, 56, or 57 from Downtown; where they run down 3rd Avenue, and then cross the West Seattle Bridge. RapidRide C runs south on California Avenue SW, the 21 on 35th Avenue SW. Bus 55 then goes north to the Admiral District, and buses 56 and 57 continue on to the western edge of Alki Beach.

West Seattle is sprawling, and easiest to traverse by car. However, if you arrived by West Seattle Water Taxi (a passenger- and bicycle-only ferry that travels from Pier 50, along the waterfront Downtown, to Seacrest Park at the peninsula's eastern shore), you have several transit options: two shuttles run from the dock, 773 to the Alaska Junction and 775 to Alki and Admiral; or, you can hop on Bus 37, which travels around the peninsula almost as far as Lincoln Park.

QUICK BITES

Bakery Nouveau Bakery Nouveau has an exquisite selection of pastries, sandwiches, croissants, and baguettes. ✉ *4737 California Ave. SW, West Seattle* ☎ *206/923–0534* 🌐 *www.bakerynouveau.com* 💳 *No credit cards.*

Elliott Bay Brewing Company Elliott Bay Brewing Company serves craft beers and sandwiches and salads. ✉ *4720 California Ave. SW, Seattle* ☎ *206/932–8695* 🌐 *www.elliottbaybrewing.com* 💳 *No credit cards.*

Husky Deli Grab a handcrafted ice-cream cone at Husky Deli, a Seattle icon. ✉ *4721 California Ave. SW, West Seattle* ☎ *206/937–2810* 🌐 *www.husky-deli.com* 💳 *No credit cards.*

Marination Ma Kai Hawaiian- and Korean-inspired tacos and sandwiches served from a bright seafood shack. ✉ *Water Taxi Dock, 1660 Harbor Ave SW,, West Seattle* ☎ *206/328-8226.*

PLANNING YOUR TIME

- Head to Alki Beach and follow a path around the peninsula, enjoying the shore, Alki Point Lighthouse, and Lincoln Park. This is easiest to do by car. If you arrived by water taxi from Downtown, you can rent a bicycle by the terminal; the trip by bike takes roughly 35 minutes. California Avenue, which is in the center of the peninsula, can be your last stop, for sustenance.

TOP REASONS TO GO

- Any trip to West Seattle should include some time on Alki Beach, but be sure to make it around the western edge of the peninsula to see the **Alki Point** lighthouse and the spot where the first settlers landed.
- Dine on **California Avenue SW.** The stretch between SW Genesee and SW Edmonds streets has most of West Seattle's notable eateries.
- Cool off in the saltwater swimming pool at **Lincoln Park.**
- Catch the ferry to **Vashon Island** where you can visit orchards, farms, and wineries.
- Climb **Schurman Rock,** an outdoor climbing gym next to the West Seattle Golf Course.

Cross the bridge to West Seattle and it's another world altogether. Jutting out into Elliott Bay and Puget Sound, separated from the city by the Duwamish waterway, this out-of-the-way neighborhood covers most of the city's western peninsula—and, indeed, it has an identity of its own. In summer, throngs of people hang out at Alki Beach—Seattle's taste of California—while others head for the trails and playgrounds of Lincoln Park to the west.

The first white settlers parked their boat at Alki Point in 1851, planning to build a major city here until they discovered a deeper logging port at today's Pioneer Square. This makes West Seattle technically the city's oldest neighborhood. West Seattle is huge, and within it are more than a dozen neighborhoods. The two most-visited neighborhoods are Alki and West Seattle (Or Alaska) Junction—the former includes the shoreline and Alki Point; the Alki Point Lighthouse sits on the peninsula's northwest tip, a place for classic sunset views. The main shopping and dining areas line Alki Avenue, next to the beach, and California and Fauntleroy Avenues on the way to the ferry docks. The latter neighborhood, named for a spot where old streetcar lines crisscrossed, is the fastest-growing part of West Seattle and has its own thriving dining scene. It also has most of the area's good shopping and ArtsWest, a community theater and gallery.

The Admiral neighborhood, on the northern bluff, is less vital, but it does have an important old movie house that is one of the venues for the Seattle International Film Festival. Fauntleroy has two main attractions: the lovely Lincoln Park and a ferry terminal with service to Vashon Island and Southworth on the Kitsap Peninsula.

Sights

★ **Alki Point and Beach**

BEACH—SIGHT | **FAMILY** | In summer, this is as close to California as Seattle gets—and some hardy residents even swim in the cold, salty waters of Puget Sound here (water temperature ranges from 46°F to 56°F). This 2½-mile stretch of sand has views of the Seattle skyline and the Olympic Mountains, and the beachfront promenade is especially popular with skaters, joggers, strollers, and cyclists. Year-round, Seattleites come

Sights

1 Alki Point and Beach... **B3**

2 The Museum of Flight... **E7**

3 West Seattle Junction Murals **D6**

Restaurants

1 Harry's Beach House... **B3**

2 Il Nido **B3**

3 Ma'ono Fried Chicken & Whiskey............... **D6**

4 Marination Ma Kai....... **E2**

5 Salty's on Alki **E2**

Quick Bites

1 Bakery Nouveau........ **D6**

Parks Close to Alki

Lincoln Park Along the neighborhood's southwest edge, near the Fauntleroy ferry terminal, Lincoln Park sets acres of old forests, rocky beaches, waterfront trails, picnic tables, and a historic saltwater pool against views of Puget Sound. **■ TIP→ Colman Pool is a Seattle landmark you won't want to miss in summer. It's located on the water toward the north end of the park. Public swims often sell out on nice days, so get there early.** ✉ *8011 Fauntleroy Way SW, West Seattle* ☎ *206/684–4075 park, 206/684–7494 Colman pool* 🌐 *www.seattle.gov/parks* 🎟 *$6 for pool.*

Schmitz Preserve Park Marvel at the lustrous 53 acres of rugged forest at Schmitz Preserve, about 15 blocks east of Alki Point. The Preserve was donated to the city in pieces between 1908 and 1912, and features one of the remaining stands of old-growth forest in Seattle. ✉ *5551 SW Admiral Way, West Seattle* 🌐 *www.seattle.gov/parks.*

to build sand castles, beachcomb, and fly kites; in winter, storm-watchers come to see the crashing waves. Facilities include drinking water, grills, picnic tables, phones, and restrooms; restaurants line the street across from the beach. To get here from Downtown, take either Interstate 5 south or Highway 99 south to the West Seattle Bridge (keep an eye out, as this exit is easy to miss) and exit onto Harbor Avenue SW, turning right at the stoplight. Alki Point is the place where David Denny, John Low, and Lee Terry arrived in September 1851, ready to found a city. The Alki Point Lighthouse dates from 1913. One of 195 Lady Liberty replicas found around the country lives near the 2700 block of Alki Avenue SW. Miss Liberty (or Little Liberty) is a popular meeting point for beachfront picnics and dates. ✉ *1702 Alki Ave. SW, West Seattle.*

The Museum of Flight

MUSEUM | Boeing, the world's largest builder of aircrafts, was founded in Seattle in 1916. This facility at Boeing Field, between Downtown and Sea-Tac airport, houses one of the city's best museums, and it's especially fun for kids, who can climb in many of the aircraft and pretend to fly, make flight-related crafts, or attend special programs. The Red Barn, Boeing's original airplane factory, houses an exhibit on the history of flight. The Great Gallery, a dramatic structure designed by Ibsen Nelson, contains more than three dozen vintage airplanes. The Personal Courage Wing showcases World War I and World War II fighter planes, and the Charles Simonyi Space Gallery is home to the NASA Full Fuselage Space Shuttle Trainer. ✉ *9404 E Marginal Way S, Tukwila* ✥ *Take I–5 south to Exit 158, turn right on Marginal Way S* ☎ *206/764–5720* 🌐 *www.museumofflight.org* 🎟 *$25.*

West Seattle Junction Murals

PUBLIC ART | Located in Seattle's business district are 10 murals depicting local history. Some are trompe-l'œils, like the realistic 1918 street scene, "The Junction," which

Located in Seattle's business district are 10 murals depicting local history. Some are trompe-l'œils, like the realistic 1918 street scene, "The Junction," which ✉ *Along California Ave. SW and Fauntleroy Way SW, between 44th and 47th Aves., West Seattle.*

Restaurants

West Seattle is enough of a trek from Seattle's central neighborhoods that some restaurants have, historically, had a hard time filling their seats. Luckily, West Seattleites love to eat out, and a new culinary energy is taking hold, making even gourmands from Ballard make the trek. The real superstar here is Ma'ono (formerly known as Spring Hill), but plenty of other neighborhood joints are top-notch and inviting. A walk up and down California Avenue will offer up plenty of choices, and with the 2019 openings of Il Nido and Harry's Beach House, Alki has joined the competition for good eating.

Harry's Beach House

$$$ | **AMERICAN** | Harry's Beach House, where the breeze is always scented with saltwater, is a casual yet exciting restaurant that opened in an old coffee shop in 2019. Spacious, warmly lit, and friendly, it's the perfect place to enjoy a long brunch or a quick drink and a snack after a day on the beach. **Known for:** great decor; Harry's burger; excellent cocktails. *Average main: $26 2676 Alki Ave. SW, West Seattle Closed Mon.-Tues.*

Il Nido

$$$ | **ITALIAN** | Housed in a historic log cabin a block from Alki Beach, Il Nido (the nest) is the sibling to chef Mike Easton's wildly popular Il Corvo (the crow). Here, Easton expands on his pasta expertise with the same playful look at Italian culinary traditions. **Known for:** house-made pasta; reservations a must; Italian drinks. *Average main: $29 2717 61st Ave. SW, West Seattle 206/466–6265 www.ilnidoseattle.com Closed Sun.–Mon.*

Ma'ono Fried Chicken & Whiskey

$$ | **HAWAIIANKOREAN FUSION** | A quietly hip vibe pervades this culinary beacon in West Seattle, where the vast bar surrounds an open kitchen. Diners of all stripes relish the Hawaiian spin on fresh and high-quality Pacific Northwest bounty. **Known for:** fried chicken; whiskey. *Average main: $18 4437 California Ave. SW, West Seattle 206/935–1075 www.maonoseattle.com No lunch weekdays.*

★ **Marination Ma Kai**

$ | **HAWAIIAN** | The best view of Downtown comes at a most affordable price: the brightly colored Adirondack chairs outside this Korean-Hawaiian fish shack offer a panoramic view of the entire Downtown area. Inside, you'll find tacos filled with Korean beef or "sexy tofu," Spam slider sandwiches, and a classic fish-and-chips—served with kimchi tartar sauce. **Known for:** views; Spam sliders; shave ice. *Average main: $10 1660 Harbor Ave. SW, West Seattle 206/328–8226 www.marinationmobile.com Breakfast Fri.–Sun. only.*

Salty's on Alki

$$$$ | **SEAFOOD** | It's undeniably touristy, but the views simply can't be beat on a summer afternoon. Famed for its Sunday and holiday brunches and view of Seattle's skyline across the harbor, Salty's offers more in the way of quantity than quality—and sometimes a bit too much of its namesake ingredient—but it's a couple of steps up from the mainstream seafood chains. **Known for:** views; brunch buffet. *Average main: $45 1936 Harbor Ave. SW, just past port complex, West Seattle 206/937–1600 www.saltys.com.*

Coffee and Quick Bites

Bakery Nouveau

$ | **CAFÉ** | Widely considered one of the best bakeries in the city, Bakery Nouveau has perfected many things, including cakes, croissants, and tarts. Their chocolate cake, in particular, might make you swoon, though twice-baked almond croissants are so good you might think you're in France when you take a bite—and owner William Leaman did lead a U.S. team to victory in France's Coupe du

Did You Know?

Construction on the Alki Point Lighthouse, which is perched on the edge of Elliott Bay, was completed in 1913. It is a beloved West Seattle landmark.

"The Junction" depicts Seattle in 1918 and is one of ten notable murals in the area.

Monde de la Boulangerie. **Known for:** closes early (7 pm); delicious chocolate cake; great savory options for lunch. *Average main: $6* *4737 California Ave. SW, West Seattle* *206/923–0534* *www.bakerynouveau.com* *No dinner.*

Hotels

It may be a trek from the rest of the city, but West Seattle is a true gem, especially come summertime when its beachfront comes alive with walkers, volleyball enthusiasts, and cyclists. California Avenue has some fabulous dining and shopping. But do keep in mind that this neighborhood is removed from city center. There is one traditional hotel (The Grove *3512 SW Alaska Street*), but the best bet for spending a night on this side of town would be to look on home rental sites for Alki area options. For the budget-conscious, Camp Long offers 10 rustic cabins (think indoor camping) for $50 a night, March through October.

Nightlife

Despite the party atmosphere of Alki Beach, the best scene in the evening moves up the hill to various points along California Ave SW. A devotion to local beers, wine, ciders, and spirits runs through the neighborhood's mostly small, independent bars. Removed from the rest of the city by bridge, residents tend to stick close to home, so chat up your neighbor at the bar and you're likely to get an insider's view of the area.

BARS AND LOUNGES

New Luck Toy

BARS/PUBS | In the skeleton of a classic Chinese-American dive bar, chef Mark Fuller created his own spin on the genre. Under the low lights and a ceiling of red lanterns, bartenders serve pink guava palomas and passion fruit caipirinhas. There's Skee-ball, karaoke, and pinball, and a menu with twists on General Tso's chicken, and honey pecan prawns. *5905 California Ave. SW, West Seattle* *www.newlucktoy.bar.*

The Nook

BARS/PUBS | This Admiral cocktail bar is housed in a cozy old home and leans into that feeling with wingback chairs, mid-century couches, and antique lighting. It's a little like drinking at home, if you lived in a fancy old mansion with bartenders who turn out intriguing craft cocktails. Not far from Alki, it makes a great post-beach stop if you need to wait out rush hour before heading back Downtown. ✉ *West Seattle* ☎ *206/420–7414* 🌐 *www.thenookseattle.com.*

Shopping

For blocks and blocks along California Avenue SW around the Junction, independent, family-owned shops thrive, and boutiques sell quirky goods. If you're stopping for lunch nearby, definitely plan a postprandial stroll through the business district to do a little window shopping and maybe pick up a souvenir or two.

Click! Design That Fits

HOUSEHOLD ITEMS/FURNITURE | This design shop serves as a repository for all things eye-catching, including but not limited to art, jewelry, clothing, accessories, furniture, and knickknacks. Click! is welcoming and inclusive, not just in how they design the store and treat their customers, but also in the pricing, which makes this a great stop for an affordable gift or souvenir. ✉ *4540 California Ave. SW, West Seattle* ☎ *206/328–9252* 🌐 *www.clickdesignthatfits.com.*

Easy Street Records

MUSIC STORES | Opened in 1988 and still thriving, this record store will make you feel cool enough to wander the aisles and browse the new and used vinyl, even if you've never dropped a needle in your life. A staple of Seattle's music scene, it hosts free live in-store performances by bands you've probably heard of (Pearl Jam has played here), along with selling records, CDs, cassettes, and DVDs. Listening stations let you preview albums before purchasing, and the attached café offers the kind of breakfast you'd want after a night of rocking out. ✉ *4559 California Ave. SW, West Seattle* ☎ *206/938-3279* 🌐 *www.easystreetonline.com.*

Activities

GOLF

Interbay Family Golf Center

GOLF | About a 10-minute drive from Downtown, Interbay is the city's most convenient course. It has a wildly popular driving range ($10 for 70 balls, $12 for 108, $15 for 160), a 9-hole executive course ($17 on weekends, $15.25 on weekdays), and a miniature golf course ($9). The range and miniature golf course are open daily approximately 7 am–10 pm March–October and 7 am–9 pm November–February; the executive course is open dawn to dusk year-round. ✉ *2501 15th Ave. W, Magnolia* ☎ *206/285–2200* 🌐 *www.premiergc.com/interbay.*

West Seattle Golf Course

GOLF | This 18-hole course has a reputation for being tough but fair—and for some excellent views of Downtown. Greens fees are around $40 but are dynamic, depending on demand. The front 9 will challenge you, while the back 9 will reward you with views of Elliott Bay and the skyline. ✉ *4600 35th Ave. SW, West Seattle* ☎ *206/935–5187* 🌐 *www.seattlegolf.com.*

ROCK CLIMBING

Schurman Rock

CLIMBING/MOUNTAINEERING | The nation's first man-made climbing rock was designed in the 1930s by local climbing expert Clark Schurman. Generations of climbers have practiced here, from beginners to rescue teams to such legendary mountaineers as Jim Whittaker, the first American to conquer Mt. Everest. Don't expect something grandiose—the rock is only 25 feet high. It's open for climbs Tuesday–Saturday 10–6. Camp Long (where the park is located) also rents cabins for $50 a night. ✉ *Camp Long, 5200 35th Ave. SW, West Seattle* ☎ *206/684–7434* 🌐 *www.seattle.gov/parks/find/centers/camp-long/schurman-rock-at-camp-long.*

TOURS

Alki Kayak Tours & Adventure Center

BOATING | For a variety of daylong guided kayak outings—from a Seattle sunset sea kayak tour to an Alki Point lighthouse tour—led by experienced, fun staff, try this great outfitter in West Seattle. In addition to kayaks, you can also rent stand-up paddleboards, skates, and longboards here. Custom sea-kayaking adventures can be set up, too. To rent a kayak without a guide, you must be an experienced kayaker; otherwise, sign up for one of the fascinating guided outings (the popular sunset tour is $69 per person). ✉ *1660 Harbor Ave. SW, West Seattle* ☎ *206/953–0237* 🌐 *kayakalki.com.*

Chapter 14

THE EASTSIDE

Updated by
Naomi Tomky

Sights	Restaurants	Hotels	Shopping	Nightlife
★★☆☆☆	★★★☆☆	★★★☆☆	★★★★☆	★★★☆☆

NEIGHBORHOOD SNAPSHOT

PLANNING YOUR TIME

There are quite a few hotels on the Eastside, mainly in Bellevue, Kirkland, and Woodinville, but unless you're planning an overnight at Willows Lodge after touring Woodinville's wineries, it's not worth staying here. You won't save any money—Bellevue's hotels are just as pricey as and far less interesting than Seattle's—and no local would recommend a daily commute to or from Seattle, especially with the 520 bridge toll.

Instead, plan targeted day trips to the Eastside: a shopping or museum excursion to Bellevue followed by a meal at one of the city's hot restaurants; a winery or brewery crawl in Woodinville; or a day of hiking, biking, or horseback riding that ends in time to return to Seattle for a shower and a nap before a night out.

TOP REASONS TO GO

Explore **Tiger Mountain,** the most popular hiking (and biking) spot, just a hop, skip, and jump from Seattle, with a large trail system and something for everyone, from grandparents to trail runners.

Visit the **Bellevue Botanical Gardens,** a 36-acre park with colorful gardens and trails.

Splurge at the **Shops at the Bravern** in Bellevue. The city has many malls, but the Bravern is the ritziest—one-stop shopping for major international labels like Jimmy Choo, Ferragamo, and Hermès.

Sample Northwest wines in **Woodinville.** The town has more than 140 wineries, wine bars, and tasting rooms, most within easy reach of each other.

GETTING HERE AND AROUND

■ Buses run to the Eastside, but it's easier to get here by car, though you'll pay a toll crossing the 520 floating bridge, and rush-hour traffic is a nightmare. The other route to the Eastside is I–5 South to I–90 East. Bellevue is the most accessible town by public transportation (🌐 *www.soundtransit.org*). It has a bus hub that's within walking distance of the art museum. The most direct bus route to central Bellevue is the Bus 550. RapidRide B connects Bellevue, Kirkland, and Redmond.

QUICK BITES

■ **Noodle Boat** If you're craving Thai food, try delicious Noodle Boat. ✉ *700 NW Gilman Blvd., Issaquah* ☎ *425/391–8096* 🌐 *www.noodleboat.com.*

■ **Deru Market** An organic cafe with everything you need to grab a picnic to-go or to sit down for a leisurely lunch. ✉ *723 9th Ave, Kirkland* ☎ *425/298–0268* 🌐 *www.derumarket.com/* ⏲ *Closed Mon.–Tues.*

■ **Twisted Cuban Cafe** This Cuban eatery serves tasty sandwiches and entrées, as well as mojitos. ✉ *12631 NE Woodinville Dr., Woodinville* ☎ *425/806–7203* 🌐 *www.twistedcubancafe.com.*

The suburbs east of Lake Washington can easily supplement any Seattle itinerary. The center of East King County is Bellevue, a fast-growing city with its own downtown core and high-end shopping. Kirkland, north of Bellevue, has a few shops and an increasingly notable restaurant scene (including fabulous Café Juanita) plus lakefront promenades.

Redmond and Issaquah, to the northeast and southeast respectively, are gateways to greenery. Woodinville, north of Redmond, is the ambassador for Washington State's wine industry, with many wineries and tasting rooms, as well as a growing number of breweries and distilleries. Redmond itself is home to Microsoft's gigantic campus. Drivers now have to pay a toll to cross the 520 Bridge to the Eastside.

Three-quarters of a century ago, Bellevue was a pleasant little town in the country, with rows of shops along Main Street serving the local strawberry farmers. Today it's fast becoming a destination in itself, with snazzy shopping malls, restaurants, and a strong art museum.

Kirkland's business district, along the Lake Street waterfront, is lined with shops, restaurants, pubs, and parks. At the height of summer, it's often warm enough to swim in the sheltered waters of Lake Washington; Juanita Beach Park is a popular spot with an enclosed swimming area.

A string of pretty parks makes Redmond an inviting place to experience the outdoors, and the 11-mile Sammamish River Trail is an attraction for locals and tourists alike. The rapidly expanding city is today one of the country's most powerful business capitals, thanks to the presence of such companies as Microsoft, Nintendo, and Eddie Bauer. Although there are several good malls and a lot of generic strip-mall stores, this isn't a place to shop—locals come here either to work or to play outdoors.

Issaquah is experiencing rapid (and not terribly attractive) development, but it's what lies beyond the subdivisions that counts. The surrounding Cougar, Tiger, and Squak mountain foothills—dubbed the Issaquah Alps—are older than the Cascade Range and pocketed with caves, parks, and trails. This area has some of the most accessible hiking and mountain biking in the Seattle area; Seattleites often use these trails to train on in early spring before the more arduous trails in the Cascades and Olympics open for hiking season.

Woodinville is perhaps the Eastside's most popular day trip. It's the home of Chateau Ste. Michelle and dozens of other wineries, plus destination restaurant The Herbfarm. Additionally, luxurious Willows Lodge is walking distance from the main attractions, making Woodinville an ideal place for a romantic getaway.

Sights

Bellevue Arts Museum

MUSEUM | A real feather in Bellevue's cap, this museum presents sophisticated exhibits on craft and design, with a focus on regional artists. Past exhibitions have included *High Fiber Diet*—focusing on underexposed media in contemporary art—and *Modern Twist: Contemporary Japanese Bamboo Art*. The dramatic puzzle-piece-looking building, which really stands out in Bellevue's somewhat uninspired downtown core, is worth the trip alone. Tours happen daily at 1 pm, and workshops for kids, teens, and adults are offered regularly. In late July, the museum hosts the BAM ARTSfair, a prestigious, high-end street festival held at Bellevue Square and Bellevue Arts Museum. ✉ *510 Bellevue Way NE, Bellevue* ☎ *425/519–0770* 🌐 *www.bellevuearts.org* 🎫 *$15* ⏲ *Closed Mon.–Tues.*

Bellevue Botanical Gardens

GARDEN | This beautiful 53-acre public area next to Wilburton Hill Park and just a short drive from downtown Bellevue is encircled by spectacular perennial borders, brilliant rhododendron displays, and patches of alpine and rock gardens. The Ravine Experience encompasses a 5-acre area in the heavily forested southwest corner of the gardens with a 1/3-mile nature trail. A 150-foot suspension bridge crosses a deep ravine in one of the most pristine spaces, allowing visitors to observe unique topography and soaring conifers without disturbing the forest floor. Docents lead tours of the gardens Saturdays and Sundays (April through October), beginning at the visitor center at noon. The Yao Japanese garden is especially beautiful in fall. One of the most interesting features of the park is the Waterwise Garden, which was planted with greenery that needs little water in summer. During the holiday season (late November–late December), the gardens are lit up nightly from 5 to 10 pm for Garden d'Lights, one of the area's most popular seasonal attractions. From downtown Bellevue, head south on 116th to SE 1st Street and take a right on Main Street. ✉ *12001 Main St., Bellevue* ☎ *425/452–2750* 🌐 *www.bellevuebotanical.org* 🎫 *Free; winter Garden d'Lights festival, $5.*

Burke-Gilman/Sammamish River Trail

TRAIL | **FAMILY** | Approximately 27 miles long, the paved, flat, tree-lined Burke-Gilman Trail runs from Seattle's Gas Works Park, on Lake Union, east along an old railroad right-of-way along the ship canal, and then north along Lake Washington's eastern shore. At Blyth Park in Bothell, the trail becomes the Sammamish River Trail and continues for 10 miles to Marymoor Park in Redmond. Except for a stretch of the Sammamish River Trail between Woodinville and Marymoor Park, where horses are permitted on a parallel trail, the path is limited to walkers, runners, and bicyclists. **■ TIP→ There are a handful of bike rental shops on Sand Point Way, just north of the University of Washington, an easy access point for the trail. For additional access points, view the map online at www.seattle.gov/transportation/burkegilmantrailmaps.htm.** ✉ *Seattle* 🌐 *www.ci.seattle.wa.us/parks/burkegilman/bgtrail.htm.*

Chateau Ste. Michelle Winery

WINERY/DISTILLERY | One of the state's oldest wineries lies 15 miles northeast of Seattle. Once part of the estate of lumber baron Fred Stimson, these 107 acres include the original trout ponds, a carriage house, a caretaker's cottage, formal gardens, and the 1912 family manor house (which is on the National Register of Historic Places). Complimentary wine

Did You Know?

The Bellevue Botanical Gardens have an impressive Christmas lights display with over half a million colorful lights during the holiday season.

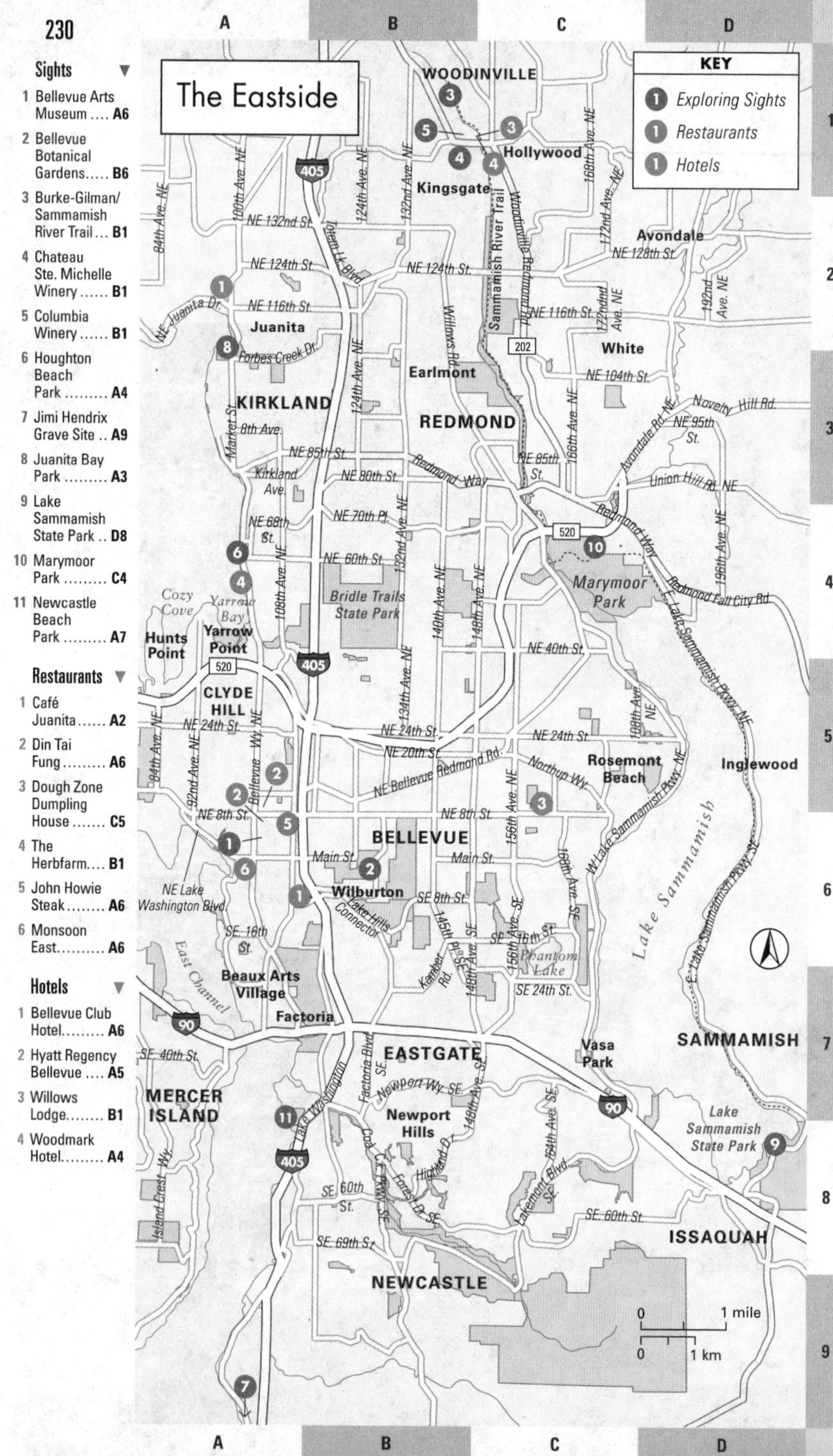
The Eastside
Sights
1 Bellevue Arts Museum A6
2 Bellevue Botanical Gardens..... B6
3 Burke-Gilman/ Sammamish River Trail ... B1
4 Chateau Ste. Michelle Winery B1
5 Columbia Winery B1
6 Houghton Beach Park A4
7 Jimi Hendrix Grave Site .. A9
8 Juanita Bay Park A3
9 Lake Sammamish State Park .. D8
10 Marymoor Park C4
11 Newcastle Beach Park A7
Restaurants
1 Café Juanita A2
2 Din Tai Fung A6
3 Dough Zone Dumpling House C5
4 The Herbfarm.... B1
5 John Howie Steak A6
6 Monsoon East.......... A6
Hotels
1 Bellevue Club Hotel......... A6
2 Hyatt Regency Bellevue A5
3 Willows Lodge........ B1
4 Woodmark Hotel......... A4
KEY
Exploring Sights
Restaurants
Hotels
A
B
C
D
1
2
3
4
5
6
7
8
9
WOODINVILLE
Hollywood
Kingsgate
Avondale
Juanita
White
Earlmont
KIRKLAND
REDMOND
Marymoor Park
Bridle Trails State Park
Cozy Cove
Yarrow Bay
Hunts Point
Yarrow Point
CLYDE HILL
Rosemont Beach
Inglewood
BELLEVUE
Wilburton
Lake Sammamish
Phantom Lake
East Channel
Beaux Arts Village
Factoria
EASTGATE
Vasa Park
SAMMAMISH
MERCER ISLAND
Newport Hills
Lake Sammamish State Park
ISSAQUAH
NEWCASTLE
405
520
90
202
NE 132nd St.
NE 124th St.
NE 116th St.
NE 128th St.
NE 104th St.
NE 95th St.
NE 85th St.
NE 80th St.
NE 70th Pl.
NE 68th St.
NE 60th St.
NE 40th St.
NE 24th St.
NE 20th St.
NE 8th St.
Main St.
SE 8th St.
SE 16th St.
SE 24th St.
SE 40th St.
SE 60th St.
SE 69th St.
84th Ave. NE
100th Ave. NE
124th Ave. NE
132nd Ave. NE
168th Ave. NE
172nd Ave. NE
192nd Ave. NE
166th Ave. NE
196th Ave. NE
108th Ave. NE
140th Ave. NE
148th Ave. NE
134th Ave. NE
94th Ave. NE
92nd Ave. NE
156th Ave. NE
148th Ave. SE
156th Ave. SE
164th Ave. SE
Totem Lk. Blvd.
Woodinville Redmond Rd.
Sammamish River Trail
Willows Rd.
NE Juanita Dr.
Forbes Creek Dr.
Market St.
8th Ave.
Kirkland Ave.
Redmond Way
Novelty Hill Rd.
Avondale Rd. NE
Union Hill Rd. NE
Redmond Fall City Rd.
E. Lake Sammamish Pkwy. NE
W Lake Sammamish Pkwy. NE
E. Lake Sammamish Pkwy. SE
NE Bellevue Redmond Rd.
Northup Wy.
Bellevue Wy. NE
NE Lake Washington Blvd.
Lake Hills Connector
145th Pl. SE
Kamber Rd.
Factoria Blvd. SE
Newport Wy. SE
Lake Washington
Coal Cr. Pkwy. SE
Forest Dr. SE
Highland Dr.
Lakemont Blvd. SE
Island Crest Wy.
0
1 mile
1 km

tastings and cellar tours run throughout the day. Specialty tours and tastings (vintage reserve tastings and theme tastings) start at $15. You're also invited to picnic and explore the grounds on your own; the wine shop sells delicatessen items. In summer Chateau Ste. Michelle hosts nationally known performers and arts events in its amphitheater. ✉ *14111 NE 145th St., Woodinville* ✣ *From Downtown Seattle take I–90 east to north I–405; take Exit 23 east (Hwy. 522) to Woodinville exit* ☎ *425/488–1133* 🌐 *www.ste-michelle.com* 🎫 *Free.*

Columbia Winery

WINERY/DISTILLERY | A group of UW professors cofounded this winery in 1962, making it the state's oldest. Using only European vinifera-style grapes grown in eastern Washington, the founders' aim was to take advantage of the fact that the vineyards share the same latitude as the best wine-producing areas of France. Wine tastings are held daily. ✉ *14030 NE 145th St., Woodinville* ✣ *From Downtown Seattle take I–90 east to north I–405; take Exit 23 east (Hwy. 522) to Woodinville exit, go right. Go right again on 175th St., and left on Hwy. 202* ☎ *425/482–7490, 800/488–2347* 🌐 *www.columbiawinery.com* 🎫 *Winery visit free; wine tastings $15.*

Houghton Beach Park

BEACH—SIGHT | On hot days, sun worshippers, swimmers, and the beach-volleyball crowd flock to this beach south of downtown Kirkland on the Lake Washington waterfront. The rest of the year, the playground attracts families, and the fishing pier stays busy with anglers. Facilities include drinking water, picnic tables, a beach volleyball court, phones, and restrooms. Perfect Wave offers stand-up paddleboard and kayak rentals at the north end of the park. Park the car and slip on some good walking shoes; it's a lovely walk along the waterfront to the shops and restaurants of either Carillon Point or downtown Kirkland. ✉ *5811 Lake Washington Blvd., Kirkland* ☎ *425/587–3000* 🌐 *www.kirklandwa.gov/depart/parks.*

Jimi Hendrix Grave Site

MEMORIAL | Since his death in 1970, the famed guitarist has rested in Greenwood Cemetery. The site includes a memorial with a domed roof and granite columns. ✉ *350 Monroe Ave. NE, Renton* ✣ *Take I–5 south to I–405 north and WA–169 south (SE Maple Valley Hwy.) exit, keeping left at fork in ramp. Merge onto SE Maple Valley Hwy./WA–169 north. Take right on Sunset Blvd. N, then right at NE 3rd St. Continue 1 mile, as NE 3rd St. becomes NE 4th St. Turn right at 3rd light* 🌐 *www.jimihendrixmemorial.com.*

Juanita Bay Park

NATURE PRESERVE | **FAMILY** | A 110-acre urban wildlife habitat, this marshy wetland is the perfect spot to don your binoculars to spot songbirds, shorebirds, turtles, beavers, and other small mammals. Interpretive signs are located throughout the park for self-guided tours along paved trails and boardwalks; or take one of the guided tours conducted by volunteer park rangers from the Eastside Audubon Society. ■ **TIP→ Just to the north of Juanita Bay Park is Juanita Beach Park, a great spot for picnicking, sunbathing, and swimming. On Friday night, June through September, there's a farmers' market.** ✉ *2201 Market St., Kirkland* ☎ *425/576–8805 Eastside Audubon Society* 🌐 *www.kirklandwa.gov/depart/parks.*

Lake Sammamish State Park

NATIONAL/STATE PARK | **FAMILY** | Two sandy beaches anchor this 531-acre park, with plenty of picnic tables (though it's best to bring your own basket rather than test the concessions), a playground, and seasonal kayak and paddleboard rentals. There are a few shady walking trails, which offer good bird-watching and wildlife viewing. If you head east, you can connect to the Sammamish River Trail and walk or bike all the way to Marymoor Park. ✉ *2000 NW Sammamish Rd., Issaquah* ✣ *From I–90, drive east to Exit*

Chateau Ste. Michelle winery hosts dinners, tours, tastings, and concerts.

15 and follow signs ☎ *425/455–7010* 🌐 *www.parks.wa.gov/parks/?selectedpark=lake%20sammamish* 🎫 *Discover Pass required ($10/day or $30/yr).*

Marymoor Park

NATIONAL/STATE PARK | FAMILY | It's not just famous for its Marymoor Velodrome, the Pacific Northwest's sole cycling arena. This 640-acre park also has a 45-foot-high climbing rock, game fields, tennis courts, a model airplane launching area, a huge off-leash dog park, and the Pea Patch community garden. You can row on Lake Sammamish or head straight to the picnic grounds or to the Willowmoor Farm, an estate inside the park.

Marymoor has some of the best bird-watching in this largely urban area. It's possible to spot some 24 resident species, including great blue herons, belted kingfishers, buffleheads, short-eared and barn owls, and red-tailed hawks. Occasionally, bald eagles soar past the lakefront. The Sammamish River, which flows through the western section of the park, is an important salmon spawning stream.

Ambitious bikers can follow the Burke-Gilman Sammamish River Trail to access the park; Marymoor is just over 20 miles from Seattle, and it's a flat ride most of the way. ✉ *6046 W Lake Sammamish Pkwy. NE, Redmond* ✣ *Take Rte. 520 east to W Lake Sammamish Pkwy. exit. Turn right (southbound) on W Lake Sammamish Pkwy. NE. Turn left at traffic light* ☎ *206/296–8687* 🌐 *www.kingcounty.gov/recreation/parks/inventory/marymoor.aspx.*

Newcastle Beach Park

BEACH—SIGHT | The most popular beach park in the Bellevue park system, this large park has a big swimming beach, seasonal lifeguards, a fishing dock, nature trails, restrooms, and a large grassy area with picnic tables. The playground is a favorite, thanks to a train that tots can sit in and older kids can climb on and hop from car to car. ✉ *4400 Lake Washington Blvd. SE, off 112th SE exit from I–405, Bellevue*

Woodinville Wineries

Walla Walla wine country is too far to go from Seattle if you've only got a few days. Instead, check out Woodinville's excellent wineries, only about 22 miles from Seattle's city center. You'll need a car unless you sign up for a guided tour. Check out 🌐 *www.woodinvillewinecountry.com* for a full list of wineries and touring maps. If you plan to spend a day or two in Woodinville, consider picking up a Passport to Woodinville Wine Country for $75. It includes a standard wine tasting at more than 60 participating wineries and tasting rooms (🌐 *www.woodinvillewinecountry.com/passport*).

Wineries

There are more than 50 wineries in Woodinville, though most of them don't have tasting rooms. This list provides a good survey, from the big guys to the smallest boutique producers:

Chateau Ste. Michelle is the grande dame of the Woodinville wine scene, and perhaps the most recognizable name nationwide. Guided tours of the winery and grounds (which include a chateau) are available daily; there's also a tasting room. Check the website for special events like dinners and concerts. 🌐 *www.ste-michelle.com*

Columbia Winery is another major player with a grand house anchoring its winery. Columbia's tasting room is open daily for regular tastings and private tastings. 🌐 *www.columbiawinery.com*

DeLille Cellars is on the list of nearly every fancy restaurant in Seattle. Most recently it's garnered national acclaim for the predominantly cab-sauv blend Chaleur Estate. The Carriage House tasting room, slightly north of the winery, is open daily. 🌐 *www.delillecellars.com*

Mark Ryan is an indie winery that has earned praise nationwide for its use of mostly Red Mountain AVA grapes—especially for the Dead Horse reds. The winery has a small tasting room open daily. 🌐 *www.markryanwinery.com*

Novelty Hill-Januik is often described as the most Napa-esque experience in Woodinville. The tasting room for these sister wineries is sleek and modern and brick-oven pizza is available on weekends. 🌐 *www.noveltyhill-januik.com*

The Woodinville Warehouse District is a collective of dozens of wineries, breweries, and distilleries around Woodinville. Print out a map for a self-guided tour if you want to explore the area 🌐 *www.woodinvillewinecountry.com/wine/maps*.

Dining and Lodging

One of the swankiest hotels in the Puget Sound region, **Willows Lodge** (🌐 *www.willowslodge.com*) is only a few minutes away from the major wineries and next door to destination restaurant the **Herbfarm**. The hotel's restaurant, **Barking Frog**, is also superb. For a simpler meal with an equally intense focus on wine, check out the Woodinville outpost of the **Purple Café and Wine Bar**.

☎ 425/452–6885 🌐 *www.ci.bellevue.wa.us/newcastle_beach_park.htm.*

Bellevue, Kirkland, and Woodinville are theoretically easy to get to from Downtown Seattle: the 520 (toll bridge) and I–90 bridges both are accessible from I–5. However, traffic is always an issue and grinds to a halt during rush hour. Don't plan a culinary expedition unless you already plan to visit this side of things—unless, of course, you have reservations at Café Juanita, the beloved and critically acclaimed restaurant that is more than worth the trek.

★ Café Juanita

$$$$ | ITALIAN | There are so many ways for a pricey "destination restaurant" to go overboard, making itself nothing more than a special-occasion spectacle, but Café Juanita manages to get everything just right. This Kirkland space, remodeled in 2015, is refined without being overly posh, and the food—much of which has a northern Italian influence—is also perfectly balanced. **Known for:** service; tasting menus. 💲 *Average main: $55* ✉ *9702 N.E. 120th Pl., Kirkland* ☎ *425/823–1505* 🌐 *www.cafejuanita.com* ⏲ *Closed Sun.–Mon. No lunch.*

Din Tai Fung

$$ | CHINESE | Watch dumplings being pleated by hand through the large glass windows in the waiting area for this restaurant on the second floor of Lincoln Square mall—it's a good thing the sight is so entertaining, because there's often a long wait. The *xiao long bao*, or "soup dumplings," are morsels of meat tucked into dough wrappers along with a slurp of broth, and are the famous attraction at Din Tai Fung, a U.S. branch of the famed Taipei-based chain. **Known for:** soup dumplings; rice cakes; pork chop. 💲 *Average main: $12* ✉ *700 Bellevue Way, Lincoln Square Mall, Bellevue* ☎ *425/698–1095* 🌐 *www.dintaifungusa.com.*

Dough Zone Dumpling House

$ | CHINESE | This place lives up to its name, serving freshly made carb-filled delights of many types: noodles, flatbreads, crepes, and dumplings. Hearty northern Chinese foods are carefully crafted in view of diners. **Known for:** soup dumplings; noodles. 💲 *Average main: $8* ✉ *15920 N.E. 8th St., #3, Bellevue* ☎ *425/641–8000.*

The Herbfarm

$$$$ | PACIFIC NORTHWEST | You might consider fasting before dining at the Herbfarm. It's prix-fixe only and you'll get nine courses—dinner takes at least four hours and includes six fine wines (you might also want to arrange for transportation there and back). **Known for:** tasting menu; farm tours. 💲 *Average main: $265* ✉ *14590 N.E. 145th St., Woodinville* ☎ *425/485–5300* 🌐 *www.theherbfarm.com* ⏲ *Closed Mon.–Wed. No lunch.*

John Howie Steak

$$$$ | STEAKHOUSE | An upscale Northwest steak house in the Shops at the Bravern, John Howie is well-known for its USDA Prime 28-day, 35-day, and 42-day custom-aged, American Wagyu beef. Steaks are tender, juicy, and perfectly executed and salmon is always available. **Known for:** steak; sandwiches. 💲 *Average main: $75* ✉ *11111 N.E. 8th St., Shops at the Bravern, Bellevue* ☎ *425/440–0880* 🌐 *www.johnhowiesteak.com* ⏲ *No lunch weekends.*

Monsoon East

$$$ | VIETNAMESE | The Eastside sibling of Capitol Hill's darling Vietnamese eatery is utterly polished and sleek—and much fancier than the original restaurant. The Vietnamese dishes are the favorites: diners love the *bo la lot* beef, crispy drunken chicken, catfish clay pot, and barbecued hoisin pork ribs. **Known for:** wine; drunken chicken. 💲 *Average main: $27* ✉ *10245 Main St., Bellevue* ☎ *425/635–1112* 🌐 *www.monsooneast.com.*

Marymoor Park has an outdoor concert series in the summer.

Hotels

Bellevue Club Hotel

$$$ | **HOTEL** | **FAMILY** | Fitness buffs will particularly enjoy the perks of this architectural jewel in downtown Bellevue because guests have use of the Bellevue Club's 200,000-square-foot private athletic club—though the luxurious rooms will please even travelers whose most strenuous form of exercise is lifting the remote. **Pros:** amazing gym and pools; indoor and outdoor tennis courts; complimentary town-car service to area shopping; good on-site restaurant. **Cons:** outside of downtown Bellevue; hotel can feel a bit corporate; books up well in advance. *Rooms from: $360* *11200 S.E. 6th St., Bellevue* *425/454–4424, 800/579–1110* *www.thehotelbellevue.com* *67 rooms* *No meals.*

Hyatt Regency Bellevue

$$ | **HOTEL** | Near Bellevue Square and other downtown Bellevue shopping centers, the Hyatt looks like any other sleek high-rise but its interior is adorned with huge displays of fresh flowers and elegant touches such as marble floors and a grand piano. **Pros:** free parking on weekends; great location in the heart of Bellevue; great staff. **Cons:** readers complain of spotty housekeeping; decor could use an update. *Rooms from: $209* *900 Bellevue Way NE, Bellevue* *425/462–1234* *www.bellevue.hyatt.com* *732 rooms* *No meals.*

★ Willows Lodge

$$$$ | **HOTEL** | Timbers salvaged from a 19th-century warehouse are rustic counterpoints to sleek, modern design of this elegant spa hotel in the heart of Woodinville wine country. **Pros:** a truly romantic getaway; great for foodies and wine people; lovely spa; impeccable service. **Cons:** not really for families; far from Downtown; rooms a bit dark. *Rooms from: $459* *14580 N.E. 145th St., Woodinville* *425/424–3900, 877/424–3930* *www.willowslodge.com* *84 rooms* *No meals.*

Woodmark Hotel

$$ | **HOTEL** | Boat tours, waterside views, and complimentary kayak usage make this Kirkland hotel and yacht club, just 9 miles from Seattle on the shores of Lake Washington, a great bet. **Pros:** great staff; boat tours, paddle boarding, and kayak rentals; free late-night snacks. **Cons:** rooms not facing the water have rotten views of an office park; wedding weekends can get a bit lively. *Rooms from: $249* *1200 Carillon Point, Kirkland* *425/822–3700, 800/822–3700* *www.thewoodmark.com* *100 rooms* *No meals.*

Performing Arts

The Theatre at Meydenbauer Center

ARTS CENTERS | Children's theater troupes, Ballet Bellevue, Bellevue City Opera, the Bellevue Civic Theater, and other groups perform here, where the equipment is state-of-the-art and the acoustics are excellent. *11100 N.E. 6th St., Bellevue* *425/637–1020* *www.meydenbauer.com.*

Shopping

The core of Bellevue's growing shopping district is the Bellevue Collection (Bellevue Square Mall, Lincoln Center, and Bellevue Place) and the sparkling upscale mall called the Bravern. The community's retail strip stretches from Bellevue Square between NE 4th and 8th Streets to the community-centered Crossroads Shopping Center several miles to the east.

Best shopping: Bellevue Square and The Shops at the Bravern.

The Bellevue Collection

SHOPPING CENTERS/MALLS | **FAMILY** | In this impressive trifecta of shopping centers, you'll find just about any chain store you've heard of (and some that you haven't). Bellevue Square's wide walkways and benches, its many children's clothing stores, the first-floor play area, and a children's museum on the third floor make this a great place for kids, too. You can park for free in the attached garage. Take the sky bridge to Lincoln Center, to catch a flick at their 16-screen cinema, organize your life at the Container Store, or sample an assortment of other retail and several popular chain restaurants. Bellevue Place, across from Lincoln Center, hosts a variety of retail along with the ever-popular Daniel's Broiler. *Bellevue Way, 575 Bellevue Sq., Bellevue* *425/454–8096* *www.bellevuecollection.com.*

Crossroads Shopping Center

SHOPPING CENTERS/MALLS | Bellevue's most laid-back and least ritzy mall has become something of an old town square to the residential community around it. Midlevel retail, like Old Navy, Dress Barn, and Bed Bath & Beyond surround the open Public Market Stage and community rooms, where there's free live music, story hours, tax workshops, Tai Chi, knitting, and meditation workshops. A giant chessboard and playground are packed with families, and the Crossroads Cinema anchors the southeast corner. If you're hungry, there are more than 20 restaurants; on Tuesday from June to September you can grab a bite at the farmers' market (noon to 6 pm). *NE 8th St. and 156th Ave., Bellevue* *425/644–1111* *www.crossroadsbellevue.com.*

The Shops at the Bravern

SHOPPING CENTERS/MALLS | If you have some serious cash to burn, the sleek, upscale Bravern might be the Eastside spot for you. With high-end shops like Neiman Marcus, Hermès, Jimmy Choo, Salvatore Ferragamo, and Louis Vuitton, it's tempting to empty your wallet—but save room for a spa treatment at the Gene Juarez Salon & Spa or a meal at luxury Chinese hot-pot spot the Dolar Shop. Valet and complimentary parking (with validation) are available. *11111 NE 8th St., Bellevue* *425/456–8780* *www.thebravern.com.*

Chapter 15

SIDE TRIPS FROM SEATTLE

Updated by
AnnaMaria Stephens

Sights	Restaurants	Hotels	Shopping	Nightlife
★★★★★	★★★★★	★★★★★	★★☆☆☆	★★☆☆☆

WELCOME TO SIDE TRIPS FROM SEATTLE

TOP REASONS TO GO

★ **Idyllic Surrounds.** Experience peace and quiet for a day or overnight away from the city, and appreciate just how majestic the islands outside Seattle can be.

★ **Incredible Seafood.** Top-notch oysters and mussels paired with equally delicious wine make for an unforgettable dining experience.

From the stunning National Parks to the jaw-dropping islands all just a ferry's distance from the city, whichever trip (or trips) you choose to take from Seattle, you'll be amazed at the scenery and wilderness that are immediately evident upon exiting the city. As you leave the city by ferry, the gorgeous Seattle skyline starts to fade as you get closer to the craggy, forested islands. As you drive toward your destination, whether into the Cascade National Park or toward Mt. Rainier, you'll encounter huge evergreen trees surrounding the road.

1 **Puget Sound Islands.** A highly popular destination for day-trips, the Puget Sound Islands include the well known Bainbridge, Vashon, and Whidbey. All are unique with their own character.

2 **San Juan Islands.** The waters of the Pacific Northwest's Salish Sea, between mainland Washington and Vancouver Island, contain hundreds of islands, some little more than rocky reefs, others rising to nearly 2,500 feet. Among these, the San Juans are considered by many to be the loveliest.

3 **Mount Rainier National Park.** Mount Rainier is the mountain scene in the distance of every quitessential Seattle panorama. The mountain holds the largest glacial system in the contiguous United States, with more than two dozen major glaciers.

4 **Olympic National Park.** A spellbinding setting is tucked into the country's far northwestern corner, within the heart-shape Olympic Peninsula.

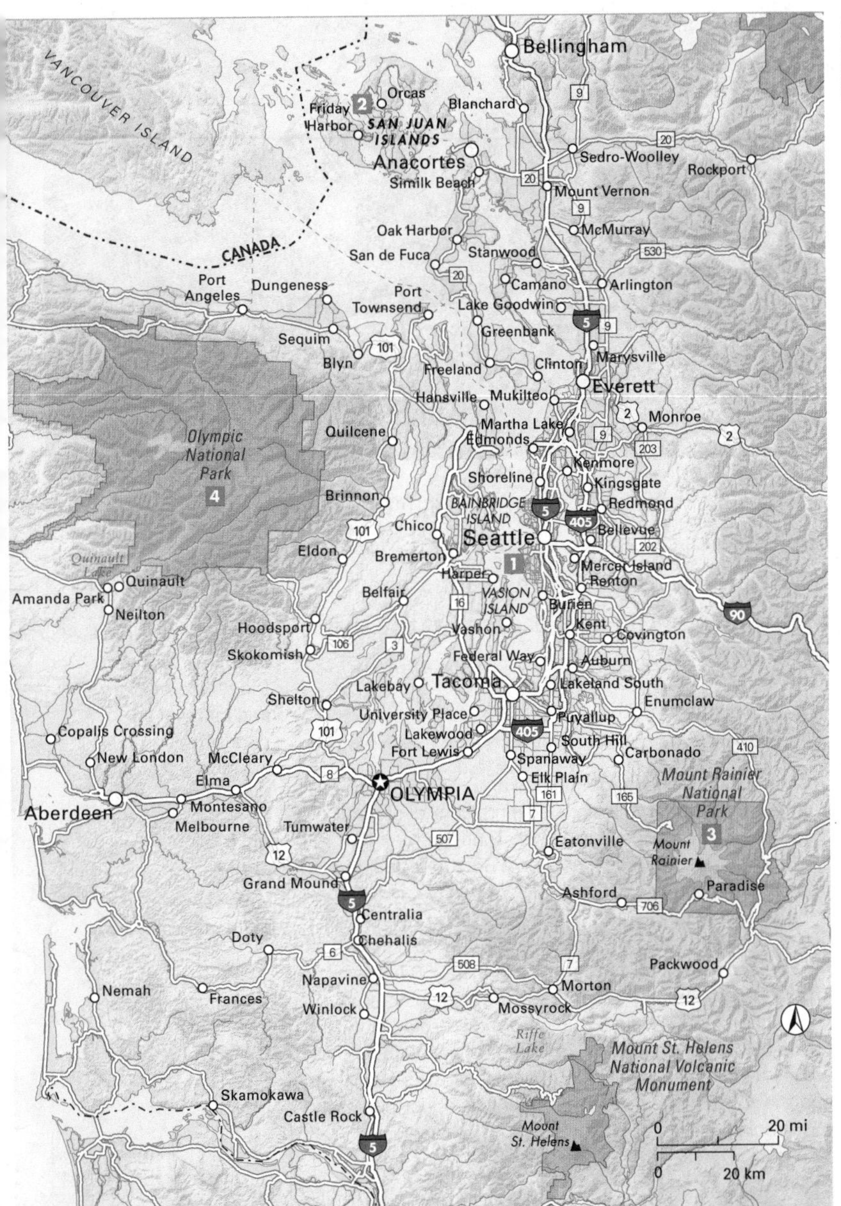
Bellingham
VANCOUVER ISLAND
CANADA
Orcas
Friday Harbor
SAN JUAN ISLANDS
2
Blanchard
Anacortes
Similk Beach
Sedro-Woolley
Rockport
Mount Vernon
McMurray
Oak Harbor
San de Fuca
Stanwood
Camano
Arlington
Port Angeles
Dungeness
Port Townsend
Lake Goodwin
Sequim
Blyn
Greenbank
Freeland
Clinton
Marysville
Everett
Hansville
Mukilteo
Monroe
Martha Lake
Edmonds
Quilcene
Olympic National Park
4
Kenmore
Shoreline
Kingsgate
Brinnon
BAINBRIDGE ISLAND
Redmond
Bellevue
Chico
Seattle
Eldon
Bremerton
1
Mercer Island
Quinault Lake
Quinault
Harper
Renton
Amanda Park
Neilton
Belfair
VASHON ISLAND
Burien
Hoodsport
Vashon
Kent
Covington
Skokomish
Federal Way
Auburn
Lakebay
Tacoma
Lakeland South
Shelton
University Place
Enumclaw
Puyallup
Copalis Crossing
Lakewood
New London
Fort Lewis
South Hill
Carbonado
McCleary
Spanaway
Elma
Elk Plain
OLYMPIA
Mount Rainier National Park
3
Aberdeen
Montesano
Melbourne
Tumwater
Eatonville
Mount Rainier
Grand Mound
Ashford
Paradise
Centralia
Doty
Chehalis
Packwood
Napavine
Nemah
Frances
Morton
Winlock
Mossyrock
Riffe Lake
Mount St. Helens National Volcanic Monument
Skamokawa
Castle Rock
Mount St. Helens
0
20 mi
0
20 km

MT. ST. HELENS

One of the most prominent peaks in the Northwest's rugged Cascade Range, Mount St. Helens National Volcanic Monument affords visitors an up-close look at the site of the most destructive volcanic blast in U.S. history.

Just 55 miles northeast of Portland and 155 miles southeast of Seattle, this once soaring, conical summit stood at 9,667 feet above sea level. Then, on May 18, 1980, a massive eruption launched a 36,000-foot plume of steam and ash into the air and sent nearly 4 million cubic yards of debris through the Toutle and Cowlitz river valleys. The devastating eruption leveled a 230-square-mile area, claiming 57 lives and more than 250 homes. The mountain now stands at 8,365 feet, and a horseshoe-shape crater—most visible from the north—now forms the scarred summit. A modern, scenic highway carries travelers to within about 5 miles of the summit, and the surrounding region offers thrilling opportunities for climbing, hiking, and learning about volcanology.

BEST TIME TO GO

It's best to visit from mid-May through late October, as the last section of Spirit Lake Highway, Johnston Ridge Observatory, and many of the park's forest roads are closed the rest of the year. The other visitor centers along the lower sections of the highway are open year-round, but overcast skies typically obscure the mountain's summit in winter.

PARK HIGHLIGHTS

Ape Cave Measuring nearly 2½ miles in mapped length, Ape Cave is the longest continuous lava tube in the continental United States. Two routes traverse the tube. The lower route is an easy hour-long hike; the upper route is more challenging and takes about three hours. The park recommends bringing at least two light sources (you can rent lanterns from the headquarters for $5 in summer) and warm clothing. In high season ranger-led walks are sometimes available; inquire at the **Apes' Headquarters** (*360/449–7800*), off Forest Service Road 8303, 3 miles north of the junction of Forest Roads 83 and 90. Although Ape Cave is open year-round, the headquarters closes November through April. A Northwest Forest Pass ($5 daily) is required for parking (or a Sno-Park permit during winter). ✉ *Cougar* ☎ *360/449–7800* 🌐 *www.fs.usda.gov/giffordpinchot.*

Johnston Ridge Observatory The visitor center closest to the summit is named for scientist David Johnston, who died in the mountain's immense lateral blast. Inside are fascinating exhibits on the mountain's geology, instruments measuring volcanic and seismic activity, and a theater that shows a riveting film that recounts the 1980 eruption. Several short trails afford spectacular views of the summit. E2400 Spirit Lake Hwy., Toutle P360/274–2140 wwww.fs.usda.gov/giffordpinchot A$8 parking CClosed mid-May–early Nov.

Spirit Lake Highway Officially known as Highway 504, this winding road rises 4,000 feet from the town of Castle Rock (just off I–5, Exit 49) to within about 5 miles of the Mt. St. Helens summit. Along this road are several visitor centers that explain the region's geology and geography, and several turnouts afford views of the destruction wrought upon the Toutle and Cowlitz river valleys. Don't miss the Mt. St. Helens Visitor Center at Silver Lake (E Hwy. 504, 5 miles east of I–5, 360/274–0962 wwww.parks.wa.gov) in Seaquest State Park, which shows video footage of the eruption and houses a scale model of the mountain that you can actually climb through.

STAY THE NIGHT

Fire Mountain Grill For good burgers, sandwiches, and beer and a memorable setting midway up Spirit Lake Highway, drop by this rustic roadhouse with a veranda overlooking the North Fork Toutle River. Be sure to save room for the fresh mountain-berry cobbler. **Known for:** scenic river views; tasty desserts; comfort food. ✉ *9440 Spirit Lake Hwy., Toutle* ☎ *360/274–5217* ⏲ *Closed late Nov.–late Mar. No dinner.*

McMenamins Kalama Harbor Lodge A 20-minute drive from the start of Spirit Lake Highway but also relatively close to Portland, this lodge with rooms overlooking the Columbia River is part of the funky McMenamins hotel and tavern chain. **Pros:** good base for Mt. St. Helens activities; pleasant views of the Columbia River; on-site food and drinks options. **Cons:** noise from passing trains; small bathrooms; food quality is uneven. ✉ *215 N. Hendrickson Dr.* ☎ *360/673–6970* 🌐 *www.mcmenamins.com/kalama-harbor-lodge* *11 rooms* *No meals.*

The beauty of Seattle is enough to wow most visitors, but it can't compare to the splendor of the state that surrounds it. You simply must put aside a day or two to venture out to one of the islands of Puget Sound or do a hike or scenic drive in one of the spectacular mountain ranges a few hours outside the city.

If you head west to Olympic National Park, north to North Cascades National Park, or east to the Cascade Range, you can hike, bike, or ski. Two and a half hours southeast of Seattle is majestic Mt. Rainier, the fifth-highest mountain in the contiguous United States. Two hours beyond Rainier, close to the Oregon border, is the Mount St. Helens National Volcanic Monument. The state-of-the-art visitor centers here show breathtaking views of the crater and lava dome and the spectacular recovery of the areas surrounding the 1980 blast.

You can get a taste of island life on Bainbridge, Whidbey, or Vashon—all easily accessible for day trips—or settle in for a few days on one of the San Juan Islands, where you can hike, kayak, or spot migrating whales and resident sea lions or otters.

WHAT IT COSTS IN U.S. DOLLARS

$	$$	$$$	$$$$
RESTAURANTS			
under $16	$16–$22	$23–$30	over $30
HOTELS			
under $150	$150–$225	$226–$300	over $300

The Puget Sound Islands

The islands of Puget Sound—particularly Bainbridge, Vashon, and Whidbey—are easy and popular day trips for Seattle visitors, and riding the Washington State ferries is half the fun. There are a few classic inns and B&Bs in the historic towns of Langley and Coupeville if you want to spend the night. It's definitely worth planning your trip around mealtimes because the islands of Puget Sound have top-notch restaurants serving local foods—including locally grown produce, seafood, and even island-raised beef. On Vashon Island, Earthen is at the top of the locavore pack; Bainbridge, Whidbey, and the San Juans also have a myriad of small farms and charming restaurants worth a visit. Seafood, of course, is a big draw. Local crab, salmon, and shellfish should be on your not-to-miss list, including the world-renowned Penn Cove mussels from Whidbey Island.

Whidbey Island has the most spectacular natural attractions, but it requires the biggest time commitment to get to (it's 30 miles northwest of Seattle). Bainbridge is the most developed island—it's something of a moneyed bedroom community—with higher-end restaurants and

Where to See Whales

The Salish Sea—which includes the Puget Sound and Straits of Georgia and Juan de Fuca—is teeming with incredibly diverse marine life. The area has even been called the American Serengeti. Seeing whales up close makes for a spectacular, memorable experience, from the huge migrating humpbacks with their powerful blows and tail slaps to the area's playful resident orca pods. The orcas, which face critical challenges with climate change, have an important role in the Pacific Northwest identity; many coastal indigeneous people consider them the guardians of the sea and honor them in their culture and artwork.

With a good pair of binoculars, you can see whales from the shore in a few spots, including Lime Kiln Park on San Juan Island, but your best bet is to get out on the water. You'll find many tour options throughout the Puget Sound and San Juan Islands; most start at around $100 and they typically offer guarantees—if you don't see any whales, you can return for free. If you don't have enough time to explore the islands during your visit to Seattle, consider taking a half-day tour out of Edmonds, just north of Seattle, on the Puget Sound Express, which zips over to prime whale-watching spots near the San Juan Islands on a boat.

shops supplementing its natural attractions. It's also the easiest to get to—just hop on a ferry from Pier 52 on the Downtown Seattle waterfront. Vashon is the most pastoral of the islands—if you don't like leisurely strolls, beachcombing, or bike rides, you might get bored there quickly. Bainbridge and Whidbey get tons of visitors in summer. Though you'll be able to snag a walk-on spot on the ferry, spaces for cars can fill up, so arrive early. Whidbey is big, so you'll most likely want to tour by car (you can actually drive there, too, as the north end of the island is accessible via Deception Pass), and a car is handy on Bainbridge as well, especially if you want to tour the entire island or visit spectacular Bloedel Reserve. Otherwise, Bainbridge is your best bet if you want to walk on the ferry and tour by foot.

★ **Puget Sound Express**

BOATING | FAMILY | If an island side trip isn't an option, you don't have to cut whale-watching from your wish list. Departing from Edmonds, about 45 minutes north of Seattle, this friendly family-owned outfitter offers half-day tours on superfast boats that zip over to prime whale-watching territory around the San Juan Islands. A naturalist provides details on what you're seeing during the 4.5-hour excursion and you can purchase hot drinks and delicious blueberry buckle cake on board. Tickets are $135 for adults. ✉ *459 Admiral Way, Edmonds* ☎ *360/385–5288* 🌐 *www.pugetsoundexpress.com.*

Bainbridge Island

35 mins west of Seattle by ferry.

Of the three main islands in Puget Sound, Bainbridge has by far the largest population of Seattle commuters. Certain parts of the island are dense enough to have rush-hour traffic problems, while other areas retain a semirural, small-town vibe. Longtime residents work hard to keep parks and protected areas out of the hands of condominium builders, and despite the increasing number of stressed-out commuters, the island still has resident artists, craftspeople, and old-timers who can't be bothered to venture into the big city. Though not as dramatic as Whidbey or as idyllic as Vashon, Bainbridge always makes for a pleasant day trip.

The ferry, which departs from the Downtown terminal at Pier 52, drops you off in the charming village of Winslow. Along its compact main street, Winslow Way, it's easy to while away an afternoon among the antiques shops, art galleries, bookstores, and cafés. There are two bike-rental shops in Winslow, too, if you plan on touring the island on two wheels. Getting out of town on a bike can be a bit nerve-racking, as the traffic to and from the ferry terminal is thick, and there aren't a lot of dedicated bike lanes, but you'll soon be on quieter country roads. Be sure to ask for maps at the rental shop, and if you want to avoid the worst of the island's hills, ask the staff to go over your options with you before you set out.

Many of the island's most reliable dining options are in Winslow—or close to it. You'll also find the delightful Town & Country supermarket on the main stretch if you want to pick up some provisions for a picnic, though you can also easily do that in Seattle at the Pike Place Market before you get on the ferry.

GETTING HERE AND AROUND

Unless you're coming from Tacoma or points farther south, or from the Olympic Peninsula, the only way to get to Bainbridge is via the ferry from Pier 52 Downtown. Round-trip fares start at $8.65 per person; round-trip fare for a car and driver is $24.70. Crossing time is 35 minutes. If you confine your visit to the village of Winslow, as many visitors do, then you won't need anything other than a pair of walking shoes. Out on the island, besides driving or biking, the only way to get around is on buses provided by Kitsap Transit. Fares are only $2 one way (ORCA cards accepted), but note that since routed buses are for commuters, they may not drop you off quite at the entrance of the park or attraction you're headed to. Be sure to study the route map carefully or call Kitsap at least a day in advance of your trip to inquire about their Dial-A-Ride services.

CONTACTS Bainbridge Chamber of Commerce. ☎ *206/842–3700* 🌐 *www.bainbridgechamber.com.* **Kitsap Transit.** ☎ *800/501–7433* 🌐 *www.kitsaptransit.com.*

Sights

Bainbridge Island Studio Tour

TOUR—SIGHT | Twice a year (the second weekend in August and the first weekend in December), the island's artists and craftspeople are in the spotlight when they put their best pieces on display for these three-day events, and you can buy anything from watercolors to furniture directly from the artists. Even if you can't make the official studio tours, check out the website, which has maps and information on studios and shops throughout the island, as well as links to artists' websites. Many of the shops have regular hours, and you can easily put together your own tour. ✉ *Bainbridge Island* 🌐 *www.bistudiotour.com.*

Bainbridge Vineyards

WINERY/DISTILLERY | Under cooperative ownership since 2013, this longtime certified-organic winery 5 miles from the ferry landing produces around 1,200 bottles a year from entirely island-grown varietals that thrive in the Puget Sound region. The winemakers compare their offerings to those that come from the Alsace or Loire Valley in France—on the light and fruity side—and you can enjoy a tasting of five pours for $8 on the winery's lovely sun-dappled patio (kids will want to say hi to the draft horses that help till the fields). The tasting room is open Friday to Sunday from 12 to 5 pm. ✉ *8989 Day Rd. E* ☎ *206/842–9463*

⊕ *www.bainbridgevineyards.com* ⊗ *Closed Mon.–Thu.*

★ Bloedel Reserve
NATIONAL/STATE PARK | This 150-acre internationally recognized preserve is a stunning mix of natural woodlands and beautifully landscaped gardens—including a moss garden, Japanese garden, a reflection pool, and the impressive former Bloedel estate home. Dazzling rhododendrons and azaleas bloom in spring, and Japanese maples colorfully signal autumn's arrival. Picnicking is not permitted, and you'll want to leave the pooch behind—pets are not allowed on the property, even if they stay in the car. Check the website's events page for special events, lectures, and exhibits. ✉ *7571 NE Dolphin Dr., 6 miles west of Winslow, via Hwy. 305* ☎ *206/842–7631* ⊕ *www.bloedelreserve.org* 🎫 *$17.*

Fletcher Bay Winery
WINERY/DISTILLERY | A boutique winery with stylish coastal decor, Fletcher Bay focuses on Bordeaux grapes along with Tempranillo and Sangiovese sourced from Washington State's Yakima and Walla Walla valleys. The casual, dog-friendly winery, set in the Coppertop Business Park (next door to Bainbridge Island Brewery), has a kids' play area with a DVD player, an enclosed patio with a fireplace and heat lamps, and live music every Wednesday from 6 to 8 pm. There's also a tasting room right in town (500 Winslow Way E) with live music every Thursday from 5:30 to 7:30 pm. ✉ *9415 Coppertop Loop NE* ☎ *206/780–9463* ⊕ *www.fletcherbaywinery.com* ⊗ *Closed Mon.*

Fort Ward Park
NATIONAL/STATE PARK | On the southwest side of the island is this lovely and tranquil 137-acre park. There are 2 miles of hiking trails through forest, a long stretch of (sometimes) sun-drenched rocky beach, several picnic tables, a boat launch, and even an underwater park for scuba diving. Along with views of the water and the Olympic Mountains, you might be lucky and get a peek of Mt. Rainier—or of the massive sea lions that frequent the near-shore waters. A loop trail through the park is suitable for all ability levels, and will take you past vestiges of the park's previous life as a military installation. ✉ *Fort Ward Hill Rd. NE* ✥ *Take Hwy. 305 out of Winslow; turn west on High School Rd. and follow signs to park* ☎ *206/842–3931* ⊕ *www.biparks.org/parksandfacilities/pkftward.html.*

Restaurants

Harbour Public House
$ | **SEAFOOD** | An 1881 estate home overlooking Eagle Harbor was renovated to create this casual pub and restaurant at Winslow's Harbor Marina, where a complimentary boat tie-up is available for pub patrons. Local seafood—including steamed mussels, clams, and oyster sliders—plus burgers, fish-and-chips, and poutine are typical fare, and there are 12 beers on tap. **Known for:** destination for kayakers; harbor views; open mic Tuesday night. $ *Average main: $16* ✉ *231 Parfitt Way SW, Winslow* ☎ *206/842–0969* ⊕ *www.harbourpub.com.*

Streamliner Diner
$ | **DINER** | **FAMILY** | It may be a no-frills diner, but Streamliner is a local institution on Bainbridge Island thanks to its hearty breakfasts and vegetarian-friendly options. Many travelers grab a quick bite here when they hop off the ferry at the nearby ferry landing, though you'll see just as many locals lining up for breakfast and lunch. **Known for:** family-friendly casual spot; vegan menu selections; quick and friendly service. $ *Average main: $10* ✉ *397 Winslow Way E.*

Coffee and Quick Bites

Blackbird Bakery
$ | **BAKERY** | A great place to grab a cup of coffee and a snack before exploring the

Bloedel Reserve is150-acres of gardens and woodlands.

island serves up rich pastries and cakes along with quiche, soups, and a good selection of teas and espresso drinks. Though there is some nice window seating that allows you to watch the human parade on Winslow Way, the place gets very crowded, especially when the ferries come in, so you might want to take your order to go. **Known for:** draws big crowds; delicious pastries. *Average main: $5* *210 Winslow Way E, Winslow* *206/780–1322* *www.blackbirdbakery.com* *No credit cards* *No dinner.*

Vashon Island

20 mins by ferry from West Seattle.

Vashon is the most peaceful and rural of the islands easily reached from the city, home to fruit growers, commune dwellers, and Seattle commuters.

Biking, beachcombing, picnicking, and kayaking are the main activities here. A tour of the 13-mile-long island will take you down country lanes and past orchards and lavender farms. There are several artists' studios and galleries on the island, as well as a small commercial district in the center of the island, where a farmers' market is a highlight every Saturday from April to October (and Wednesday afternoons, as well, from June to September). The popular Strawberry Festival takes place every July. The Vashon Ciderfest takes place in early October.

GETTING HERE

Washington State Ferries leave from Fauntleroy in West Seattle (about 9 miles southwest of Downtown) for the 20-minute ride to Vashon Island. The ferry docks at the northern tip of the island. Round-trip fares are $5.95 per person or $20.85 for a car and driver. A water taxi also goes to Vashon from Pier 50 on the Seattle waterfront, but it's primarily for commuters, operating only on weekdays during commuter hours (no holiday service). One-way fares are $6.75. There's limited bus service on the island; the best way to get around is by car or by bicycle (bring your own or rent in Seattle. Note that there's the huge hill as you immediately disembark the ferry dock and head up to town). The site 🌐 *www.vashonchamber.com* is also a good source of information.

VISITOR INFORMATION

Vashon-Maury Island Chamber of Commerce
The office is open Monday to Friday 10 to 3. ✉ *17141 Vashon Hwy. SW, Vashon* ☎ *206/463–6217* 🌐 *www.vashonchamber.com.*

Sights

Jensen Point and Burton Acres Park
NATIONAL/STATE PARK | Vashon has many parks and protected areas. This park, on the lush Burton Peninsula overlooking Quartermaster Harbor, is home to 64 acres of secluded hiking and horseback-riding trails. The adjacent Jensen Point, a 4-acre shoreline park, has picnic tables, a swimming beach, and kayak and paddleboard rentals (May through September). ✉ *8900 SW Harbor Dr., Vashon* ✣ *From ferry terminal, take Vashon Hwy. SW to SW Burton Dr. and turn left. Turn left on 97 Ave. SW and follow it around as it becomes SW Harbor Dr.* 🌐 *www.vashonparks.org.*

Point Robinson Park
NATIONAL/STATE PARK | You can stroll along the beach, which is very picturesque thanks to **Point Robinson Lighthouse.** The lighthouse is typically open to the public from noon to 4 on Sunday during the summer; call to arrange a tour or rent out one of the historic beachfront Keepers' Quarters (two multibedroom houses) by the week. If you're lucky, you might even see an orca swim surprisingly close to the shore. ✉ *3705 SW Pt. Robinson Rd., Vashon* ☎ *206/463–9602* 🌐 *www.vashonparks.org.*

Vashon Allied Arts
ARTS VENUE | The best representative of the island's diverse arts community presents monthly exhibits and events that span all mediums, including dance, chamber music, and art lectures. The gallery's exhibits rotate monthly, featuring local and Northwest artists, and Heron's Nest (17600 Vashon Highway SW, 206/463–5252), the affiliated gift shop in town, is where you'll find fine art and handcrafted items by local artists. ✉ *19704 Vashon Hwy.* ☎ *206/463–5131* 🌐 *www.vashonalliedarts.org.*

Restaurants

Hardware Store
$$ | **AMERICAN** | This all-day restaurant's unusual name comes from its former life as a mom-and-pop hardware shop—it occupies the oldest commercial building on Vashon, and certainly looks like a relic from the outside. Inside, you'll find a bistro-meets-upscale-diner serving "Northwest Americana" cuisine, with classic dishes ranging from rustic French toast for breakfast to buttermilk-fried chicken and meatloaf for dinner. **Known for:** iconic Vashon Island building; refined takes on diner favorites; decent wine list with Northwest options. $ *Average main: $19* ✉ *17601 Vashon Hwy. SW, Vashon* ☎ *206/463–1800* 🌐 *www.thsrestaurant.com.*

★ **May Kitchen + Bar**
$$ | **THAI** | This is where sophisticated foodies swoon over delectable and highly authentic Thai dishes. The ambience is scene-y (atypical for Vashon): dark with fully paneled walls in mahogany and teak—wood that owner May Chaleoy had shipped from Thailand, where it previously lived in the interior of a 150-year-old home. **Known for:** real-deal Thai food that goes way beyond pad Thai; vibrant atmosphere; unique cocktails. $ *Average main: $18* ✉ *17614 Vashon Hwy. SW, Vashon* ☎ *206/408–7196* 🌐 *www.maykitchen.com* ⏲ *Closed Mon.–Tue.*

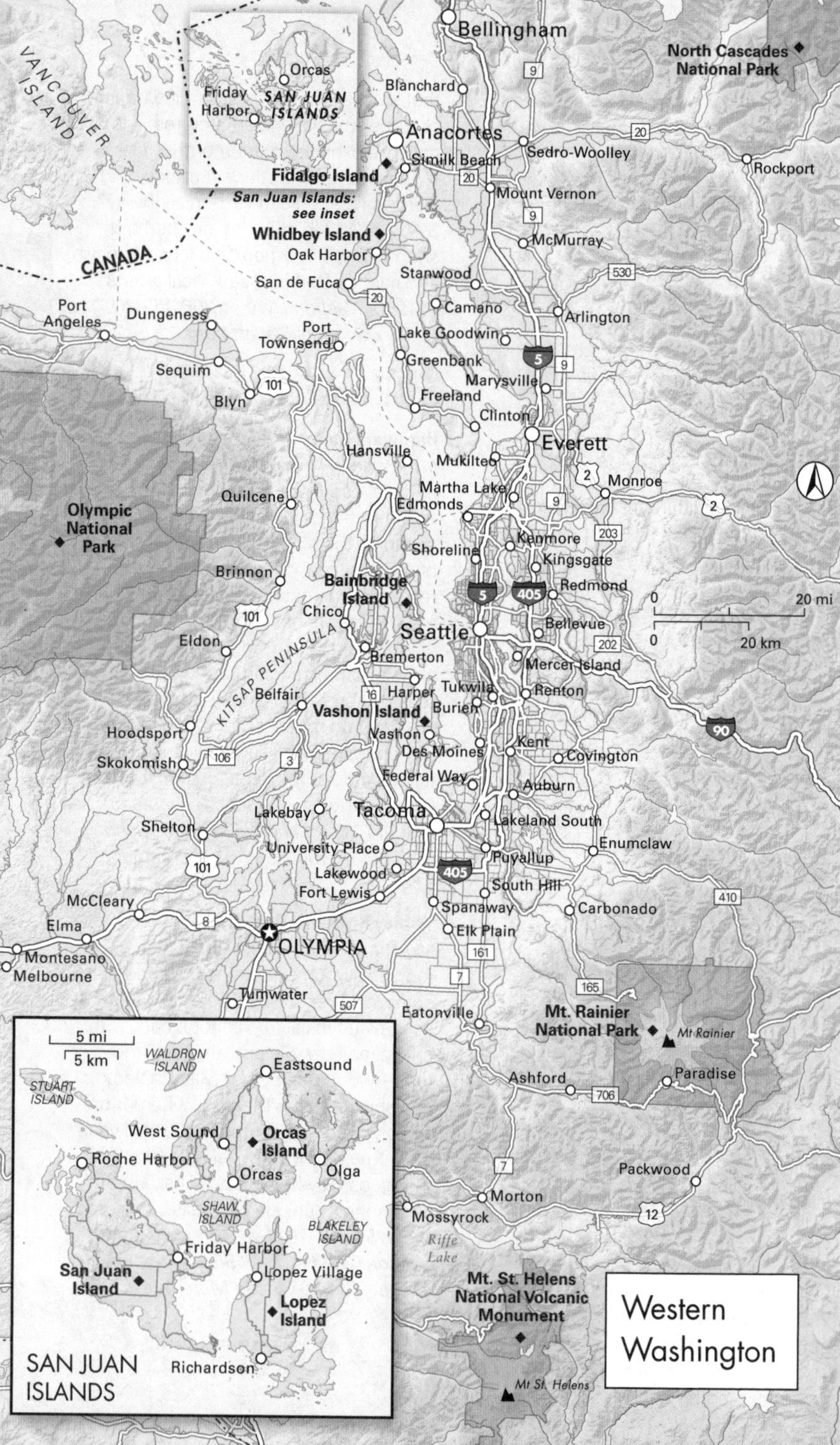
Western Washington
Bellingham
North Cascades National Park
VANCOUVER ISLAND
Orcas
Friday Harbor
SAN JUAN ISLANDS
Blanchard
Anacortes
Similk Beach
Fidalgo Island
Sedro-Woolley
Rockport
Mount Vernon
San Juan Islands: see inset
Whidbey Island
McMurray
CANADA
Oak Harbor
Stanwood
San de Fuca
Camano
Arlington
Port Angeles
Dungeness
Port Townsend
Lake Goodwin
Greenbank
Sequim
Marysville
Blyn
Freeland
Clinton
Everett
Hansville
Mukilteo
Monroe
Martha Lake
Edmonds
Quilcene
Olympic National Park
Kenmore
Shoreline
Kingsgate
Brinnon
Bainbridge Island
Redmond
Chico
Seattle
Bellevue
Eldon
KITSAP PENINSULA
Bremerton
Mercer Island
Harper
Tukwila
Renton
Belfair
Vashon Island
Burien
Vashon
Hoodsport
Des Moines
Kent
Covington
Skokomish
Federal Way
Auburn
Lakebay
Tacoma
Lakeland South
Shelton
University Place
Enumclaw
Puyallup
Lakewood
Fort Lewis
South Hill
McCleary
Spanaway
Carbonado
Elma
Elk Plain
Montesano
OLYMPIA
Melbourne
Tumwater
Eatonville
Mt. Rainier National Park
Mt Rainier
Ashford
Paradise
Packwood
Morton
Mossyrock
Riffe Lake
Mt. St. Helens National Volcanic Monument
Mt St. Helens
0 20 mi
0 20 km
5 mi
5 km
WALDRON ISLAND
Eastsound
STUART ISLAND
West Sound
Orcas Island
Roche Harbor
Orcas
Olga
SHAW ISLAND
BLAKELEY ISLAND
Friday Harbor
San Juan Island
Lopez Village
Lopez Island
Richardson
SAN JUAN ISLANDS

Whidbey Island

20 mins by ferry from Mukilteo (20 miles north of Seattle) to Clinton, at the southern end of Whidbey Island, or drive north 87 miles to Deception Pass at the north end of the island.

Whidbey is a blend of low pastoral hills, evergreen and oak forests, meadows of wildflowers (including some endemic species), sandy beaches, and dramatic bluffs with a few pockets of unfortunate suburban sprawl. It's a great place for a scenic drive, viewing sunsets over the water, taking ridge hikes that give you uninterrupted views of the Strait of Juan de Fuca, walking along miles of rugged seaweed-strewn beaches, and for boating or kayaking along the protected shorelines of Saratoga Passage, Holmes Harbor, Penn Cove, and Skagit Bay.

The best beaches are on the west side, where wooded and wildflower-bedecked bluffs drop steeply to sand or surf—which can cover the beaches at high tide and can be unexpectedly rough on this exposed shore. Both beaches and bluffs have great views of the shipping lanes and the Olympic Mountains. Maxwelton Beach, with its sand, driftwood, and amazing sunsets, is popular with the locals. Possession Point includes a park and a beach, but it's best known for its popular boat launch. West of Coupeville, Ft. Ebey State Park has a sandy spread and an incredible bluff trail; West Beach is a stormy patch north of the fort with mounds of driftwood. At 35 miles long, Whidbey's island vibe is split between north and south; the historic southern and central towns of Langley and Coupeville are quaint and offer the most to do; Clinton (near the ferry terminal) isn't much of a destination, nor is the sprawling Navy town of Oak Harbor farther north. Yet Deception Pass at the island's northern tip offers the most jaw-dropping splendor, so plan enough time to visit both ends of the island. One fun way to see it all is to arrive via the Clinton ferry and drive back to Seattle via Deception Pass, or vice versa.

GETTING HERE

You can reach Whidbey Island by heading north from Seattle on I–5, west on Route 20 onto Fidalgo Island, and south across Deception Pass Bridge. The Deception Pass Bridge links Whidbey to Fidalgo Island. From the bridge it's just a short drive to Anacortes, Fidalgo's main town and the terminus for ferries to the San Juan Islands. It's easier—and more pleasant—to take the 20-minute ferry trip from Mukilteo (30 miles northwest of Seattle) to Clinton, on Whidbey's south end, as long as you don't time your trip on a Friday evening, which could leave you waiting in the car line for hours. Fares are $5.20 per person for walk-ons (round-trip) and $14.80 per car and driver (round trip). Be sure to look at a map before choosing your point of entry; the ferry ride may not make sense if your main destination is Deception Pass State Park. Buses on Whidbey Island, provided by Island Transit, are free. Routes are fairly comprehensive, but keep in mind that Whidbey is big—it takes at least 35 minutes just to drive from the southern ferry terminal to the midway point at Coupeville—and if your itinerary is far-reaching, a car is your best bet.

CONTACT Island Transit. ☎ *800/240–8747* 🌐 *www.islandtransit.org.*

VISITOR INFORMATION

Langley Chamber of Commerce
Start off the "Langley Loop"—an 8-mile scenic driving or biking tour—at the Chamber offices, which will point you in the right direction for South Whidbey's eclectic mix of restaurants, galleries, wineries, and markets. ✉ *208 Anthes Ave., Langley* ☎ *360/221–6765* 🌐 *www.visitlangley.com.*

LANGLEY

The historic village of Langley, 7 miles north of Clinton on Whidbey Island, is above a 50-foot-high bluff overlooking Saratoga Passage, which separates Whidbey from Camano Island. A grassy terrace just above the beach is a great place for viewing birds on the water or in the air. On a clear day you can see Mt. Baker in the distance. Upscale boutiques selling art, glass, jewelry, books, and clothing line 1st and 2nd streets in the heart of town.

Restaurants

Prima Bistro

$$ | **BISTRO** | Langley's most popular gathering spot occupies a second-story space on 1st Street, right above the Star Store Grocery. Northwest-inspired French cuisine is the headliner here; classic bistro dishes like steak frites, salade nicoise, and confit of duck leg are favorites. **Known for:** Penn Cove mussels and oysters; patio views of Saratoga Passage and Camano Island; live music on Thursday nights. *Average main: $22* ✉ *201½ 1st St., Langley* ☎ *360/221–4060* 🌐 *www.primabistro.com.*

Hotels

★ **Inn at Langley**

$$$$ | **B&B/INN** | Perched on a bluff above the beach, this concrete-and-wood Frank Lloyd Wright–inspired structure is just steps from the center of town. **Pros:** no children under 12; stunning views of the Saratoga Passage; destination restaurant (with priority seating for inn guests). **Cons:** some rooms can be on the small side; expensive for the area; not family-friendly for young kids. *Rooms from: $375* ✉ *400 1st St., Langley* ☎ *360/221–3033* 🌐 *www.innatlangley.com* *28 rooms* *Free Breakfast.*

Saratoga Inn

$$ | **B&B/INN** | At the edge of Langley, this cedar-shake, Nantucket-style inn features cozy decor and fireplaces in every room. **Pros:** wraparound porches with rocking chairs; some rooms have water and mountain views; afternoon tea. **Cons:** a bit rustic; some small bathrooms; no on-site restaurant. *Rooms from: $195* ✉ *201 Cascade Ave., Langley* ☎ *360/221–5801, 800/698–2910* 🌐 *www.saratogainnwhidbeyisland.com* *15 rooms, 1 carriage house* *Free Breakfast.*

Shopping

Moonraker Books

BOOKS/STATIONERY | Langley's independent bookshop, an institution since 1972, stocks a wonderful and eclectic array of fiction, nonfiction, cookbooks—and, according to the owners, "books you didn't even know you wanted until you stepped inside." ✉ *209 1st St., Langley* ☎ *360/221–6962.*

Museo

ART GALLERIES | This contemporary fine art gallery focused on Northwest and regional artists is known for its glass art, sculpture, and handcrafted jewelry. Artist receptions are held on the first Saturday of each month from 5 to 7 pm, part of Langley's First Saturday Art Walk ✉ *215 1st St., Langley* ☎ *360/221–7737* 🌐 *www.museo.cc.*

GREENBANK

About halfway up Whidbey Island, 14 miles northwest of Langley, is the hamlet of Greenbank, home to a former farm turned multiuse attraction encircled by views of the Olympic and Cascade ranges.

Sights

Greenbank Farm

FARM/RANCH | **FAMILY** | You can't miss the huge, chestnut-color, two-story barn out front—the centerpiece to this picturesque, 150-acre property, a former working farm that now houses two art galleries, a café, and several shops.

Did You Know?

The Admiralty Head Lighthouse, in Whidbey Island's Fort Casey State Park, was built in 1861 and then rebuilt in 1903; the lighthouse was decommissioned and its lens turned off in 1922.

Greenbank's grounds include a demonstration garden and lovely walking trails, many of which are dog-friendly. ✉ *765 Wonn Rd., Greenbank* ☎ *360/678–7700* 🌐 *www.greenbankfarm.com* 🎫 *Free.*

Meerkerk Rhododendron Gardens
GARDEN | The 53-acre Meerkerk Rhododendron Gardens contain 1,500 native and hybrid species of rhododendrons and more than 100,000 spring bulbs on 10 acres of display gardens with more than 4 miles of nature trails. The flowers are in full bloom in April and May; summer flowers and fall color provide interest later in the year. The 43 remaining acres are kept wild as a nature preserve. Leashed pets are permitted on the gravel paths. ✉ *Hwy. 525 and Resort Rd., Greenbank* ☎ *360/678–1912* 🌐 *www.meerkerkgardens.org* 🎫 *$5.*

COUPEVILLE

Restored Victorian houses grace many of the streets in quiet Coupeville, Washington's second-oldest city, on the south shore of Penn Cove, 12 miles north of Greenbank. It also has one of the largest national historic districts in the state and has been used for filming movies depicting 19th-century New England villages. Stores above the waterfront have maintained their old-fashioned character. Captain Thomas Coupe founded the town in 1852. His house was built the following year, and other houses and commercial buildings were built in the late 1800s. Even though Coupeville is the island county seat, the town has a laid-back, almost 19th-century air.

Sights

★ Ebey's Landing National Historic Reserve
BEACH—SIGHT | **FAMILY** | The reserve encompasses a sand-and-cobble beach, bluffs with dramatic views down the Strait of Juan de Fuca, two state parks (Ft. Casey and Ft. Ebey; see separate listings), and several privately held pioneer farms homesteaded in the early 1850s. The first and largest reserve of its kind holds nearly 400 nationally registered historic structures (including those located within the town of Coupeville), most of them from the 19th century. Miles of trails lead along the beach and through the woods. Cedar Gulch, south of the main entrance to Ft. Ebey, has a lovely picnic area in a wooded ravine above the beach. ✉ *Coupeville* ✥ *From Hwy. 20, turn south on Main St. in Coupeville. This road turns into Engles Rd. as you head out of town. Turn right on Hill Rd. and follow it to reserve* 🌐 *www.nps.gov/ebla.*

Ft. Casey and Keystone State Park
NATIONAL/STATE PARK | **FAMILY** | The 467-acre Ft. Casey State Park, on a bluff overlooking sweeping views of Strait of Juan de Fuca and the Port Townsend ferry landing, was one of three forts (the "Triangle of Death") built after 1890 to protect the entrance to Admiralty Inlet from a naval invasion. Look for the concrete gun emplacement and a couple of 8-inch "disappearing" guns. The charming Admiralty Head Lighthouse Interpretive Center is north of the gunnery emplacements. There are also grassy picnic sites, rocky fishing spots, waterfront campsites, and a boat launch. A Washington State Discover Pass is required ($30/year or $10/day; see *www.discoverpass.wa.gov*). Once you're done exploring the park, take the ferry from here to Port Townsend for a quick side trip or long lunch. ✉ *2 miles west of Rte. 20, Coupeville* ☎ *360/678–4519* 🌐 *www.parks.wa.gov/parks* 🎫 *Discover Pass required; $30/year or $10/day.*

Ft. Ebey State Park
NATIONAL/STATE PARK | **FAMILY** | In late May and early June, Ft. Ebey State Park blazes with native rhododendrons. West of Coupeville on Point Partridge, it has 3 miles of shoreline, campsites in the woods, trails to the headlands, a freshwater lake for fishing, World War II gun emplacements, wildflower meadows, spectacular views down the Strait

This Historic Ferry House is part of Ebey's Landing National Historic Reserve on Whidbey Island.

of Juan de Fuca, and miles of hiking and biking trails. A Washington State Discover Pass is required. ✉ *3 miles west of Rte. 20, Coupeville* ☎ *360/678–4636* 🌐 *www.parks.wa.gov* 🎟 *Washington State Discover Pass required ($30/year or $10/day).*

Island County Historical Museum
HISTORIC SITE | FAMILY | Collections include Ice Age relics, mammoth remains, and a strong Native American collection, including cedar dugout canoes. The square-timber **Alexander Blockhouse** outside dates from 1855. Note the squared logs and dovetail joints of the corners—no overlapping log ends. This construction technique was favored by many western Washington pioneers. ✉ *908 NW Alexander St., Coupeville* ☎ *360/678–3310* 🎟 *Free (donations welcomed).*

Restaurants

Currents Bistro
$$ | PACIFIC NORTHWEST | Formerly known as Christopher's on Whidbey, this warm and casual place is in a house one block from the waterfront. The seafood-centric menu features many island favorites, including local mussels and clams, a wonderful calamari and seafood stew; the meat and pasta dishes are good, too. **Known for:** Penn Cove mussels; extensive wine list; calamari Caesar salad. $ *Average main: $22* ✉ *103 NW Coveland, Coupeville* ☎ *360/678–5480* 🌐 *www.christophersonwhidbey.com* ⏲ *Closed Mon.*

★ The Oystercatcher
$$$$ | SEAFOOD | A dining destination for foodies from across the Northwest renowned for its local-inspired cuisine, the Oystercatcher features a simple menu that's heavily influenced by fresh in-season ingredients. The intimate, romantic dining space in the heart of town serves lunch Friday through Sunday, but **Known for:** pretty views of Penn Cove; farm-to-table; stellar wine list.

A dining destination for foodies from across the Northwest renowned for its local-inspired cuisine, the Oystercatcher features a simple menu that's heavily influenced by fresh in-season ingredients. The intimate, romantic dining space in the heart of town serves lunch Friday through Sunday, but **Known for:** pretty views of Penn Cove; farm-to-table; stellar wine list. *Average main: $38 901 Grace St. NW, Coupeville 360/678–0683 www.oystercatcherwhidbey.com Closed Mon.–Tues. No lunch weekdays.*

Hotels

Captain Whidbey Inn

$$ | **B&B/INN** | Over a century old and steps from the shorefront of Penn Cove, this venerable historic lodge surrounded by old-growth firs was recently purchased by a young trio of investors from Portland, who refreshed the place with more of a hip boutique hotel vibe (think Ace Hotel) while maintaining the rustic charm that's made it a favorite for decades. **Pros:** a few lodging options, including private cabins with hot tubs; secluded "upscale summer camp" vibe; pedestal sinks in rooms. **Cons:** shared bathrooms; poor soundproofing in the main motel; spotty cell phone coverage. *Rooms from: $215 2072 Captain Whidbey Inn Rd., off Madrona Way, Coupeville 360/678–4097, 800/366–4097 www.captainwhidbey.com 29 rooms, 2 suites, 4 cabins Free Breakfast.*

Compass Rose Bed and Breakfast

$ | **B&B/INN** | Inside this stately 1890 Queen Anne Victorian on the National Register of Historic Places, a veritable museum of art, artifacts, and antiques awaits you. **Pros:** wonderful, interesting hosts; elegant breakfast with china, silver, linen, and lace; lots of eye candy for antiques lovers. **Cons:** only two rooms, so it gets booked up fast; too old-fashioned for some travelers; not kid-friendly (too many things to break). *Rooms from: $140 508 S Main St., Coupeville 360/678–5318, 800/237–3881 www.compassrosebandb.com No credit cards 2 rooms Free Breakfast.*

OAK HARBOR

Oak Harbor, about 10 miles north of Coupeville, is the least attractive and least interesting part of Whidbey—it mainly exists to serve the Whidbey Island Naval Air Station, and has none of the historic or pastoral charm of the rest of the island. It is, however, the largest town on the island and the one closest to Deception Pass State Park. If you need to stock up on provisions, you'll find all the big-box stores here, in addition to major supermarkets. In town, the marina, at the east side of the bay, has a picnic area with views of Saratoga Passage and the entrance of Penn Cove.

Sights

Deception Pass State Park

NATIONAL/STATE PARK | **FAMILY** | The biggest draw of the park is the historic two-lane Deception Pass Bridge connecting Whidbey Island to Fidalgo Island, about 9 miles north of Oak Harbor. Park the car and walk across in order to get the best views of the dramatic saltwater gorges and churning whirlpools below. Then spend a few hours walking the 19 miles of rocky shore and beaches, exploring three freshwater lakes, or walking along the many forest and meadow trails. *Rte. 20, 9 miles north of Oak Harbor, Oak Harbor 360/675–2417 www.parks.wa.gov Daily Discover pass $10 per vehicle; annual $30 (valid at all state parks); campsite fees vary.*

The San Juan Islands

About 100 miles northwest of Seattle, these romantic islands abound with breathtaking rolling pastures, rocky shorelines, and thickly forested ridges, and their quaint villages draw art lovers, foodies, and city folk seeking serenity.

Inns are easygoing and well appointed, and many restaurants are helmed by highly talented chefs emphasizing local ingredients.

Each of the San Juans maintains a distinct character, though all share in the archipelago's blessings of serene farmlands, unspoiled coves, blue-green or gray tidal waters, and radiant light. Offshore, seals haul out on sandbanks and orcas patrol the deep channels. You may see the occasional minke whale frolicking in the kelp, and humpback whales have become increasingly visible around the islands. You'll very rarely spy gray whales, which stay closer to Washington's mainland.

There are 172 named islands in the archipelago. Sixty are populated (though most have only a house or two), and 10 are state marine parks, some of which are accessible only to nonmotorized craft—kayakers, canoes, small sailboats—navigating the Cascadia Marine Trail.

The San Juan Islands have valleys and mountains where eagles soar and forests and leafy glens where the small island deer browse. Even a species of prickly pear cactus (*Opuntia fragilis*) grows here. Beaches can be of sand or shingle (covered in small pebbles). The islands are home to ducks and swans, herons and hawks, otters and whales. The main draw is the great outdoors, but there's plenty to do once you've seen the whales or hiked. Each island, even tiny Lopez, has at least one commercial center, where you'll find shops, restaurants, and history museums. Not surprisingly, many artists take inspiration from the dramatic surroundings, and each island has a collection of galleries; Friday Harbor even has an impressive sculpture park and art museum. Lavender and alpaca farms, spas and yoga studios, a whale museum and lighthouse tours—the San Juans have a little bit of everything.

Planning

WHEN TO GO

This part of Washington has a mild, maritime climate. Winter temperatures average in the low 40s, while summer temps hover in the mid 70s. July and August are by far the most popular months to visit the three main islands—they can get busy during this time, with resorts, boating tours, and ferries often at capacity. To beat the crowds and avoid the worst of the wet weather, visit in late spring or early fall—September and early October can be fair and stunningly gorgeous, as can May and early June. Hotel rates are generally lower everywhere during these shoulder seasons—and even lower once often drizzly winter starts.

Orcas, Lopez, and San Juan islands are extremely popular in high season; securing hotel reservations in advance is essential. If you're bringing a car to the islands, be sure to book a ferry reservation well in advance. Or if you're traveling light and plan to stay put in one place in the islands, consider walking or biking. Lot parking at Anacortes is $10 per day and $40 per week in summer and half that October–April.

■ TIP→ Though a few places close or have limited hours and the incredible views are frequently obscured by drizzle during the winter, the San Juan Islands are still worth a visit in the off-season, except in January, when many spots shutter for the entire month.

FESTIVALS

Orcas Island Chamber Music Festival

FESTIVALS | Around for more than two decades, this music festival comprises more than two weeks of "classical music with a view" in August. These concerts are immensely popular with chamber-music fans around the Pacific Northwest. ✉ *Orcas Island* ☎ *866/492–0003* 🌐 *www.oicmf.org.*

Savor the San Juans
FESTIVALS | Autumn has become increasingly popular thanks to the growth of this culinary festival, which runs about six weeks. It consists of an islands-wide series of events and gatherings celebrating local foods and beverages, including farm tours, film screenings, and harvest dinners. ☎ *360/378–3277* 🌐 *www.visitsanjuans.com/savor.*

GETTING HERE AND AROUND

AIR

Port of Friday Harbor is the main San Juan Islands airport, but there are also small airports on Lopez, Shaw, and Orcas Islands. Seaplanes land on the waterfront at Friday Harbor and Roche Harbor on San Juan Island; Rosario Resort, Deer Harbor, and West Sound on Orcas Island; and Fisherman Bay on Lopez Island. Daily scheduled flights link the San Juan Islands with mainland airports at Anacortes, Bellingham, and Lake Washington, Renton, and Boeing Field near Seattle. Some airlines also offer charter services.

If traffic and ferry lines really aren't your thing, consider hopping aboard a seaplane for the quick flight from Seattle. **Kenmore Air** offers several daily departures from Lake Union, Lake Washington, and Boeing Field, and from May through September **Friday Harbor Seaplanes** has up to four daily departures from Renton to Friday Harbor. Flying isn't cheap—around $130–$170 each way—but the scenic, hour-long flight is an experience in itself. Flights on **San Juan Airlines** from Bellingham and Anacortes run about $96 each way.

AIR CONTACTS Friday Harbor Seaplanes. ☎ *425/277–1590,* 🌐 *www.fridayharborseaplanes.com.* **Kenmore Air.** ☎ *425/486–1257, 866/435–9524* 🌐 *www.kenmoreair.com.* **San Juan Airlines.** ☎ *800/874–4434* 🌐 *www.sanjuanairlines.com.*

CAR

Most visitors arrive by car, which is the best way to explore these mostly rural islands comprehensively, especially if you plan on visiting for more than a couple of days. You can also park your car at the Anacortes ferry terminal ($10 per day or $40 per week high season, and half that fall through spring), as fares are cheaper and lines much shorter for passengers without cars. B&B owners can often pick guests up at the ferry terminal by prior arrangement, and you can rely on bikes and occasional taxis or on-island car or moped rentals (on San Juan and Orcas) for getting around. Also, in summer, a shuttle bus makes its way daily around San Juan Island and on weekends on Orcas and Lopez islands. From Seattle, it's a 90-minute drive via Interstate 5 north and Highway 20 west to reach Anacortes.

Island roads are narrow and often windy, with one or two lanes. Slow down and hug the shoulder when passing another car on a one-lane road. Expect rough patches, some unpaved lanes, deer and rabbits, bicyclists, and other hazards—plus the distractions of sweeping water views. There are a few car-rental agencies on San Juan and Orcas, with daily rates running about $60 to $100 in summer, and as much as 25% less off-season. You'll likely save money renting a car on the mainland, even factoring in the cost of ferry transport (which in high season is about $45 to $65 for a standard vehicle including driver, plus around $14 per passenger, depending on which island you're headed to).

RENTAL CAR CONTACTS M and W Rental Cars. ✉ *725 Spring St., Friday Harbor* ☎ *360/376–5266 Orcas, 360/378–2794 San Juan* 🌐 *www.sanjuanauto.com.* **Orcas Island Rental Cars.** ☎ *360/376–7433* 🌐 *www.orcasislandshuttle.com.* **Susie's Mopeds.** ✉ *125 Nichols St., Friday Harbor* ☎ *360/378–5244, 800/532–0087* 🌐 *www.susiesmopeds.com.*

FERRY

The Washington State Ferries system can become overloaded during peak travel times. Thankfully, a reservations system makes it far easier to plan trips and avoid lines. Reservations are highly recommended, especially in summer and on weekends, although a small number of spaces on every sailing are always reserved for standby. Always arrive at least 45 minutes ahead of your departure, and as much as two hours ahead at busy times if you don't have a reservation. You'll find information on the Washington State Ferries website on up-to-the-minute wait times as well as tips on which ferries tend to be the most crowded. It's rarely a problem to get a walk-on spot, although arriving a bit early to ensure you get a ticket is wise. **■ TIP→ Avoid returning to Anacortes on the daily ferries that originate in Sidney, BC; though they're more direct routes, domestic passengers have to wait in the Customs and Border Protection line to exit along with Canadian passengers, which can take a very long time.**

FERRY CONTACTS Washington State Ferries. ✉ *2100 Ferry Terminal Rd., Anacortes* ☎ *206/464–6400, 888/808–7977* 🌐 *www.wsdot.wa.gov/ferries.*

RESTAURANTS

The San Juans have myriad small farms and restaurants serving local foods and fresh-harvested seafood, and culinary agritourism—visiting local farmers, growers, and chefs at their places of business—is on the rise.

HOTELS

With the exception of Lopez Island, which has just a handful of inns, accommodations in the San Juans are quite varied and tend be plush, if also expensive during the high summer season. Rosario Resort & Spa on Orcas Island and Roche Harbor Resort on San Juan Island are favorite spots for special-occasion splurges, and both islands have seen an influx of either new or luxuriously updated inns in recent years. These places often have perks like lavish breakfasts and on-site outfitters and tour operators. *Hotel reviews have been shortened. For full information, visit Fodors.com.*

VISITOR INFORMATION

Look to the San Juan Islands Visitors Bureau for general information on all the islands—the website is very useful.

CONTACTS San Juan Islands Visitors Bureau. ✉ *The Technology Center, 640 Mullis St., Suites 210–211, Friday Harbor* ☎ *360/378–3277, 888/468–3701* 🌐 *www.visitsanjuans.com.*

Lopez Island

45 mins by ferry from Anacortes.

Known affectionately as "Slow-pez," the closest significantly populated island to the mainland is a broad, bay-encircled bit of terrain set amid sparkling blue seas, a place where cabinlike homes are tucked into the woods, and boats are moored in lonely coves. Of the three San Juan Islands with facilities to accommodate overnight visitors, Lopez has the smallest population (approximately 2,200), and with its old orchards, weathered barns, and rolling green pastures, it's the most rustic and least crowded in the archipelago. Gently sloping roads cut wide curves through golden farmlands and trace the edges of pebbly beaches, while peaceful trails wind through thick patches of forest. Sweeping country views make Lopez a favorite year-round biking locale, and except for the long hill up from the ferry docks, most roads and designated bike paths are easy for novices to negotiate.

The only settlement is Lopez Village, really just a cluster of cafés and boutiques, as well as a summer market and outdoor theater, an upscale inn, a visitor information center, and a grocery store. Other attractions—such as seasonal berry-picking farms, small wineries, kitschy galleries, intimate restaurants, and one secluded bed-and-breakfast—are scattered around the island.

GETTING HERE AND AROUND

The Washington State Ferries crossing from Anacortes take about 45 minutes; round-trip peak-season fares are about $14 per person, $45 for a car and driver. One-hour flights from Seattle cost about $130 to $170 each way. You can get around the island by car (bring your own—there are no rentals) or bike; there are bike-rental facilities by the ferry terminal.

ESSENTIALS

VISITOR INFORMATION Lopez Island Chamber of Commerce. ✉ *Lopez Rd., at Tower Rd., Lopez* ☎ *360/468–4664* 🌐 *www.lopezisland.com.*

Sights

Lopez Island Historical Museum
MUSEUM | Artifacts from the region's Native American tribes and early settlers include some impressive ship and small-boat models and maps of local landmarks. You can also listen to fascinating digital recordings of early settlers discussing life on Lopez Island. ✉ *Weeks Rd. and Washburn Pl., Lopez* ☎ *360/468–2049* 🌐 *www.lopezmuseum.org* 🎫 *Free* 🕒 *Closed Mon.–Tues. and Oct.–Apr.*

★ **Shark Reef Sanctuary**
TRAIL | A quiet forest trail along beautiful Shark Reef leads to an isolated headland jutting out above the bay. The sounds of raucous barks and squeals mean you're nearly there, and eventually you may see throngs of seals and seagulls on the rocky islets across from the point. Bring binoculars to spot bald eagles in the trees as you walk and to view sea otters frolicking in the waves near the shore. The trail starts at the Shark Reef Road parking lot south of the airport, and it's a 15-minute walk to the headland. ✉ *Shark Reef Rd., Lopez* ✣ *2 miles south of Lopez Island Airport* 🎫 *Free.*

Spencer Spit State Park
NATIONAL/STATE PARK | Set on a spit along the Cascadia Marine Trail for kayakers, this popular spot for summer camping is on former Native American clamming, crabbing, and fishing grounds. A variety of campsites is available, from primitive tent sites to full hookups. This is one of the few Washington beaches where cars are permitted. ✉ *521 A Bakerview Rd., Lopez* ☎ *360/468–2251* 🌐 *www.parks.wa.gov/parks* 🎫 *$10.*

Restaurants

Haven Kitchen & Bar
$$ | AMERICAN | You'll find something for everyone at this Lopez eatery, which seems to have picked favorite dishes from various cuisines and created solid versions of them, sometimes with inventive twists (tater tots in a burrito, for example); they've got everything from Thai fresh rolls to gamberoni linguine with fresh, locally made pasta. **Known for:** eclectic menu; expansive flower-lined outdoor deck; well-crafted artisanal cocktails. $ *Average main: $22* ✉ *9 Old Post Rd., Lopez* ☎ *360/468–3272* 🌐 *www.lopezhaven.com* 🕒 *Closed Sun.–Tues.*

Ursa Minor
$$$$ | PACIFIC NORTHWEST | One of the latest upscale farm-to-table restaurants to put the San Juan Islands on the culinary map (reservations strongly recommended), Ursa Minor is helmed by Nick Coffey, formerly of the now-closed Sitka & Spruce in Seattle. He celebrates the Islands' incredible bounty with a creative seasonal menu featuring seafood, foraged mushrooms, and products from Lopez's longtime Jones Family Farm, which raises grass-fed livestock and cultivates a few types of shellfish, including a pink scallop that has Seattle chefs wait-listing for orders. **Known for:** airy, serene organic-modern space; island-sourced ingredients; unique Northwest fare. $ *Average main: $40* ✉ *210 Lopez Rd., Lopez* ☎ *360/622–2730*

The view from Mount Constitution on Orcas Island, the highest point in the San Juans

www.ursaminorlopez.com Closed Mon.–Thu. and Jan.

Coffee and Quick Bites

Holly B's Bakery

$ | **BAKERY** | Tucked into a small, cabinlike strip of businesses set back from the water, this cozy wood-paneled bakery has been a source of delicious fresh ham-and-Gruyère croissants, marionberry scones, slices of pizza, and other savory and sweet treats since 1977. Sunny summer mornings bring diners out onto the patio, where kids play and parents relax. **Known for:** ginormous, decadent cinnamon rolls; pizza by the slice; scones flavored with seasonal fruit. *Average main: $7 Lopez Plaza, 211 Lopez Rd., Lopez 360/468–2133 www.hollybsbakery.com No credit cards Closed Dec.–Mar. No dinner.*

Isabel's Espresso

$ | **CAFÉ** | A favorite of Lopez locals, Isabel's sources its coffee from Fair Trade suppliers and its creamy dairy from the mainland's small Fresh Breeze Organic Dairy Farm. Housed in a charming rustic building in Lopez's tiny "downtown," the café also serves light fare like pastries and sandwiches. **Known for:** good coffee; outdoor seating with views. *Average main: $6 308 Lopez Rd., Lopez 360/468–4114 www.isabelsespresso.com.*

Vita's Wildly Delicious

$ | **CAFÉ** | At this gourmet market and wine shop (open primarily during the daytime but until 8 pm on Friday), the proprietors create a daily-changing assortment of prepared foods and some made-to-order items, such as Reuben panini sandwiches. Other favorites include Dungeness crab cakes, hearty meat loaf, lobster mac-and-cheese, and an assortment of tempting desserts. **Known for:** Dungeness crab cakes; pretty garden-dining area; gourmet picnic supplies. *Average main: $11 77 Village Rd., Lopez 360/468–4268 www.vitasonlopez.com Closed Sun., Mon., and late fall–late spring. No dinner.*

Hotels

Edenwild Inn

$$$ | **B&B/INN** | Thoughtful and friendly owners Anthony and Crystal Rovente operate this large Victorian-style farmhouse surrounded by gardens and framed by Fisherman Bay, where spacious rooms are each painted or papered in different pastel shades and furnished with simple antiques; some have claw-foot tubs and brick fireplaces. **Pros:** lovely outdoor spaces, including an outdoor veranda; nice breakfast buffet using local produce and homemade baked goods; handy location close to village restaurants. **Cons:** no TVs in rooms; decor is a bit plain; two-night minimum. *Rooms from: $229* *132 Lopez Rd., Lopez* *360/468–3238* *www.edenwildinn.com* *9 rooms* *Free Breakfast.*

★ **Mackaye Harbor Inn**

$$ | **B&B/INN** | This former sea captain's house, built in 1904, rises two stories above the beach at the southern end of the island and accommodates guests in cheerfully furnished rooms with golden-oak and brass details and wicker furniture; three have views of MacKaye Harbor. **Pros:** fantastic water views; mountain bikes (free) and kayaks (reasonable daily fee) available; friendly and attentive hosts. **Cons:** on far end of the island; several miles from the ferry terminal and airport; some bathrooms are across the hall from rooms. *Rooms from: $195* *949 MacKaye Harbor Rd., Lopez* *360/468–2253, 888/314–6140* *www.mackayeharborinn.com* *5 rooms* *Free Breakfast.*

Activities

BIKING

Bike rental rates start at around $7 an hour and $30 a day. Reservations are recommended, particularly in summer.

Lopez Bicycle Works

BICYCLING | At the marina 4 miles from the ferry, this full-service operation can bring bicycles right to you. In addition to cruisers and mountain bikes, the shop also rents tandem and recumbent bikes. *2847 Fisherman Bay Rd., Lopez* *360/468–2847* *www.lopezbicycleworks.com.*

Village Cycles

BICYCLING | This aptly named full-service rental and repair shop is in the heart of Lopez Village. *214 Lopez Rd., Lopez* *360/468–4013* *www.villagecycles.net.*

SEA KAYAKING

Cascadia Kayaks

KAYAKING | This company rents kayaks for half days or full days. The outfitter also organizes half-day, full-day, and two- to three-day guided tours. Hour-long private lessons are available, too, if you need a little coaching before going out on your own. *135 Lopez Rd., Lopez* *360/468–3008* *www.cascadiakayaks.com.*

Lopez Island Sea Kayak

KAYAKING | Open May to September at Fisherman Bay, this outfitter has a huge selection of kayaks, both plastic and fiberglass touring models. Rentals are by the hour or day, and the company can deliver kayaks to any point on the island for an additional fee. *2845 Fisherman Bay Rd., Lopez* *360/468–2847* *www.lopezkayaks.com.*

Shopping

Chimera Gallery

ART GALLERIES | This local artists' cooperative exhibits and sells crafts, jewelry, and fine art. *Lopez Plaza, 211 Lopez Rd., Lopez* *360/468–3265* *www.chimeragallery.com.*

Lopez Bookshop

BOOKS/STATIONERY | This longtime bookseller is stocked with publications on

San Juan Islands history and activities, as well as tomes about the Pacific Northwest. There's also a good selection of mysteries, literary novels, children's books, and craft kits, plus greeting cards, art prints, and maps. Many of the items sold here are the works of local writers, artists, and photographers. ✉ *Lopez Plaza, 211 Lopez Rd., Lopez* ☎ *360/468–2132* 🌐 *www.lopezbookshop.com.*

Orcas Island

75 mins by ferry from Anacortes.

Orcas Island, the largest of the San Juans, is blessed with wide, pastoral valleys and scenic ridges that rise high above the neighboring waters. (At 2,409 feet, Orcas's Mt. Constitution is the highest peak in the San Juans.) Spanish explorers set foot here in 1791, and the island is actually named for one of these early visitors, Juan Vicente de Güemes Padilla Horcasitas y Aguayo—not for the black-and-white whales that frolic in the surrounding waters. The island was also the home of Native American tribes, whose history is reflected in such places as Pole Pass, where the Lummi people used kelp and cedar-bark nets to catch ducks, and Massacre Bay, where in 1858 a tribe from southeast Alaska attacked a Lummi fishing village.

Today farmers, fishermen, artists, retirees, and summer-home owners make up the population of about 4,500. Houses are spaced far apart, and the island's few hamlets typically have just one major road running through them. Low-key resorts dotting the island's edges are evidence of the thriving local tourism industry, as is the gradual but steady influx of urbane restaurants, boutiques, and even a trendy late-night bar in the main village of Eastsound. The beauty of this island is beyond compare; Orcas is a favorite place for weekend getaways from the Seattle area any time of the year, as well as one of the state's top settings for summer weddings.

The main town on Orcas Island lies at the head of the East Sound channel, which nearly divides the island in two. More than 20 small shops and boutiques here sell jewelry, pottery, and crafts by local artisans, as well as gourmet edibles, from baked goods to chocolates.

GETTING HERE AND AROUND

The Washington State Ferries crossing from Anacortes to Orcas Village, in the island's Westsound area, takes about 75 minutes; peak-season round-trip fares are about $14 per person, $55 for a car and driver. One-hour flights from Seattle cost about $130 to $170 each way. Planes land at Deer Harbor, Eastsound, Westsound, and at the Rosario Resort and Spa.

The best way to get around the island is by car—bikes will do in a pinch, but the hilly, curvy roads that generally lack shoulders make cycling a bit risky. Most resorts and inns offer transfers from the ferry terminal.

ESSENTIALS

VISITOR INFORMATION Orcas Island Chamber of Commerce & Visitor Center. ✉ *65 N Beach Rd.* ☎ *360/376–2273* 🌐 *www.orcasislandchamber.com.*

Sights

Moran Museum at Rosario

ARTS VENUE | This 1909 mansion that forms the centerpiece of Rosario Resort was constructed as the vacation home of Seattle shipping magnate and mayor Robert Moran. On the second floor is this fascinating museum that spans several former guest rooms and includes old photos, furniture, and memorabilia related to the Moran family, the resort's history, and the handsome ships built by Moran and his brothers. A highlight is the music room, which contains an incredible two-story 1913 aeolian pipe organ and an ornate, original Tiffany chandelier. Renowned musician Christopher Peacock discusses the resort's history and performs on the 1900 Steinway grand piano daily (except Sunday) at 4 pm in summer and on Saturday at 4 the rest of the year. The surrounding grounds make for a lovely stroll, which you might combine with lunch or a cocktail in one of the resort's water-view restaurants. ✉ *1400 Rosario Rd.* ☎ *360/376–2222* 🌐 *www.rosarioresort.com/museum* 🎫 *Free.*

★ Moran State Park

NATIONAL/STATE PARK | **FAMILY** | This pristine patch of wilderness comprises 5,252 acres of hilly, old-growth forests dotted with sparkling lakes, in the middle of which rises the island's highest point, 2,409-foot Mt. Constitution. A drive to the summit affords exhilarating views of the islands, the Cascades, the Olympics, and Vancouver Island, and avid hikers enjoy the strenuous but stunning 7-mile round-trip trek from rippling Mountain Lake to the summit (some 38 miles of trails traverse the entire park). The observation tower on the summit was built by the Civilian Conservation Corps in the 1930s. In summer, you can rent boats to paddle around beautiful Cascade Lake. ✉ *Mt. Constitution Rd.* ☎ *360/376–2326* 🌐 *www.parks.wa.gov/parks* 🎫 *Discover Pass (annual $30/day pass $10).*

Orcas Island Historical Museum

HISTORIC SITE | Surrounded by Eastsound's lively shops and cafés, this museum comprises several reassembled and relocated late-19th-century pioneer cabins. An impressive collection of more than 6,000 photographs, documents, and artifacts tells the story of the island's Native American and Anglo history, and in an oral-history exhibit longtime residents of the island talk about how the community has evolved over the decades. The museum also operates the 1888 Crow Valley Schoolhouse, which is open on summer Wednesdays and Saturdays; call the museum for hours and directions. ✉ *181 N Beach Rd.* ☎ *360/376–4849* 🌐 *www.orcasmuseum.org* 🎫 *$5* ⏲ *Closed Oct.–May, Sun.–Tues.*

Orcas Island Winery

WINERY/DISTILLERY | **FAMILY** | This boutique winery known on the island for its reds is under new ownership—a young married couple from Los Angeles was so awed by the area that they jumped at the chance to take over and have transformed the winery into a modern farmhouse-chic gathering space with picnic-table outdoor seating perfect for a sunny afternoon spent sipping wine and listening to concerts. ✉ *2371 Crow Valley Rd.* ☎ *360/797–5062* 🌐 *www.orcasislandwinery.com* ⏲ *Closed Mon.–Tue. and Jan.*

★ Turtleback Mountain Preserve

NATURE PRESERVE | A more peaceful, less crowded hiking and wildlife-watching alternative to Moran State Park, this 1,576-acre expanse of rugged ridges, wildflower-strewn meadows, temperate rain forest, and lush wetlands is one of the natural wonders of the archipelago. Because the San Juan County Land Bank purchased this land in 2006, it will be preserved forever for the public to enjoy. There are 8 miles of well-groomed trails, including a steep trek up to 1,519-foot-elevation Raven Ridge and a windy hike to Turtlehead Point, a soaring bluff with spectacular views west of San Juan Island and Vancouver Island beyond that—it's an amazing place to watch the sunset. You can access the preserve either from the North Trailhead, which is just 3 miles southwest of Eastsound on Crow Valley Road, or the South Trailhead, which is 3 miles northeast of Deer Harbor off Wild Rose Lane—check the website for a trail map and detailed directions. ✉ *North Trailhead parking, Crow Valley Rd., just south of Crow Valley Schoolhouse* ☎ *360/378–4402* 🌐 *www.sjclandbank.org/turtle_back.html* 🎫 *Free.*

Restaurants

★ Doe Bay Cafe

$$$ | **PACIFIC NORTHWEST** | Most of the tables in this warmly rustic dining room at Doe Bay Resort overlook the tranquil body of water for which the café is named. This is a popular stop for brunch or dinner before or after hiking or biking in nearby Moran State Park—starting your day off with smoked-salmon Benedict with Calabrian-chili hollandaise sauce will provide you with plenty of fuel for recreation. **Known for:** locally sourced and foraged ingredients; smoked-salmon Benedict; funky, rustic vibe. *Average main: $23 107 Doe Bay Rd. 360/376–8059 www.doebay.com Closed Tues.–Wed. Limited hrs Oct.–May; call ahead.*

★ Hogstone's Wood Oven

$$ | **PIZZA** | An intimate, minimalist space with large windows and just a handful of tables, this hip locavore-minded pizza joint (a James Beard Award semifinalist in 2019) serves wood-fired pies with creative toppings—consider the one with new potatoes, crispy pork fat, chickweed, cultured cream, and uncured garlic. The bounteous, farmers'-market-sourced salads are another strength, and the wine list, with varietals from the Northwest and Europe, is exceptional. **Known for:** wildly inventive pizzas with unusual toppings; extensive wine list; long wait on the weekend (reservations not accepted). *Average main: $22 460 Main St. 360/376–4647 www.hogstone.com Closed Tues.–Wed. (check for winter hours).*

Inn at Ship Bay

$$$ | **PACIFIC NORTHWEST** | This restaurant at this stylish, contemporary inn just a mile from Eastsound offers among the most memorable dining experiences on the island. Tucked into a renovated 1869 farmhouse, the dining room and bar serve food that emphasizes local, seasonal ingredients. **Known for:** outstanding wine list; house-made sourdough bread made from a century-old starter yeast; ingredients from on-site garden and orchard. *Average main: $26 326 Olga Rd. 360/376–5886 www.innatshipbay.com Closed Sun. and Mon. and mid-Dec.–mid-Mar. No lunch.*

The Kitchen

$ | **ASIAN** | Seating at this casual, affordable Asian restaurant adjacent to the distinctive boutiques of Prune Alley is in a compact dining room or, when the weather is nice, at open-air picnic tables in a tree-shaded garden. The pan-Asian food here is filling and simple, using local seafood and produce, with plenty of vegetarian options. **Known for:** hearty ramen and Thai noodle soups; sustainable practices; nice selection of craft brews on tap. *Average main: $10 249 Prune Alley 360/376–6958 www.thekitchenorcas.com Closed Sun.*

Mansion Restaurant

$$$$ | **PACIFIC NORTHWEST** | For a special-occasion dinner (or lunch on weekends), it's worth the drive to this grandly romantic dining room inside the historic main inn at Rosario Resort, which recently tapped a heavy-hitter restaurant-industry veteran from San Francisco to oversee the dining program at the historic hotel. Though some changes are in store, you'll still be treated to polished service, sweeping bay views, and exquisitely plated seasonal Northwest cuisine. **Known for:** lovely views of Cascade Bay; dinner service in the mahogany-clad fireside Moran Lounge; small portions for the price. *Average main: $40 1400 Rosario Rd. 360/376–2222 www.rosarioresort.com No lunch Mon.–Thurs.*

Mijitas

$$ | **MEXICAN** | **FAMILY** | A bustling family-friendly Mexican restaurant with a cozy dining room and a sprawling shaded garden patio is helmed by Raul Rios, who learned to cook during his years growing up outside Mexico City. The flavorful food

here isn't entirely authentic—expect a mix of Mexican and Mexican-American dishes, many featuring local ingredients. **Known for:** sweet, tangy margaritas; expansive garden patio; braised short ribs with blackberry mole sauce. *Average main: $21 310 A St. 360/376–6722 No lunch.*

Roses Bakery & Cafe
$$ | **MODERN AMERICAN** | Set inside a cheerfully renovated former Eastsound fire station, this bustling café known for its house-baked breads and an impressive selection of artisanal gourmet groceries (from cheeses to fine wines) is also a fine spot for breakfast or lunch. The fare is French-Italian influenced but using local ingredients: try the croque monsieur or house-cured gravlax in the morning. **Known for:** rhubarb galette with fennel ice cream; outstanding assortment of cheese, sweets, and wines to go; budget-friendly premade sandwiches for picnic lunches. *Average main: $19 382 Prune Alley www.rosesbakerycafe.com No dinner.*

Coffee and Quick Bites

Brown Bear Baking
$ | **BAKERY** | You might make it a point to get to this wildly popular village bakery by late morning—come midafternoon, many of the best treats are sold out. Delectables here include flaky almond-coated bear paw pastries, rich croque monsieur sandwiches, hubcap-size "Sasquatch" cookies, Tuscan olive bread, and moist blueberry muffins. **Known for:** almond-coated bear paw; French pastries; alfresco dining on the patio. *Average main: $7 29 N Beach Rd. 360/855–7456 www.facebook.com/brownbearbaking.*

Catkin Cafe
$ | **CAFÉ** | Attached to the visit-worthy Artworks Gallery, this lovely little café with rustic charm serves breakfast and lunch all day, including locally roasted coffee, fresh pastries and baked goods, and a small selection of soups, sandwiches, and salads. **Known for:** housed in a historic former strawberry barreling plant; friendly service; local ingredients. *Average main: $8 11 Pt. Lawrence Rd 360/376-3242 www.catkincafe.com Closed Mon.–Tues. No dinner.*

Hotels

Doe Bay Resort + Retreat
$$$ | **RESORT** | **FAMILY** | The family-friendly Doe Bay Resort has definite hippie roots, and some of that vibe remains intact—its large communal hot tubs overlooking a lovely little bay are still clothing optional—but the current owners have restored the charming rustic cabins that dot the 38-acre waterfront resort, all of which are clean and comfortable; the treehouse, boasting a lofted bed and an indoor bathroom with a window that hugs a tree trunk, is probably the hardest to snag during summer. **Pros:** some cabins have bathrooms, kitchens, and great views; home to the popular grassroots Doe Bay Fest; kayaks available for rent. **Cons:** many cabins have shared bathroom facilities; farther from Eastsound than most lodging (a mile from Moran State Park); two-night minimum stay. *Rooms from: $256 107 Doe Bay Rd 206/376–2291 www.doebay.com 26 cabins (yurts and geodesic domes also available) No meals.*

Kangaroo House
$$$ | **B&B/INN** | Set back from the road behind a large garden overlooked by a lovely covered porch, this 1907-built B&B in a local landmark Craftsman has an interesting history: it's named for a Depression-era resident kangaroo that provided entertainment for islanders (ask the friendly, knowledgeable hosts for the story), as well as nicely appointed private rooms, all with en suite bathrooms, and a deck dotted with busy bird feeders. **Pros:** garden hot tub with a sign-up sheet for privacy; 5-minute walk to beach and

Eastsound; fabulous multicourse organic breakfast. **Cons:** 3-night minimum for visits that include Sat.; kids must be 12 to stay here; 8-step stoop and only one downstairs room. *Rooms from: $246 1459 N Beach Rd 360/376–2175 www.kangaroohouse.com 5 rooms Free Breakfast.*

Kingfish Inn

$$$ | B&B/INN | Spacious units in this atmospheric 1902 house are equipped with a king or queen bed, private bath, and all the serenity a guest could ever want. **Pros:** decor is tasteful and contemporary; good café; water views. **Cons:** somewhat small bathrooms in some rooms; although on the lesser-visited shore of West Sound, the rooms do get some noise from road and busy marina; two-night minimum. *Rooms from: $240 Crow Valley Rd., at Deer Harbor Rd. 360/376–2500 www.kingfishinn.com Closed Jan. 4 rooms Free Breakfast.*

★ Outlook Inn

$ | HOTEL | This nice range of accommodations in the center of Eastsound includes small budget-oriented rooms with twin beds and shared bathrooms, rooms with queen or double beds, and rambling bay-view suites with gas fireplaces, kitchenettes, and two-person Jacuzzi tubs. **Pros:** steps from Eastsound dining and shops (and great restaurant on-site); friendly and helpful staff; broad mix of rates. **Cons:** in-town location can be a little noisy; only some rooms have water view; least expensive rooms have shared bath. *Rooms from: $124 171 Main St. 360/376–2200, 888/688–5665 www.outlookinn.com 54 rooms No meals.*

★ Rosario Resort and Spa

$$ | RESORT | FAMILY | Shipbuilding magnate Robert Moran built this Arts and Crafts–style waterfront mansion in 1909, and it is now the centerpiece of a gorgeous 40-acre resort that comprises several different buildings with sweeping views of Cascade Bay and Rosario Point—accommodations range from moderately priced standard guest rooms to deluxe one- and two-bedroom suites with fireplaces, decks, and full kitchens. **Pros:** water views from all buildings and many rooms; management continues to make improvements; first-rate spa and adults-only pool. **Cons:** often busy with weddings and special events; some rooms/common spaces need updating; 15-minute drive to Eastsound. *Rooms from: $185 1400 Rosario Rd. 360/376–2222, 800/562–8820 www.rosarioresort.com 67 rooms No meals.*

Nightlife

★ The Barnacle

BARS/PUBS | This quirky hole-in-the-wall bar with an insider-y, speakeasy vibe is across the lawn from the Kitchen restaurant, and has developed a cult following for its sophisticated, well-made craft cocktails—many infused with house-made bitters and local herbs and berries—and interesting wines. On this quiet, early-to-bed island, it's a nice late-night option. Light tapas are served, too. *249 Prune Alley 206/679–5683.*

Champagne Champagne

WINE BARS—NIGHTLIFE | Champagne Champagne—just a minute's walk from the ferry landing—is a charming little spot with panoramic views of the Salish Sea that showcases an excellent selection of wines (there's also a small bottle shop, the Bodega) and light bites like oysters, crudo, ceviche, and tartare. *8292 Orcas Rd., Suite A 617/449–8297 www.champagnechampagne.me.*

Island Hoppin' Brewery

LOCAL SPECIALTIES | Set in an otherwise inauspicious industrial area near the airport, this craft brewery and taproom (open nightly till 9 pm) has quickly earned a reputation throughout the archipelago—and even on the mainland as far away as Seattle—for well-made beers, including the faintly citrusy Elwha Rock IPA and the silky Old Salts Brown Ale. Smoked salmon, cheese and crackers, and a few other snacks are sold in the homey taproom. ✉ *33 Hope La.* ☎ *360/376–6079* 🌐 *www.islandhoppinbrewery.com.*

Activities

BIKING

Mountain bikes rent for about $30 per day or $100 per week. Tandem, recumbent, and electric bikes rent for about $50 per day.

Wildlife Cycles

BICYCLING | This trusty shop rents bikes and can recommend great routes all over the island. ✉ *350 N Beach Rd.* ☎ *360/376–4708* 🌐 *www.wildlifecycles.com.*

BOATING AND SAILING

Kruger Escapes

BOATING | Three-hour day adventures and sunset cruises around the islands are offered on two handsome sailboats that were both designed and formerly used for racing. The boats are also available for multiday charters. ✉ *Orcas Island* ☎ *360/201–0586* 🌐 *www.krugerescapes.com.*

Orcas Boat Rentals

BOATING | You can rent a variety of sailboats, outboards, and skiffs for full- and half-day trips, as well as book custom charter cruises, with this company. ✉ *5164 Deer Harbor Rd.* ☎ *360/376–7616* 🌐 *www.orcasboatrentals.com.*

West Beach Resort Marina

BOATING | This is a good option for renting motorized boats, kayaks and canoes, and fishing gear on the island's northwest shore. The resort is also a popular spot for divers, who can fill their tanks here. ✉ *190 Waterfront Way* ☎ *360/376–2240, 877/937–8224* 🌐 *www.westbeachresort.com.*

SEA KAYAKING

All equipment is usually included in a rental package or tour. Three-hour trips cost around $80; day tours, $110 to $135.

Orcas Outdoors Sea Kayak Tours

KAYAKING | This outfitter offers one-, two-, and three-hour journeys, as well as day trips, overnight tours, and rentals. ✉ *Orcas Ferry Landing* ☎ *360/376–4611* 🌐 *www.orcasoutdoors.com.*

Shearwater Kayak Tours

KAYAKING | This established company holds kayaking classes and runs three-hour, day, and overnight tours from Rosario, Deer Harbor, West Beach, and Doe Bay resorts. ✉ *138 N Beach Rd.* ☎ *360/376–4699* 🌐 *www.shearwaterkayaks.com.*

WHALE-WATCHING

Cruises, which run about four hours, are scheduled daily in summer and once or twice weekly at other times. The cost is around $100 to $120 per person, and boats hold 20 to 40 people. Wear warm clothing and bring a snack.

Deer Harbor Charters

BOATING | This eco-friendly tour company (the first in the San Juans to use biodiesel) offers whale-watching cruises around the island straits, with departures from both Deer Harbor Marina and Rosario Resort. Outboards and skiffs are also available, as is fishing gear. ✉ *Deer Harbor Rd.* ☎ *360/376–5989, 800/544–5758* 🌐 *www.deerharborcharters.com.*

Orcas Island Eclipse Charters

WHALE-WATCHING | In addition to tours that search around Orcas Island for whale pods and other sea life, this charter company offers lighthouse tours. ✉ *Orcas Island Ferry Landing* ☎ *360/376–6566* 🌐 *www.orcasislandwhales.com.*

Shopping

Darvill's Bookstore

BOOKS/STATIONERY | This island favorite, with a coffee bar and a couple of cozy seats with panoramic views of the water, specializes in literary fiction and nautical literature. ✉ *296 Main St.* ☎ *360/376–2135* 🌐 *www.darvillsbookstore.com.*

★ **Doe Bay Wine Co.**
WINE/SPIRITS | Owned by an Orcas Island–born sommelier who worked at restaurants in Vail and Vegas before returning home, this cheerful little bottle shop and tasting room in Eastsound has a great selection of wine, beer, and cider from around the world, including a wine series, the Orcas Project, that is produced in collaboration with Pacific Northwest winemakers and artists. Sample flights of Orcas Project wines daily. ✉ *109 N Beach Rd.* ☎ 🌐 *www.doebaywinecompany.com.*

Island Thyme and Crow Valley Shop and Gallery
ART GALLERIES | This colorful shop/gallery in Eastsound's village sells locally made soap and skin-care products and hosts occasional gallery shows. ✉ *296 Main St.* ☎ *360/376–4260* 🌐 *www.crowvalley.com.*

Kathryn Taylor Chocolates
FOOD/CANDY | This sweet sweetshop in Eastsound village sells the creative bonbons (pistachio-fig, black raspberry) of Kathryn Taylor. It's also a good stop for ice cream and Stumptown coffee drinks. ✉ *68 N Beach Rd.* ☎ *360/376–1030* 🌐 *www.kathryntaylorchocolates.com.*

★ **Orcas Island Artworks Gallery**
ART GALLERIES | Stop by this cooperative gallery to see the impressive displays pottery, sculpture, jewelry, art glass, paintings, and quilts by resident artists, including an upstairs gallery devoted to current original paintings by well-known Northwest landscape artist James Hardman. You'll find gifts in a wide price range at this wonderful space. ✉ *11 Point Lawrence Rd.* ☎ *360/376–4408* 🌐 *www.orcasartworks.com.*

★ **Orcas Island Pottery**
ART GALLERIES | A stroll through the historic house, outbuildings, and gardens of this enchanting arts complex on a bluff overlooking President Channel and Waldron Island is more than just a chance to browse beautiful pottery—it's a great spot simply to relax and soak up the views. More than a dozen regular and guest potters exhibit and sell their wares here, everything from functional dinnerware and mugs to fanciful vases and wall hangings. ✉ *338 Old Pottery Rd.* ☎ *360/376–2813* 🌐 *www.orcasislandpottery.com.*

San Juan Island

45 mins by ferry from Orcas Island, 75–90 mins by ferry from Anacortes or Sidney, BC (near Victoria).

San Juan is the cultural and commercial hub of the archipelago that shares its name. Friday Harbor, the county seat, is larger, more vibrant, and more crowded than any of the towns on Orcas or Lopez, yet San Juan still has miles of rural roads, uncrowded beaches, and rolling woodlands. It's easy to get here, too, making San Juan the preferred destination for travelers who have time to visit only one island.

Several different Coast Salish tribes first settled on San Juan, establishing encampments along the north end of the island. North-end beaches were especially busy during the annual salmon migration, when hundreds of tribal members would gather along the shoreline to fish, cook, and exchange news. Many of the indigenous early inhabitants were killed by smallpox and other imported diseases in the 18th and 19th centuries. Smallpox Bay was where tribal members plunged into the icy water to cool the fevers that came with the disease.

The 18th century brought explorers from England and Spain, but the island remained sparsely populated until the mid-1800s. From the 1880s, Roche Harbor and its newspaper were controlled by lime-company owner and Republican bigwig John S. McMillin, who virtually ran this part of the island as a personal fiefdom from 1886 until his death in 1936. Friday Harbor ultimately emerged as the island's largest community. The town's main street, rising from the harbor and ferry landing up the slopes of a modest hill, hasn't changed much in the past few decades, though the cafés, inns, and shops have become increasingly urbane.

GETTING HERE AND AROUND

With ferry connections from both Anacortes and Sidney, BC (on Vancouver Island, near Victoria), San Juan is the most convenient of the islands to reach, and the island is easily explored by car; public transportation and bicycles also work but require a bit more effort. However, if you're staying in Friday Harbor, you can get from the ferry terminal to your hotel as well as to area shops and restaurants easily on foot.

One-hour flights from Seattle to San Juan Airport, Friday Harbor, or Roche Harbor cost about $130 to $170 each way.

San Juan Transit & Tours operates shuttle buses daily from mid-May to mid-September. Hop on at Friday Harbor, the main town, to get to all the island's significant points and parks, including the San Juan Vineyards, Krystal Acres Alpaca Farm, Lime Kiln Point State Park, and Snug Harbor and Roche Harbor resorts. Different buses call on different stops, so be sure to check the schedule before you plan your day. Tickets are $5 one-way or $15 for a day pass. From mid-June through mid-September, the Friday Harbor Jolly Trolley offers trips around the island—also stopping at all of the key attractions—in an old-fashioned trolley-style bus; tickets cost $20 and are good for the entire day.

CONTACT Friday Harbor Jolly Trolley. ☎ *360/298–8873* 🌐 *www.fridayharborjollytrolley.com.* **San Juan Transit & Tours.** ✉ *Cannery Landing, Friday Harbor* ☎ *360/378–8887* 🌐 *sanjuantransit.com.*

The Washington State Ferries crossings from Anacortes to Friday Harbor takes about 75 to 90 minutes; round-trip fares in high season are about $14 per person, $65 for a car and driver. It's about the same distance from Sidney, BC, on Vancouver Island—this service is available twice daily in summer and once daily spring and fall (there's no BC service in winter). Round-trip fares are about $25 per person, $85 for car and driver. Clipper Navigation operates the passenger-only *San Juan Clipper* jet catamaran service between Pier 69 in Seattle and Friday Harbor. Boats leave Seattle daily mid-June–early September, Thursday–Monday mid-May–mid-June, and weekends early September–early October at 8:15 am and return from Friday Harbor at 5 pm; reservations are strongly recommended. During peak season, fares start at $160 for a round-trip ticket, depending on the day and whether you purchase in advance (advance tickets are cheaper). Clipper also offers optional whale-watching excursions, which can be combined with ferry passage.

■ TIP→ Some points on the west end of San Juan Island are so close to BC, Canada (which is visible across the Haro Straight), that cell phones switch to roaming; it's a good idea to turn roaming off while touring the island to avoid unexpected charges.

CONTACTS Clipper Navigation. ☎ *206/448–5000, 800/888–2535* 🌐 *www.clippervacations.com.*

ESSENTIALS

The San Juan Island Chamber of Commerce has a visitor center (open daily 10 to 4) in Friday Harbor where you can grab brochures and ask for advice.

VISITOR INFORMATION San Juan Island Chamber of Commerce. ✉ *165 1st St., Friday Harbor* ☎ *360/378–5240* 🌐 *www.sanjuanisland.org.*

Sights

Krystal Acres Alpaca Farm

FARM/RANCH | **FAMILY** | Kids and adults love admiring the more than 70 alpacas from South America at this sprawling 80-acre ranch on the west side of the island. The shop in the big barn displays beautiful, high-quality clothing and crafts, all handmade from alpaca hair. ✉ *152 Blazing Tree Rd., Friday Harbor* ☎ *360/378–6125* 🌐 *www.krystalacres.com* 🎟 *Free.*

★ Lime Kiln Point State Park

NATIONAL/STATE PARK | **FAMILY** | To watch whales cavorting in Haro Strait, head to these 36 acres on San Juan's western side just 9 miles from Friday Harbor. A rocky coastal trail leads to lookout points and a little 1919 lighthouse. The best time to spot whales is from the end of April through September, but resident pods of orcas regularly cruise past the point. This park is also a beautiful spot to soak in a summer sunset, with expansive views of Vancouver Island and beyond. ✉ *1567 Westside Rd.* ☎ *360/378–2044* 🌐 *www.parks.wa.gov/parks* 🎟 *$10* ⏲ *Interpretive center closed mid-Sept.–late May.*

Pelindaba Lavender Farm

FARM/RANCH | **FAMILY** | Wander a spectacular 20-acre valley smothered with endless rows of fragrant purple-and-gold lavender blossoms. The oils are distilled for use in therapeutic, botanical, and household products, all created on-site. The farm hosts the very popular San Juan Island Lavender Festival in mid- to late July. If you can't make it to the farm, stop at the outlet in the Friday Harbor Center at 150 1st Street, where you can buy their products and sample delicious lavender-infused baked goods, ice cream, and beverages. ✉ *33 Hawthorne La., Friday Harbor* ☎ *360/378–4248, 866/819–1911* 🌐 *www.pelindabalavender.com* 🎟 *Free* ⏲ *Closed Nov.–Apr.*

★ Roche Harbor

TOWN | **FAMILY** | It's hard to believe that fashionable Roche Harbor at the northern end of San Juan Island was once the most important producer of builder's lime on the West Coast. In 1882, John S. McMillin gained control of the lime company and expanded production. But even in its heyday as a limestone quarrying village, Roche Harbor was known for abundant flowers and welcoming accommodations. McMillin transformed a bunkhouse into private lodgings for his invited guests, who included such notables as Teddy Roosevelt. The guesthouse is now the Hotel de Haro, which displays period photographs and artifacts in its lobby. The staff has maps of the old quarry, kilns, and the Mausoleum, an eerie Greek-inspired memorial to McMillin.

McMillin's heirs operated the quarries and plant until 1956, when they sold the company to the Tarte family, who developed it into an upscale resort (but no longer own it)—the old lime kilns still stand below the bluff. Locals say it took two years for the limestone dust to wash off the trees around the harbor. McMillin's former home is now a restaurant, and workers' cottages have been transformed into comfortable visitors' lodgings. With its rose gardens, cobblestone waterfront, and well-manicured lawns, Roche Harbor retains the flavor of its days as a hangout for McMillin's powerful friends—especially since the sheltered harbor is very popular with well-to-do pleasure boaters. ✉ *End of Roche Harbor Rd.* 🌐 *www.rocheharbor.com.*

★ San Juan Island National Historic Park

NATIONAL/STATE PARK | **FAMILY** | Fortifications and other 19th-century military installments commemorate the Pig War, in which the United States and Great Britain nearly went into battle over their respective claims on the San Juan Islands. The dispute began in 1859 when an American settler killed a British settler's pig and escalated until roughly 500 American soldiers and 2,200 British soldiers with five warships were poised for battle. Fortunately, no blood was spilled, and the disagreement was finally settled in 1872 in the Americans' favor, with Kaiser Wilhelm I of Germany as arbitrator.

The park comprises two separate areas on opposite sides of the island. English Camp, in a sheltered cove of Garrison Bay on the northern end, includes a blockhouse, a commissary, and barracks. A popular (though steep) hike is to the top of Young Hill, from which you can get a great view of the northwest side of the island. American Camp, on the southern end, has a visitor center and the remains of fortifications; it stretches along driftwood-strewn beaches. Many of the American Camp's walking trails are through prairie; in the evening, dozens of rabbits emerge from their warrens to nibble in the fields. Great views greet you from the top of the Mt. Finlayson Trail—if you're lucky, you might be able to see Mt. Baker and Mt. Rainier along with the Olympics. From June to August you can take guided hikes and see reenactments of 1860s-era military life. ✉ *Park headquarters, 125 Spring St., American Camp, 6 miles southeast of Friday Harbor; English Camp, 9 miles northwest of Friday Harbor, Friday Harbor* ☎ *360/378–2240* 🌐 *www.nps.gov/sajh* 🎟 *Free* 🕑 *American Camp visitor center closed mid-Dec.–Feb. English Camp visitor center closed early Sept.–late May.*

San Juan Islands Museum of Art

MUSEUM | Housed in a sleek, contemporary building, SJIMA presents rotating art shows and exhibits with an emphasis on island and Northwest artists, including the highly touted Artists' Registry Show in winter, which features works by nearly 100 San Juan Islands artists.

Housed in a sleek, contemporary building, SJIMA presents rotating art shows and exhibits with an emphasis on island and Northwest artists, including the highly touted Artists' Registry Show in winter, which features works by nearly 100 San Juan Islands artists. ✉ *540 Spring St., Friday Harbor* ☎ *360/370–5050* 🌐 *www.sjima.org* 🎟 *$10* 🕑 *Closed Tue.–Wed. in summer, Tue.–Thu. off season.*

San Juan Islands Sculpture Park

PUBLIC ART | **FAMILY** | At this serene 20-acre park near Roche Harbor, you can stroll along five winding trails to view more than 150 colorful, in many cases large-scale sculptures spread amid freshwater and saltwater wetlands, open woods, blossoming fields, and rugged terrain. The park is also a haven for birds; more than 120 species nest and breed here. It's a great spot for picnicking, and dogs are welcome. ✉ *Roche Harbor Rd., just before entrance to Roche Harbor Resort, Roche Harbor* 🌐 *www.sjisculpturepark.com* 🎟 *$5 donation recommended.*

San Juan Historical Museum

MUSEUM | This museum in an old farmhouse presents island life at the turn of the 20th century through historic photography, documents, and buildings. ✉ *405 Price St., Friday Harbor* ☎ *360/378–3949* 🌐 *www.sjmuseum.org* 🎟 *$5* 🕑 *Closed Nov.–Mar. except by appointment.*

San Juan Vineyard

WINERY/DISTILLERY | A remodeled 1895 schoolhouse serving estate-grown wines, this picturesque winery is worth a visit for the scenery and its award-winning Siegerrebe and Madeleine Angevine varietals (the winery belongs to the Puget Sound AVA, the coolest-climate growing region in Washington State). In 2018, the winery was purchased by new owners who also own other wineries and vineyards in Eastern Washington. The vineyard's wines show up on many local menus. ✉ *3136 Roche Harbor Rd.* ☎ *360/378–9463* 🌐 *www.sanjuanvineyard.com.*

Whale Museum

MUSEUM | **FAMILY** | A dramatic exterior mural depicting several types of whales welcomes you into a world that is all about these behemoth beauties. Visitors will find models of whales and large whale skeletons, recordings of whale sounds, videos of whales, and information about the plight of the three local orca pods. Head around to the back of the first-floor gift shop to view maps of the latest orca trackings in the area. ✉ *62 1st St. N, Friday Harbor* ☎ *360/378–4710* 🌐 *www.whalemuseum.org* 🎫 *$9.*

Restaurants

★ Backdoor Kitchen

$$$ | **ECLECTIC** | This local favorite has become well-known beyond the San Juans, thanks to the stellar service and inventive, globally inspired cuisine and craft cocktails. As the name might indicate, it's a bit hard to find, tucked in an elegant courtyard a few blocks uphill from the water, but worth the search for dishes that include pan-seared scallops with ginger-sake beurre blanc, and pork chops topped with a poblano–goat cheese sauce and served with caramelized onions and smoked bacon. **Known for:** "noodle Bowl Monday" lunch specials; some of the best pan-Asian dishes on the island; relaxing and scenic outdoor dining in a landscaped courtyard. *$ Average main: $23* ✉ *400b A St., Friday Harbor* ☎ *360/378–9540* 🌐 *www.backdoorkitchen.com* 🕓 *Closed Mon., Tues., and additional days in winter; call off-season. No lunch Tues.–Sun.*

Cask and Schooner

$$$ | **AMERICAN** | This convivial pub decked out with nautical trappings and steps from the ferry terminal serves reliably filling, tasty pub fare with contemporary twists. Among the popular dishes are spicy braised short ribs with mashed potatoes and horseradish crème, and a lamb burger with tomato chutney, watercress, and feta; the Anglophile-friendly spot even sent its chef abroad for a stint to master classic English pub dishes like cod fish-and-chips, shepherd's pie, and bangers and mash. **Known for:** friendly ambience; excellent brunch; strong selection of craft beers. *$ Average main: $23* ✉ *1 Front St., Friday Harbor* ☎ *360/378–2922* 🌐 *www.caskandschooner.com* 🕓 *Closed Tues.*

Downriggers

$$$ | **PACIFIC NORTHWEST** | This snazzy, contemporary, seafood-driven restaurant overlooking the harbor is helmed by one of the most celebrated chefs in the islands, Aaron Rock. The light-filled dining room is a terrific spot to watch boats and ferries come and go while sampling such tempting fare as Penn Cove mussels and pan-seared sockeye salmon with sweet-corn grits, and caramel-chicken and ginger-spiced waffles drizzled with warm honey. **Known for:** pub fare with creative twists; extensive list of craft cocktails; Asian-inspired chicken and waffles. *$ Average main: $23* ✉ *10 Front St., Friday Harbor* ☎ *360/378–2700* 🌐 *www.downriggerssanjuan.com.*

Ernie's Cafe

$ | **ECLECTIC** | Ask a local for the best lunch recommendation in town, and you may be surprised by the answer—plenty of folks will send you to this casual diner at the airport, where you can watch planes take off while you eat. You'll find a few Asian-fusion dishes on the menu, including Korean-style *bulgogi* (grilled marinated beef), and hearty noodle bowls, plus diner classics like hefty cheeseburgers, breakfast sandwiches, and flaky popovers. **Known for:** popovers at breakfast; several Korean-inspired dishes; watching airplanes. *$ Average main: $12* ✉ *744 Airport Circle Dr., Friday Harbor* ☎ *360/378–6605* 🕓 *Closed weekends. No dinner.*

★ Restaurant at Friday Harbor House

$$$ | **PACIFIC NORTHWEST** | Ingenuity and dedication to local ingredients are hallmarks of this stylish, contemporary restaurant, where locals and tourists alike come for dishes such as baked oysters, mushroom panzanella, San Juan Island–raised lamb shoulder cooked in fig leaves, and a popular house burger; during the summer, the hotel's outdoor

Raw Bar serves up seafood and frozen cocktails. The brunch burger, topped with a fried egg and green-tomato-and-bacon jam, and breakfast poutine with duck confit and cheese curds make for decadent starts to your day. **Known for:** excellent cocktails with unique ingredients; a popular daily breakfast (until noon on the weekend); panoramic views of Friday Harbor. *Average main: $30 Friday Harbor House, 130 West St., Friday Harbor 360/378–8455 www.fridayharborhouse.com No dinner Tues. and Wed.*

San Juan Island Brewing

$ | **AMERICAN** | The island's local brewery, just a few short blocks from the ferry landing, has a nice selection of suds brewed on site, along with standard brew-pub fare (pretzels, cheese curds, chicken wings) and surprisingly good individual pizzas. **Known for:** craft beer made on site; light eats and pizza. *Average main: $12 410 A St., Friday Harbor 360/378–2017 www.sanjuanbrew.com Closed Tue.*

Coffee and Quick Bites

Bakery San Juan

$ | **BAKERY** | The fabulous aroma lets you know you're in for a treat at this popular island bakery, which makes fresh bread, cakes and pastries, sandwiches, and pizza. **Known for:** wild-yeasted baked goods; nice place for morning coffee. *Average main: $6 775 Mullis St. 360/378–5810.*

The Bean Cafe

$ | **CAFÉ** | This friendly coffee shop has a ferry cam so you can keep track of your ride back to the mainland while enjoying espresso drinks, baked goods, and a selection of breakfast and lunch items. **Known for:** voted best latte on the island; handmade caramels; wine and beer options. *Average main: $6 150 B 1st Street 360/370–5858 www.thebeancafe.com.*

The Market Chef

$ | **CAFÉ** | Only 50 yards from the ferry holding area (though that includes a lot of stairs), this pleasant little café and specialty grocery store makes fantastic sandwiches (try the roast-beef-and-rocket version, which is served on a house-baked roll with spicy chili aioli). The soups and deli items—including a decadent macaroni and cheese—are also top-notch. **Known for:** strong coffee; picnic and to-go lunches; gourmet locally made goods. *Average main: $10 225 A St., Friday Harbor 360/378–4546 Closed weekends. No dinner.*

Hotels

Birdrock Hotel

$$$ | **HOTEL** | The charming lodging options range from affordable, compact rooms that have private baths down the hall to downright cushy two-bedroom suites with gas fireplaces, spacious sitting rooms, pitched ceilings, and terrific harbor views. **Pros:** handy downtown Friday Harbor location; tasteful, unfussy furnishings; continental breakfast and fresh-baked afternoon cookies. **Cons:** central location means some street noise and crowds; some rooms are small; no on-site dining. *Rooms from: $228 35 1st St., Friday Harbor 360/378–5848, 800/352–2632 www.birdrockhotel.com 10 rooms, 5 suites Free Breakfast.*

★ **Friday Harbor House**

$$$$ | **HOTEL** | At this bluff-top getaway with floor-to-ceiling windows, sleek, modern wood furnishings, and fabrics in beige hues fill the rooms—all of which have gas fireplaces, deep jetted tubs, Chemex pour-over coffee carafes, and at least partial views of the marina, ferry landing, and San Juan Channel below (the ferries are especially enjoyable to watch dock after dark, when they're all lit up). **Pros:** some room views are breathtaking (request at booking); excellent restaurant and bar with views; free parking and just steps from downtown shopping

and dining. **Cons:** two-night minimum at peak season; among the priciest hotels in the San Juan Islands; some early-morning noise from the ferry landing. *Rooms from: $429* *130 West St., Friday Harbor* *360/378–8455, 866/722–7356* *www.fridayharborhouse.com* *23 rooms* *Free Breakfast.*

★ Island Inn at 123 West

$$$ | **HOTEL** | There's a pretty striking contrast of accommodation styles at this cosmopolitan complex that tumbles down a hillside overlooking Friday Harbor, from intimate Euro-style rooms that lack exterior windows to expansive suites with water views to ginormous bilevel penthouses with two bedrooms, private decks, gorgeous full kitchens, and astounding views. **Pros:** penthouse suites are great for luxurious family getaways; Euro-style standard rooms are a good deal; handy in-town location. **Cons:** suites are quite spendy; standard rooms have no views; no on-site dining. *Rooms from: $279* *123 West St., Friday Harbor* *360/378–4400, 877/512–9262* *www.123west.com* *16 rooms* *No meals.*

Kirk House Bed & Breakfast

$$$ | **B&B/INN** | Rooms are all differently decorated in this 1907 Craftsman bungalow, the one-time summer home of steel magnate Peter Kirk: the Garden Room has a botanical motif, the sunny Trellis Room is done in soft shades of yellow and green, and the Arbor Room has French doors leading out to the garden. **Pros:** gorgeous house full of stained glass and other lovely details; within walking distance of town; nice breakfast in the parlor or in bed served on Limoges china. **Cons:** occasional noise from nearby airport; a couple of the rooms are on the small side; with only 4 rooms, inn itself may feel too cozy for some. *Rooms from: $245* *595 Park St., Friday Harbor* *360/378–3757, 800/639–2762* *www.kirkhouse.net* *4 rooms* *Free Breakfast.*

★ Lakedale Resort at Three Lakes

$$$ | **RESORT** | **FAMILY** | This 82-acre property may not have invented glamping, but it was one of the first to nail the travel trend, and the resort's hip 450-square-foot yurts—which share a private lakefront beach and fire pit—are as luxurious as they come, with fireplaces, kitchenettes, spacious bathrooms, and private decks with hot tubs; other options include real log cabins and the lodge, which sits on a scenic lake frequented by swans and geese. **Pros:** pretty grounds and fun amenities; close to Friday Harbor but feels secluded; serene hotel rooms at the lakefront lodge (16 and up only) were just renovated. **Cons:** some noise from nearby Roche Harbor Road; the grounds include a lot of camping spots, so the resort can feel crowded; books up way in advance. *Rooms from: $295* *4313 Roche Harbor Rd.* *360/378–2350* *www.lakedale.com* *10 rooms, 7 yurts, 6 cabins* *Free Breakfast.*

★ Roche Harbor Resort

$$$ | **RESORT** | This sprawling resort, with several types of accommodations ranging from historic hotel rooms to luxurious contemporary waterfront suites, occupies the site of the lime works that made John S. McMillin his fortune in the late 19th century. **Pros:** lots of different options for families and groups; several on-site restaurants; gorgeous full-service spa. **Cons:** condos have less character and are away from the waterfront; a bit isolated from the rest of the island if you don't have a car; the least expensive rooms in Hotel de Haro have shared baths. *Rooms from: $277* *248 Reuben Memorial Dr., Roche Harbor* *360/378–2155, 800/451–8910* *www.rocheharbor.com* *16 rooms, 18 suites, 9 cottages, 20 condos* *No meals.*

Snug Harbor Resort

$$$$ | **RESORT** | **FAMILY** | At this popular cottage resort and marina on the northwest side of the island, all of the units were completely rebuilt in 2014 with tall windows overlooking the water, high ceilings, well-equipped kitchens, knotty-pine wood paneling, gas fireplaces, and private decks. **Pros:** beautiful, contemporary decor; quiet location with a coffeehouse and small camp store; nice views of the harbor. **Cons:** no pets; 20-minute drive from Friday Harbor; expensive and two-night minimum stay required. *Rooms from: $399 ✉ 1997 Mitchell Bay Rd., Friday Harbor ☎ 360/378–4762 🌐 www.snugresort.com 17 cottages No meals.*

Activities

BEACHES

San Juan County Park

BEACH—SIGHT | You'll find a wide gravel beachfront at this park 10 miles west of Friday Harbor, overlooking waters where orcas often frolic in summer, plus grassy lawns with picnic tables and a small campground. **Amenities:** parking (free); toilets. **Best for:** walking. *✉ 380 Westside Rd., Friday Harbor ☎ 360/378–8420 🌐 www.co.san-juan.wa.us.*

South Beach at American Camp

BEACH—SIGHT | This 2-mile public beach on the southern end of the island is part of San Juan Island National Historical Park. **Amenities:** parking (free); toilets. **Best for:** solitude; walking. *✉ Off Cattle Point Rd. 🌐 www.nps.gov/sajh.*

BIKING

You can rent standard, mountain, and BMX bikes for $40 to $50 per day or about $200 to $240 per week. Tandem, recumbent, and electric-assist bikes rent for about $55 to $80 per day.

Discovery Adventure Tours

BICYCLING | The noted Friday Harbor outfitter (aka Discovery Sea Kayaks) also rents conventional road bikes and electric-assist bikes. *✉ 260 Spring St., Friday Harbor ☎ 360/378–2559, 866/461–2559 🌐 www.discoveryadventuretours.com.*

Island Bicycles

BICYCLING | This full-service shop rents bikes. *✉ 380 Argyle Ave., Friday Harbor ☎ 360/378–4941 🌐 www.islandbicycles.com.*

BOATING AND SAILING

At public docks, high-season moorage rates are $1.10 to $2.10 per foot (of vessel) per night.

Port of Friday Harbor

BOATING | The marina at the island's main port offers guest moorage, vessel assistance and repair, bareboat and skippered charters, overnight accommodations, and wildlife- and whale-watching cruises. *✉ 204 Front St., Friday Harbor ☎ 360/378–2688 🌐 www.portfridayharbor.org.*

Roche Harbor Marina

BOATING | The marina at Roche Harbor Resort has a fuel dock, pool, grocery, and other guest services. *✉ 248 Reuben Memorial Dr., Roche Harbor ☎ 360/378–2155 🌐 www.rocheharbor.com.*

Snug Harbor Resort Marina

BOATING | This well-located marina adjoins a popular, upscale small resort. It provides van service to and from Friday Harbor and rents small powerboats. *✉ 1997 Mitchell Bay Rd., Friday Harbor ☎ 360/378–4762 🌐 www.snugresort.com.*

SEA KAYAKING

One of the best ways to take in the island's stunning views and get up close to the resident orcas is in a kayak. You'll find many places to rent kayaks in Friday Harbor, as well as outfitters providing classes and guided tours. Be sure to make reservations in summer. Three-hour tours run about $75 to $100, day tours cost around $110 to $125, and overnight tours start around $175 per day. Equipment is always included in the cost.

Crystal Seas Kayaking

KAYAKING | Sunset trips and multisport tours that might include biking, kayaking, yoga, and camping are among the options with this respected guide company. ✉ *40 Spring St., Friday Harbor* ☎ *360/378–4223, 877/732–7877* 🌐 *www.crystalseas.com.*

Discovery Sea Kayaks
KAYAKING | This outfitter offers both sea-kayaking adventures, including sunset trips and multiday excursions and whale-watching paddles. ✉ *260 Spring St., Friday Harbor* ☎ *360/378–2559, 866/461–2559* 🌐 *www.discoveryseakayak.com.*

San Juan Kayak Expeditions
KAYAKING | This reputable company has been running kayaking and camping tours in two-person kayaks since 1980. ✉ *85 Front St., Friday Harbor* ☎ *360/378–4436* 🌐 *www.sanjuankayak.com.*

Sea Quest Expeditions
KAYAKING | Kayak eco-tours with guides who are trained naturalists, biologists, and environmental scientists are available through this popular outfitter. ✉ *Friday Harbor* ☎ *360/378–5767, 888/589–4253* 🌐 *www.sea-quest-kayak.com.*

WHALE-WATCHING

Whale-watching expeditions usually run three to four hours and cost around $100–$120 per person. Note that tours departing from San Juan Island typically get you to the best whale-watching waters faster than those departing from the mainland. ■ **TIP→ For the best experience, look for tour companies with small boats that carry under 30 people**. Bring warm clothing even if it's a warm day.

★ **Maya's Legacy Whale Watching**
WHALE-WATCHING | These informative tours on small, modern, and speedy boats ensure great views for every passengers; departures are from Friday Harbor and Snug Harbor Marina. ✉ *14 Cannery Landing, Friday Harbor* ☎ *360/378–7996* 🌐 *www.sanjuanislandwhalewatch.com.*

San Juan Excursions
WHALE-WATCHING | Whale-watching cruises are offered aboard a converted 1941 U.S. Navy research vessel. ✉ *40 Spring St., Friday Harbor* ☎ *360/378–6636, 800/809–4253* 🌐 *www.watchwhales.com.*

San Juan Island Whale & Wildlife Tours
WHALE-WATCHING | Tours from Friday Harbor leave daily at noon and are led by highly knowledgeable marine experts. ✉ *1 Front St., Friday Harbor* ☎ *360/298–0012* 🌐 *www.sanjuanislandwhales.com.*

Western Prince Whale & Wildlife Tours
WHALE-WATCHING | Narrated whale-watching tours last three to four hours. ✉ *1 Spring St., Friday Harbor* ☎ *360/378–5315, 800/757–6722* 🌐 *www.orcawhale-watch.com.*

Shopping

Friday Harbor is the main shopping area, with dozens of shops selling a variety of art, crafts, and clothing created by residents, as well as a bounty of island-grown produce.

Arctic Raven Gallery
ART GALLERIES | The specialty here is Northwest native art, including scrimshaw and wood carvings. ✉ *130 S. 1st St., Friday Harbor* ☎ *360/378–3433* 🌐 *www.arcticravengalleryfridayharbor.com.*

Friday Harbor Chocolates
FOOD/CANDY | The artisan chocolates at this friendly little shop come from all over the Pacific Northwest, including a nice assortment of confections sold by the piece, and the proprietor also stocks a selection of fine domestic and imported ports, dessert wines, and drinking wines. ✉ *255 Spring St., Friday Harbor* ☎ *360/370–0050* 🌐 *www.fridayharbor-chocolates.com.*

San Juan Island Farmers Market
OUTDOOR/FLEA/GREEN MARKETS | From April through October, this open-air market

with more than 30 vendors selling local produce and crafts takes place at Friday Harbor Brickworks on Saturdays from 9:30 to 1. The market is also open once or twice a month on Saturdays in winter; check the website for the schedule. ✉ *150 Nichols St., Friday Harbor* 🌐 *www.sjifarmersmarket.com.*

Waterworks Gallery

ART GALLERIES | This respected gallery represents about 30 eclectic, contemporary artists, from painters to jewelers. ✉ *315 Argyle Ave., Friday Harbor* ☎ *360/378–3060* 🌐 *www.waterworksgallery.com.*

Westcott Bay Shellfish Co

FOOD/CANDY | This rustic oyster farm is tucked into a small bay 2 miles south of Roche Harbor; the best time to buy oysters is November through April, and you can buy, shuck, and eat them on site; the farm sells local bakery bread, cheese, charcuterie, salads, and wine if you want to make a meal of it. ✉ *904 Westcott Dr., off Roche Harbor Rd., Friday Harbor* ☎ *360/378–2489* 🌐 *www.westcottbay.com.*

Mount Rainier National Park

Mt. Rainier is the centerpiece of its namesake park. The impressive volcanic peak stands at an elevation of 14,411 feet, making it the fifth-highest peak in the lower 48 states. Nearly 2 million visitors a year enjoy spectacular views of the mountain and return home with a lifelong memory of its image.

On the lower slopes you find silent forests made up of cathedral-like groves of Douglas fir, western hemlock, and western red cedar, some more than 1,000 years old. Water and lush greenery are everywhere in the park, and dozens of thundering waterfalls, accessible from the road or by a short hike, fill the air with mist.

Planning

WHEN TO GO

Rainier is the Puget Sound's weather vane: if you can see it, skies will be clear. Visitors are most likely to see the summit July through September. Crowds are heaviest in summer, too, meaning the parking lots at Paradise and Sunrise often fill before noon, campsites are reserved months in advance, and other lodgings are reserved as much as a year ahead.

True to its name, Paradise is often sunny during periods when the lowlands are under a cloud layer. The rest of the year, Rainier's summit gathers flying-saucer-like lenticular clouds whenever a Pacific storm approaches; once the peak vanishes from view, it's time to haul out rain gear. The rare periods of clear winter weather bring residents up to Paradise for cross-country skiing.

PLANNING YOUR TIME

MT. RAINIER IN ONE DAY

The best way to get a complete overview of Mt. Rainier in a day is to enter via Nisqually and begin your tour by browsing in **Longmire Museum.** When you're done, get to know the environment in and around Longmire Meadow and the overgrown ruins of Longmire Springs Hotel on the ½-mile **Trail of the Shadows** nature loop.

From Longmire, Highway 706 East climbs northeast into the mountains toward Paradise. Take a moment to explore two-tiered **Christine Falls,** just north of the road 1½ miles past Cougar Rock Campground, and the cascading **Narada Falls,** 3 miles farther on; both are spanned by graceful stone footbridges. Fantastic mountain views, alpine meadows crosshatched with nature trails, a welcoming lodge and restaurant, and the excellent **Jackson Memorial Visitor Center** combine to make lofty Paradise the primary goal of most park visitors. One outstanding (but challenging) way to explore the high country is to hike the 5-mile round-trip **Skyline Trail** to Panorama Point, which rewards you with stunning 360-degree views.

Continue eastward on Highway 706 East for 21 miles and leave your car to explore the incomparable, 1,000-year-old **Grove of the Patriarchs.** Afterward, turn your car north toward White River and **Sunrise Visitor Center,** where you can watch the alpenglow fade from Mt. Rainier's domed summit.

GETTING HERE AND AROUND

AIR

Seattle–Tacoma International Airport, 15 miles south of downtown Seattle, is the nearest airport to the national park.

CAR

The Nisqually entrance is on Highway 706, 14 miles east of Route 7; the Ohanapecosh entrance is on Route 123, 5 miles north of U.S. 12; and the White River entrance is on Route 410, 3 miles north of the Chinook and Cayuse passes. These highways become mountain roads as they reach Rainier, winding up and down many steep slopes, so cautious driving is essential: use a lower gear, especially on downhill sections, and take care not to overheat brakes by constant use. These roads are subject to storms any time of year and are repaired in the summer from winter damage and washouts.

Side roads into the park's western slope are narrower, unpaved, and subject to flooding and washouts. All are closed by snow in winter except Highway 706 to Paradise and Carbon River Road, though the latter tends to flood near the park boundary. (Route 410 is open to the Crystal Mountain access road entrance.)

Park roads have a maximum speed of 35 mph in most places, and you have to watch for pedestrians, cyclists, and wildlife. Parking can be difficult during peak summer season, especially at Paradise, Sunrise, Grove of the Patriarchs, and at the trailheads between Longmire and Paradise; arrive early if you plan to visit these sites. All off-road-vehicle use—4X4 vehicles, ATVs, motorcycles, snowmobiles—is prohibited in Mount Rainier National Park.

PARK ESSENTIALS

ACCESSIBILITY

The only trail in the park that is fully accessible to those with impaired mobility is Kautz Creek Trail, a ½-mile boardwalk that leads to a splendid view of the mountain. Parts of the Trail of the Shadows at Longmire and the Grove of the Patriarchs at Ohanapecosh are also accessible. Campgrounds at Cougar Rock and Ohanapecosh have several accessible sites. All main visitor centers, as well as National Park Inn at Longmire, are accessible. Wheelchairs are available at the Jackson Visitor Center for guests to use in the center.

PARK FEES AND PERMITS

The entrance fee of $30 per vehicle and $15 for those on foot, motorcycle, or bicycle is good for seven days. Annual passes are $55. Climbing permits are $51 per person per climb or glacier trek. Wilderness camping permits must be obtained for all backcountry trips, and advance reservations are highly recommended.

PARK HOURS

Mount Rainier National Park is open 24/7 year-round, but with limited access in winter. Gates at Nisqually (Longmire) are staffed year-round during the day; facilities at Paradise are open daily from late May to mid-October; and Sunrise is open daily July to early September. During off-hours you can buy passes at the gates from machines that accept credit and debit cards. Winter access to the park is limited to the Nisqually entrance, and the Jackson Memorial Visitor Center at Paradise is open on weekends and holidays in winter. The Paradise snow-play area is open when there is sufficient snow.

CELL PHONE RECEPTION

Cell phone reception is unreliable throughout much of the park, although access is clear at Paradise, Sunrise, and Crystal Mountain. Public telephones are at all park visitor centers, at the National Park Inn at Longmire, and at Paradise Inn at Paradise.

EDUCATIONAL OFFERINGS

RANGER PROGRAMS

Junior Ranger Program

NATIONAL/STATE PARK | FAMILY | Youngsters ages 6 to 11 can pick up an activity booklet at a visitor center and fill it out as they explore the park. When they complete it, they can show it to a ranger and receive a Mount Rainier Junior Ranger badge. ✉ *Visitor centers, Mt. Rainier National Park* ☎ *360/569–2211* 🌐 *www.nps.gov/mora/learn/kidsyouth* 🎟 *Free with park admission.*

Ranger Programs

NATIONAL/STATE PARK | FAMILY | Park ranger-led activities include **guided snowshoe walks** in the winter (most suitable for those older than eight) as well as **evening programs** during the summer at Longmire/Cougar Rock, Ohanapecosh, and White River campgrounds, and at the Paradise Inn. Evening talks may cover subjects such as park history, its flora and fauna, or interesting facts on climbing Mt. Rainier. There are also daily guided programs that start at the Jackson Visitor Center, including meadow and vista walks, tours of the Paradise Inn, a morning ranger chat, and evening astronomy program. ✉ *Visitor centers, Mt. Rainier National Park* ☎ *360/569–2211* 🌐 *www.nps.gov/mora/planyourvisit/rangerprograms.htm* 🎟 *Free with park admission.*

RESTAURANTS

A limited number of restaurants are inside the park, and a few worth checking out lie beyond its borders. Mt. Rainier's picnic areas are justly famous, especially in summer, when wildflowers fill the meadows. Resist the urge to feed the yellow pine chipmunks darting about.

HOTELS

The Mt. Rainier area is remarkably bereft of quality lodging. Rainier's two national park lodges, at Longmire and Paradise, are attractive and well maintained. They exude considerable history and charm, especially Paradise Inn, but unless you've made summer reservations a year in advance, getting a room can be a challenge. Dozens of motels, cabin complexes, and private vacation-home rentals are near the park entrances; while they can be pricey, the latter are convenient for longer stays. *Hotel reviews have been shortened. For full information, visit Fodors.com.*

VISITOR INFORMATION

PARK CONTACT INFORMATION Mount Rainier National Park. ✉ *55210 238th Ave. East, Ashford* ☎ *360/569–2211, 360/569–6575* 🌐 *www.nps.gov/mora.*

VISITOR CENTERS

Jackson Memorial Visitor Center

INFO CENTER | High on the mountain's southern flank, this center houses exhibits on geology, mountaineering, glaciology, and alpine ecology. Multimedia programs are staged in the theater; there's also a snack bar and gift shop. This is the park's most popular visitor destination, and it can be quite crowded in summer. ✉ *Hwy. 706 E, 19 miles east of Nisqually park entrance, Mt. Rainier National Park* ☎ *360/569–6571* 🌐 *www.nps.gov/mora/planyourvisit/paradise.htm* ⏲ *Closed weekdays mid-Oct.–Apr.*

Longmire Museum and Visitor Center

INFO CENTER | Glass cases inside this museum preserve the park's plants and animals, including a stuffed cougar. Historical photographs and geographical displays provide a worthwhile overview of the park's history. The adjacent visitor center has some perfunctory exhibits on the surrounding forest and its inhabitants, as well as pamphlets and information about park activities. ✉ *Hwy. 706, 10 miles east of Ashford, Longmire* ☎ *360/569–6575* 🌐 *www.nps.gov/mora/planyourvisit/longmire.htm.*

Sunrise Visitor Center

INFO CENTER | Exhibits at this center explain the region's sparser alpine and subalpine ecology. A network of nearby loop trails leads you through alpine meadows and forest to overlooks that have broad views of the Cascades and Rainier. The visitor center has a snack bar and gift shop. ✉ *Sunrise Rd., 15 miles from White River park entrance, Mt. Rainier National Park* ☎ *360/663–2425* 🌐 *www.nps.gov/mora/planyourvisit/sunrise.htm* ⏲ *Closed mid-Sept.–June.*

Sights

Chinook Pass Road

SCENIC DRIVE | Route 410, the highway to Yakima, follows the eastern edge of the park to Chinook Pass, where it climbs the steep, 5,432-foot pass via a series of switchbacks. At its top, take in broad views of Rainier and the east slope of the Cascades. The pass usually closes for the winter in November and reopens by late May. ✉ *Mt. Rainier National Park* 🌐 *www.wsdot.wa.gov/traffic/passes/chinook-cayuse.*

Christine Falls

BODY OF WATER | These two-tiered falls were named in honor of Christine Louise Van Trump, who climbed to the 10,000-foot level on Mt. Rainier in 1889 at the age of nine, despite having a crippling nervous-system disorder. ✉ *Next to Hwy. 706, about 2½ miles east of Cougar Rock Campground, Mt. Rainier National Park* 🌐 *www.nps.gov/mora.*

★ **Grove of the Patriarchs**

TRAIL | Protected from the periodic fires that swept through the surrounding areas, this small island of 1,000-year-old trees is one of Mount Rainier National Park's most memorable features. A 1½-mile loop trail heads through the old-growth forest of Douglas fir, cedar, and hemlock. ✉ *Rte. 123, west of the Stevens Canyon entrance, Mt. Rainier National Park* 🌐 *www.nps.gov/mora/planyourvisit/ohanapecosh.htm.*

Plants and Wildlife

Wildflower season in the meadows at and above timberline is mid-July through August. Large mammals like deer, elk, black bears, and cougars tend to occupy the less accessible wilderness areas of the park and thus elude the average visitor. The best times to see wildlife are at dawn and dusk at the forest's edge, though you'll occasionally see bears ambling through meadows in the distance during the day. Fawns are born in May, and the bugling of bull elk on the high ridges can be heard in late September and October.

Mowich Lake Road

SCENIC DRIVE | In the northwest corner of the park, this 24-mile mountain road begins in Wilkeson and heads up the Rainier foothills to Mowich Lake, traversing beautiful mountain meadows along the way. Mowich Lake is a pleasant spot for a picnic. The road is open mid-July to mid-October. ✉ *Mt. Rainier National Park* 🌐 *www.nps.gov/mora/planyourvisit/carbon-and-mowich.htm* ⏲ *Closed mid-Oct.–mid-July.*

Narada Falls

BODY OF WATER | A steep but short trail leads to the viewing area for these spectacular 168-foot falls, which expand to a width of 75 feet during peak flow times. In winter the frozen falls are popular with ice climbers. ✉ *Along Hwy. 706, 1 mile west of turnoff for Paradise, 6 miles east of Cougar Rock Campground, Mt. Rainier*

National Park ⊕ www.nps.gov/mora/planyourvisit/longmire.htm.

National Park Inn

BUILDING | Even if you don't plan to stay overnight, you can stop by year-round to view the architecture of this inn, built in 1917 and on the National Register of Historic Places. While you're here, relax in front of the fireplace in the lounge, stop at the gift shop, or dine at the restaurant. ✉ *Longmire Visitor Complex, Hwy. 706, 10 miles east of Nisqually entrance, Longmire* ☎ *360/569–2411* ⊕ *www.mtrainierguestservices.com/accommodations/national-park-inn.*

Paradise Road

SCENIC DRIVE | This 9-mile stretch of Highway 706 winds its way up the mountain's southwest flank from Longmire to Paradise, taking you from lowland forest to the ever-expanding vistas of the mountain above. Visit early on a weekday if possible, especially in peak summer months, when the road is packed with cars. The route is open year-round, though there may be some weekday closures in winter. From November through April, all vehicles must carry chains. ✉ *Mt. Rainier National Park* ⊕ *www.nps.gov/mora/planyourvisit/paradise.htm.*

Sunrise Road

SCENIC DRIVE | This popular (and often crowded) scenic road to the highest drivable point at Mt. Rainier carves its way 11 miles up Sunrise Ridge from the White River Valley on the northeast side of the park. As you top the ridge there are sweeping views of the surrounding lowlands. The road is usually open July through September. ✉ *Mt. Rainier National Park* ⊕ *www.nps.gov/mora/planyourvisit/sunrise.htm* ⏲ *Usually closed Oct.–June.*

Tipsoo Lake

BODY OF WATER | **FAMILY** | The short, pleasant trail that circles the lake—ideal for families—provides breathtaking views. Enjoy the subalpine wildflower meadows during the summer months; in late summer to early fall there is an abundant supply of huckleberries. ✉ *Off Cayuse Pass east on Hwy. 410, Mt. Rainier National Park* ⊕ *www.nps.gov/mora/planyourvisit/sunrise.htm.*

Activities

MULTISPORT OUTFITTERS

RMI Expeditions

CLIMBING/MOUNTAINEERING | Reserve a private hiking guide through this highly regarded outfitter, or take part in its one-day mountaineering classes (mid-May through late September), where participants are evaluated on their fitness for the climb and must be able to withstand a 16-mile round-trip hike with a 9,000-foot gain in elevation. The company also arranges private cross-country skiing and snowshoeing guides. ✉ *30027 Hwy. 706 E, Ashford* ☎ *888/892–5462, 360/569–2227* ⊕ *www.rmiguides.com* 🎫 *From $1,118 for 4-day package.*

Whittaker Mountaineering

TOUR—SPORTS | You can rent hiking and climbing gear, cross-country skis, snowshoes, and other outdoor equipment at this all-purpose Rainier Base Camp outfitter, which also arranges for private cross-country skiing and hiking guides. If you forget to bring tire chains (which all vehicles are required to carry in the national park in winter), they rent those too. ✉ *30027 SR 706 E, Ashford* ☎ *800/238–5756, 360/569–2982* ⊕ *www.whittakermountaineering.com.*

BIRD-WATCHING

Be alert for kestrels, red-tailed hawks, and, occasionally, golden eagles on snags in the lowland forests. Also present at Rainier, but rarely seen, are great horned owls, spotted owls, and screech owls. Iridescent rufous hummingbirds flit from blossom to blossom in the drowsy summer lowlands, and sprightly water ouzels flutter in the many forest creeks. Raucous Steller's jays and gray jays scold passersby from trees, often darting boldly down to steal morsels from unguarded picnic tables. At higher elevations, look for the pure white plumage of the white-tailed ptarmigan as it hunts for seeds and insects in winter. Waxwings, vireos, nuthatches, sapsuckers, warblers, flycatchers, larks, thrushes, siskins, tanagers, and finches are common throughout the park.

HIKING

Although the mountain can seem remarkably benign on calm summer days, hiking Rainier is not a city-park stroll. Dozens of hikers and trekkers annually lose their way and must be rescued—and lives are lost on the mountain each year. Weather that approaches cyclonic levels can appear quite suddenly, any month of the year. All visitors venturing far from vehicle access points, with the possible exception of the short loop hikes listed here, should carry day packs with warm clothing, food, and other emergency supplies.

Nisqually Vista Trail

HIKING/WALKING | Equally popular in summer and winter, this trail is a 1¼-mile round-trip through subalpine meadows to an overlook point for Nisqually Glacier. The gradually sloping path is a favorite venue for cross-country skiers in winter; in summer, listen for the shrill alarm calls of the area's marmots. *Easy.* ✉ *Mt. Rainier National Park* ✣ *Trailhead: at Jackson Memorial Visitor Center, Rte. 123, 1 mile north of Ohanapecosh, at high point of Hwy. 706* 🌐 *www.nps.gov/mora/planyourvisit/day-hiking-at-mount-rainier.htm.*

★ Skyline Trail

HIKING/WALKING | This 5-mile loop, one of the highest trails in the park, beckons day-trippers with a vista of alpine ridges and, in summer, meadows filled with brilliant flowers and birds. At 6,800 feet, Panorama Point, the spine of the Cascade Range, spreads away to the east, and Nisqually Glacier tumbles downslope. *Moderate.* ✉ *Mt. Rainier National Park* ✣ *Trailhead: Jackson Memorial Visitor Center, Rte. 123, 1 mile north of Ohanapecosh at high point of Hwy. 706* 🌐 *www.nps.gov/mora/planyourvisit/skyline-trail.htm.*

Sunrise Nature Trail

HIKING/WALKING | The 1½-mile-long loop of this self-guided trail takes you through the delicate subalpine meadows near the Sunrise Visitor Center. A gradual climb to the ridgetop yields magnificent views of Mt. Rainier and the more distant volcanic cones of Mt. Baker, Mt. Adams, and Glacier Peak. *Easy.* ✉ *Mt. Rainier National Park* ✣ *Trailhead: at Sunrise Visitor Center, Sunrise Rd., 15 miles from White River park entrance* 🌐 *www.nps.gov/mora/planyourvisit/sunrise.htm.*

Trail of the Shadows

HIKING/WALKING | This ¾-mile loop is notable for its glimpses of meadowland ecology, its colorful soda springs (don't drink the water), James Longmire's old homestead cabin, and the foundation of the old Longmire Springs Hotel, which was destroyed by fire around 1900. *Easy.* ✉ *Mt. Rainier National Park* ✣ *Trailhead: at Hwy. 706, 10 miles east of Nisqually entrance* 🌐 *www.nps.gov/mora/planyourvisit/day-hiking-at-mount-rainier.htm.*

Van Trump Park Trail

HIKING/WALKING | You gain an exhilarating 2,200 feet on this route while hiking through a vast expanse of meadow with views of the southern Puget Sound and Mt. Adams and Mt. St. Helens. On the way up is one of the highest water falls in the park, Comet Falls. The 5¾-mile track provides good footing, and the average hiker can make it up and back in five hours. *Moderate.* ✉ *Mt. Rainier National Park* ✣ *Trailhead: Hwy. 706 at Christine Falls, 4½ miles east of Longmire* 🌐 *www.nps.gov/mora/planyourvisit/van-trump-trail.htm.*

Bridle Trails State Park

HIKING/WALKING | Though most of the travelers on the trails in this Bellevue park are on horseback, the 28 miles of paths are popular with hikers, too. The 489-acre park consists mostly of lowland forest, with Douglas firs, big-leaf maples, mushrooms, and abundant birdlife. Note that horses are given the right-of-way on all trails; if you encounter riders, stop and stand to the side until the horses pass. ✉ *Bridle Trails State Park, Bellevue* ✣ *From Downtown Seattle take I–90 or 520 E and get on I–405 N. Take Exit 17 and turn right onto 116 Ave. NE. Follow that road to park entrance* 🌐 *parks.state.wa.us/481/Bridle-Trails.*

Cougar Mountain Regional Wildland Park
HIKING/WALKING | This spectacular park in the "Issaquah Alps" has more than 38 miles of hiking trails and 12 miles of bridle trails within its 3,000-plus acres. The Indian Trail, believed to date back 8,000 years, was part of a trade route that Native Americans used to reach North Bend and the Cascades. Thick pine forests rise to spectacular mountaintop views; there are waterfalls, deep caves, and the remnants of a former mining town. Local residents include deer, black bears, bobcats, bald eagles, and pileated woodpeckers, among many other woodland creatures. ✉ *18201 SE Cougar Mountain Dr., Issaquah* ✣ *From Downtown Seattle take I–90 E; follow signs to park beyond Issaquah.*

Larrabee State Park
HIKING/WALKING | This favorite spot has two lakes, a coastline with tidal pools, and 15 miles of hiking trails. The Interurban Trail, which parallels an old railway line, is perfect for leisurely strolls or trail running. Head up Chuckanut Mountain to reach the lakes and to get great views of the San Juan Islands. ✉ *245 Chuckanut Dr., Bellingham* ✣ *Take I–5 N to Exit 231. Turn right onto Chuckanut Dr. and follow that road to park entrance.*

Mt. Si
HIKING/WALKING | This thigh-buster is where mountaineers train to climb grueling Mt. Rainier. Mt. Si offers a challenging hike with views of a valley (slightly marred by the suburbs) and the Olympic Mountains in the distance. The main trail to Haystack Basin, 8 miles round-trip, climbs some 4,000 vertical feet, but there are several obvious places to rest or turn around if you'd like to keep the hike to 3 or 4 miles. Note that solitude is in short supply here—this is an extremely popular trail thanks to its proximity to Seattle. On the bright side, it's one of the best places to witness the local hikers and trail runners in all their weird and wonderful splendor. ✉ *North Bend* ✣ *Take I–90 E to Exit 31 (toward North Bend). Turn onto North Bend Way and then make left onto Mt. Si Rd. and follow that road to trailhead parking lot.*

★ **Snow Lake**
HIKING/WALKING | One of Washington State's most popular wilderness trails may be crowded at times, but the scenery and convenience of this hike make it a classic. Though very rocky in stretches—you'll want to wear sturdy shoes—the 8-mile round-trip sports a relatively modest 1,300-foot elevation gain; the views of the Alpine Lakes Wilderness are well worth the sweat. The glimmering waters of Snow Lake await hikers at the trail's end; summer visitors will find abundant wildflowers, huckleberries, and wild birds. ✉ *Snoqualmie Pass* ✣ *Take I–90 E to Exit 52 (toward Snoqualmie Pass West). Turn left (north), cross under freeway, and continue on to trailhead, located in parking lot at Alpental Ski Area* 🌐 *www.wta.org/go-hiking/hikes/snow-lake-1.*

MOUNTAIN CLIMBING

Climbing Mt. Rainier is not for amateurs; each year adventurers die on the mountain, and many get lost and must be rescued. Near-catastrophic weather can appear quite suddenly any month of the year. If you're experienced in technical, high-elevation snow, rock, and ice-field adventuring, Mt. Rainier can be a memorable adventure. Climbers can fill

Mount Rainier, Looking North
MOUNT RAINIER
Liberty Cap 14,122 ft
Columbia Crest 14,411 ft
Point Success 14,153 ft
SUNSET AMPHITHEATER
St. Andrews Rock 10,992 ft
Gibraltar Rock 12,660 ft
Disappointment Cleaver
Little Tahoma Peak 11,138 ft
CATHEDRAL ROCKS
Ingraham Glacier
Camp Muir 10,188 ft
Anvil Rock 9,584 ft
Muir Snowfield
Paradise Glaciers
Nisqually Glacier
Wilson Glacier
Van Trump Glaciers
Panorama Point 6,800 ft
McClure Rock 7,385 ft
Skyline Trail
Alta Vista
Henry M. Jackson Memorial Visitor Center
Paradise
Louise Lake
The Castle
Reflection Lakes
Pinnacle Peak 6,562 ft
Plummer Peak 6,370 ft
Lane Peak 6,012 ft
Wahpenayo Peak 6,231 ft
Chutla Peak
Eagle Peak 5,958 ft
Unicorn Peak 6917 ft
TATOOSH RANGE
Tokaloo Rock 7,684 ft
PUYALLUP CLEAVER
Tahoma Glacier
GLACIER ISLAND
South Tahoma Glacier
SUCCESS DIVIDE
SUCCESS CLEAVER
Success Glacier
Pyramid Glaciers
Kautz Glacier
WAPOWETY CLEAVER
Pyramid Peak 6,937 ft
EMERALD RIDGE
Iron Mountain 6,283 ft
PYRAMID PARK
Mildred Point
VAN TRUMP PARK
CUSHMAN CREST
Pyramid Creek
Rampart Ridge Trail
RAMPART RIDGE
THE RAMPARTS
Cougar Rock
Longmire
KEY
Paved Roads
Hiking Trails
Climbing Routes

out a climbing card at the Paradise, White River, or Carbon River ranger station and lead their own groups of two or more. Climbers must register with a ranger before leaving and check out on return. A $51 annual climbing fee applies to anyone heading above 10,000 feet or onto one of Rainier's glaciers. During peak season it is recommended that climbers make their camping reservations ($20 per site) in advance; reservations are taken by fax and mail beginning in mid-March on a first-come, first-served basis (find the reservation form at 🌐 *www.nps.gov/mora/planyourvisit/climbing.htm*).

SKIING AND SNOWSHOEING

Mt. Rainier is a major Nordic ski center for cross-country and telemark skiing. Although trails are not groomed, those around Paradise are extremely popular. If you want to ski with fewer people, try the trails in and around the Ohanapecosh–Stevens Canyon area, which are just as beautiful and, because of their more easterly exposure, slightly less subject to the rains that can douse the Longmire side, even in the dead of winter. Never ski on plowed main roads, especially around Paradise—the snowplow operator can't see you. Rentals aren't available on the eastern side of the park.

Deep snows make Mt. Rainier a snowshoeing pleasure. The Paradise area, with its network of trails, is the best choice. The park's east-side roads, Routes 123 and 410, are unplowed and provide other good snowshoeing venues, although you must share the main routes with snowmobilers.

Paradise Snowplay Area and Nordic Ski Route

SKIING/SNOWBOARDING | Sledding on flexible sleds (no toboggans or runners), inner tubes, and plastic saucers is allowed only in the Paradise snow-play area adjacent to the Jackson Visitor Center. The area is open when there is sufficient snow, usually from late December through mid-March. The easy 3½-mile Paradise Valley Road Nordic ski route begins at the Paradise parking lot and follows Paradise Valley/Stevens Canyon Road to Reflection Lakes. Equipment rentals are available at Whittaker Mountaineering in Ashford or at the National Park Inn's General Store in Longmire. ✉ *Adjacent to Jackson Visitor Center at Paradise, Mt. Rainier National Park* ☎ *360/569–2211* 🌐 *www.nps.gov/mora/planyourvisit/winter-recreation.htm.*

TOURS AND OUTFITTERS

General Store at the National Park Inn

SKIING/SNOWBOARDING | The store at the National Park Inn in Longmire rents cross-country ski equipment and snowshoes. It's open daily in winter, depending on snow conditions. ✉ *National Park Inn, Longmire* ☎ *360/569–2411* 🌐 *www.mtrainierguestservices.com/activities-and-events/winter-activities/cross-country-skiing.*

What's Nearby

Ashford sits astride an ancient trail across the Cascades used by the Yakama Indians to trade with the coastal tribes of western Washington. The town began as a logging railway terminal; today it's the main gateway to Mt. Rainier—and the only year-round access point to the park—with lodges, restaurants, grocery stores, and gift shops. Surrounded by Cascade peaks, **Packwood** is a pretty mountain village on U.S. 12, below White Pass. Between Mt. Rainier and Mt. St. Helens, it's a perfect jumping-off point for exploring local wilderness areas.

VISITOR INFORMATION Destination Packwood Association. ✉ *13011B U.S. Hwy. 12, Packwood* ☎ *360/492–7365* 🌐 *www.destinationpackwood.com.* **Mount Rainier Visitor Association.** ✉ *30027 SR 706 E, Ashford* ☎ *360/569–0910, 877/617–9951* 🌐 *www.mt-rainier.com.*

Sights

Goat Rocks Wilderness

NATIONAL/STATE PARK | The crags in Gifford Pinchot National Forest, south of Mt. Rainier, are aptly named. You often see mountain goats here in this vast and unspoiled 108,000-acre wilderness, especially when you hike into the backcountry. Goat Lake is a particularly good spot for viewing these elusive creatures. See the goats without backpacking by taking Forest Road 21 to Forest Road 2140, south from U.S. 12. The goats will be on Stonewall Ridge looming up ahead of you. ✉ *NF-21 and NF-2140, Randle* ☎ *360/891–5000* 🌐 *www.fs.usda.gov/giffordpinchot.*

Mount St. Helens Science and Learning Center

INFO CENTER | The Mount St. Helens Institute operates this center, which offers family camps, field trips, and learning experiences throughout the year. It's open to the public on weekends in the off-season when the Johnston Ridge Observatory is closed. Exhibits document the great 1980 blast of Mt. St. Helens and its effects on the surrounding 150,000 acres. A ¼-mile trail leads from the visitor center to Coldwater Lake. ✉ *Rte. 504, 43 miles east of I–5, 19000 Spirit Lake Hwy., Toutle* ☎ *360/274–2131* 🌐 *www.mshslc.org* ⏲ *Closed May–Oct. and weekdays except special events.*

Mount St. Helens Visitor Center

INFO CENTER | This facility, one of several visitor centers along Route 504 on the west side of the mountain, has exhibits documenting the eruption, plus a walk-through volcano. ✉ *Rte. 504, 5 miles east of I–5, 3029 Spirit Lake Hwy., Silver Lake* ☎ *360/274–0962* 🌐 *parks.state.wa.us/245/Mount-St-Helens* 🎫 *$5* ⏲ *Closed Tues., Wed., and federal holidays during Nov.–Feb.*

Mt. Rainier Scenic Railroad and Museum

TOUR—SIGHT | FAMILY | This trip takes you through lush forests and across scenic bridges, covering 14 miles of incomparable beauty. Trains depart from Elbe, 11 miles west of Ashford, then bring passengers to a lovely picnic area near Mineral Lake before returning. The trains run weekends from mid-May to June, then Friday–Sunday from July through Labor Day weekend, and Saturday through mid-October. Special pumpkin patch excursions operate for two weekends in late October, and Winter Polar Express trains run from mid-November to December on weekends (and daily during winter break, except Christmas Day). Prices start at $41 for basic excursions; special events—including wine and craft beer trains—cost more. At Mineral Lake, guests can tour the museum containing old train memorabilia and artifacts and exhibits on the area's old railroad camps. ✉ *54124 Mountain Hwy. E, Elbe* ☎ *360/492–6000* 🌐 *www.mtrainierrailroad.com* ⏲ *Closed Nov.–Apr. (except for holiday excursions).*

Northwest Trek Wildlife Park

NATURE PRESERVE | FAMILY | This spectacular, 723-acre wildlife park 30 miles southeast of Tacoma is devoted to native creatures of the Pacific Northwest. Walking paths wind through natural surroundings—so natural that a cougar once entered the park and started snacking on the deer (it was finally trapped and relocated to the North Cascades). See beavers, otters, and wolverines; get close to wolves, foxes, coyotes; and observe several species of big cats and bears in wild environments. Admission includes a 40-minute tram ride through fields of wandering moose, bighorn sheep, elk, bison, and mountain goats. The most adventurous way to see the park is via one of six zip lines, which traverse the park canopy and is part of a series of different adventure courses. Rides are available late May through late September. ✉ *11610 Trek Dr. E, Eatonville* ☎ *360/832–6117* 🌐 *www.nwtrek.org* 🎫 *$25* ⏲ *Closed Mon.–Thurs. in Oct.–mid-Mar.*

Did You Know?

Named after British admiral Peter Rainier in the late 18th century, Mt. Rainier had an earlier name. Tahoma (also Takhoma), its American Indian name, means "the mountain that was God." Various unsuccessful attempts have been made to restore the aboriginal name to the peak. Of course, to most Puget Sound residents, Rainier is simply "the mountain."

Restaurants

National Park Inn Dining Room
$$$ | **AMERICAN** | Photos of Mt. Rainier taken by top photographers adorn the walls of this inn's large dining room, a bonus on the many days the mountain refuses to show itself. Meals are simple but tasty: rib-eye steak, lamb chops, cedar-plank trout, and blackberry cobbler à la mode. **Known for:** only restaurant open year-round in the park; hearty breakfast options. *Average main: $25* *Hwy. 706, Longmire* *360/569–2411* *www.mtrainierguestservices.com.*

Paradise Camp Deli
$ | **AMERICAN** | **FAMILY** | Grilled meats, sandwiches, salads, and soft drinks are served daily from May through early October and on weekends and holidays the rest of the year. **Known for:** a quick bite to eat. *Average main: $10* *Jackson Visitor Center, Paradise Rd. E, Paradise* *360/569–6571* *www.mtrainierguestservices.com* *Closed weekdays early Oct.–Apr.*

Paradise Inn
$$$ | **AMERICAN** | Tall windows in this historic timber lodge provide terrific views of Rainier, and the warm glow of native wood permeates the large dining room, where hearty Pacific Northwest fare is served. Sunday brunch is legendary and served during the summer months; on other days and during the shoulder season there's a breakfast buffet. **Known for:** bourbon buffalo meat loaf; warm liquor drinks. *Average main: $27* *E. Paradise Rd., near Jackson Visitor Center, Paradise* *360/569–2275, 855/755–2275* *www.mtrainierguestservices.com* *Closed Oct.–mid-May.*

Sunrise Day Lodge Food Service
$ | **AMERICAN** | **FAMILY** | A cafeteria and grill serve tasty hamburgers, chili, hot dogs, and soft-serve ice cream from July through September. **Known for:** only food service in this part of the park; often busy. *Average main: $10* *Sunrise Rd., 15 miles from White River park entrance, Mt. Rainier National Park* *360/663–2425* *www.mtrainierguestservices.com* *Closed Oct.–June.*

PICNIC AREAS

Park picnic areas are usually open only from late May through September.

Paradise Picnic Area
NATIONAL/STATE PARK | This site has great views on clear days. After picnicking at Paradise, you can take an easy hike to one of the many waterfalls in the area—Sluiskin, Myrtle, or Narada, to name a few. *Hwy. 706, 11 miles east of Longmire, Mt. Rainier National Park* *www.nps.gov/mora.*

Sunrise Picnic Area
NATIONAL/STATE PARK | Set in an alpine meadow that's filled with wildflowers in July and August, this picnic area provides expansive views of the mountain and surrounding ranges in good weather. *Sunrise Rd., 11 miles west of White River entrance, Mt. Rainier National Park* *www.nps.gov/mora/planyourvisit/sunrise.htm* *Road to Sunrise usually closed Oct.–June.*

Hotels

National Park Inn
$$ | **B&B/INN** | A large stone fireplace warms the common room of this country inn, the only one of the park's two inns that's open year-round, while rustic details such as wrought-iron lamps and antique bentwood headboards adorn the small rooms. **Pros:** classic national park lodge ambience; on-site restaurant with simple American fare; winter packages with perks like breakfast and free snowshoe use. **Cons:** jam-packed in summer; must book far in advance; some rooms have a shared bath. *Rooms from: $187* *Longmire Visitor Complex, Hwy. 706, 6 miles east of Nisqually entrance,*

Best Campgrounds in Mount Rainier

Three drive-in campgrounds are in the park—Cougar Rock, Ohanapecosh, and White River—with almost 500 sites for tents and RVs. None has hot water or RV hookups. The nightly fee is $20. The more primitive Mowich Lake Campground has 10 walk-in sites for tents only; no fee is charged. For backcountry camping, get a free wilderness permit at a visitor center on a first-come, first-served basis. Primitive sites are spaced at 7- to 8-mile intervals along the Wonderland Trail.

Cougar Rock Campground. A secluded, heavily wooded campground with an amphitheater, Cougar Rock is one of the first to fill up. Reservations are accepted for summer only. ✉ *2½ miles north of Longmire* ☎ *877/444–6777* 🌐 *www.recreation.gov* for reservations.

Mowich Lake Campground. This is Rainier's only lakeside campground and has just 10 primitive campsites. At 4,959 feet, it's also peaceful and secluded. ✉ *Mowich Lake Rd., 6 miles east of park boundary* ☎ *360/569–2211.*

Ohanapecosh Campground. This lush, green campground in the park's southeast corner has an amphitheater and self-guided trail. It's one of the first campgrounds to open for the season. ✉ *Rte. 123, 1½ miles north of park boundary* ☎ *877/444–6777* 🌐 *www.recreation.gov* for reservations.

White River Campground. At an elevation of 4,400 feet, White River is one of the park's highest and least wooded campgrounds. Here you can enjoy campfire programs, self-guided trails, and partial views of Mt. Rainier's summit. ✉ *5 miles west of White River entrance* ☎ *360/569–2211.*

Longmire ☎ *360/569–2275, 855/755–2275* 🌐 *www.mtrainierguestservices.com* *43 rooms* *No meals.*

★ Paradise Inn

$$ | HOTEL | With its hand-carved Alaskan cedar logs, burnished parquet floors, stone fireplaces, Indian rugs, and glorious mountain views, this 1917 inn is a classic example of a national park lodge. **Pros:** central to trails; pristine vistas; nature-inspired details. **Cons:** rooms are small and basic; many rooms have shared bathrooms; no elevators, air-conditioning, cell service, TV, or Wi-Fi. *Rooms from: $138* ✉ *E Paradise Rd., near Jackson Visitor Center, Paradise* ☎ *360/569–2275, 855/755–2275* 🌐 *www.mtrainierguest-services.com* *Closed mid-Oct.–mid-May* *121 rooms* *No meals.*

Activities

SKIING

Crystal Mountain Ski Area

HIKING/WALKING | Washington State's biggest and best-known ski area has nine lifts (plus a children's lift and a gondola) and 57 runs. In summer, it's open for hiking, rides on the Mt. Rainier Gondola, and meals at the Summit House, all providing sensational views of Rainier and the Cascades. **■ TIP→ Because of recent episodes of overcrowding at the ski resort, during which many people were turned away, Crystal no longer sells day-of tickets on weekends during peak winter season.** **Facilities:** 57 trails; 2,600 acres; 3,100-foot vertical drop; 11 lifts. ✉ *33914 Crystal Mountain Blvd. , off Rte. 410, Crystal Mountain* ☎ *360/663–2265* 🌐 *www.crystalmountainresort.com* *From $24.*

Olympic National Park

Edged on all sides by water, the forested landscape is remote and pristine, and works its way around the sharpened ridges of the snowcapped Olympic Mountains. Big lakes cut pockets of blue in the rugged blanket of pine forests.

Planning

WHEN TO GO

Summer, with its long stretches of sun-filled days, is prime touring time for Olympic National Park. June through September are the peak months; Hurricane Ridge, the Hoh Rain Forest, Lake Crescent, and Ruby Beach are bustling by 10 am.

Late spring and early autumn are also good bets for clear weather; anytime between April and October, you'll have a good chance of fair skies. Between Thanksgiving and Easter, it's a toss-up as to which days will turn out fair; prepare for heavy clouds, rain showers, and chilly temperatures, then hope for the best.

Winter is a great time to visit if you enjoy isolation. Locals are usually the only hardy souls here during this time, except for weekend skiers heading to the snowfields around Hurricane Ridge. Many visitor facilities have limited hours or are closed from October to April.

PLANNING YOUR TIME

OLYMPIC IN ONE DAY

Start at the **Lake Quinault Lodge** in the park's southwest corner. From here, drive a half hour into the Quinault Valley via **South Shore Road.** Tackle the forested **Graves Creek Trail,** then head up **North Shore Road** to the Quinault Rain Forest Interpretive Trail. Next, head back to U.S. 101 and drive to **Ruby Beach,** where a shoreline walk presents a breathtaking scene of sea stacks and sparkling, pink-hue sands.

Forks and its **Timber Museum** are your next stop; have lunch here, then drive 20 minutes to the beach at **La Push.** Next, head to **Lake Crescent** around the corner to the northeast, where you can rent a boat, take a swim, or enjoy a picnic next to the sparkling teal waters. Drive through **Port Angeles** to **Hurricane Ridge**; count on an hour's drive from bottom to top if there aren't too many visitors. At the ridge, explore the visitor center or hike the 3-mile loop to **Hurricane Hill,** where you can see over the entire park north to Vancouver Island and south past Mt. Olympus.

GETTING HERE AND AROUND

You can enter the park at a number of points, but because the park is 95% wilderness, access roads do not penetrate far. The best way to get around and to see many of the park's top sites is on foot.

AIR

Seattle–Tacoma International Airport is the nearest airport to Olympic National Park. It's roughly a two-hour drive from the park.

BOAT

Ferries provide another unique (though indirect) link to the Olympic area from Seattle; contact **Washington State Ferries** (☎ *800/843–3779, 206/464–6400* 🌐 *www.wsdot.wa.gov/ferries*) for information.

BUS

Grays Harbor Transit runs buses Monday through Saturday from Aberdeen and Hoquiam to Amanda Park, on the west end of Lake Quinault. Jefferson Transit operates a Forks–Amanda Park route Monday through Saturday.

BUS CONTACTS Grays Harbor Transit. ☎ *360/532–2770, 800/562–9730* 🌐 *www.ghtransit.com.* **Jefferson Transit.** ☎ *800/371–0497, 360/385–4777* 🌐 *www.jeffersontransit.com.*

Good Reads

- Robert L. Wood's *Olympic Mountains Trail Guide* is a great resource for both day hikers and those planning longer excursions.
- Craig Romano's *Day Hiking Olympic Peninsula: National Park/Coastal Beaches/Southwest Washington* is a detailed guide to day hikes in and around the national park.
- Stephen Whitney's *A Field Guide to the Cascades and Olympics* is an excellent trailside reference, covering more than 500 plant and animal species found in the park.
- The park's newspaper, the *Olympic Bugler*, is a seasonal guide for activities and opportunities in the park. You can pick it up at the visitor centers.
- A handy online catalog of books, maps, and passes for northwest parks is available from Discover Your Northwest (🌐 *www.discovernw.org*).

CAR

U.S. 101 essentially encircles the main section of Olympic National Park, and a number of roads lead from the highway into the park's mountains and toward its beaches. You can reach U.S. 101 via Interstate 5 at Olympia, via Route 12 at Aberdeen, or via Route 104 from the Washington state ferry terminals at Bainbridge or Kingston.

PARK ESSENTIALS

ACCESSIBILITY

There are wheelchair-accessible facilities—including trails, campgrounds, and visitor centers—throughout the park; contact visitor centers for information.

ADMISSION FEES AND PERMITS

Seven-day vehicle admission is $25; an annual pass is $50. Individuals arriving on foot, bike, or motorcycle pay $10. An overnight wilderness permit, available at visitor centers and ranger stations, is $7 per person per night. An annual wilderness camping permit costs $45. Fishing in freshwater streams and lakes within Olympic National Park does not require a Washington state fishing license; however, anglers must acquire a salmon-steelhead catch record card when fishing for those species. Ocean fishing and harvesting shellfish require licenses, which are available at sporting-goods and outdoor-supply stores.

ADMISSION HOURS

Six park entrances are open 24/7; gate kiosk hours (for buying passes) vary according to season and location, but most are staffed during daylight hours. Olympic National Park is in the Pacific time zone.

CELL PHONE RECEPTION

Note that cell reception is sketchy in wilderness areas. There are public telephones at the Olympic National Park Visitor Center, Hoh River Rain Forest Visitor Center, and lodging properties within the park—Lake Crescent, Kalaloch, and Sol Duc Hot Springs. Fairholme General Store also has a phone.

EDUCATIONAL OFFERINGS

CLASSES AND SEMINARS

NatureBridge

COLLEGE | **FAMILY** | This rustic educational facility offers talks and excursions focusing on park ecology and history. Trips range from canoe trips to camping excursions, with a strong emphasis on family programs. ✉ *111 Barnes Point Rd.,*

Port Angeles ☎ *360/928–3720* 🌐 *www.naturebridge.org/olympic.*

RANGER PROGRAMS

Junior Ranger Program

TOUR—SIGHT | FAMILY | Anyone can pick up the booklet at visitor centers and ranger stations and follow this fun program, which includes assignments to discover park flora and fauna, ocean life, and Native American lore. Kids get a badge when they turn in the finished work. Kids can also earn an "Ocean Steward" badge by doing activities in another booklet that teaches about the park's coastal ecosystem. ✉ *Olympic National Park* ☎ *360/565–3130* 🌐 *www.nps.gov/olym/learn/kidsyouth/beajuniorranger.htm.*

RESTAURANTS

The major resorts are your best bets for eating out in the park. Each has a main restaurant, café, and/or kiosk, as well as casually upscale dinner service, with regional seafood, meat, and produce complemented by a range of microbrews and good Washington and international wines. Reservations are either recommended or required.

Outside the park, small, easygoing cafés and bistros line the main thoroughfares in Sequim, Port Angeles, and Port Townsend, offering cuisine that ranges from hearty American-style fare to more eclectic local flavor.

HOTELS

Major park resorts run from good to terrific, with generally comfortable rooms, excellent facilities, and easy access to trails, beaches, and activity centers. Midsize accommodations, like Sol Duc Hot Springs Resort, are often shockingly rustic—but remember, you're here for the park, not for the rooms.

The towns around the park have motels, hotels, and resorts for every budget. For a full beach-town vacation experience, base yourself in a home or cottage in the coastal community of Seabrook (near Pacific Beach). Sequim and Port Angeles have many attractive, friendly B&Bs, plus lots of inexpensive chain hotels and motels. Forks has mostly motels, with a few guesthouses on the fringes of town.

Hotel reviews have been shortened. For full information, visit Fodors.com.

VISITOR INFORMATION

PARK CONTACT INFORMATION Olympic National Park. ✉ *Olympic National Park Visitor Center, 3002 Mount Angeles Rd., Port Angeles* ☎ *360/565–3130* 🌐 *www.nps.gov/olym.*

VISITOR CENTERS

Hoh Rain Forest Visitor Center

INFO CENTER | Pick up park maps and pamphlets, permits, and activities lists in this busy, woodsy chalet; there's also a shop and exhibits on natural history. Several short interpretive trails and longer wilderness treks start from here. ✉ *Hoh Valley Rd., Forks* ✢ *31 miles south of Forks* ☎ *360/374–6925* 🌐 *www.nps.gov/olym/planyourvisit/visitorcenters.htm* ⏲ *Closed Jan.–Feb., and Mon.–Thurs. off-season.*

Hurricane Ridge Visitor Center

INFO CENTER | The upper level of this visitor center has exhibits and nice views; the lower level has a gift shop and snack bar. Guided walks and programs start in late June. In winter, find details on the surrounding ski and sledding slopes and take guided snowshoe walks. ✉ *Hurricane Ridge Rd., Olympic National Park* ☎ *360/565–3131 for road conditions* 🌐 *www.nps.gov/olym/planyourvisit/visitorcenters.htm* ⏲ *Operating hrs/days vary off-season.*

Olympic National Park Visitor Center

INFO CENTER | This modern, well-organized facility, staffed by park rangers, provides everything: maps, trail brochures, campground advice, weather forecasts, listings of wildlife sightings, educational programs and exhibits, information on road and trail closures, and a gift shop. ✉ *3002 Mount Angeles Rd., Port Angeles* ☎ *360/565–3130* 🌐 *www.nps.gov/olym/planyourvisit/visitorcenters.htm.*

South Shore Quinault Ranger Station

INFO CENTER | The National Forest Service's ranger station near the Lake Quinault Lodge has maps, campground information, and program listings. ✉ *353 S Shore Rd., Quinault* ☎ *360/288–2525* 🌐 *www.fs.usda.gov/main/olympic/home* ⏲ *Closed weekends after Labor Day until Memorial Day weekend.*

Wilderness Information Center (WIC)

INFO CENTER | Located behind Olympic National Park Visitor Center, this facility provides all the information you'll need for a trip in the park, including trail conditions, safety tips, and weather bulletins. The office also issues camping permits, takes campground reservations, and rents bear-proof food canisters. ✉ *3002 Mount Angeles Rd., Port Angeles* ☎ *360/565–3100* 🌐 *www.nps.gov/olym/planyourvisit/wic.htm* ⏲ *Hrs vary during off-season.*

Sights

Most of the park's attractions are found either off U.S. 101 or down trails that require hikes of 15 minutes or longer. The west-coast beaches are linked to the highway by downhill tracks; the number of cars parked alongside the road at the start of the paths indicates how crowded the beach will be.

★ Hoh River Rain Forest

FOREST | South of Forks, an 18-mile spur road links Highway 101 with this unique temperate rain forest, where spruce and hemlock trees soar to heights of more than 200 feet. Alders and big-leaf maples are so densely covered with mosses they look more like shaggy prehistoric animals than trees, and elk browse in shaded glens. Be prepared for precipitation: the region receives 140 inches or more each year. ✉ *Olympic National Park* ✣ *From Hwy. 101, at about 20 miles north of Kalaloch, turn onto Upper Hoh Rd. 18 miles east to Hoh Rain Forest Visitor Center* ☎ *360/374–6925* 🌐 *www.nps.gov/olym/planyourvisit/visiting-the-hoh.htm.*

★ Hurricane Ridge

MOUNTAIN—SIGHT | The panoramic view from this 5,200-foot-high ridge encompasses the Olympic range, the Strait of Juan de Fuca, and Vancouver Island. Guided tours are given in summer along the many paved and unpaved trails, where wildflowers and wildlife such as deer and marmots flourish. ✉ *Hurricane Ridge Rd., Olympic National Park* ✣ *17 miles south of Port Angeles* ☎ *360/565–3130 visitor center* 🌐 *www.nps.gov/olym/planyourvisit/visiting-hurricane-ridge.htm* ⏲ *Closed when road is closed.*

Kalaloch

BEACH—SIGHT | With a lodge and restaurant, a huge campground, miles of coastline, and easy access from the highway, this is a popular spot. Keen-eyed beachcombers may spot sea otters just offshore; they were reintroduced here in 1970. ✉ *Hwy. 101, Kalaloch* ✣ *32 miles northwest of Lake Quinault* ☎ *360/565–3130 visitor center, 360/962–2283 ranger station* 🌐 *www.nps.gov/olym/planyourvisit/visiting-kalaloch-and-ruby-beach.htm.*

Lake Crescent

BODY OF WATER | Visitors see Lake Crescent as Highway 101 winds along its southern shore, giving way to gorgeous views of teal waters rippling in a basin formed by Tuscan-like hills. In the evening, low bands of clouds caught between the surrounding mountains often linger over its reflective surface. ✉ *Hwy. 101, Olympic National Park* ✣ *16 miles west of Port Angeles and 28 miles northeast of Forks* ☎ *360/565–3130 visitor center* 🌐 *www.nps.gov/olym/planyourvisit/visiting-lake-crescent.htm.*

Lake Ozette

BEACH—SIGHT | The third-largest glacial impoundment in Washington anchors the coastal strip of Olympic National Park at its north end. The small town of Ozette, home to a coastal tribe, is the trailhead

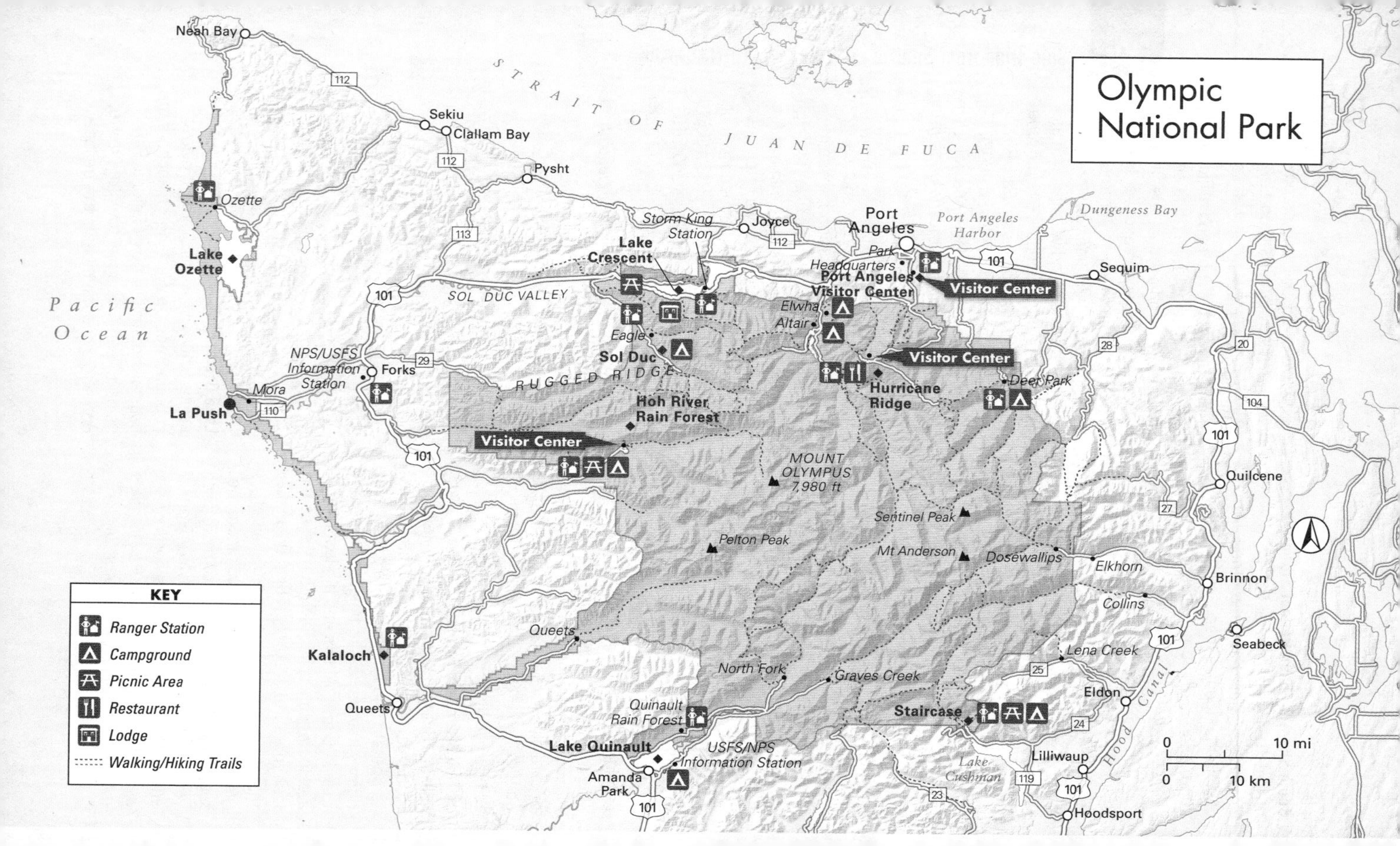
Olympic National Park
STRAIT OF JUAN DE FUCA
Pacific Ocean
Neah Bay
Sekiu
Clallam Bay
Pysht
Ozette
Lake Ozette
La Push
Mora
NPS/USFS Information Station
Forks
SOL DUC VALLEY
Storm King Station
Joyce
Lake Crescent
Eagle
Sol Duc
RUGGED RIDGE
Hoh River Rain Forest
Visitor Center
Port Angeles
Port Angeles Harbor
Dungeness Bay
Park Headquarters
Port Angeles Visitor Center
Visitor Center
Sequim
Elwha
Altair
Visitor Center
Hurricane Ridge
Deer Park
MOUNT OLYMPUS 7,980 ft
Sentinel Peak
Pelton Peak
Mt Anderson
Dosewallips
Elkhorn
Brinnon
Quilcene
Collins
Seabeck
Lena Creek
Hood Canal
Eldon
Staircase
Lake Cushman
Lilliwaup
Hoodsport
Graves Creek
North Fork
Queets
Quinault Rain Forest
USFS/NPS Information Station
Lake Quinault
Amanda Park
Kalaloch
Queets
101
112
113
110
29
28
20
104
27
25
24
23
119
0
10 mi
10 km
KEY
Ranger Station
Campground
Picnic Area
Restaurant
Lodge
Walking/Hiking Trails

Plants and Wildlife in Olympic

Along the high mountain slopes hardy cedar, fir, and hemlock trees stand tough on the rugged land; the lower montane forests are filled with thickets of silver firs; and valleys stream with Douglas firs and western hemlock. The park's famous temperate rain forests are on the peninsula's western side, marked by broad western red cedars, towering red spruces, and ferns festooned with strands of mosses and patchwork lichens. This lower landscape is also home to some of the Northwest's largest trees: massive cedar and Sitka spruce near Lake Quinault can measure more than 700 inches around, and Douglas firs near the Queets and Hoh rivers are nearly as wide.

These landscapes are home to a variety of wildlife, including many large mammals and 15 creatures found nowhere else in the world. Hikers often come across Roosevelt's elk, black-tailed deer, mountain goats, beavers, raccoons, skunks, opossums, and foxes; Douglas squirrels and flying squirrels populate the heights of the forest. Less common are black bears (most prevalent from May through August); wolves, bobcats, and cougars are rarely seen. Birdlife includes bald eagles, red-tailed hawks, osprey, and great horned owls. Rivers and lakes are filled with freshwater fish, while beaches hold crabs, sea stars, anemones, and other shelled creatures. Get out in a boat on the Pacific to spot seals, sea lions, and sea otters—and perhaps a pod of porpoises, orcas, or gray whales.

Beware of jellyfish around the shores—beached jellyfish can still sting. In the woods, check for ticks after every hike and after each shower. Biting nasties include black flies, horseflies, sand fleas, and the ever-present mosquitoes. Yellow-jacket nests populate tree hollows along many trails; signs throughout the Hoh Rain Forest warn hikers to move quickly through these sections. If one or two chase you, remain calm and keep walking; these are just "guards" making sure you're keeping away from the hive. Poison oak is common, so familiarize yourself with its appearance. Bug repellent, sunscreen, and long pants and sleeves will go a long way toward making your experience more comfortable.

for two of the park's better one-day hikes. Both 3-mile trails lead over boardwalks through swampy wetland and coastal old-growth forest to the ocean shore and uncrowded beaches. ✉ *Ozette* ✣ *At end of Hoko-Ozette Rd., 26 miles southwest of Hwy. 112 near Sekiu* ☎ *360/565–3130 Ozette Ranger Station* 🌐 *www.nps.gov/olym/planyourvisit/visiting-ozette.htm.*

Lake Quinault

BODY OF WATER | This glimmering lake, 4½ miles long and 300 feet deep, is the first landmark you'll reach when driving the west-side loop of U.S. 101. The rain forest is thickest here, with moss-draped maples and alders, and towering spruce, fir, and hemlock. Enchanted Valley, high up near the Quinault River's source, is a deeply glaciated valley that's closer to the Hood Canal than to the Pacific Ocean. A scenic loop drive circles the lake and travels around a section of the Quinault River. ✉ *Hwy. 101, Olympic National Park* ✣ *38 miles north of Hoquiam* ☎ *360/288–2525 Quinault Rain Forest ranger station* 🌐 *www.nps.gov/olym/planyourvisit/visiting-quinault.htm.*

La Push

BEACH—SIGHT | At the mouth of Quileute River, La Push is the tribal center of the Quileute Indians. In fact, the town's name is a variation on the French *la bouche,* which means "the mouth." Offshore rock spires known as sea stacks dot the coast here, and you may catch a glimpse of bald eagles nesting in the nearby cliffs. ✉ *Rte. 110, La Push* ✣ *14 miles west of Forks* 🌐 *www.nps.gov/olym/planyourvisit/upload/mora.pdf.*

★ Port Angeles Visitor Center to Hurricane Ridge

VIEWPOINT | The premier scenic drive in Olympic National Park is a steep ribbon of curves that climbs from thickly forested foothills and subalpine meadows into the upper stretches of pine-swathed peaks. At the top, the visitor center at Hurricane Ridge has some spectacular views over the heart of the peninsula and across the Strait of Juan de Fuca. A mile past the visitor center, there are picnic tables in open meadows with photo-worthy views of the mountains to the east. Hurricane Ridge also has an uncommonly fine display of wildflowers in spring and summer. In winter, vehicles must carry chains, and the road is usually open Friday to Sunday only (call first to check conditions). ✉ *Olympic National Park* 🌐 *www.nps.gov/olym.*

Second and Third Beaches

BEACH—SIGHT | During low tide these flat, driftwood-strewn expanses are perfect for long afternoon strolls. Second Beach, accessed via an easy forest trail through Quileute lands, opens to a vista of Pacific Ocean and sea stacks. Third Beach offers a 1¼-mile forest hike for a warm-up before reaching the sands. ✉ *Hwy. 101, Olympic National Park* ✣ *32 miles north of Lake Quinault* ☎ *360/565–3130 visitor center* 🌐 *www.nps.gov/olym.*

Sol Duc

BODY OF WATER | Sol Duc Valley is one of those magical places where all the Northwest's virtues seem at hand: lush lowland forests, sparkling river scenes, salmon runs, and serene hiking trails. Here, the popular Sol Duc Hot Springs area includes three attractive sulfuric pools ranging in temperature from 98°F to 104°F (admission to the pools costs $15). ✉ *Sol Duc Rd., Olympic National Park* ✣ *South of U.S. 101, 12 miles past west end of Lake Crescent* ☎ *360/565–3130 visitor center* 🌐 *www.nps.gov/olym/planyourvisit/visiting-the-sol-duc-valley.htm.*

Staircase

INFO CENTER | Unlike the forests of the park's south and west sides, Douglas fir is the dominant tree on the east slope of the Olympic Mountains. Fire has played an important role in creating the majestic forest here, as the Staircase Ranger Station explains in interpretive exhibits. ✉ *Olympic National Park* ✣ *At end of Rte. 119, 15 miles from U.S. 101 at Hoodsport* ☎ *360/565–3130 visitor center* 🌐 *www.nps.gov/olym/planyourvisit/visiting-staircase.htm.*

Activities

BICYCLING

The rough gravel car tracks to some of the park's remote sites were meant for four-wheel-drive vehicles but can double as mountain-bike routes. The Quinault Valley, Queets River, Hoh River, and Sol Duc River roads have bike paths through old-growth forest. Graves Creek Road, in the southwest, is a mountain-bike path; Lake Crescent's north side is also edged by the bike-friendly Spruce Railroad Trail. More bike tracks run through the adjacent Olympic National Forest. Note that U.S. 101 has heavy traffic and isn't recommended for cycling, although the western side has broad roads with beautiful scenery and can be biked off-season. Bikes are not permitted on foot trails.

TOURS AND OUTFITTERS

Sound Bike & Kayak

BICYCLING | This sports outfitter rents and sells bikes, and sells kayaks, climbing gear, and related equipment. They offer several guided mountain climbs, day hikes, and custom trips, and a climbing wall to practice skills. Bike rentals start at $10 per hour and $45 per day. ✉ *120 E Front St., Port Angeles* ☎ *360/457–1240* 🌐 *www.soundbikeskayaks.com.*

CLIMBING

At 7,980 feet, Mt. Olympus is the highest peak in the park and the most popular climb in the region. To attempt the summit, climbers must register at the Glacier Meadows Ranger Station. Mt. Constance, the third-highest Olympic peak at 7,743 feet, has a well-traversed climbing route that requires technical experience; reservations are recommended for the Lake Constance stop, which is limited to 20 campers. Mt. Deception is another possibility, though tricky snows have caused fatalities and injuries in the last decade.

Climbing season runs from late June through September. Note that crevasse skills and self-rescue experience are highly recommended. Climbers must register with park officials and purchase wilderness permits before setting out. The best resource for climbing advice is the Wilderness Information Center in Port Angeles.

TOURS AND OUTFITTERS

Mountain Madness

CLIMBING/MOUNTAINEERING | Adventure through the rain forest to the glaciated summit of Mt. Olympus on a five-day trip, offered several times per year by Mountain Madness. ☎ *800/328–5925, 206/937–8389* 🌐 *www.mountainmadness.com* 🎟 *From $1,390 for 5-day climb.*

FISHING

There are numerous fishing possibilities throughout the park. Lake Crescent is home to cutthroat and rainbow trout, as well as petite kokanee salmon; lakes Cushman, Quinault, and Ozette have trout, salmon, and steelhead. As for rivers, the Bogachiel and Queets have steelhead salmon in season. The glacier-fed Hoh River is home to chinook salmon April to November, and coho salmon from August through November; the Sol Duc River offers all five species of salmon. The Elwha River has been undergoing restoration since two dams were removed; strong salmon and steelhead runs are expected to return, although a fishing moratorium has been in place for several years. Other places to go after salmon and trout include the Dosewallips, Duckabush, Quillayute, Quinault, Salmon, and Skokomish rivers. A Washington state punch card is required during salmon-spawning months; fishing regulations vary throughout the park, and some areas are for catch and release only. Punch cards are available from sporting-goods and outdoor-supply stores.

TOURS AND OUTFITTERS

Piscatorial Pursuits

FISHING | This company, based in Forks, offers salmon and steelhead fishing trips around the Olympic Peninsula from mid-October through May. ✉ *Forks* ☎ *866/347–4232* 🌐 *www.piscatorialpursuits.com* 🎟 *From $225 (rate per person for parties of two or more).*

HIKING

Know your tides, or you might be trapped by high water. Tide tables are available at all visitor centers and ranger stations. Remember that a wilderness permit is required for all overnight backcountry visits.

KAYAKING AND CANOEING

Lake Crescent, a serene expanse of teal-color waters surrounded by deep-green pine forests, is one of the park's best

Did You Know?

Encompassing more than 70 miles of beachfront, Olympic is one of the few national parks of the West with an ocean beach (Redwood, Channel Islands, and some of the Alaskan parks are the others). The park is therefore home to many marine animals, including sea otters, whales, sea lions, and seals.

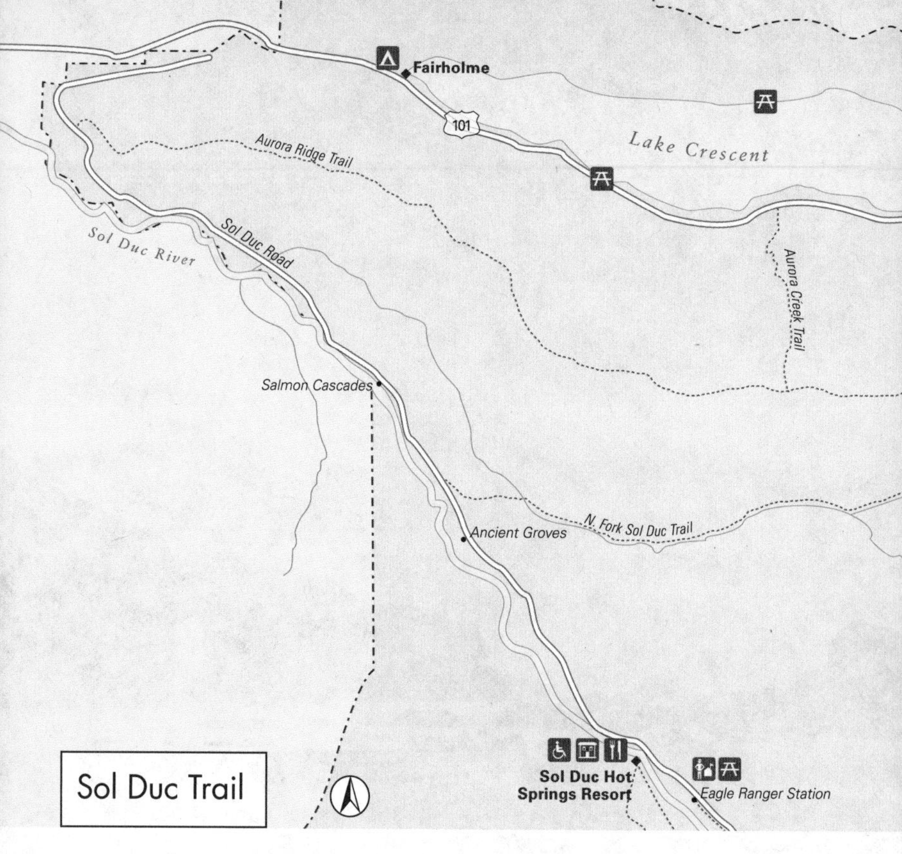

boating areas. Note that the west end is for swimming only; no speedboats are allowed here.

Lake Quinault has boating access from a gravel ramp on the north shore. From U.S. 101, take a right on North Shore Road, another right on Hemlock Way, and a left on Lakeview Drive. There are plank ramps at Falls Creek and Willoughby campgrounds on South Shore Drive, 0.1 mile and 0.2 mile past the Quinault Ranger Station, respectively.

Lake Ozette, with just one access road, is a good place for overnight trips. Only experienced canoe and kayak handlers should travel far from the put-in, since fierce storms occasionally strike—even in summer.

TOURS AND OUTFITTERS

Fairholme General Store

CANOEING/ROWING/SKULLING | Kayaks and canoes on Lake Crescent are available to rent from $20 per hour to $60 for eight hours. The store is at the lake's west end, 27 miles west of Port Angeles. Closed after Labor Day until Memorial Day weekend. ✉ *221121 U.S. 101, Port Angeles* ☎ *360/928–3020* 🌐 *www.olympicnationalparks.com* 🕒 *Closed after Labor Day–Apr. and Mon.–Thurs. in May.*

Lake Crescent Lodge

CANOEING/ROWING/SKULLING | You can rent canoes, kayaks, and paddleboards here for $20 per hour and $60 for a full day. Two-hour guided kayak tours are offered and include instruction; they cost $55 in a single kayak and $75 in a double kayak. ✉ *416 Lake Crescent Rd., Olympic National Park* ☎ *360/928–3211* 🌐 *www.*

olympicnationalparks.com ⏲ *Closed Jan.–Apr.*

Log Cabin Resort

CANOEING/ROWING/SKULLING | This resort, 17 miles west of Port Angeles, has paddle boat, kayak, canoe, and paddleboard rentals for $20 per hour and $60 per day. The dock provides easy access to Lake Crescent's northeast section. ✉ *3183 E Beach Rd., Port Angeles* ☎ *360/928–3325* 🌐 *www.olympicnationalparks.com*. ⏲ *Closed Oct.–mid-May.*

Rainforest Paddlers

KAYAKING | This company takes kayakers down the Hoh River to explore the rain forest, and down the Quillayute through the estuary to La Push. Rafting trips are offered on both the Hoh and Sol Duc rivers. They also rent kayaks and mountain bikes. ✉ *4883 Upper Hoh Rd., Forks* ☎ *360/374–5254, 866/457–8398* 🌐 *www.rainforestpaddlers.com* 🎫 *Tours from $44; kayak rentals from $11/hr.*

RAFTING

Olympic has excellent rafting rivers, with Class II to Class V rapids. The Elwha River is a popular place to paddle, with some exciting turns. The Hoh is better for those who like a smooth, easy float.

WINTER SPORTS

Hurricane Ridge is the central spot for winter sports. Miles of downhill and Nordic ski tracks are open late December through March, and a ski lift, towropes, and ski school are open 10 to 4 weekends and holidays. A snow-play area for children ages eight and younger is near the Hurricane Ridge Visitors Center. Hurricane Ridge Road is open Friday through Sunday in the winter season; all vehicles are required to carry chains.

Hurricane Ridge Visitor Center

SNOW SPORTS | Rent snowshoes and ski equipment here December through March. ✉ *Hurricane Ridge Rd., Port Angeles* ☎ *360/565–3131 road condition information* 🌐 *www.nps.gov/olym/planyourvisit/hurricane-ridge-in-winter.htm* ⏲ *Closed Mon.–Thurs.*

Hurricane Ridge Ski and Snowboard Area

SKIING/SNOWBOARDING | The cross-country trails here, in Olympic National Park, begin at the lodge and have great views of Mt. Olympus. A small downhill ski and snowboarding area is open weekends and holidays; lift tickets are $17–$40. There's also a tubing/sledding hill. The Hurricane Ridge Visitor Center has a small restaurant, an interpretive center, and restrooms. Admission to the park is $30 per vehicle. Call ahead for road conditions before taking the three-hour drive from Seattle. ✉ *Olympic National Park, 17 miles south of Port Angeles, Seattle* ☎ *360/565–3100, 360/565–3131 for road reports* 🌐 *www.hurricaneridge.com.*

Nearby Towns

Although most Olympic Peninsula towns have evolved from their exclusive reliance on timber, **Forks,** outside the national park's northwest tip, remains one of the region's logging capitals. Washington state's wettest town (100 inches or more of rain a year), it's a small, friendly place with just under 3,800 residents and a modicum of visitor facilities. **Port Angeles,** a city of around 20,000, focuses on its status as the main gateway to Olympic National Park and Victoria, British Columbia. Set below the Strait of Juan de Fuca and looking north to Vancouver Island, it's an enviably scenic settlement filled with attractive, Craftsman-style homes.

The Pacific Northwest has its very own "Banana Belt" in the waterfront community of **Sequim,** 15 miles east of Port Angeles along U.S. 101. The town of 6,900 is in the rain shadow of the Olympics and receives only 16 inches of rain per year (compared with the 140 to 170 inches that drench the Hoh Rain Forest just 40 miles away). The beach community of **Seabrook,** near Pacific Beach, is 25 miles from the southeast corner of the national park via the Moclips Highway. Created in 2004 as a pedestrian-friendly beach town, many of its several hundred Cape Cod–style cottage homes are available for short-term rentals; the community has parks, swimming pools, bike trails, beach access, special events, and a growing retail district.

VISITOR INFORMATION Forks Chamber of Commerce Visitor Center. ✉ *1411 S Forks Ave. (U.S. 101), Forks* ☎ *800/443–6757, 360/374–2531* 🌐 *www.forkswa.com.* **Port Angeles Chamber of Commerce Visitor Center.** ✉ *121 E Railroad Ave., Port Angeles* ☎ *360/452–2363* 🌐 *www.portangeles.org.* **Sequim-Dungeness Valley Chamber of Commerce.** ✉ *1192 E Washington St., Sequim* ☎ *360/683–6197, 800/737–8462* 🌐 *www.sequimchamber.com.*

Restaurants

Creekside Restaurant

$$$ | **AMERICAN** | A tranquil country setting and ocean views at Kalaloch Lodge's restaurant create the perfect backdrop for savoring Pacific Northwest dinner specialties like grilled salmon, fresh shellfish, and elk burgers. Tempting seasonal desserts include local fruit tarts and cobblers in summer and organic winter squash bread pudding in winter; flourless chocolate torte is enjoyed year-round. **Known for:** locally sourced food; Washington wines. $ *Average main: $28* ✉ *157151 Hwy. 101, Forks* ☎ *866/662–9928, 360/962–2271* 🌐 *www.thekalalochlodge.com/dine-and-shop/creekside-restaurant.*

Lake Crescent Lodge

$$$ | **AMERICAN** | Part of the original 1916 lodge, the fir-paneled dining room overlooks the lake; you won't find a better spot for sunset views. Dinner entrées include wild salmon, brown butter–basted halibut, grilled steak, and roasted chicken breast; the lunch menu features elk cheeseburgers, inventive salads, and a variety of sandwiches. **Known for:** award-winning Pacific Northwest wine list; house-made lavender lemonade; certified green restaurant. $ *Average main: $29* ✉ *416 Lake Crescent Rd., Port Angeles* ☎ *360/928–3211* 🌐 *www.olympicnationalparks.com/lodging/dining/lake-crescent-lodge/* ⏲ *Closed Jan.–Apr.*

The Springs Restaurant

$$$ | **AMERICAN** | The main Sol Duc Hot Springs Resort restaurant is a rustic, fir-and-cedar-paneled dining room surrounded by trees. In summer big breakfasts are turned out daily—hikers can fill up on biscuits and sage-pork-sausage gravy, Grand Marnier French toast, and omelets before hitting the trails; for lighter fare, there's steel cut oatmeal and yogurt and granola parfaits. **Known for:** three breakfast mimosa choices; boxed lunches. $ *Average main: $24* ✉ *12076 Sol Duc Rd. , at U.S. 101, Port Angeles* ☎ *360/327–3583* 🌐 *www.olympicnationalparks.com/stay/dining/sol-duc-hot-springs-resort-.aspx* ⏲ *Closed Nov.–late Mar.*

PICNIC AREAS

All Olympic National Park campgrounds have adjacent picnic areas with tables, some shelters, and restrooms, but no cooking facilities. The same is true for major visitor centers, such as Hoh Rain Forest. Drinking water is available at ranger stations, interpretive centers, and inside campgrounds.

East Beach Picnic Area

Set on a grassy meadow overlooking Lake Crescent, this popular swimming spot has six picnic tables and vault toilets. ✉ *E Beach Rd., Port Angeles* ⊕ *At far east end of Lake Crescent, off Hwy. 101, 17 miles west of Port Angeles.*

La Poel Picnic Area

Tall firs lean over a tiny gravel beach at this small picnic area, which has several picnic tables and a splendid view of Pyramid Mountain across Lake Crescent. It's closed October to April. ✉ *Olympic National Park* ⊕ *Off Hwy.*

101, 22 miles west of Port Angeles ⏲ *Closed mid-Oct.–mid-May.*

Rialto Beach Picnic Area
Relatively secluded at the end of the road from Forks, this is one of the premier day-use areas in the park's Pacific coast segment. This site has 12 picnic tables, fire grills, and vault toilets. ✉ *Rte. 110, 14 miles west of Forks, Forks.*

Hotels

★ Kalaloch Lodge
$$$$ | HOTEL | FAMILY | Overlooking the Pacific, Kalaloch has cozy lodge rooms with sea views and separate cabins along the bluff. **Pros:** ranger tours; clam digging; supreme storm-watching in winter. **Cons:** no Internet and most units don't have TVs; some rooms are two blocks from main lodge; limited cell phone service. 💲 *Rooms from: $292* ✉ *157151 U.S. 101, Forks* ☎ *360/962–2271, 866/662–9928* 🌐 *www.thekalalochlodge.com* 🛏 *64 rooms* 🍽 *No meals.*

Lake Crescent Lodge
$$$ | HOTEL | Deep in the forest at the foot of Mt. Storm King, this 1916 lodge has a variety of comfortable accommodations, from basic rooms with shared baths to spacious two-bedroom fireplace cottages. **Pros:** gorgeous setting; free wireless access in the lobby; lots of opportunities for off-the-grid fun outdoors. **Cons:** no laundry; Roosevelt Cottages often are booked a year in advance for summer stays; crowded with nonguest visitors. 💲 *Rooms from: $152* ✉ *416 Lake Crescent Rd., Port Angeles* ☎ *360/928–3211, 888/896–3818* 🌐 *www.olympicnationalparks.com* ⏲ *Closed Jan.–Apr., except Roosevelt fireplace cabins open weekends* 🛏 *52 rooms* 🍽 *No meals.*

Lake Quinault Lodge
$$$$ | HOTEL | On a lovely glacial lake in Olympic National Forest, this beautiful early-20th-century lodge complex is within walking distance of the lakeshore and hiking trails in the spectacular old-growth forest. **Pros:** boat tours of the lake are interesting; family-friendly ambience; year-round pool and sauna. **Cons:** no TV in some rooms; some units are noisy and not very private; service could be friendlier. 💲 *Rooms from: $341* ✉ *345 South Shore Rd., Quinault* ☎ *360/288–2900, 888/896–3818* 🌐 *www.olympicnationalparks.com* 🛏 *92 rooms* 🍽 *No meals.*

Log Cabin Resort
$$ | HOTEL | FAMILY | This rustic resort has an idyllic setting at the northeast end of Lake Crescent with lodging choices that include A-frame chalet units, standard cabins, small camper cabins, motel units, and RV sites with full hookups. **Pros:** boat rentals available on-site; convenient general store; pets allowed in some cabins. **Cons:** cabins are extremely rustic; no plumbing in the camper cabins; no TVs. 💲 *Rooms from: $104* ✉ *3183 E Beach Rd., Port Angeles* ☎ *888/896–3818, 360/928–3325* 🌐 *www.olympicnationalparks.com* ⏲ *Closed Oct.–late May* 🛏 *4 rooms, 20 cabins* 🍽 *No meals.*

Sol Duc Hot Springs Resort
$$$$ | HOTEL | Deep in the brooding forest along the Sol Duc River and surrounded by 5,000-foot-tall mountains, the main draw of this remote 1910 resort is the pool area, with soothing mineral baths and a freshwater swimming pool. **Pros:** nearby trails; peaceful setting; some units are pet-friendly. **Cons:** units are dated; no air-conditioning, TV, or Internet access; pools get crowded. 💲 *Rooms from: $215* ✉ *12076 Sol Duc Hot Springs Rd., Olympic National Park* ☎ *888/896–3818* 🌐 *www.olympicnationalparks.com* ⏲ *Closed Nov.–late Mar.* 🛏 *32 cabins, 1 suite, 17 RV sites* 🍽 *No meals.*

Activities

★ Dungeness Spit
BEACH—SIGHT | FAMILY | Curving 5½ miles into the Strait of Juan de Fuca, the longest natural sand spit in the United States is a wild, beautiful section of shoreline. More

than 30,000 migratory waterfowl stop here each spring and fall, but you'll see plenty of birdlife any time of year. The entire spit is part of the **Dungeness National Wildlife Refuge.** Access it through the **Dungeness Recreation Area,** which serves as a portal to the shoreline. ✉ *554 Voice of America Rd., Sequim* ✣ *Entrance 3 miles north from U.S. 101, 4 miles west of Sequim* ☎ *360/457–8451 wildlife refuge* 🌐 *www.clallam.net/parks/dungeness.html (recreation area); www.fws.gov/refuge/Dungeness (wildlife refuge)* 🎟 *$3 per family.*

New Dungeness Lighthouse

BEACH—SIGHT | At the end of the Dungeness Spit is the towering white 1857 New Dungeness Lighthouse; tours are available, though access is limited to those who can hike or kayak out 5 miles to the end of the spit. Guests also have the opportunity to serve as lighthouse keepers for a week at a time. An adjacent, 66-site camping area, on the bluff above the Strait of Juan de Fuca, is open year-round. ✉ *Sequim* ✣ *Entrance 3 miles north of Hwy. 101 via Kitchen Dick Rd.* ☎ *360/683–6638* 🌐 *www.newdungenesslighthouse.com.*

Olympic Discovery Trail

TRAIL | Eventually, 140 miles of nonmotorized trail will lead from Port Townsend west to the Pacific Coast. As of this writing, 80 miles of the paved trail are complete and available for use by hikers, bikers, equestrians, and disabled users. The trail has been conceived as the northern portion of a route that will eventually encircle the entire Olympic Peninsula. 🌐 *www.olympicdiscoverytrail.org.*

Port Angeles Fine Arts Center

MUSEUM | This small, sophisticated museum is inside the former home of late artist and publisher Esther Barrows Webster, one of Port Angeles's most energetic and cultured citizens; displays are modern, funky, and intriguing. Outside, Webster's Woods Art Park is dotted with oversize sculptures set before a vista of the city and harbor. Exhibitions emphasize the works of emerging and well-established Pacific Northwest artists. ✉ *1203 E Lauridsen Blvd., Port Angeles* ☎ *360/457–3532* 🌐 *www.pafac.org* 🎟 *Free* ⏲ *Closed Oct.–Mar.*

Timber Museum

MUSEUM | The museum highlights Forks's logging history since the 1870s; a garden and fire tower are also on the grounds. ✉ *1421 S Forks Ave., Forks* ☎ *360/374–9663* 🌐 *www.forkstimbermuseum.org* 🎟 *$3.*

SKIING AND SNOWBOARDING

Snow sports are one of the few reasons to look forward to winter in Seattle. Ski season usually lasts from late November until late March or early April. A one-day adult lift ticket at an area resort averages around $80; most resorts rent equipment and have restaurants.

Cross-country trails range from undisturbed backcountry routes to groomed resort tracks. To ski on state park trails you must purchase a Sno-Park Pass, available at most sporting goods stores, ski shops, and forest service district offices. Always call ahead for road conditions, which might prevent trail access or require you to put chains on your tires.

The Summit at Snoqualmie

SKIING/SNOWBOARDING | Chances are good that any local skier you ask took his or her first run at Snoqualmie, the resort closest to the city. With four ski areas, gentle-to-advanced slopes, rope tows, moseying chairlifts, a snowboard park, and dozens of educational programs, it's the obvious choice for an introduction to the slopes. One-day lift tickets cost $58–$97 for adults; equipment packages are $45 a day. The Nordic Center at Summit East is the starting point for 31 miles of cross-country trails. Guided snowshoe hikes are offered here on Friday and weekends. ✉ *Exit 52 off I–90, Snoqualmie Pass, Seattle* ☎ *425/434–7669, 206/434–6708 for Nordic center* 🌐 *www.summitatsnoqualmie.com.*

Best Campgrounds in Olympic

Note that only a few places take reservations; if you can't book in advance, you'll have to arrive early to get a place. Each site usually has a picnic table and grill or fire pit, and most campgrounds have water, toilets, and garbage containers; for hookups, showers, and laundry facilities, you'll have to head into the towns or stay at a privately owned campground. Firewood is available from camp concessions, but if there's no store you can collect dead wood within 1 mile of your campsite. Dogs are allowed in campgrounds, but not on most trails or in the backcountry. Trailers should be 21 feet long or less (15 feet or less at Queets Campground), though a few campgrounds can accommodate up to 35 feet. There's a camping limit of two weeks. Nightly rates run $15–$22 per site.

If you have a backcountry pass, you can camp virtually anywhere throughout the park's forests and shores. Overnight wilderness permits are $8 per person per night and are available at visitor centers and ranger stations. Note that when you camp in the backcountry, you must choose a site at least ½ mile inside the park boundary.

Kalaloch Campground. Kalaloch is the biggest and most popular Olympic campground, and it's open all year. Its vantage of the Pacific is unmatched on the park's coastal stretch. ✉ *U.S. 101, ½ mile north of Kalaloch Information Station, Olympic National Park* ☎ 877/444–6777 or 🌐 *www.recreation.gov* for reservations.

Lake Quinault Rain Forest Resort Village Campground. Stretching along the south shore of Lake Quinault, this RV campground has many recreation facilities, including beaches, canoes, ball fields, and horseshoe pits. The 31 RV sites, which rent for $36 per night, are open year-round, but bathrooms are closed in winter. ✉ *3½ miles east of U.S. 101, South Shore Rd., Lake Quinault* ☎ *360/288–2535, 800/255–6936* 🌐 *www.rainforestresort.com.*

Mora Campground. Along the Quillayute estuary, this campground doubles as a popular staging point for hikes northward along the coast's wilderness stretch. ✉ *Rte. 110, 13 miles west of Forks* ☎ *No phone.*

Ozette Campground. Hikers heading to Cape Alava, a scenic promontory that is the westernmost point in the lower 48 states, use this lakeshore campground as a jumping-off point. ✉ *Hoko-Ozette Rd., 26 miles south of Hwy. 112* ☎ *No phone.*

Sol Duc Campground. Sol Duc resembles virtually all Olympic campgrounds save one distinguishing feature—the famed hot springs are a short walk away. ✉ *Sol Duc Rd., 11 miles south of U.S. 101* ☎ *877/444–6777* or 🌐 *www.recreation.gov* for reservations.

Staircase Campground. In deep woods away from the river, this campground is a popular jumping-off point for hikes into the Skokomish River Valley and the Olympic high country. ✉ *Rte. 119, 16 miles northwest of U.S. 101* ☎ *No phone.*

★ Whistler Blackcomb

SKIING/SNOWBOARDING | Whistler, 200 miles north of Seattle, is best done as a three-day weekend trip. (Just make sure your car has chains or snow tires.) And you really can't call yourself a skier here and not go to Whistler at least once. The massive resort is renowned for its nightlife, which is just at the foot of the slopes. When you arrive, you abandon your car outside the village—you can reach the entire hotel/dining/ski area on foot. A one-day adult lift ticket costs about $160 at the window, which includes access to the famous Peak 2 Peak gondola, a hair-raising ride between Whistler and Blackcomb mountains; you'll save if you buy a multiday pass in advance online. The area includes more than 17 miles of cross-country trails, usually open November–March. For diehard skiers and boarders who want an extended season, there's summer skiing on Blackcomb Glacier through July. ✉ *Hwy. 99, Whistler* ☎ *866/218–9690* 🌐 *www.whistlerblackcomb.com.*

GOLF

Gold Mountain Golf Complex

GOLF | Most people make the trek to Bremerton to play the Olympic Course, a beautiful and challenging par 72 that is widely considered the best public course in Washington. The older, less-sculpted Cascade Course is also popular; it's better suited to those new to the game. There are four putting greens, a driving range, and a striking clubhouse with views of the Belfair Valley. Rates vary but start as low as $20 for midweek, off-season tee times booked online. Carts are $16.50 prior to twilight and $10 after. You can drive all the way to Bremerton via Interstate 5, or you can take the car ferry to Bremerton from Pier 52. The trip will take roughly 1½ hours no matter which way you do it, but the ferry ride (60 minutes) might be a more pleasant way to spend a large part of the journey. Note, however, that the earliest departure time for the ferry is 6 am, so this option won't work for very early tee times. ✉ *7263 W Belfair Valley Rd., Bremerton* ☎ *360/415–5433* 🌐 *www.goldmt.com.*

The Golf Club at Newcastle

GOLF | Probably the best option on the Eastside, this golf complex, which includes a pair of courses and an 18-hole putting green, has views, views, and more views. From the hilly greens you'll see Seattle, the Olympic Mountains, and Lake Washington. The 7,000-yard, par-72 Coal Creek course is the more challenging of the two, though the China Creek course has its challenges and more sections of undisturbed natural areas. This is the Seattle area's most expensive golf club—greens fees for Coal Creek range from $140 to $195 depending on the season; fees for China Creek range from $100 to $140. Newcastle is about 35 minutes from Downtown—if you don't hit traffic. ✉ *15500 Six Penny La., Newcastle, Seattle* ☎ *425/793–5566* 🌐 *www.newcastlegolf.com.*

Jefferson Park

GOLF | This golf complex has views of the city skyline *and* Mt. Rainier. The par-27, 9-hole course has a lighted driving range with heated stalls that's open from dusk until midnight. And the 18-hole, par-69 main course is one of the city's best. Greens fees are around $30 but are dynamic based on demand, so you could get a great deal on an off-time or weekday option. ✉ *4101 Beacon Ave. S., Beacon Hill* ☎ *206/762–4513* 🌐 *www.seattlegolf.com.*

Index

A

B

C

U

V

W

X

Y

Z